A NEW ECONOMIC HISTORY
OF COLONIAL INDIA

A New Economic History of Colonial India provides a new perspective on Indian economic history. Using economic theory and quantitative methods, it shows how the discipline is being redefined and how new scholarship on India is beginning to embrace and make use of concepts from the larger field of global economic history and economics.

The book discusses the impact of property rights, the standard of living, the labour market and the aftermath of the Partition. It also addresses how education and work changed, and provides a rethinking of traditional topics including deindustrialization, industrialization, railways, balance of payments and the East India Company. Writing in an accessible way, the contributors – all leading experts in their fields – firmly place Indian history in the context of world history.

An up-to-date critical survey and novel resource on Indian Economic History, this book will be useful for undergraduate and postgraduate courses on Economic History, Indian and South Asian Studies, Economics and Comparative and Global History.

Latika Chaudhary is Associate Professor of Economics in the Graduate School of Business and Public Policy at the Naval Postgraduate School, USA.

Bishnupriya Gupta is Associate Professor of Economics at the University of Warwick, UK.

Tirthankar Roy is Professor of Economic History at the London School of Economics, UK.

Anand V. Swamy is Professor of Economics at Williams College in Massachusetts, USA.

A NEW ECONOMIC HISTORY OF COLONIAL INDIA

Edited by
Latika Chaudhary, Bishnupriya Gupta,
Tirthankar Roy and Anand V. Swamy

Routledge
Taylor & Francis Group

LONDON AND NEW YORK

First published 2016
by Routledge
2 Park Square, Milton Park, Abingdon, Oxon OX14 4RN

and by Routledge
711 Third Avenue, New York, NY 10017

Routledge is an imprint of the Taylor & Francis Group, an informa business

British Library Cataloguing in Publication Data
A catalogue record for this book is available from the British Library

Library of Congress Cataloging-in-Publication Data
A new economic history of colonial India / Edited by Latika Chaudhary,
    Bishnupriya Gupta, Tirthankar Roy and Anand V. Swamy.
        pages cm
    1. India—Economic conditions.   2. India—Social conditions.
3. Business—India—History.   4. Economic history.   I. Chaudhary, Latika,
editor.   II. Gupta, Bishnupriya, editor.   III. Roy, Tirthankar.
    HC433.N49 2016
    330.954'035—dc23
    2015008638

ISBN: 978-1-138-77971-6 (hbk)
ISBN: 978-1-138-77972-3 (pbk)
ISBN: 978-1-315-77108-3 (ebk)

Typeset in Bembo
by Apex CoVantage, LLC

Printed and bound by CPI Group (UK) Ltd, Croydon, CR0 4YY

CONTENTS

FIGURES

TABLES

BOXES

CONTRIBUTORS

Gopalan Balachandran is Professor of International History at the Graduate Institute in Geneva. His research focuses on globalization, especially in relation to South Asia. His book *Globalizing Labour? Indian Seafarers and World Shipping, c. 1870–1945* was published by Oxford University Press in 2012.

Prashant Bharadwaj is Assistant Professor in the Department of Economics at the University of California, San Diego. His research is in Development Economics. He has published several papers on the economic consequences of the partition of India, including "Partition, Migration and Jute Cultivation in India" (with James Fenske) in the *Journal of Development Studies* in 2012.

Dan Bogart is Associate Professor of Economics at the University of California, Irvine. His research focuses on Indian railways, British institutions, property rights and infrastructure. His paper entitled "Engines of Growth: The Productivity Advance of Indian Railways, 1874–1912" (with Latika Chaudhary) won the Cole Prize for best article in the *Journal of Economic History* in 2013.

Steven Broadberry is Professor of Economic History at the London School of Economics. His recent research interests include Global Economic History and Economic History in the Long Run. He has co-edited (with Kevin O'Rourke) *The Cambridge Economic History of Modern Europe* (two volumes), published by Cambridge University Press in 2010.

Latika Chaudhary is Associate Professor of Economics in the Graduate School of Business and Public Policy at the Naval Postgraduate School, Monterey, CA. Her research interests include the provision of public goods in colonial India. Recent publications include "Determinants of Primary Schooling in British India" (*Journal of Economic History*, 2009).

Bishnupriya Gupta is Associate Professor of Economics in the University of Warwick. Her research interests include industrial organization in colonial India and the divergence in living standards between Europe and Asia. Her recent publications include "Discrimination or Social Networks? Industrial Investment in Colonial India" (*Journal of Economic History*, 2014).

Santhi Hejeebu is Associate Professor of Economics and Business at Cornell College. Her research focuses on the organizational structure of the East India Company in papers such as "Contract Enforcement in the English East India Company," published by the *Journal of Economic History* in 2005.

Lakshmi Iyer is Associate Professor at Harvard Business School with research interests in Political Economy and Development Economics. Her influential work on the long-run impact of colonial institutions in India includes "Direct versus Indirect Colonial Rule in India: Long-term Consequences," published by the *Review of Economics and Statistics* in 2010.

Kevin Quirolo graduated Magna Cum Laude from the University of California, San Diego, in 2012. In 2013 he moved to New York City where he has worked and interned at the Drug Policy Alliance conducting strategic research, as well as working in grass-roots criminal justice reform organizations.

Indrajit Ray is Professor at the Department of Commerce, University of North Bengal, Darjeeling. He has worked on the history of industrialization in Bengal. His book *Bengal Industries and the British Industrial Revolution 1757–1857* was published by Routledge in 2011.

Tirthankar Roy is a Professor of Economic History at the London School of Economics. His research field is the economic history of South Asia. Recent publications include *An Economic History of Early Modern India* (Routledge, 2013) and *India in the World Economy From Antiquity to the Present* (Cambridge University Press, 2012).

Anand V. Swamy is a Professor of Economics at Williams College in Massachusetts U.S.A. His research focuses on colonial India. His publications include "Contracts, Hold-Up and Exports: Textiles and Opium in Colonial India," *American Economic Review* (2008), written jointly with Rachel Kranton.

Susan Wolcott is Associate Professor of Economics at Binghamton University. Her research has focused on labour productivity in colonial India, and she has authored several articles on the Indian textile industry. Her recent work includes "Strikes in Colonial India," forthcoming in *Industrial and Labor Relations Review*.

ACKNOWLEDGMENTS

This project began with a conference at the University of Warwick in July 2011. The conference was funded by the Department of Economics at Warwick, and CAGE (Center for Advantage in the Global Competitive Economy). We thank them for their generosity. Early encouragement from Steve Broadberry played an important role in turning the papers presented at the conference into the volume you are now reading. Once the project was under way the various contributors were patient with delays, and responsive to our requests for changes, making the editors' task easier. Our greatest collective obligation is perhaps to Johann Custodis, who took on the onerous task of editing the entire volume, and accomplished it with a degree of thoroughness that can only be described as awe inspiring.

The editors of this book received support from different sources. Anand V. Swamy's research was supported by Williams College and specifically its extraordinarily helpful and resourceful Inter-Library Loan Service. Earlier versions of the chapter contributed by Tirthankar Roy were prepared for a project on labour history led by the International Institute of Social History, Amsterdam, and for the annual conference of the Indian Society of Labour Economics, Banaras, 2012. He is grateful to the participants and organizers of these bodies for helpful comments. Latika Chaudhary's research was supported by the Lowe Institute of Political Economy at Claremont McKenna College. Bishnupriya Gupta acknowledges the generous support of the Department of Economics at the University of Warwick in the successful completion of this project.

Latika Chaudhary
Bishnupriya Gupta
Tirthankar Roy
Anand V. Swamy

1

INTRODUCTION

Latika Chaudhary, Bishnupriya Gupta,
Tirthankar Roy and Anand V. Swamy

The aim

In this book we aim to provide the students of Economics, History, Development Studies and Global History with a handy textbook on the Economic History of colonial India. Over the last two decades, many papers have been published in Economics and Economic History journals using tools from Economics to analyse the development experience of colonial India. This literature is not necessarily a critique of the existing debates on the role of colonialism, but takes a more thematic approach to situate the history of India in the context of developments in the writing of the Economic History of Europe, Asia, Africa and the Americas. These themes range from the impact of property rights, the provision of public goods, standard of living, institutional specificities and labour markets to the investments in human capital and infrastructure, and economic impacts of shocks such as the partition. This book contains a collection of essays by subject experts, all of whom have been associated with teaching Economic History and have published original articles in the field in recent times.

Presently, teachers have a few resources when teaching the Economic History of India. One of these is *The Cambridge Economic History of India, vol. 2* (Kumar and Desai 1983, hereafter *CEHI 2*), a collection of papers on different aspects of the economy. There are textbooks on the subject (Roy 2011a; Tomlinson 1982; Rothermund 2000) and more focussed monographs such as *Bagchi (1972)* or *Blyn (1962)*. There are edited collections that republish essays written over several decades. Yet the new research on the Economic History of colonial India is yet to find its way into texts and readers. This book is an attempt to make this research accessible to students of Indian Economic History. The chapters have grown out of the research interests of the contributors as well as discussions and feedback from students and colleagues. This volume of readings aims to show how the discipline is being redefined in the present time, and how, in that process, the new scholarship on India is beginning to embrace and make use of concepts from the larger field of global Economic History and Economics.

What is this book *not* trying to be? It is not intended to replace or update existing texts and reference works. With all its limitations of coverage, the *CEHI 2* remains indispensable as a research tool, or even as a teaching aid in a research-oriented course. This book does not want to be, and cannot be, a systematic summary of everything one needs to know on the subject. It collects a set of reflective reviews by a number of active practitioners of the field. In that sense, it shows how the field has changed.

A survey of the field

The time span of interest to the book is colonial India, roughly 1757 to 1947, though individual chapters define their time spans flexibly. Over almost 200 years, India experienced the full effects of three world-changing forces: the British Empire, the Industrial Revolution, and the first period of globalization that saw a massive increase in trade, investment and labour migration. The Empire represented a diverse collection of world regions with a shared official language and mutually compatible legal regimes. Colonization and globalization brought new institutions and new responses from economic agents in agriculture and industry. The interactions with European trading companies and the Asian trading networks in the seventeenth and eighteenth centuries opened up new opportunities for weavers, artisans and merchants. The thriving world of commerce in pre-British India has been the subject of extensive research (Bayly 1983; Chaudhuri 1978). The rising trade in textiles brought prosperity to weavers and merchants and made India the main supplier in the world market. In the three principal port cities, the merchants made money in maritime trade and the financing of trade. The 'deindustrialization' of India that coincided with colonization also coincided with one of the most important economic events in the world, the 'Industrial Revolution', which transformed the technology of textile production. From an exporter of cotton goods, India became locked in a colonial relationship with Britain in an international division of labour. The process of nineteenth-century deindustrialization was the mirror image of rising commercialization of agriculture. With the rise of modern industries from the middle of the century, the textile factories that started in Bombay and Ahmedabad once again became a dynamic sector of the economy. But in the vast backdrop of an agrarian society, these ports-cum-mill-towns were mere islands. How did the two forces shape prospects of economic growth?

The oldest and the most enduring conception in Indian Economic History has focussed on the balance of payments, or colonial India's transactions with the nineteenth-century world economy. Two stylized facts influenced the arguments surrounding economic growth, or rather the lack thereof in the region: first, a persistent surplus of exports over imports, and second, a persistent net payment deficit on the invisibles account. The Indian nationalist critics of imperial rule called the net payment deficit on the invisibles account 'drain'. The notion behind the drain was that these payments, which potentially reduced domestic savings, and consisted of payments on account of services purchased from Britain on private and government account, reflected India's subservient political status to Britain. The nationalists saw market integration with the international economy as a colonial construct which transformed the pattern of merchandise trade from exports of manufactured goods into exports of primary agricultural commodities. Colonial policy stunted the pattern of development by denying autonomy in trade policy. Railways too became a vehicle for reinforcing the pattern of colonial trade. Land was another area of debate.

Land

Even at the peak of India's industrial success, she was primarily an agricultural economy. The impact of colonial rule on agriculture is thus key to accounting for the overall economy's progress or failure. The first steps of the colonial rulers were to introduce relatively clearly defined property rights in land in the late eighteenth century. Three variants of a system that was to incentivize the landowner to improve productivity ranged from the *zamindari* system that gave property rights and tax responsibility to the landlord to the *ryotwari* that gave the same to the owner-cultivator and finally the *mahalwari* that allowed communal ownership and tax responsibility. The Crown inherited this system of land rights just when a long period of boom in the terms of trade was beginning. During 1860–1920, agricultural prices steadily increased in relation to non-agricultural prices. Export of agricultural products became more profitable. The peasant with secure rights and some surplus crops to sell gained; so did the economy of Britain, which wanted Indian cotton and wheat in exchange for textiles, and the Indian state for which land tax was the main income. The British state embarked on a programme of investment in infrastructure, particularly railways and to a limited extent irrigation to aid the process of integrating India into the global economy. The newly constructed railway network reduced transport costs and helped increase trade. It also brought in capital flows from London. In this period of colonial rule, GDP per capita witnessed a slightly positive growth.

But these processes also exposed, and possibly intensified, regional and other types of inequality. As canal-rich Punjab saw agricultural growth, the dry-land and rain-fed peninsula saw repeated occurrences of devastating famines and mass death. In *zamindari* areas, landlords with secure land titles lived off rent. They often lived in the cities and neglected investments, whereas hard-working tenant farmers had little incentive to spend money on land improvement. Throughout India, trade encouraged the business of rural lending. In the *ryotwari* areas, land titles began to be mortgaged to finance investment or consumption. In a bad year, the debts could be ruinous for the peasant. New research in the 1970s and the 1980s focussed on the interaction between commodity markets, credit markets and rural property rights to reveal emerging patterns of inequality and their consequences for conditions of living (see essays in Raj, Bhattacharya, Guha and Padhi 1985; Bose 1994; Ludden

1994). The scholarship was characterized by disagreement over whether the net effect of all this was good or bad for agriculture. Predictably, the answer varied according to the region studied. Some studies emphasized the negative effects of the *zamindari* and related colonial institutions on agriculture in Bengal while others highlighted the achievements of the Canal Colonies in Punjab. But even within regions, the assessments often differed quite sharply, for example, on the role of irrigation in the United Provinces (Stone 1984; Whitcombe 1972).

Industry

Similar debates surround the study of industry. The standard trade model predicts that a region scarce in capital but abundant in land should see manufacturing retreat and agriculture expand as costs of conducting trade falls. In colonial India there was a retreat of manufacturing and a growth of agriculture. Still, India is more of an anomaly than a confirmation of the model's predictions, especially when compared with tropical commodity exporters in Asia, Africa and Latin America. India specialized in export agriculture far less than these regions, and far from losing its manufactures, experienced robust industrialization after 1850. Between 1860 and 1940, modern industry emerged and grew significantly. Employment in factories increased from less than 100,000 to 2 million (Roy 2011a, p. 201). Real GDP at factor cost originating in factories rose at the rate of 4 per cent per year between 1900 and 1947 (calculation based on Sivasubramonian 2000). However, the share of modern industry in employment was small.

Studies on industrialization stressed two indigenous advantages: cheap labour and a strong mercantile tradition (Morris 1983; Bagchi 1972; Ray 1982). By many accounts, colonial policies hindered the entry of Indian entrepreneurs into a number of fast-growing industries. The presence of Indian mercantile networks in western India was described as a result of a less imposing position of British capital. Such narratives are fraught with problems of identifying the direction of causality. In reality, the entry of Indian merchant groups into modern industry in western India provided a strong contrast to the British domination of eastern India. New studies on Indian industrialization remained essentially within the field of business history (Tripathi 2004). A range of institutional details, such as law and aspects of business organization, were under-researched if not overlooked. Notable exceptions are the histories of labour in Bombay's cotton mills and Calcutta's jute mills that bear the common theme of a slow and late emergence of a 'working class' identity for migrant workers from a world of self-employment in rural India to crowded urban centres (Chakrabarty 1989; Chandavarkar 1994).

Against this backdrop significant revisions and rethinking have happened along a small range of themes, for example, the role of artisans. The real surprise of Indian industrialization is artisanal production of cotton textiles following deindustrialization. This business, along with a few other craft enterprises, experienced a significant revival from 1900. Beginning in the late 1980s, a group of historians have tried to explain this counter-intuitive stylized fact. Like mercantile heritage in the case of factories, another part of indigenous tradition, the accumulated skill and craftsmanship has also received particular attention in the revisionist account (Roy 1999; Haynes 2012).

Measurement

With such diverging accounts of agriculture and industry, aggregate measures such as GDP are necessary to understand how India performed under colonial rule. The first systematic measures of gross domestic product (1900–1947) were prepared in 1965, even though the work was not published in full detail until 2000 (Sivasubramonian 2000). Because of the long publication lag, a number of other crude figures circulated around, principally those by Maddison (1971) and Mukherjee (1965). Mukherjee's method had the virtue of being amenable to extrapolation back in time, at least to the 1860s. But almost all these estimates suffered from assumptions recycled from the literature rather than a careful study of the data. By contrast, Sivasubramonian (2000) is a careful measurement project, and therefore became a benchmark to test some of the predictions in the nationalist-imperialist debate.

Combining the disparate estimates shows that colonial India did not experience a single pattern of GDP growth. There was positive growth, significant in comparison with the world average, during 1860–1920, and a deceleration thereafter. Whereas the factory sector, small industry, trade, transport and public administration performed well, agriculture, which determined average trends, did well until 1920 and badly thereafter. After 1920, acceleration in population growth further suppressed average incomes.

A new paradigm

Global history and economics have experienced a resurgence in the study of colonialism and institutions. In accounting for the wide scope of development experiences in the early modern period, researchers have drawn on themes in analytical Economic History, economic theory and the new institutional economics. Questions about how institutions formed, how the state worked and how individuals learned to do different things have demanded a fresh look at the colonial experience of India and other parts of the world.

Inherent in neoclassical models and Marxist accounts of modern economic growth is a strong Eurocentrism. In these accounts, western Europe invented industrialization and the non-Western world either passively followed, or was obstructed by the colonizers and by its own internal conditions. The reaction to these old discourses has led to a crop of new interpretations of the non-Western regions, which recognize the potential for growth within these societies. This literature is variously called the 'Great Divergence' debate after the title of Pomeranz (2000) or 'New Comparative History' after the title of a collection of essays in Hatton, O'Rourke and Taylor (2007). By shifting the explanations for world inequality into the seventeenth and eighteenth century or even earlier, the rethinking also underscored the need to gather more data on comparative living standards on a long time scale. Seeing colonial India in the backdrop of global history and the comparative experience of colonial and independent economies became part of the new research agenda. The reorientation stimulated fresh work on India, much of it published in international journals read by economists. These writings introduced four themes. Between 1999 and 2010, a series of articles participated in the debate on the Great Divergence with Indian evidence (Broadberry and Gupta 2006; Allen 2007). These contributions were in part a response to one article that pioneered the use of agricultural wages to infer patterns of international inequality (Parthasarathi 1999). Through these writings, historical national accounts have acquired a relevance that they lacked before.

A second new direction views culture as a determinant of growth. Using the cotton textile industry as an example, Susan Wolcott and Gregory Clark have placed culture, efficiency and work ethic in a discussion on comparative economic growth (Clark 1987; Wolcott and Clark, 1999). These papers have become influential, as well as controversial, because they convincingly united two discourses, world inequality and shop-floor practices, something the earlier literature had not done.

A third set of articles has focussed on institutions, more specifically, the microeconomics of contracting in early modern export trade and in nineteenth-century rural credit markets. In both cases, the transaction process was beset by potential contract enforcement failure, partially addressed by means of informal arrangements or, in the case of credit, new courts of law (Kranton and Swamy 1998; 2008; Roy 2011b). Through these writings, the notion of the market is beginning to change, from one where capitalists or expatriates necessarily enjoy more bargaining power, to one where all parties are subject to information deficit and a lack of adequate formal mechanisms to redress contract failure. Lastly, one group of articles has focussed on public goods (Banerjee and Iyer 2005; Iyer 2010; Chaudhary 2010). The older literature had explained the supply of public goods largely with reference to colonial policy and political calculation. Such overarching explanations may hold for canals or railways, but not for education, health or roads, where local conditions and administrative practices mattered a great deal. This new scholarship, therefore, is more mindful of regional differences in institutions, governance, and fiscal conditions, once again a field of enquiry largely neglected in the received narratives of Indian history.

The idea of this book developed partly in response to this new corpus of work. In the next section, we summarize the individual contributions.

The essays

Chapter 2, by Broadberry and Gupta, contributes to the discussion on the Great Divergence in living standards with new statistical methodology. The authors argue that, in terms of real wages, the Indian subcontinent was lagging behind western Europe by the early eighteenth century. A key issue here is the unit of measurement of the wage. Broadberry and Gupta rely on a useful insight from the theory of international trade: prices will tend to equalize for traded goods, but not for non-traded goods. Since cloth was traded for silver, the silver price of cloth would tend to equalize between India and Britain. High silver wages reflect high labour productivity in the sector producing the trading good. However, there was nothing to equalize the price of non-traded food, which was more expensive in the richer economy. The gap in silver wages in Britain and India was large. The purchasing power of the silver wage in terms of the quantity of grain it would buy is the grain wage and the purchasing power of silver wage in terms of the cloth it would buy is the cloth wage. Both are crude measures of the standard of living. However, in an economy close to subsistence, the grain wage may be a better indicator. Thus, the Indian grain wage was closer to the British grain wage, but the cloth wage was much higher in Britain. The declining trend in the grain wage is supported by the declining trend in GDP per capita. The trend shows that Indian GDP per capita compared well with Britain in 1600, but there was a systematic decline starting in the late seventeenth century and stagnation in the nineteenth and early twentieth century. The cloth wage shows a different trend as the cloth became cheaper in the nineteenth century.

In an innovative rereading of the history of the East India Company, in Chapter 3 Hejeebu returns us to the very beginning of the colonial period. In line with a rich tradition of scholars like Peter Marshall, she examines the changes in the internal organization of the Company as it went from a trading enterprise to enjoying territorial power. To begin with, the Company was primarily focussed on procuring cheap Indian textiles for sale in Europe. At this stage, its civilian employees were the most prominent. As its army began to demonstrate its prowess, military officials became more influential, and there were tensions with the civilians. The subsequent acquisition of Indian territory meant that Indian land revenues were available, as were other opportunities for the Company's officials to enrich themselves. This undermined trust between officials in India and their superiors in Britain. As controversy around the Company grew, it was increasingly regulated by Parliament. Hejeebu identifies 1784 as the decisive date when under Pitt's India Act, the Parliament established a 'Board of Control' to supervise the Company. From this date on, she suggests, the East India Company became primarily an administrative rather than a commercial entity.

India's shrinking share of the world textile market after the Industrial Revolution is widely viewed in the literature as a period of 'deindustrialization', as Ray documents in a systematic way. This has been the subject of much debate (Thorner and Thorner 1962; Bagchi 1976; Vicziany 1979; Twomey 1983; Clingingsmith and Williamson 2008). There are three issues: (a) How do we define deindustrialization? (b) Did it actually occur? and (c) If so, what were the reasons for it? In Chapter 4 Indrajit Ray provides a succinct overview of this wide-ranging debate, illustrating the variety of intellectual frameworks that have been brought to bear on this issue, from traditional Marxist approaches to World-Systems theories, to neoclassical Economics, and even long-term climatic changes. The chapter discusses the arguments of the nationalist/Marxist view of India's changing position in world manufacturing as a result of colonial policy. The Company's capture of state power reduced the bargaining power of Indian weavers and merchants and undermined the textile industry. In turn, modern industry was slow to develop. Ray also brings together alternative explanations such as the change in the terms of trade between agriculture and industry as political conflict and weather shocks raised agricultural prices, making this sector more attractive to economic agents.

The trajectory of modern industry in colonial India poses something of a puzzle. Why did this sector develop at all given the colonial emphasis on India as an agricultural producer catering to the needs of an industrial core? By the end of the colonial period there was a significant modern industrial sector – textiles, steel, paper, jute, tea and coal, among others. Although still small as a fraction of output and even more so of employment, this became the most dynamic sector of the economy in terms of labour productivity and technology. Capital per unit of labour was higher compared to other sectors of the Indian economy, but low compared to how similar technology was used in other producing countries, certainly in the core, but also elsewhere. An obvious explanation for this is the scarcity of capital: modern industry requires significant investment, but factor prices determine the capital labour ratio. Prominent scholars like Amiya Bagchi (1972) and Rajat Ray (1982) have also argued that Indian industrialization was inhibited by the discrimination faced by Indian capital. This view stands in contrast to Max Weber's view of industrialization, where the lack of the 'Protestant ethic' inhibited entrepreneurship and industrialization. Gupta takes on both formulations in Chapter 5. On the issue of discrimination, she points out that while British capital was dominant in eastern India, Indian capital had the lion's share of the textile industry in western India. Therefore, as an explanation for patterns of investment, the discrimination story is, at least, incomplete. Gupta answers the question with reference to the role of social networks and information behind the formation of investment patterns.

In Chapter 6, Balachandran picks up on the theme of changing structure of trade in colonial India from the exporter of textiles to agricultural goods, but then follows the timeline to the early twentieth century when India emerges once again as an exporter of industrial goods such as cotton and jute products, although on a limited scale. The chapter broadens the theme to look at the impact of the specifically *colonial* nature of the Indian economy and the interconnections between trade, capital flows and banking. This exploration paints the big picture of a colonial economy interlocked with the imperial economy both in relationships of exploitation and economic gain. The discussion of the literature ranges across a broad spectrum bounded by Naoroji and Dutt's 'drain theory' on one side and Davis and Huttenback's view that the empire 'did not pay' on the other side. Balachandran comments on the still unresolved problems of the size and importance of the 'drain'. But his central argument is that the grand themes of 'colonialism', 'empire' and 'globalization' have led to a neglect of important relationships between India and the world that are not obvious under these rubrics. He points, for instance, to the extent of involvement of Indian workers and entrepreneurs in international merchant shipping.

Two-thirds of the employed population in colonial India lived on agriculture or natural resource extraction. Agriculture, therefore, merits a detailed consideration. It is also the most intensively researched theme in the field. Chapter 7, by Chaudhary, Gupta, Roy and Swamy, therefore, is intended more as a review of current research than a comprehensive survey. It has four parts: land tenure and institutions, productivity growth, public investment, and famines. The chapter focuses on slow productivity growth in agriculture arising from a failure to bring about technological change. Investment in irrigation by public and private sectors brought about changes in some regions and increased regional diversity, but did not succeed in generating major gains in productivity. One of the reflections of this failure was the famine of 1943. The chapter summarizes two competing explanations of the famine: the first in terms of sheer availability of goods, and the second focusing on access or 'entitlement' to available food.

Colonial rule led to greater integration with the world economy, with some regions participating more than others. Also, different political realignments occurred across the subcontinent. How was regional inequality affected? We can, in principle, ask two questions: (a) How did outcomes differ between the Princely States and British India? and (b) How much of this difference across regions is *because* some regions were under British rule and others were ruled indirectly? Iyer's contribution addresses the causal impact of indirect rule, question (b). Chapter 8 provides an excellent illustration of the direction taken by recent research in studying the persistent effects of historical institutions in economic development. Empirical work in economics has always suffered in comparison with fields like medical research because of its reliance on observational data: when one cannot conduct experiments, it is harder to establish causality. Over the last decade, economists have raised their standards on this issue in part because they have started to do experiments. But even in Economic History economists have begun to look for 'natural experiments', changes that, for statistical purposes, can be considered 'as good as random'. Iyer exploits a mid-nineteenth century British policy, the 'Doctrine of Lapse', according to which Princely States in which the ruler died without an heir were annexed by the East India Company. If this event (death without an heir) occurred randomly, its impact on future outcomes would reflect the role of direct British rule, as compared to rule by an Indian prince. Iyer finds that the regions ruled by Indian princes have better present-day outcomes in health and education, and she is able to claim that this impact is causal. In another exercise, Iyer conducts a careful examination of political and administrative history to find variation in land tenure that can be considered 'exogenous' or de facto random. She finds that landlord-dominated regions produced an institutional overhang: even though they did better in the colonial period, their legacy for the post-colonial period has been harmful in various dimensions, including agricultural productivity, health and education.

The provision of social and physical infrastructure in economic development has emerged as a major theme in economics. The Economic History literature on the industrial countries has discussed the role of such investments. Chaudhary picks up these themes in the chapters on education and railways. Starting with railways in Chapter 9 (the first of these two chapters), Bogart and Chaudhary provide a comprehensive overview of the literature. This is another area where the nationalist view emphasized the adverse consequences of colonial policy. According to this view the railways were constructed to facilitate trade between Britain and India and, by guaranteeing positive rates of return, assisted British companies. Bogart and Chaudhary discuss the more recent literature on the impact of the railways that relates to the broader issues of infrastructural development. Two particularly interesting links with the existing literature on public ownership are discussed. First, they argue that in hindsight the notorious scheme of guaranteed returns to British investors in railroad construction can be assessed more favourably: given demand and cost uncertainties, even present-day developing countries have difficulty in attracting foreign investment in infrastructure unless they offer subsidies, implicit or explicit. Second, contrary to the negative view of government ownership in much of present-day discussion, the Government of India's eventual takeover of privately owned lines *lowered* costs. Railways were one of the most successful industries in terms of productivity and a reduction in costs. The railways integrated markets, reduced price fluctuations and therefore reduced the negative shocks of famines.

Education is a surprisingly neglected field in Indian Economic History. In Chapter 10 Chaudhary shows the inequalities in literacy across region, gender and caste. These are analysed in terms of opportunity cost of attending school and returns to education. The evidence suggests that returns to education were high despite poverty and a lack of alternative employment opportunities in agriculture. Chaudhary's findings are in the spirit of recent research from different parts of the world showing that there is opposition to mass education in stratified and fragmented societies. She finds that primary education, in particular, was underfunded in colonial India, with the colonial state not investing enough in education – and where it did, opposition from upper castes and landed elites prevented a primary school movement. Secondary education, more likely to be accessed by elites, did far better and was surprisingly on a par with some advanced European countries.

The emergence and impact of the Indian working class as the economy underwent structural change is the theme of the next two chapters. In Chapter 11 Roy documents the shift from self- employment to wage earning over the twentieth century. Although the emergence of a working-class identity was a slow process as documented by labour historians, the absolute number and the share of wage earners in total employment rose during colonial rule. In the course of a little over 100 years spanning colonial and postcolonial times, most of these workers had moved from a variety of self-employment situations to wage employment or working. The shift of work from self-employment to wage employment is regarded as one of the most fundamental transformations of Indian society in this time. The dominant view in the literature sees the shift with reference to crises in self-employment brought on by colonial interventions and commercialization, which forced peasants and artisans to become wage earners. Roy instead favours an explanation that allows the worker the capacity to choose, and suggests how we can read these choices on the basis of historical evidence.

A significant number of the new wage workers ended up in the factories of Bombay and Calcutta. The second chapter on labour, Chapter 12 by Susan Wolcott, focuses on the wage earners in modern industry. Here she sees them as a powerful interest group. The existing literature on labour utilization in modern industry has emphasized the low cost of this workforce. Wolcott's chapter breaks with that tendency. In contrast to the usual emphasis on the low cost of Indian workers, she highlights their low productivity and artificially high cost. This is reflected, for instance, in high worker-to-machine ratios in textiles. This evidence is viewed differently by Gupta's chapter on industrialization, which emphasized the high worker/machine ratios as the profit maximizing response to the low cost of Indian labour. Wolcott's chapter emphasizes the bargaining power of Indian labour, which, she argues, raised labour costs. While formal unions were not very effective, caste and kinship networks facilitated collective bargaining. This is reflected in the relatively high incidence of strikes. The important link between social differentiation and organizational cultures is invoked very differently by Gupta and Wolcott: in Gupta's work they facilitate industrialization by allowing information sharing and capital mobilization whereas in Wolcott's they undermine industrialization by lowering worker productivity and raising labour costs.

Much of the economic activity described involved interactions between 'principals' (the landlords, merchants, lenders and planters) and 'agents' (the borrowers, artisans and workers). These interactions were often fraught with conflict, violence and many changes in the regulatory and legal settings. Much of the existing work has emphasized the political power and coercive capacity of the principals, especially those of European origin. In Chapter 13 Swamy complicates the picture, using a simple framework from contract theory. The argument is that within the prevailing power structure, contracts had to satisfy two features: a 'participation constraint' (unless the worker was entirely coerced) and an 'incentive compatibility constraint', which means that the worker had to be motivated to fulfil at least part of the contract to which she/he was committed. Swamy argues that the need to satisfy these constraints placed limits on the manner and extent to which principals could use coercion, notwithstanding the support of the colonial state. He also documents the state's struggle to find an appropriate regulatory framework in various settings: textiles, opium and tea.

Finally, in Chapter 14 Bharadwaj and Quirolo provide one of the first economic analyses of the last, and traumatic, event of the colonial era: Partition. The authors look at different aspects of migration. Migration flows are explained by the difficulty of moving, that is, the distance from the border and how hostile the home environment was, which is indicated by the share of the minority population. Migrants are analysed in terms of education, gender and occupation. An interesting finding is that more educated people migrated and entered into non-agricultural occupations at their destination. In situations where they entered into agricultural occupations, such as migrants from the geographical boundary of present-day Bangladesh to present-day West Bengal, they contributed to jute production not simply by increasing labour input, but through specialized knowledge or human capital.

Conclusion

We do not wish to suggest to the student that the essays compiled here have left conventional themes behind. On the contrary, much of this new literature will not make sense without reference to the long-standing debates within the field. Nor do we suggest that the book is a comprehensive survey of the literature. The contributions do share an awareness of the main organizing ideas of the field. But they are also willing to think outside them. What we try to capture here are attempts by a number of scholars to push the boundaries of the field and connect Indian history with economics and global history. The book represents the first coordinated move to draw attention to this enterprise.

References

Allen, R. C. (2007). 'India in the Great Divergence', in T.J. Hatton, K.H. O'Rourke and A. M. Taylor, eds., *The New Comparative Economic History: Essays in honor of Jeffrey G. Williamson*, Cambridge, MA: MIT Press, pp. 9–32.

Bagchi, A. K. (1972). *Private Investment in India, 1900–1939*, Cambridge: Cambridge University Press.

———. (1976). 'Deindustrialization in India in the Nineteenth Century: Some Theoretical Implications', *Journal of Development Studies*, 12 (2), pp. 135–164.

Banerjee, A., and L. Iyer (2005). 'History, Institutions, and Economic Performance: The Legacy of Colonial Land Tenure Systems in India', *American Economic Review*, 95 (4), pp. 1190–1213.

Bayly, C.A. (1983). *Rulers, Townsmen and Bazaars: North Indian Society in the Age of British Expansion, 1770–1870*, Cambridge: Cambridge University Press.

Blyn, G. (1962). *Agricultural Trends in India, 1891–1947: Output, Availability and Productivity*, Philadelphia: University of Pennsylvania Press.

Bose, S., ed. (1994). *Credit, Markets and the Agrarian Economy*, Delhi: Oxford University Press.

Broadberry, S., and B. Gupta (2006). 'The Early Modern Great Divergence: Wages, Prices and Economic Development in Europe and Asia, 1500–1800', *Economic History Review*, 59 (1), pp. 2–31.

Chakrabarty, D. (1989). *Rethinking Working-class History: Bengal, 1890–1940*, Princeton: Princeton University Press.

Chandavarkar, R. (1994). *The Origins of Industrial Capitalism in India*, Cambridge: Cambridge University Press.

Chaudhary, L. (2010). 'Land Revenues, Schools and Literacy: A Historical Examination of Public and Private Funding of Education', *Indian Economic and Social History Review*, 47 (2), pp. 179–204.

———. (1978). *The Trading World of Asia and the English East India Company: 1660–1760*, Cambridge: Cambridge University Press.

Clark, G. (1987). 'Why Isn't the Whole World Developed? Lessons from the Cotton Mills', *Journal of Economic History*, 49 (3), pp. 107–114.

Clingingsmith, D., and J. Williamson (2008). 'Deindustrialization in 18th and 19th Century India: Mughal Decline, Climate Shocks and British Industrial Ascent', *Explorations in Economic History, 45 (3)*, pp. 209–234.

Hatton, T.J., K.H. O'Rourke, and A. M. Taylor, eds. (2007). *The New Comparative Economic History: Essays in honor of Jeffrey G. Williamson*, Cambridge, MA: MIT Press.

Haynes, D. (2012). *Small Town Capitalism in Western India – Artisans, Merchants, and the Making of the Informal Economy, 1870–1960*, Cambridge: Cambridge University Press.

Iyer, L. (2010). 'Direct versus Indirect Colonial Rule in India: Long-term Consequences', *Review of Economics and Statistics, 92 (4)*, pp. 693–712.

Kranton, R., and A.V. Swamy (1998). 'The Hazards of Piecemeal Reform: British Civil Courts and the Credit Market in Colonial India', *Journal of Development Economics, 58 (1)*, pp. 1–24.

———. (2008). 'Contracts, Hold-up, and Exports: Textiles and Opium in Colonial India', *American Economic Review, 98 (3)*, pp. 967–989.

Kumar, D., and M. Desai, eds. (1983). *The Cambridge Economic History of India, Vol. II, c.1757–1970*, Cambridge: Cambridge University Press.

Ludden, D., ed. (1994). *Agricultural Production in Indian History*, Delhi: Oxford University Press.

Maddison, A. (1971). *Class Structure and Economic Growth, India and Pakistan since the Moghuls*, London: Routledge.

Morris, M. D. (1983). 'The Growth of Large-scale Industry to 1947', in D. Kumar and M. Desai, eds., *The Cambridge Economic History of India, Vol. II, c.1757–1970*, Cambridge: Cambridge University Press.

Mukherjee, M. (1965). *National Income of India*, Calcutta: Firma KLM.

Parthasarathi, P. (1999). 'Rethinking Wages and Competitiveness in the Eighteenth Century: Britain and South India', *Past and Present, 158 (1)*, pp. 79–109.

Pomeranz, K. (2000). *The Great Divergence: China, Europe, and the Making of the Modern World Economy*, Princeton: Princeton University Press.

Raj, K. N., N. Bhattacharya, S. Guha, and S. Padhi, eds. (1985). *Essays on the Commercialization of Indian Agriculture*, Delhi: Oxford University Press.

Ray, R. K. (1982). *Industrialization in India. Growth and Conflict in the Private Corporate Sector, 1914–1947*, Delhi: Oxford University Press.

Rothermund, D. (2000). *An Economic History of India: From Pre-colonial Times to 1991*, London: Routledge.

Roy, T. (1999). *Traditional Industry in the Economy of Colonial India*, Cambridge: Cambridge University Press.

———. (2011a). *The Economic History of India 1857–1947*, Delhi: Oxford University Press.

———. (2011b). 'Indigo and Law in Colonial India', *Economic History Review, 64 (S1)*, pp. 60–75.

Sivasubramonian, S. (2000). *National Income of India in the Twentieth Century*, Delhi: Oxford University Press.

Stone, I. (1984). *Canal Irrigation in British India*, Cambridge: Cambridge University Press.

Thorner, D., and A. Thorner (1962). *Land and Labour in India*, New York: Asia Publishing House.

Tomlinson, B. R. (1982). *The Political Economy of the Raj: The Decline of Colonialism*, London: Macmillan.

Tripathi, D. (2004). *The Oxford History of Indian Business*, Delhi: Oxford University Press.

Twomey, M.J. (1983). 'Employment in Nineteenth Century Indian Textiles', *Explorations in Economic History, 20 (1)*, pp. 37–57.

Vicziany, M. (1979). 'The De-industrialisation of India in the Nineteenth Century: A Methodological Critique of Amiya Kumar Bagchi', *Indian Economic and Social History Review, 16 (2)*, pp. 105–146.

Whitcombe, E. (1972). *Agrarian Conditions in Northern India, Vol. 1,* Berkeley and Los Angeles: University of California Press.

Wolcott, S., and G. Clark (1999). 'Why Nations Fail: Managerial Decisions and Performance in Indian Cotton Textiles, 1890–1938', *Journal of Economic History, 59 (2)*, pp. 397–423.

2

INDIAN ECONOMIC PERFORMANCE AND LIVING STANDARDS

1600–2000

Stephen Broadberry and Bishnupriya Gupta

Introduction

Why did India fall behind Europe in terms of economic performance and living standards? Colonization and unequal exchange in trade have been suggested as explanations of the impoverishment of India and China in the nineteenth century (Frank 1998; Bagchi 1976; Amin 1976). This raises two questions: How far back did India look similar to the economies in western Europe, and did the divergence coincide with the colonization of India? This date is the conquest of Bengal by the East India Company in 1757. This chapter takes a long-run view and presents evidence on living standards in India going back to 1595. Our key indicators are based on the purchasing power of the wages of unskilled workers and gross domestic product per capita. By taking a long-run view we can try to pinpoint when the living standards began to decline and how they compared with European standards in the sixteenth and seventeenth centuries, before India became part of an international division of labour through the trading nexus established by the European trading companies. The discussion is situated in the context of Pomeranz's (2000) picture of the Great Divergence between Europe and Asia. The same indicators can also be used to trace the evolution of Indian economic performance during the colonial and post-colonial years.

The chapter proceeds as follows. We begin with a brief survey of the existing literature on the wealth and poverty of the Indian people. This is followed by a more detailed discussion of the Great Divergence, focusing on Indian wages and prices in an international comparative framework. Finally, we consider India's economic performance by making use of a historical national accounting framework to analyze GDP per capita and sectoral performance.

India's long-run economic performance

India's economic performance since the late sixteenth century has been the subject of enduring controversy. The travelogues of Europeans to India in the sixteenth and seventeenth centuries often described great wealth and opulence, but it is not difficult to see this as reflecting their contact with the ruling classes, who enjoyed a luxurious lifestyle with consumption of high-quality food, clothing and ornaments, as well as imported luxury products. The middle class was small and the merchants that European travellers most frequently came into contact with also enjoyed a comfortable lifestyle (Moreland 1923). However, most travel accounts of Mughal India and the Deccan noted that the majority of Indians lived in poverty (Chandra 1982; Fukazawa 1982). The labouring classes were seen as living in mud huts with thatched roofs, eating inferior grains and wearing rudimentary clothing. The use of footwear was relatively unknown. Wheat was not widely consumed and inferior grains such as *jowar* and *bajra* were grown everywhere (Moreland 1923, pp. 197–203).

Based on temple donation records in southern India, Ramaswamy (1985) confirms a similar picture. The nobility was prosperous, a small group of weavers formed a middle class, and the rural poor and low caste artisans were at the bottom of the social hierarchy. The rich and the middle classes consumed rice, but others could only afford *ragi* or rye (Ramaswamy 1985, pp. 99–100). The middle-class weavers earned a little more than unskilled workers in the seventeenth and eighteenth centuries.

The continuity in living standards of the majority of the population over the eighteenth and nineteenth centuries was noted by several writers on the economy of this period. Buchanan (1807) found that although weavers enjoyed a comfortable lifestyle in the early nineteenth century, the mass of cultivators lived in poverty. Moreland (1923) suggests that living standards of the majority were little different in the early twentieth century, although the middle class could have been larger in the later period. The evidence therefore suggests that people in agricultural occupations were poor. This was where the majority of the population lived and worked. While cultural and climatic conditions may explain some of the consumption differences between India and Europe, most writers were in little doubt that the average Indian lived in poverty. The picture of the prosperous weaver or the rich nobility did not represent the majority of the Indian population.

The reign of Akbar is usually seen as the peak of economic well-being. It is well documented in Abū 'l-Fazl's (1595) *Ā' īn–i-Akbarī*, which meticulously reported wages and prices in the region of Agra. This has provided a reference point for real wage comparisons with later years. Desai (1972) made the striking claim that at best, the average standard of living in 1961 was no higher than in 1595, when although the average wage would buy fewer industrial goods such as clothing, it could buy more food, with the changing relative prices reflecting the changing productivity trends in agriculture and industry. This paper provoked some controversy over the details of the calculations (Heston 1977; Moosvi 1973, 1977; Desai 1978). Nevertheless, most writers seem to accept the idea of a downward real wage trend during the seventeenth and eighteenth centuries before recovery during the twentieth century, a pattern first suggested by Mukerjee (1967).

This view of Mughal India as a relatively backward economy has been challenged recently by the work of revisionist economic historians, whose work must be assessed within the wider context of changing views on the Great Divergence of living standards between Asia and Europe. Parthasarathi's (1998; 2011) characterization of south Indian real wages as on a par with English real wages during the eighteenth century is strikingly at variance with the older literature, but fits well with the claims of Pomeranz (2000), Frank (1998) and other world historians that the most developed parts of Asia were on the same development level as the most developed parts of Europe such as Britain and the Netherlands as late as 1800. Bayly's (1983) description of a thriving market economy in north India during the eighteenth century leaves a similar impression. More recently, Sivramkrishna (2009) has argued that living standards calculated in terms of consumption of a cheaper inferior grain rather than rice in the state of Mysore in southern India were comparable to the advanced parts of Europe in the early nineteenth century.

All of this qualitative and quantitative evidence has given us the first steps towards understanding the early modern economy of India, but falls short of establishing trends in living standards. The first attempt may be found in Mukerjee's (1967) estimates of real wages from 1600. The book puts together data on wages and prices and is valuable. Broadberry and Gupta (2006) present systematic evidence of wages to establish what Indian living standards might have looked like relative to the well-known prosperous societies of northwest Europe, and we shall examine this evidence in more detail in the next section.

The availability of statistical information on India improved greatly from the late nineteenth century, so that from the time of the first census in 1871 it is possible to build up a much more systematic picture of Indian economic performance (Roy 2011; Gupta 2012). A picture has emerged of some growth of per capita incomes during the late nineteenth century, but stagnation during the first half of the twentieth century and the beginning of modern economic growth after independence in 1947.

Wages and prices

The established practice in the literature on measuring living standards across time and place has been to gather data on money wages of unskilled and skilled workers. For Europe, there has been a long tradition of collecting such data on the wages of building workers, which have been converted to a common unit of grams of silver to yield the silver wage. At a time of a silver standard, the conversion of money wages paid in particular currencies to this common basis facilitates international comparisons. To establish the purchasing power of these wages, it has been common to divide the silver wage by the silver price of the common local grain to yield the grain wage, which has often been taken as a crude measure of the standard of living. The closer an economy is to subsistence, the more accurate is the grain wage as a measure of living standards since people then have to spend a large part of their income on food to survive.

Trends in silver and grain wages, 1600–1871

Broadberry and Gupta (2006) assemble a database of wages and grain prices in India, allowing for regional variation, and make comparisons with similar data for Britain.

Part A of Table 2.1 provides data on silver wages and grain wages in northern and western India, drawing largely on sources for Agra and Surat. Wage rates are provided for both unskilled and skilled workers, although we shall focus primarily on unskilled workers in the international comparisons. Wages in rupees are converted to silver using information from Habib (1982) and Chaudhuri (1978). The broad trend was for the silver wage to rise, with the skilled wage being roughly twice the unskilled wage. Note that the rising silver wage is consistent with the constancy of the money wage expressed in copper *dams* per day, since the price of silver depreciated relative to copper (Habib 1982, p. 370). Grain wages in northern and western India were obtained by dividing the silver wages by the price of wheat, also expressed in terms of silver. In contrast to the rising trend of silver wages, grain wages trended downwards in northern and western India, as money wages failed to keep up with the rising trend in grain prices, particularly during the early seventeenth century.

Turning to southern India in Part B of Table 2.1, the wage and price data are drawn largely from the area around Madras, with the wage rates often referring to skilled and unskilled weavers. Money wage rates here are usually available in units of the *pagoda* (a gold coin); these pagoda rates are converted to silver rupees using East India Company standard rates from Chaudhuri (1978, p. 471). Silver wages for southern India are converted to grain wages using the price of rice as the deflator. It is worth noting that in general the levels and trends of silver and grain wages in southern India fit well with the levels and trends in the north.[1]

TABLE 2.1 Indian silver and grain wages, 1595–1874

A. Northern and western India

	Silver wage (grams per day)		Wheat grain wage (kg per day)		Rice grain wage (kg per day)	
	Unskilled	Skilled	Unskilled	Skilled	Unskilled	Skilled
1595	0.67	1.62	5.2	12.6	3.1	7.5
1616	0.86		3.0		2.4	
1623	1.08		3.8		2.9	
1637	1.08	2.37	3.8	8.3	2.9	6.5
1640	1.29		4.5		3.5	
1690	1.40		4.3			
1874	1.79	5.27	2.5	7.5		

B. Southern India

	Silver wage (grams per day)		Rice grain wage (kg per day)	
	Unskilled	Skilled	Unskilled	Skilled
1610–13	1.15		5.7	
1600–50	1.15		3.2	
1680	1.44	2.44	3.9	6.9
1741–50	1.49		2.1	
1750	(3.02)	(7.56)	(4.2)	(10.5)
1779	0.86		1.1	
1790	1.44		1.8	

Source: Broadberry and Gupta (2006, p. 14).

To make any normative statement on the standard of living, we need to know what the subsistence level is. In the simplest case of the grain wage, how many calories would meet the minimum sustenance need of a family? Brennig (1986, p. 349) argues that subsistence consumption for a household of six was 3.1 kilograms of rice per day. Taking the wheat/rice ratio of calories per pound from Parthasarathi (1998, p. 83) yields a subsistence consumption of 4.7 kilograms of wheat per day for a family of six. On this basis, grain wages were always above subsistence for skilled workers but fell below the subsistence level for unskilled workers during the early seventeenth century. This raises questions about how the families of unskilled labourers survived, to which we return in the section on real consumption wages. Here it is worth noting that we use the price of rice and wheat as the deflator, whereas poor families tended to consume cheaper grains as noted earlier. More realistic and complicated calculations of a subsistence consumption basket including clothing and shelter will be considered next.

Table 2.2 provides an Anglo-Indian comparison of silver and grain wages for unskilled labourers. In Part A, we see that Indian silver wages for unskilled workers were little more than one-fifth of the English level in the late sixteenth century and fell to just over one-seventh of the English level during the eighteenth century. The silver wage data thus show unambiguously that the Great Divergence was already well under way by the late sixteenth century.[2]

Turning to the grain wage in Part B of Table 2.2, we see that India remained closer to the English level until the end of the seventeenth century. The data indicate

TABLE 2.2 An Anglo-Indian comparison of the daily wages of unskilled labourers, 1550–1849

A. Silver wages (grams of silver per day)

Date	Southern England	India	Indian wage as % of English wage
1550–99	3.4	0.7	21
1600–49	4.1	1.1	27
1650–99	5.6	1.4	25
1700–49	7.0	1.5	21
1750–99	8.3	1.2	14
1800–49	14.6	1.8	12

B. Grain wages (kilograms of grain per day)

Date	England	India		Indian wage as % of English wage
	(wheat)	(wheat)	(rice, on wheat equivalent basis)	
1550–99	6.3	5.2		83
1600–49	4.0	3.8		95
1650–99	5.4	4.3		80
1700–49	8.0		3.2	40
1750–99	7.0		2.3	33
1800–49	8.6	2.5		29

Source: Broadberry and Gupta (2006, p. 17).

a sharp divergence during the eighteenth century, partly as a result of a rise in the English grain wage, but also partly as a result of a decline in the Indian grain wage.

Explaining international differences in silver and grain wages

How do we explain this big Anglo-Indian difference in silver wages but not in grain wages as early as the sixteenth century? Broadberry and Gupta (2006) note that this Indian pattern of comparatively low silver wages, but with grain wages much closer to the level of Britain until the eighteenth century, is also character-istic of the less-developed parts of continental Europe during the early modern period. One potential explanation of this pattern can be ruled out: the inflow of bullion from the New World causing inflation in both money wages and grain prices. While this might at first sight seem to be a promising explanation of the difference between Europe and Asia, since most of the New World bullion flowed initially into Europe, a consideration of intra-European differences immediately disposes of this argument, for the bullion flows entered Europe through Spain, which nevertheless moved from being a high-wage to a relatively low-wage region during the early modern period. Rather, it was northwest Europe, and particularly Holland and Britain, that emerged as the high wage and high price region. Instead, we need to turn to the Balassa-Samuelson approach to wage and price level dif-ferences between countries for an understanding of these trends (Balassa 1964; Samuelson 1964).

It is well known that there is a tendency for both wages and prices to be higher in developed economies, so that an international comparison of wages at the market exchange rate gives a misleading impression of the gap in living stan-dards between developed and less developed countries. Consequently, wages and per capita incomes are usually compared on a purchasing power parity (PPP) basis, taking account of the prices of consumer goods in the countries being compared. Development economists see the relationship between the PPP-converted and the exchange rate converted per capita incomes as reflecting differences in the level of development, and we can see the relationship between grain wages and silver wages in a similar light (see Box 2.1).

BOX 2.1   THE BALASSA-SAMUELSON FRAMEWORK

The Balassa-Samuelson framework can explain the difference between silver and grain wages. The overall price level tends to be higher in richer countries where wages are high. If goods are traded, then prices will tend to be equalized across countries because of the possibility of arbitrage. But for goods that are not traded, prices will be higher in richer countries. Wages in a less-developed country (LDC) meet the food needs of the population at LDC food prices, but not at developed country prices. Manufactures produced in an LDC are relatively expensive at LDC prices but competitive on the world market because of low wages in developed country prices. Applying the model to the early modern period, we assume that grain is non-tradable internationally, reflecting the fact that grain was bulky and costly to transport. Thus grain prices were not equalized between Asia and Europe. On the other hand, commodities such as cloth and bullion were widely traded internationally, with arbitrage tending to equalize prices between countries. Higher prices of non-tradables reflect higher wages and higher labour productivity in tradable goods (see Broadberry and Gupta 2006 for a theoretical analysis). Consequently we can argue that higher silver wages are a feature of a more productive economy, while grain wages are determined by the price of non-tradables (i.e. food).

Towards real consumption wages

The international comparison of silver wages and grain wages thus provides bounds for the Anglo-Indian ratio of real consumption wages. For India, Table 2.3 presents a range of measures: as well as the silver wage and the grain wage, we have the cloth wage and the real consumption wage. The cloth wage is constructed by systematically collecting evidence on the price of cotton cloth in India from the records of the East India Company for the period before 1833 and from Parliamentary Papers for subsequent years (Chaudhuri 1978; Bowen 2007; Twomey 1983; Sandberg 1974). It is interesting to note that the scale of the Indian grain wage decline is similar to that suggested by van Zanden (1999) and Allen (2001) for early modern southern and eastern Europe, where a long period of decline steadily eroded the post–Black Death doubling of grain wages.

However, note that the cloth wage declined by less than the grain wage during the seventeenth and eighteenth centuries and increased substantially during the nineteenth century. This reflects the change in the relative price of cloth in terms of the price of grain and supports the evidence from Desai (1972) that the average wage in 1961 could have bought less food but more cloth than the average wage in 1595. As a result, the real consumption wage declined by much less than the grain wage, which has often been taken as an easily available index of living standards. Our real consumption wage is a weighted average of the grain wage and the cloth wage, with a weight of two-thirds given to the former, consistent with budget studies for India during this period (Allen 2007).

Similar calculations have been made by Allen (2007) for north India and Bengal, but including data on prices for a number of other food items such as *ghee* and sugar. Allen presents his data in terms of welfare ratios, defined as the number of subsistence baskets that can be purchased by the annual earnings of a wage labourer. Allen assumes that a man needed to earn enough to buy three such baskets to support a family consisting of himself, his wife and several children. A welfare ratio above one thus indicates that wages are sufficient for a society to feed itself and

TABLE 2.3 Real wages of Indian unskilled labourers, 1600–1871 (1871 = 100)

Year	Silver wage	Grain price	Cloth price	Grain wage	Cloth wage	Real consumption wage
1600	37.7	18.3	57.1	205.9	65.9	159.7
1650	72.3	40.9	127.6	176.8	56.7	137.2
1700	78.3	46.6	150.6	168.1	52.0	129.8
1750	83.5	61.4	168.3	136.0	49.6	107.5
1801	80.3	67.6	166.7	118.9	48.2	95.5
1811	68.1	70.4	182.6	96.7	37.3	77.1
1821	69.9	67.9	180.4	103.0	38.7	81.8
1831	71.1	73.1	171.8	97.3	41.4	78.8
1841	72.3	61.3	110.3	117.9	65.5	100.7
1851	72.9	63.3	89.0	115.1	81.9	104.1
1861	98.8	105.6	100.0	93.6	98.8	95.3
1871	100.0	100.0	100.0	100.0	100.0	100.0

Sources: Broadberry and Gupta (2006, p. 14), Mukerjee (1967, p. 58), Chaudhuri (1978), Bowen (2007), Twomey (1983), Sandberg (1974).

reproduce. We noted earlier that unskilled wages fell below the subsistence level of grain needed to support a family in north India during the seventeenth century, and this result is confirmed by Allen (2007), who finds welfare ratios consistently well below one using a wider basket of goods. However, as Allen (2007, pp. 22–26) notes, this welfare ratio is based on a basket of goods that includes superior-quality grains. In practice, poorer workers consumed inferior grains – which were much cheaper, but still provided sufficient kilocalories to survive and reproduce. Welfare ratios calculated using the bare-bones subsistence basket rarely fell below unity.

Allen's (2007, p. 28) international comparison of real consumption wages between England and India broadly confirms the grain wage findings of Broadberry and Gupta (2006). Real consumption wages in north India and Bengal were close to the English level in the early seventeenth century, but fell substantially behind during the eighteenth century.

The decline in the grain wage during the seventeenth and eighteenth centuries was accompanied by a substantial increase in population from 142 million in 1600 to 207 million in 1801 (Visaria and Visaria 1983, p. 466). However, caution should be exercised before drawing strong Malthusian conclusions here, since the grain wage stagnated as population rose further to 256 million by 1871, and there is much evidence to suggest the existence of surplus land as late as the early nineteenth century (Buchanan 1807; Parthasarathi 2001). Nevertheless, periodic famines did create spikes in grain prices with sometimes devastating consequences for mortality and population growth throughout this period, and indeed into the twentieth century.[3]

Real wages since 1871

The analysis of growth and living standards during the period since 1871 has mostly been conducted within a national accounting framework, drawing on the wider

TABLE 2.4 Real wages of Indian workers, 1871–1981
(1871 = 100)

	Industry	Agriculture
1871	100.0	100.0
1881	93.2	77.1
1891	80.0	
1901	82.3	105.7
1911	81.1	
1921	82.3	82.9
1929	82.3	134.3
1935	103.4	80.0
1943	78.0	51.4
1947	101.5	88.6
1951	139.9	137.1
1961	161.1	120.0
1971	185.7	120.0
1981	208.5	

Sources: Industry: Mukerjee (1967), Tulpule and Datta (1988, p. 2275).
Agriculture: Roy (2011, p. 137).

availability of statistical information after the move to Crown rule. However, before analyzing trends in GDP per capita in the next section, it will be helpful to set out the path of real wages in Indian industry and agriculture in Table 2.4. These data suggest a stagnation of living standards during the first half of the twentieth century, followed by rising living standards after independence, although real wages rose considerably faster in industry than in agriculture.

Historical national accounting

Overall economic performance before 1871

So far, we have pieced together our picture of Indian economic performance before 1871 largely on the basis of wages and prices. However, a full assessment of economic performance at this time requires information on a wider range of evidence. Broadberry, Custodis and Gupta (2015) have recently applied the methodology of historical national accounting to make use of all the currently available data series to produce the series of GDP in Table 2.5. As well as utilizing the series analyzed earlier on wages, grain prices and cloth prices, the estimation of GDP also makes use of data on agricultural and industrial exports, crop yields and cultivated acreage, cloth consumption per capita, urbanization rates and government revenue to build up to aggregate output from sectoral estimates for agriculture, industry and services.

Referring to Table 2.5, agricultural output is constructed from the demand side using data on population, wages and prices to estimate domestic demand, and data on exports for foreign demand. These demand-based estimates are then cross-checked over the long run for consistency with agricultural supply, and estimated using data on crop yields and the cultivated land area. Industrial production for the domestic market can also be estimated from information on wages and prices, but cross-checked against independent information on cloth consumption per capita. Output of the export industries is based on the excellent export data collected by the European East India companies. A weighted average of the output of home and export industries is used to chart the movement of total industry and commerce. For services, the output of the government sector is measured using data on tax revenue, while the size of the private services and rent sector is assumed to move in line with the urban population. These methods are based on approaches to historical national accounting that have been developed in the context of European economies, but have also recently been applied to Asian countries. Note that a particular feature of this approach is to build in cross-checks where possible, so that the estimates of agricultural output from both the supply and demand sides match and the estimation of home industrial output matches with independent estimates of cloth consumption per head.

In Table 2.5, we see that total industry and commerce grew rapidly between 1650 and 1801, driven particularly by exports; the agricultural sector also grew, but less rapidly. Since agriculture was the largest sector, the growth of total output was also quite modest before 1801. Total output stagnated between 1801 and 1841 as modest agricultural growth was offset by deindustrialization, due to the collapse of industrial exports as Britain replaced India as the world's major producer and exporter of cotton textiles. There was a return to modest total output growth between 1841 and 1871 as industrial growth returned and agricultural growth accelerated.

Combining the GDP series from Table 2.5 with population data, we see in Table 2.6 that India's per capita GDP declined during the seventeenth and eighteenth centuries before stabilizing during the nineteenth century. By comparing

TABLE 2.5 Indian real GDP by sector, 1600–1871 (1871 = 100)

Year	Agriculture	Home industries	Export industries	Total industry and commerce	Rent and services	Government	Total real GDP
1600	67.8	72.4	148.6	80.0	95.5	84.3	71.9
1650	63.8	67.1	148.6	75.3	95.5	48.2	67.3
1700	72.2	74.3	202.0	87.0	103.0	60.4	75.7
1750	76.8	84.0	213.6	97.0	110.8	46.9	81.3
1801	79.3	90.2	457.9	127.0	120.7	74.5	87.5
1811	76.0	82.3	304.7	104.6	125.3	77.3	82.9
1821	74.9	78.6	183.2	89.0	110.3	70.6	79.2
1831	77.5	84.3	65.2	82.4	116.2	71.3	81.8
1841	82.8	97.0	56.6	92.9	104.6	79.3	87.3
1851	91.5	105.2	49.5	99.6	114.4	87.8	95.9
1861	89.2	112.9	56.3	107.3	109.4	86.9	95.6
1871	100.0	100.0	100.0	100.0	100.0	100.0	100.0

Source: Broadberry, Custodis and Gupta (2015).

TABLE 2.6 Comparative India/GB GDP per capita, 1600–1871

	Indian GDP per capita	GB GDP per capita	India/GB GDP per capita	India/GB GDP per capita
	1871 = 100			GB = 100
1600	129.7	30.5	424.4	61.5
1650	121.2	29.9	405.2	58.8
1700	118.2	42.5	278.0	40.3
1750	109.6	46.5	234.3	34.2
1801	108.2	56.6	191.3	27.7
1811	98.8	56.2	175.8	25.5
1821	98.9	58.0	170.4	24.7
1831	97.0	63.9	151.7	22.0
1841	105.5	71.1	148.4	21.5
1851	105.8	81.5	129.8	18.8
1861	100.3	90.1	111.4	16.2
1871	100.0	100.0	100.0	14.5

Source: Broadberry, Custodis and Gupta (2015).

this with the path of GDP per capita in Great Britain (GB), we can track India's performance in an international context. Benchmarking on the comparative India/GB per capita GDP level for 1871 from Broadberry and Gupta (2010), we see in the final column of Table 2.6 that India's comparative position deteriorated from a GDP per capita of more than 60 per cent of the British level in 1600 to just 14.5 per cent by 1871. The relative decline occurred fairly steadily throughout the period. Broadberry, Custodis and Gupta (2015) provide an additional cross-check in the international comparative context, demonstrating that the level of GDP per capita in India compared with Britain can also be calculated independently at 1600 and checked for consistency with the growth rates in the two countries between 1600 and 1871.

The GDP per capita data thus confirm the findings that were already beginning to emerge from our analysis of wages and prices. There were already signs of India lagging behind the most developed parts of Europe during the seventeenth century, and by the eighteenth century, the gap had become quite large. The Great Divergence was therefore already under way during the early modern period, so that developments during the colonial period cannot be seen as the root cause of the divergence. It is worth noting that the pattern of declining GDP per capita during the seventeenth and eighteenth centuries occurred in China as well as India, and in both countries this was driven mainly by trends in agriculture, because population growth outstripped the growth of the cultivated land area and crop yields did not increase sufficiently to offset the decline in the land-labour ratio. In both countries, workers remained on the land, holding down agricultural labour productivity, in contrast to developments in the more successful economies of northwest Europe. Again in common with much of the rest of the world, India lacked the state institutions needed to underpin the hard work, investment and innovation that allowed Britain and Holland to break free from the Malthusian trap (Parthasarathi 2011).

Aggregate economic performance since 1871

We have more detailed historical national accounts for the period after 1871 constructed by Heston (1983) and Sivasubramonian (2000). The broad path of per capita GDP is shown in Table 2.7 and Figure 2.1. Per capita incomes grew slowly during the late nineteenth century, but stagnated during the first half of the twentieth century. Since 1947, the GDP per capita has grown at a positive rate, indicating

TABLE 2.7 Indian real national income growth (% per year)

	National income	*National income per capita*
A. Roy		
1860–1885	1.8	1.2
1885–1900	1.0	0.5
1900–1914	1.4	1.0
1914–1947	1.1	0.1
B. Sivasubramonian		
1900–2000	2.0	1.0
1900–1950	**1.4**	**0.0**
1950–2000	4.0	1.9
1950–1980	**3.5**	**1.4**
1980–2000	**5.5**	**3.4**
1980–1990	5.2	3.0
1990–2000	5.9	4.1

Source: Gupta (2012, p. 22), based on Roy (2011, p. 80) and Sivasubramonian (2000).

FIGURE 2.1 Indian GDP per capita, 1900–2000 (Rs at 1948–1949 prices)

Source: Derived from Sivasubramonian (2000).

a transition to modern economic growth. However, this growth rate has lagged behind that of East Asian countries coming out of colonial rule.

Statistical tests confirm that there was a significant break in 1952 for GDP and in 1967 for per capita GDP, putting India on a path of economic development (Hatekar and Dongre, 2005, Gupta 2012). However, political independence in India also coincided with a broad change in economic policy from laissez-faire and Imperial Preference under colonial rule to a highly interventionist planning aimed at industrialization. In the new regime, Soviet-style planning regulated international trade, entry of the private sector into some industrial activities was restricted and the state controlled the development of heavy industry. A full discussion of the successes and failures of this policy is outside the scope of this chapter, but the rising growth was in part due to rising agricultural growth and rapid industrial growth in the early phase of import substituting industrialization.

A much more significant turning point came around 1980 with the liberalization of the economy both in terms of industrial regulation and international trade. This general 'pro-business' shift in industrial policy in the early 1980s is regarded by Rodrik and Subramanian (2005) as the main factor to put India on a growth path. Following this shift, 'pro market' policies were introduced in the 1990s and contributed to a further rise in economic growth, in particular to the growth of the service sector.

Sectoral performance

The output and employment data from the historical national accounts have been used by Broadberry and Gupta (2010) to calculate indices of Indian labour productivity by major sector. From these indices it is possible to calculate the average annual growth rates of labour productivity by sector, which are presented here in Table 2.8. During the late nineteenth century, labour productivity growth was fastest in industry, as modern industry developed in India, and slowest in services, despite the modernization of the transport network. During the first half of the twentieth century, although there was respectable labour productivity growth in industry and services, labour productivity growth in the economy as a whole was held back by stagnation in agriculture. During the second half of the twentieth century, respectable labour productivity growth in industry and services was again offset by slow productivity growth in agriculture.

TABLE 2.8 Average annual growth rates of Indian output per employee, 1872–2000 (% per year)

	Agriculture	Industry	Services	GDP
1872/73 to 1900/01	0.4	1.1	0.0	0.4
1900/01 to 1946/47	0.0	1.4	1.0	0.5
1950/51 to 1970/71	0.9	3.4	2.8	1.9
1970/71 to 1999/00	0.9	2.7	2.3	2.5

Source: Broadberry and Gupta (2010, p. 266).

It is interesting to place this sectoral productivity performance in an international comparative perspective and to work in terms of comparative levels, as with the real wage data for the pre-1870 period. Table 2.9, taken from Broadberry and Gupta (2010), provides a breakdown of comparative India/UK labour productivity levels by the three main sectors of agriculture, industry and services. It is clear that agriculture played a key role in India's falling further behind during the period 1871/73 to 1970/71 and that it subsequently slowed down the process of catching up. In the early 1870s, an average Indian agricultural worker produced slightly more than 10 per cent of the output produced by an average British agricultural worker. By the 1970s, this had fallen to around 2 per cent, and by the 1990s to as little as 1 per cent.[4] In industry, comparative labour productivity fluctuated but remained stationary, with Indian labour productivity returning to around 15 per cent of the British level on a number of occasions. In services, the India/UK comparative labour productivity level trended upwards from around 15 per cent to around 30 per cent, although the disruption surrounding independence interrupted this upward trajectory, providing a setback to services as well as to agriculture and industry.

To fully understand the contributions of the three main sectors to comparative productivity performance, it is necessary to track their shares in economic activity as well as their comparative productivity levels. Table 2.10 shows the changing sectoral distribution of employment in India over time. The most striking finding is the dominance of agriculture as an employer of labour. For the century after 1870, agriculture's share of the labour force was around 75 per cent, and even by the end of the twentieth century, agriculture still accounted for nearly 65 per cent of Indian employment. Given this commitment of resources to an inherently low value added sector, and the poor productivity performance within that sector, it is not difficult to understand India's disappointing overall productivity performance during this period.

TABLE 2.9 Comparative India/UK labour productivity by sector, 1871–2000 (UK = 100)

	Agriculture	*Industry*	*Services*	*GDP*
1871/73	11.2	18.2	18.1	15.0
1881/83	11.3	16.8	15.9	14.1
1890/91	10.4	17.3	15.6	13.8
1900/01	10.5	18.6	15.6	13.2
1910/11	11.1	24.2	17.7	14.4
1920/21	9.8	21.1	21.1	13.4
1929/30	8.3	25.3	25.2	14.2
1935/36	7.1	21.8	23.2	12.8
1946/48	7.0	18.1	23.5	11.7
1950/51	5.4	14.6	17.5	9.3
1960/61	4.3	16.4	20.0	9.7
1970/71	2.3	17.3	22.6	8.9
1980/81	1.6	16.1	29.3	10.2
1990/91	0.9	18.3	33.0	11.0
1999/00	1.0	15.8	32.8	11.4

Source: Broadberry and Gupta (2010, p. 268).

TABLE 2.10 Indian labour force by sector, 1875–2000 (%)

	Agriculture	Industry	Services
1875	73.4	14.5	12.1
1910/11	75.5	10.3	14.2
1929/30	76.1	9.1	14.8
1950/51	73.6	10.2	16.2
1970/71	73.8	11.1	15.1
1999/00	64.2	13.9	21.9

Source: Broadberry and Gupta (2010, p. 269).

Note further, however, that the Indian development path stands out in terms of the structural change that has characterized the pattern of economic development in most industrial countries. Britain saw an early decline in the share of employment in agriculture and a rise in the share of industry and this pattern was replicated as the rest of Europe industrialized. In India, although the share of agriculture in employment has declined since the 1970s, industry has never gained the largest share in total employment. Instead the service sector has dominated. As noted by Bosworth and Collins (2008), India's development experience is therefore very different from that of China and other rapidly growing Asian economies, which have followed a process of manufacturing-led development.

Conclusions

In this chapter we have covered four centuries of Indian economic performance and living standards. Using data on real wages and GDP per capita, we have established that the Great Divergence was already under way during the early modern period. As early as 1600, living standards in India were already lower than in Britain, and the gap widened during the seventeenth and eighteenth centuries as real wages and GDP per capita fell in India and rose in Britain. By the early nineteenth century, Indian real wages and GDP per capita stabilized at a low level, and despite some signs of a small increase in the late nineteenth century, the rest of the colonial period was characterized by stagnation.

Using a national accounting framework, we can trace the sources of this stagnation in living standards to poor productivity performance, particularly in agriculture. Although economic performance improved with independence, a far more significant turning point came around 1980 with the adoption of a more liberal economic environment. Unlike China and other developing Asian economies, India has followed a distinct pattern of service-led rather than manufacturing-led development.

Finally, let us point to some areas where we think future research could usefully focus. Dealing first with the period since 1870, we think there is a pressing need to explain the poor performance of Indian agriculture, both in absolute terms and in relation to other sectors. Until this issue is resolved, many Indians will continue to live in poverty, missing out on the rapidly growing prosperity of those working in industry and services. Dealing with the period before 1870, although historical national accounts have now been pushed back to 1600, the evidential basis remains weaker than for the post-1871 period, and more work is needed to confirm the above trends. It would also be useful to confirm the aggregate trends using a regional breakdown. Roy's (2010) work on Bengal provides a useful example of what can be achieved at a regional level within a national accounting framework.

Notes

1 The only real exception to this concerns the observations for 1750 taken from the work of Parthasarathi (1998), which cannot be taken as representative of the earnings of weavers in the Madras area at this time, and are hence placed in parentheses. A more detailed critical evaluation of Parthasarathi's (1998) data is provided in Broadberry and Gupta (2006, p. 14).
2 Parthasarathi's (1998) estimates have been excluded from this table. But note that even if they were included, they would merely show a temporary boost in south Indian wages to around 40 per cent of the English level in the first half of the eighteenth century.
3 The major famine of the twentieth century was in Bengal in 1943.
4 The comparison of the agricultural productivity is somewhat misleading as it accounts for only 2 per cent of employment.

References

Abū 'l-Fazl [1595] (1927). *The Ā' īn–i-Akbarī*. H. Blochman, trans. Delhi: Low Price Publications.

Allen, R. C. (2001). 'The Great Divergence in European Wages and Prices from the Middle Ages to the First World War', *Explorations in Economic History, 38 (4)*, pp. 411–447.

———. (2007). 'India in the Great Divergence', in T.J. Hatton, K.H. O'Rourke and A. M. Taylor, eds., *The New Comparative Economic History: Essays in Honor of Jeffrey G. Williamson*, Cambridge, MA: MIT Press, pp. 9–32.

Amin, S. (1976). *Unequal Development: An Essay on the Social Formations of Peripheral Capitalism*, Hassocks: Harvester.

Bagchi, A.K. (1976). 'De-industrialization in India in the Nineteenth Century: Some Theoretical Implications', *Journal of Development Studies, 12 (2)*, pp. 135–164.

Balassa, B. (1964). 'The Purchasing-Power Parity Doctrine: A Reappraisal', *Journal of Political Economy, 72 (6)*, pp. 584–596.

Bayly, C.A. (1983). *Rulers, Townsmen and Bazaars: North Indian Society in the Age of British Expansion, 1770–1870*, Cambridge: Cambridge University Press.

Bosworth, B., and S. Collins (2008). 'Accounting for Growth: Comparing China and India', *Journal of Economic Perspectives, 22 (1)*, pp. 45–66.

Bowen, H. (2007). 'East India Company: Trade and Domestic Financial Statistics, 1755–1838', UK Data Archive, Colchester. Retrieved from http://discover.ukdataservice.ac.uk/catalogue/?sn=5690&type=Data%20catalogue.

Brennig, J. (1986). 'Textile Producers and Production in Late-Nineteenth Century Coromandel', *Indian Economic and Social History Review, 23 (4)*, pp. 333–356.

Broadberry, S., and B. Gupta (2006). 'The Early Modern Great Divergence: Wages, Prices and Economic Development in Europe and Asia, 1500–1800', *Economic History Review, 59 (1)*, pp. 2–31.

———. (2010), 'The Historical Roots of India's Service-Led development: A Sectoral Analysis of Anglo-Indian Productivity Differences, 1870–2000', *Explorations in Economic History, 47 (3)*, pp. 264–278.

Broadberry, S., J. Custodis, and B. Gupta (2015). 'India and the Great Divergence: An Anglo-Indian Comparison of GDP per capita, 1600–1871', *Explorations in Economic History, 55 (1)*, pp. 58–75.

Buchanan, F. [1807] (1999). *Journey from Madras through the countries of Mysore, Canara, and Malabar, for the express purpose of investigating the state of agriculture, arts, and commerce; the religion, manners, and customs; the history natural and civil, and antiquities, in the dominions of the Rajah of Mysore, and the countries acquired by the honourable East India Company, in the late and former wars, from Tipoo Sultan*, Delhi: Asian Education Services.

Chandra, S. (1982). 'Standard of Living 1: Mughal India', in T. Raychaudhuri and I. Habib, eds., *The Cambridge Economic History of India, Volume I, c. 1200–1750*, Cambridge: Cambridge University Press, pp. 458–471.

Chaudhuri, K.N. (1978). *The Trading World of Asia and the English East India Company, 1660–1760*, Cambridge: Cambridge University Press.

Desai, A.V. (1972). 'Population and Standards of Living in Akbar's Time', *Indian Economic and Social History Review, 9 (1)*, pp. 43–62.

———. (1978). 'Population and Standards of Living in Akbar's Time: A Second Look', *Indian Economic and Social History Review, 15 (1)*, pp. 53–79.

Frank, A. G. (1998). *ReOrient: The Silver Age in Asia and the World Economy*, Berkeley: University of California Press.

Fukazawa, H. (1982). 'Standard of Living 2: Maharashtra and the Deccan', in T. Raychaudhuri and I. Habib, eds., *The Cambridge Economic History of India, Volume I, c. 1200–1750*, Cambridge: Cambridge University Press, pp. 471–477.

Gupta, B. (2012). 'India's Growth in a Long-Run Perspective', in R. Jha, ed., *Routledge Handbook of South Asian Economics*, London: Routledge, pp. 19–31.

Habib, I. (1982). 'Population', in T. Raychaudhuri and I. Habib, eds., *The Cambridge Economic History of India, Volume I, c. 1200–c. 1750*, Cambridge: Cambridge University Press, pp. 163–171.

Hatekar, N., and A. Dongre (2005). 'Structural Breaks in India's Growth: Revisiting the Debate with a Longer Perspective', *Economic and Political Weekly, 40 (14)*, pp. 1432–1435.

Heston, A. W. (1977). 'The Standard of Living in Akbar's Time: A Comment', *Indian Economic and Social History Review, 14 (3)*, pp. 391–396.

———. (1983). 'National Income', in M. Kumar and M. Desai, eds., *The Cambridge Economic History of India, Volume II, c. 1757–c. 1970*, Cambridge: Cambridge University Press, pp. 463–532.

Moosvi, S. (1973). 'Production, Consumption and Population in Akbar's Time', *Indian Economic and Social History Review, 10 (2)*, pp. 181–195.

———. (1977). 'Note on Professor Alan Heston's 'Standard of Living in Akbar's Time: A Comment', *Indian Economic and Social History Review, 14 (3)*, pp. 397–401.

Moreland, W. H. [1923] (1990). *From Akbar to Aurangzeb: A Study in Indian Economic History*, Delhi: Low Price Publications.

Mukerjee, R. (1967). *The Economic History of India, 1600–1800*, Allahabad: Kitab Mahal.

Parthasarathi, P. (1998). 'Rethinking Wages and Competitiveness in the Eighteenth Century: Britain and South India', *Past and Present, 158 (1)*, pp. 79–109.

———. (2001). *The Transition to a Colonial Economy: Weavers, Merchants and Kings in South India, 1720–1800*, Cambridge: Cambridge University Press.

———. (2011). *Why Europe Grew Rich and Asia Did Not: Global Economic Divergence 1600–1850*, Cambridge: Cambridge University Press.

Pomeranz, K. (2000). *The Great Divergence: China, Europe, and the Making of the Modern World Economy*, Princeton: Princeton University Press.

Ramaswamy, V. (1985). *Textiles and Weavers in Medieval South India*, Delhi: Oxford University Press.

Rodrik, D., and A. Subramanian (2005). 'From Hindu Growth to Productivity Surge: The Mystery of the Indian Growth Transition', *IMF Staff Papers 52 (2)*, pp. 193–228.

Roy, T. (2010). 'Economic Conditions in Early Modern Bengal: A Contribution to the Divergence Debate', *Journal of Economic History, 70 (1)*, pp. 179–194.

———. (2011). *Economic History of India: 1857–1947*, 3rd ed., Delhi: Oxford University Press.

Samuelson, P. A. (1964). 'Theoretical Notes on Trade Problems', *Review of Economics and Statistics, 46 (2)*, pp. 145–154.

Sandberg, L. G. (1974). *Lancashire in Decline: A Study in Entrepreneurship, Technology and International Trade*, Columbus: Ohio State University Press.

Sivasubramonian, S. (2000). *The National Income of India in the Twentieth Century*, Delhi: Oxford University Press.

Sivramkrishna, S. (2009). 'Ascertaining Living Standards in Erstwhile Mysore, Southern India, from Francis Buchanan's *Journey* of 1800–01: An Empirical Contribution to the Great Divergence Debate', *Journal of the Economic and Social History of the Orient. 52 (4–5)*, pp. 695–733.

Tulpule B., and R. Datta (1988). 'Real Wages in Indian Industry', *Economic and Political Weekly, 23 (44)*, pp. 2275–2277.

Twomey, M. J. (1983). 'Employment in Nineteenth Century Indian Textiles', *Explorations in Economic History, 20 (1)*, pp. 37–57.

van Zanden, J. L. (1999). 'Wages and the Standard of Living in Europe, 1500–1800', *European Review of Economic History, 3 (2)*, pp. 175–197.

Visaria, L., and P. Visaria (1983). 'Population (1757–1947)', in M. Kumar and M. Desai, eds., *The Cambridge Economic History of India, Volume II, c. 1757–c. 1970*, Cambridge: Cambridge University Press, pp. 463–532.

3

THE COLONIAL TRANSITION AND THE DECLINE OF THE EAST INDIA COMPANY, C. 1746–1784

Santhi Hejeebu

Introduction

Across the globe, the English East India Company is remembered as a formidable organization, at once respected, feared, and loathed. In East Asia, it often symbolizes Western economic and imperial aggression. In North America, its name recalls the arrogance and privilege of entities tied closely to the government of King George III. On both the Indian subcontinent and in Britain, where the Company's legacies are indelible, the name evokes many images: the cruelty and grandeur of the British Raj, plus the closer integration of formerly distant peoples. As the breadth of its activities – commercial, administrative, and military – staggers the imagination, reactions to the Company can be complex and contradictory. Indeed the East India Company can serve as a Rorschach test of one's views toward corporate power.[1]

The Company remains an object of intense fascination in large measure because it had once been a merchant trading firm, but later morphed into a colonial state. This chapter describes that unusual transformation: the Company's loss of its commercial character. In the middle decades of the eighteenth century the Company lost its will and capacity to pursue profits from trade. The devastating impact of the Company's transformation upon Indian states and economies has often been told.[2] Less attention has been paid to the changes in the internal culture and organization of the East India Company. Between 1745 and 1784, what critical realignments took place within the Company that enabled it to transition from a trader to a military-fiscal juggernaut? This chapter explores the process of organizational change *within* the East India Company.

When the East India Company operated as a commercial entity, it cohered with the goal of generating profits for proprietors. Owners purchased and sold Company stock on London's share market and were originally called "adventurers," reflecting the great risks of trading with Asia in the early modern era. A vessel from London to Bombay could take six to nine months in each direction. With valuable bullion and goods exported to Asia and spices, textiles, tea, and raw silk among the goods exported to London, the vessels were heavily armed men-of-war. In London, the management of staff, shipping, inventory, warehouses, auction sales, finance, accounting, relations with government, etc., rested in the hands of twenty-four individuals annually elected to the "Court of Directors." Headed by a chairman and a deputy chairman, the directors were organized into subcommittees with specialized functions. The committees reported several times a week to the directors' meetings. The directors in turn advised and sought the consent of the "General Court of Proprietors," the body of shareholders, which met quarterly. The busiest times of year revolved around the quarterly auctions, especially the September auction, and the spring despatch of vessels to the East. The Company depended heavily on short-term debt financing, which in turn depended critically on successful autumn sales. Upon the close of each fiscal year on 30 June, proprietors would consult the annual "balance of accounts" and, with the advice of directors, vote upon the annual dividend, or distribution of profits.

The Company's overseas employees, called "servants," likewise ordered their lives according to the seasonal flow of commodities and the movement of ships. They contracted for the future delivery of textiles based upon musters and order lists sent from London. They inspected tea packed in warehouses and ready for export. They oversaw the loading of homeward vessels, ballasting them with saltpetre, an agent used in gunpowder. The Company's settlements, a collection of forts and factories, erupted with people, news, and activity with the November-December arrival of European ships. Yet servants remained engaged year round, contracting with Indian merchants, for both the Company's and their own private trade. If fortunate, employees would privately carry goods or consign cargo along Asia's merchant trade networks. Over many years, their toils might be rewarded with a steady accumulation of wealth. If luckier still, employees might survive long enough to return to Europe. Like merchants everywhere, their risk-filled careers were driven by the search for arbitrage opportunities.

A broader view of the Company's commercial character can be seen in the context of the states in which it operated. From the British state, the Company received numerous charters and letters patent that granted exclusive right to trade in Asia, the right to declare war on non-Christian powers, the power to establish English courts at its overseas settlements, and the power to govern its members overseas, including through court martial and capital punishment. To the British state, the Company delivered a stream of customs revenues, credit on favourable terms, and episodically offered gifts to influential members of the royal household, government office holders, and members of Parliament. Charters could be withdrawn with three years' notice.[3]

Such revenue for state privileges arrangements, as Pearson (1991, p. 110) noted, was wholly alien to Mughal governance. In the subcontinent, the Company sought and received permission to trade. The company settlements depended critically on the goodwill of the *sultans*, *subhadars*, and *rajas* who controlled strategic territory.[4] Until the mid-eighteenth century, the Company posed little threat to Indian land-based powers. The English communities were very small and subject to high mortality. Joining the Company around the age of 17, most employees were dead by the age of 30. While the boundaries between the Company and the British state were semi-permeable, this chapter looks inside the firm at a time when the lines of separating it from post-Mughal states completely dissolved.

The transformation of the East India Company underscores the dynamic, adaptive nature of global firms. Firms are not mere black boxes, reducible to a single profit function. Nor can they be summarized by static arrangements of people and assets organized as integrated systems.[5] Firms are dynamic sets of social relationships, sustained by self-enforcing, managerial practices and constrained by changing relationships with external parties, including buyers, suppliers, competitors, and governmental agencies.[6] Firms are entities in flux. During the first half of the eighteenth century, as Mughal power ebbed relative to that of regional and successor states, the Company's personnel in India believed operations were at risk of being severely limited or curtailed altogether. The Company's response to greater political uncertainty altered long-established hierarchies within the firm. The new managerial alignment steered the firm along a destructive path, involving new relationships with Indian polities and with its home government in London. The chapter identifies three key changes inside the East India Company that enabled its pivot to an imperial state. Before turning to mid-eighteenth century developments, a brief overview of earlier periods may be helpful.

BOX 3.1 KEY TERMS

Investment	financial capital allocated to the acquisition of trade goods
East Indiamen	armed sailing ships used exclusively in the trade between Asia and Europe
Piece goods	units of woven cloth of varying dimension and made of cotton, silk, or mixed cotton and silk
Diwani	grant of the land revenues of Bengal, Bihar, and Orissa
India Office Records	the records of the East India Company (1600–1858), the Board of Control (1784–1858), the India Office (1858–1947), and additional offices associated with British administration in South Asia. The records, housed at the British Library, are described here: http://www.bl.uk/reshelp/findhelpregion/asia/india/indiaofficerecords/indiaofficehub.html

---

Fits and starts, 1600–1660

The Company began modestly: 218 individuals subscribed a total of £68,373.[7] It existed only for the duration of the voyage out and back. Vessels left the Thames in early spring and, if fortunate, would return late the following summer. Once the assets were liquidated or transferred to the next joint stock, the books were closed.

Indeed there were twelve such "terminal joint stocks" during the first thirteen years. The Company's richly laden vessels were filled mainly with black pepper, used to keep meat palatable in an age without refrigeration.

Eurasian trade was for the risk-loving investor, mariner, or merchant. In the "Spice Islands," the bitter rivalry with the Dutch was epitomized by the 1623 massacre of English traders by the Dutch at Amboyna.[8] In contrast to the Dutch in Indonesia, the European companies in India did not hold monopolies over territories producing homogeneous agricultural commodities. The Company arrived in urbanized Surat in 1608, following the commercial routes established by Gujaratis, Parsis, Jews, Armenians, and other communities. They obtained permission from Crown Prince Mirza Khurram to set up a small factory, or warehouse, for purchasing and storing goods. This grant was reaffirmed by the Mughal Emperor Jahangir through the embassy of Thomas Roe. Permissions were also obtained at other Mughal port cities. Conflict arose less from indigenous suppliers and governors than from other European rivals.

At home, King Charles I subjected the Company to royal whimsy. He granted a competing syndicate license to trade in the Indies, confiscated a return cargo of pepper, and once attempted to join the Company as a member himself (Scott 1910, pp. 112–119). Through the decades of England's civil war and Cromwell's protectorate, the 1640s and 1650s, English investor confidence plummeted while the Dutch East India Company was thriving. The Dutch Company had firmly established a massive military and administrative bureaucracy based in Batavia and in this period sent out 2.5 times as many vessels as the English (Bruijn and Gaastra 1993, p. 182). Only by 1657, with a charter from Cromwell that was subsequently ratified by Charles II, did the English company begin to operate on a firmer footing.

Growth through crises, 1660–1745

The next phase in the Company's history was unquestionably one of commercial expansion, punctuated by episodic crises at home and abroad. The Company's annual "investment" in Asia grew in both scale and scope. According to Chaudhuri (1978, pp. 508–510), the total value of imports into England rose from £140,000 in 1664 to an average of £775,000 in the early 1740s. The spice trade expanded into textiles, raw silk, teas, porcelain, etc.[9] In India, the number of factories grew as the Company purchased roughly ninety different textile varieties.[10] Collections of factories grew into administrative clusters called *presidencies*. Reporting to Madras were the following subsidiaries with their year of establishment: Bantam (1603) on the island of Java, Masulipatnam (1611), Petapoli (1633), Madapollam (1676), Conimere (1682), Cuddalore (1682), Bencoolen (1687) on the island of Sumatra, and Fort St. David (1690). Bombay, founded in 1668, became the centre of operations from Gujarat and along the Konkan and Malabar coasts. Bombay's subsidiary posts included Surat (1613), Broach (1616), Cambay (1730), Karwar (1649), Rajapur (1660), Tellicherri (1683), and Anjengo (1684). Anchoring settlements in Bengal was the factory at Calcutta (1690). Calcutta's dependencies included Dacca (1666),

Kasimbazar (1658), Malda (1676), and Patna (1650s). The principal settlements of Bombay, Madras, and Calcutta thus became the seats of the Company's three Indian presidencies.[11] From the mid-seventeenth century to the early eighteenth century, the Company's volume of trade pivoted away from the Arabian Sea settlements and toward settlements around the Bay of Bengal and eastward.

Yet the path to commercial expansion was not predestined, but rather required changes in managerial practices. For example, the Company significantly improved the incentives offered to overseas employees. From the 1680s onwards, overseas employees were granted greater liberties to pursue their own private trading interests. From 1705, the Company encouraged overseas employees to remit their savings home on risk-free bills of exchange. Further, the Company's order lists adapted to both changing consumer tastes and greater restrictions that Parliament placed on the importation of Indian cloth in 1702 and 1721 (Riello and Roy 2009). In the late 1720s, the Company's legal staff instituted a system of courts, modelled after the English Court of Chancery, within the enlarging settlements.[12] The professional accounting staff also improved their processes. They systemized the annual financial reports called *balance of accounts*, which allowed for greater clarity of the firm's financial position at the close of each fiscal year. Thus the Company continued to modernize as its trade enlarged.

Threatening the administrative and commercial gains in the late seventeenth century was the belligerent leadership of Sir Josiah Child. Child first entered the Court of Directors in 1674, utterly dominated that body in the 1680s, and finally left the direction in the year of his death, 1699 (Grassby 2004). He closely aligned himself and the Company with the political interests of the later Stuart kings and opposed the trend toward Parliamentary independence. In 1688, hoping to establish a permanent foothold within Mughal dominions, Child initiated a disastrous war against Mughal Emperor Aurungzeb. The war ended three years later with the Company's complete humiliation and payment of a large indemnity to the Emperor. Fortunately for the Company, Aurungzeb did not seek retribution and quickly allowed the English to re-establish their affairs.

The Company's enemies at home were less forgiving of the arrogance embodied by Child. Influenced by rivals who resented the Company's exclusive monopoly rights to the eastern trades, Parliament voted to end the Company's charter in 1691, effective in three years. Parliament then granted another syndicate, organized as the New East India Company, the right to participate in the India trade. A brutal rivalry ensued, with contract prices rocketing in the Indies and sales prices plummeting in London. It was clear to all observers that the competition would result in the bankruptcy of one if not both the New and the Old East India companies. Plans for a merger began in 1701. Named the United Company of Merchants after 1709, the Company consolidated the assets, personnel, and privileges of the Old Company. After the age of Child, the United Company largely eschewed partisan politics throughout the first half of the eighteenth century (Sutherland 1952). In India in the first decades of the eighteenth century, the Company held a prickly defensiveness toward host governments, whom they regarded as grasping and perfidious.[13]

The western settlement of Bombay struggled to either contain or evade harassment by Maratha admiral Kanhoji Angre and his sons. Commerce at the eastern and southern settlements flourished but remained vulnerable to shifting political forces. While the Company had no interest in repeating Child's folly, directors did expect their governors and councils "when insulted, to repel force with force."[14]

A mature company facing crisis, c. 1745

By the mid-eighteenth century, the Company's trading operations had achieved an impressive level of regularity and stability. Crippling external competition from outside syndicates was a distant memory. Membership in the Court of Directors often passed from father to son. Internal competition from ship captains and employees was contained to tolerable bounds.[15] The number of settlements stabilized and the Company maintained long-term relationships with suppliers in India and buyers in London.[16] The calm was not destined to last. Before considering the major breakages that took place, we next introduce the organization of personnel at the Company's principal settlements in India.

Management was personal and hierarchical, tightly controlled by a president and a council consisting of nine to eleven senior merchants. Again, the communities were small and subject to high mortality. In 1745, the number of white civilians in Madras, Bengal, and Bombay was 152, 222, and 101 respectively.[17] A president would have known every civilian employee by first name and may have counted among them several kinsmen. Men with at least eleven years of experience in the settlement – councillors – might be heads of subsidiary factories or serve in positions such as "import warehouse keeper" or "export warehouse keeper." They attended meetings, called "consultations," when the European ships were in port and as occasion required. The president and council at Bengal, for example, would jointly decide matters involving the Company's investment, the minting of bullion, and the disposition of military forces.

Yet, at each settlement, the president was first among equals. His was the pre-eminent post, reflecting his long service in India and the high regard in which he was held by directors at home and colleagues abroad. He was the Company's chief commercial officer, chief diplomatic officer, and chief administrator at each settlement. As the directors describe in a letter of 1724:

> As the President and next to him the deputy governor are at the head of the management . . . entrusted as such, and in case they do well will have the larger share of the praise and the benefit, so on the contrary if the Company's affairs under them suffer by their connivance or want of diligence . . . they ought and shall bear the blame and making satisfaction for mismanagement because they ought to prevent them by their authority.[18]

The president's authority touched every aspect of life at the settlements. Until the mid-1740s, he also served as the commander-in-chief of the settlement's armed forces. These forces were recruited and retained by the Company and were occasionally complemented by a contingent of Royal forces. In 1744, the overall size of British military personnel was 600, 1,360, and 2,110 for Madras, Bengal, and Bombay respectively.[19] At this time the Company's forces amounted to garrison defence units made up of former seamen who were granted permission to stay in the settlements and serve as "gunnery-room boys." They had no field training and answered to a president who himself was more versed in Indian commerce than military science.

The hierarchical pattern of authority was repeated at each Indian presidency, with each reporting directly to London. Presidents and council members achieved their position by long seniority, by meritorious service, and by the active support of influential directors in London.[20] Over the course of a decade, the five or six men who held the position of chairman and deputy chairman and the five or six men who held the position of president of Bengal, Madras, or Bombay would know each other well. Through regular correspondence and exchange of account books, they would understand each other's capabilities and concerns. Directors trusted their presidents whenever possible and dismissed them when not. By virtue of their seniority and position, council members were the first to be informed of the Company's orders, spending priorities in India, information from other settlements, and private news transmitted by ship captains and crew. With the trust of the Court of Directors, presidents and councillors had better information, greater decision authority, and more control over company assets than younger, lower-ranked employees. Hejeebu (2005) has shown that seniority was highly correlated with private wealth accumulation. The president could make or break a young "griffen" or newcomer's prospects by assigning him to a barren or lucrative post. Deference and subordination to managerial hierarchy within the presidency was the best way for a young man to make his fortunes.

The nuances of Company management, of course, lay outside the concerns of the British or of Indian states. Yet the Company management was buffeted by political headwinds outside its control. An expanding fiscal and military state, Britain opposed France during the War of the Austrian Succession, 1740–1748. The conflict spilled into theatres far from Europe, including south-eastern India. The English East India Company was thus directly entangled in a military conflict not of its making. Likewise on the subcontinent, the decline of the Mughal Empire centred in Delhi corresponded with the rise of regional powers including the Marathas and successor states, including Bengal, Hyderabad, and the Carnatic. These polities faced succession crises within their borders and threats from without. Some Indian powers and banking elites were certainly willing to recruit European military force for their own ambitions.[21] At the same time, the companies sought material advantages from these opportunities. From the 1740s, changing political frameworks compounded the usual vagaries of trade.

Seeking more predictable and advantageous environments for their companies, Europeans innovatively combined European warfare with Indian military manpower. The French East India Company under Governor Dumas (1735–1741) first applied European field techniques that combined light and heavy infantry with mobile artillery (see Bryant 2004; K. Roy 2005; Lenman 2001, Chapter 3; Dodwell 1920). His innovation saw the use of European officers to train and discipline natives soldiers or sepoys from the Persian *sipahi* as regular troops, thereby greatly economizing on European soldiers. Tested at the battle of Adyar River, the new approach to land warfare humbled the Mughal provincial Nawab Anwar-ud-din, who had attempted to defend the English.[22] As H. H. Dodwell (1929, p. 122) succinctly wrote, "The terror of Asiatic armies had disappeared." The cash-strapped French supported their military campaigns by territorial revenues acquired from the Indian states they supported. The English realized that the French Company was not simply a commercial rival, but now posed an existential threat.

At home and abroad, conflict consumed the Company's resources. The Company's cash journals through the 1740s demonstrate a large spike in the spending on military stores.[23] In 1746, the French easily captured Madras. Two years later, the city's restoration followed the payment of ransom and a significant indemnity, in addition to the losses from the stoppage of trade. Numerous private individuals also petitioned the London directors for compensation associated with the loss and restoration of Madras.[24] Despite the peace treaty of 1748, the two nations remained in a state of continuous conflict in India through 1756, when the Seven Years War began. The directors were crystal clear about the devastation the Anglo-French war imposed on their treasuries and trade. By 1757, the Company's shareholders saw dividends reduced to 6 per cent per annum, their lowest point since 1708.[25] With episodic military and naval support from the British Government, the Company directors worked assiduously to fund their settlements abroad while averting a liquidity crisis at home. The Company's strategic response to war would ultimately upend the whole enterprise.

Institutional Path to Empire, 1745–1784

Simply put, the British strategy was to best the French at their own game. The English Company mimicked the application of European military techniques to the Indian countryside. The English Company sided with contestants for Indian thrones and acquired land revenue rights in the process. They too hoped that military campaigns would be short-lived and locally self-supporting, financed through the collection of local revenues dedicated for the purpose by friendly princes. By securing the hinterlands surrounding their major coastal settlements against potential challengers, the London directors hoped for the return of business on its traditional footing. Such hopes were not realized.

First, establishing a large military administration alongside the civilian commercial administration created irreconcilable goals and conflicting lines of authority. Decision making rights were split between the civilian and military leadership, with each side having little comprehension of the constraints of the other. Leadership positions in council and in select committees became accessible to military men with little history in the settlement. At the presidency level, no clear vision emerged of how military strategy *ought* to be integrated with longstanding commercial strategy. How were the material exigencies of war to be reconciled with those of long-distance commerce? Who would govern the generals?

Second, there was little clarity on how revenue collection on a large scale was to be conducted. Experimentation in various collection methods began only after 1765. Yet the hope that junior employees could extract such resources without high military costs was utterly misplaced. Company employees felt little compunction against the use of force. Instead, territorial control exposed new frontiers for the growth of private earnings, benefitting men on the spot ahead of their masters in London. As the tie between the Company's territorial control and the employees' private wealth grew stronger, the bonds of trust between directors and overseas servants rapidly corroded.

These two breaks resulted in a fatal third change: the intrusive intervention of Parliament. After the *diwani* of Bengal, the scope and scale of regulatory actions were unprecedented. All major groups of insiders – shareholders, directors, and employees – increasingly found key decisions subject to Parliamentary fiat. From 1784, the Company's political imperatives largely overshadowed the profit motive. The next sections examine the three breaks more fully.

Break 1: horizontal conflicts at the Indian settlements

Replicating the French military strategy required a new type of administration. After the fall of Madras in 1746, the English settlements became far more militarized, even in times of peace. Extended periods in camps or on the march, as well as the new battlefield techniques, precluded civilian governors from also acting as commanders-in-chief as they had done in the past. Specifically, the development of a professionally trained field army required greater specialization and division of labour between the civil and military branches. The commander-in-chief, for the first time in the Company's history, was distinct from the governor of the presidency. His critical martial talents were ill-suited to merchant affairs as the Company entered political alliances, acquired territory, and fully internalized its higher protection costs. The commander-in-chief and the hierarchy of men beneath him were not easily subordinated to the governor. Commanders – cultivated completely outside of the Company's mercantile culture – acquired seats on presidency councils and greater voices in select and secret subcommittees. Governors and the commanders competed for the direction of the settlements.

The tensions between the civilian and military leadership can be illustrated in the relationship between Madras governor Thomas Saunders (1750–1754) and the first commander-in-chief, Major-General Stringer Lawrence (1748–1766). Considered the "Father of the Indian Army," Lawrence complied with the authority of the Madras Council under certain conditions. A retired royal army captain at the time he joined the Company, Lawrence expected a satisfactory compensation. He also expected deference for his military experience, especially in the presence of other officers newly arriving to India. Tensions flared as Saunders wanted Lawrence to collaborate on commercial and military strategy. Saunders bristled at Lawrence's lack of interest in shaping the council's plans and his strong preference for fighting fresh campaigns than collecting revenues to pay for the current one. Dissatisfied with his pay in 1750, Lawrence resigned from his office at a critical juncture and returned to London. There he confronted the directors with his own estimate of his singular contribution. Sensitized to the settlements' dependency upon such able field commanders, the directors acceded to his demands and urged him back to India (Bryant 1975; Dodwell 1920; Biddulph 1901, Chapter 4).

The challenge of integrating military with civilian, commercial leadership was particularly acute in the presence of newly arrived royal navy or army officers.[26] Officially, the better-paid company officers were expected to defer to their royal counterparts of the same or higher rank. Those expectations grated on the public dignity of company officers who doubted the local knowledge and abilities of officers who had recently landed. This situation can be illustrated by the icy relationship between Captain Lawrence and Col. John Adlercron (1754–1757), Commander of the 39th Regiment of the Foot. When Col. Adlercron's regiment arrived, Lawrence refused to be subordinated to him and served instead as a volunteer, a man at liberty to leave, so long as Adlercron remained. In private correspondence, company commanders pressed the directors for greater rank and public recognition. They had little interest in the September auction.

According to Bryant (1975, Chapters 6–7), with different players, internal disputes between governors and commanders-in-chief continued to erupt over (i) rewards (pay, rank, and, if successful in battle, honours and the division of booty), (ii) operations (revenue collection or frontier patrol), and (iii) strategy (the size, dispersion or concentration of the forces). Such clashes persisted with other leaderships pairs in Madras and Bengal through the 1760s and 1770s. The specialization of labour into civilian and military branches exposed the deep fissures between mercantile men whose honour required balancing costs and benefits and military men whose honour required winning at any cost. From 1746, the Company's commercial fabric began to tear at the Indian seams.

Break 2: vertical conflicts between servants and directors

While the first institutional change can be drawn using organizational charts, the second is harder to visualize. The second moment involved the dissolution of vertical ties between servants in India and directors in London. In the first half of the eighteenth century, this employment relationship had been characterized by a workable balance of incentives and controls. Despite the long distance from headquarters, Company employees in India were provided sufficient incentives, in the form of freedom to pursue private trade, to comply with the directors' orders and instructions. When servants, especially senior servants, failed to defer to London, they risked suspension and dismissal. Individual cases of malfeasance of course occurred, but were offset by decades of predictable cooperation. From the mid-1750s to the mid-1770s, cooperation became harder to achieve. Suspicion and distrust increasingly marred the employment relationship. Hilder (1978, p. 1) described the regulation of company servants in the 1760s as a "study in failure."

Sustaining trust became more difficult as information flows multiplied and as political and commercial strategies became more deeply intertwined. The president was no longer the most authoritative source of information. Especially after the fall of Calcutta in 1756, the credibility of presidents was sharply questioned and information flows from India became highly contested. Some servants spied on behalf of directors, as was the case of Robert Orme for director John Payne (Hill 1916, p. xxi). Others promised absolute and confidential obedience to their patron among the directors. "I will obey you . . . in everything," wrote Henry Vansittart to Lawrence Sulivan, then chairman of the Court of Directors.[27] How were the directors to interpret the fundamental changes to the security and commercial prospects of their settlements except through the ears and eyes of their servants?[28] As the Company's future rested on territorial grants to subsidize their army and changing political alliances in India, servants had first-hand access to information of great value in London.[29]

Employees leveraged the information asymmetry to their advantage. Some sought to influence the Company in London through powerful patrons outside the Court of Directors altogether. Years before Britain's peace with France, for example, Robert Clive had famously written to the Prime Minister, William Pitt the Elder, indicating the ease of acquiring sovereignty in India.[30] Other servants and military officers used their insider knowledge to delegitimize the decisions of presidents and directors. For example, unprecedented in the Company's long history, in the 1760s, some dismissed servants, upon returning home, challenged the informational basis on which their dismissals were made. Other employees returned home to pen portraits vindicating their official behaviour in India. Ex-presidents and councillors felt the urgency of publicizing their actions as "disinterested" and serving the public good.[31] As private lines of communication proliferated, the squabbling between directors and servants echoed well beyond Company headquarters on Leadenhall Street.

In the mid-1750s, not only did servants acquire valuable information, they also amassed new resources. With the advent of the Company's offensive military powers, servants' private fortunes surged and the rate of wealth accumulation grew significantly. The locations of the new profit opportunities had been well established: opportunities from within the company (military and public works contracts), from direct "gifts" transferred from Indian rulers and elites, and from abuse of power in the operation of trade and revenue collection (Marshall 1976). Prior to the acquisition of territory, employee fortunes were made after long years of service and sacrifice. The common ideal was a comfortable retirement in a fine country home. In the decade following the 1757 Battle of Plassey in Bengal, however, servants returned home after a few years with unheard-of wealth. Quantitative research has shown that territorial acquisitions in Bengal led directly to hundreds of pounds of additional savings per employees per year, even after controlling for other factors (Hejeebu 2009). Londoners derided the newly rich as *nabobs*, a corruption of *nawab* or Mughal ruler. As Nechtman (2010) has shown, the nabobs attracted much public fascination and censure. Some acquired Parliamentary seats and influenced the Company from that venue. Others purchased company shares to influence

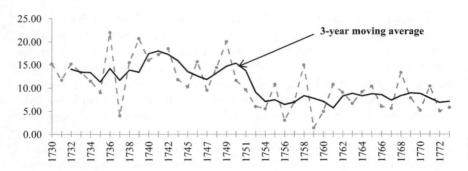

FIGURE 3.1 Average years of service by departure year, 1730–1773

Sources: British Library, OIOC, IOR/L/F/10/1-2, Bengal Establishment Lists, 1700–1784

memberships in the Court of Directors. Rarely had employees returned to England and attempted to alter the entire governance of the Company.

To visualize the deterioration in the servant-director relationship, one can examine the average length of service by year of departure. Figure 3.1 summarizes data drawn from official, annual lists of covenanted servants in Bengal during the eighteenth century. In the first two decades after 1750, men exited the Company's service after shorter careers than was the case in the prior two decades. It shows unequivocally the deep loss of mercantile experience after 1750.

Figure 3.1 suggests a connection between the average length of employment and the Company's decline as a commercial organization. As the company became a military force absorbing territorial revenues in India, servants prospered and departed earlier. A more muscular military presence in India raised the rate of private wealth accumulation, giving employees less incentive to honour the Company's hierarchy and remain at their stations.

Break 3: vertical conflicts between the company and home government

Disputes between servants and directors spilled over to the Company's relationship with Parliament. Until the late 1760s, Parliament avoided regulating relationships among stakeholders within the Company. That was about to change. The last major reconfiguration, the straw that broke the back of the Company, was the progressive intervention by Parliament. From 1767 to 1784, Parliament constrained the company on four critical points: the ownership rights of shareholders, the Company's ownership claims of territorial revenues, compensation of employees, and the official information flows between directors and leading servants. By 1784, the East India Company was no longer master of its own house.

Company-state relations took a sharp, downward turn when news arrived in April 1766 of the acquisition of the *diwani* or territorial revenue rights of Bengal, Bihar, and Orissa. Robert Clive had been sent to India to reform the Company's

civil and military services, to end wars, and to return the Company to a stable footing. Instead, by accepting the *diwani*, Clive opened a Pandora's box. He had boasted
wildly about its value and the news brought immediate public scrutiny to the servants' conduct in India and directors' and shareholders' behaviour at home. Upon
hearing the news and against the directors' advice, shareholders voted to increase
the dividend (from 6 to 10 per cent). The move precipitated Parliament's investigation in the Company's affairs. Chairman George Dudley lamented the impact of
the news to Robert Clive, then the governor of Bengal:

> I could wish also the Company's affairs at Bengal had not been set forth as so
> immensely great in its revenues without showing at the same time the doubts
> and difficulties attending the collection, as well as the stability of the same,
> as likewise the improbability of your being able to make these great acquisi-
> tions centre in England, and without which the proprietors can be very little
> benefitted.[32]

In London, the possibility that shareholders, passive members of the public, might
benefit from the spoils of Indian territories while excluding government spawned
deep resentment. Parliament imposed new rules on the election of directors, levied
a fine of £400,000 per annum, and regulated the size of the dividend.[33] Thus the
benefits of the *diwani* remained speculative, while the costs imposed on the Company were tangible.

From 1767–1772 leading directors could no longer convince the public that
directors could prudentially manage themselves while serving the national interest.
Internal attempts at regulating overseas personnel were ill-fated, openly resisted,
or stymied by a lack of continuity of leadership in the directorate. The Company's
humiliating defeat by Hyder Ali during the First Mysore War (1767–1769) and
the severity of the famine in Bengal (1770) burnished an image of incompetence
in the field. The steep climb in the Company's stock price followed by the Company's narrow escape from bankruptcy in 1772 burnished an image of corruption at
home. The exhaustive reports of Parliamentary investigations of 1772–1773 solidi-
fied the case for extreme mercantile dysfunction.

Parliament offered no remedies for problems of such complexity. Indeed it could
hardly diagnose the problem to which its own actions may have contributed.[34] The
best economic thinking of the day oddly argued that the Company's mismanagement owed fundamentally to the separation of the ownership of capital from its
management. The solution to East India Company's managerial problems, Adam
Smith proposed in 1776, was nationalization. He argued for the charter not to be
renewed and the Company's forts and territories to become public assets (Smith
1776, Book V, Ch 1, Part III, Art. I). As Parliament lacked an alternative bureaucracy
to replace the Company, such a solution was infeasible.

Parliament did the next best thing: it neutralized proprietors' claims to control
the management of capital. Instead of expropriating the Company's assets outright,
government stripped directors of their fiduciary obligations to owners. From 1773

onwards, dividends would be set by statute, making permanent the precedence of dividend capping that had begun in 1767.[35] The Act further required that dividends be treated as annual expenses of trade and tied increases to the reduction of both short-term and long-term debt. Thus Parliament effectively insulated proprietors from trade swings and internal mismanagement. With downside risks to owners eliminated, the impetus to operate as a commercial enterprise was checked. It is curious to note that the Company's annual financial statements had always referred to shareholders' equity as "By what due the adventurers." With the Regulating Act the "adventure" came to an end.

Conclusion: incompatibility of firm and state

After 1773, little of the Company's commercial ethos survived in India. The three breaks in the firm's internal management were irreparable. According to veteran director Laurence Sulivan in 1773, the newly appointed Governor-General, Warren Hastings, was now expected to do what was biblically impossible: serve two masters – the minister and the chairman.[36] The civilian service continued to devote greater attention to revenue administration than to acquiring piece goods, raw silk, or salt-petre.[37] The Company continued to ferry passengers and cargoes to and from the subcontinent, no doubt. Yet in South Asia its commercial activities could scarcely be heard above its thunderous war machine.[38] The creation of a new government department, the Board of Control under Pitt's India Act (1784), deepened and institutionalized the ministerial oversight that had begun after the *diwani*. The Act required servants returning to Britain to account for the source of their fortunes. Salaries across all ranks of servants were finally raised to levels that compensated for the loss of private trade, even as the workforce grew. No longer essential for recruiting and keeping young men in the covenanted service, private trade quickly ebbed toward private agency houses (Osborn 1999, pp. 87–88; Webster 2009). Between 1784 and the Charter Act of 1813, which ended the monopoly of trade to India, the Company was a company by name only. India's wrenching transition to British colonial rule had many casualties. A student of business history would be right to include the for-profit East India Company among them.

Notes

1 Recent surveys of the Company include T. Roy (2012), Bowen, McAleer, and Blyth (2011), Robins (2006), and Lawson (1993).
2 To scratch the surface of this vast literature, one might begin with regional investigations of the economic havoc associated with the Company's rise as a colonial state: Arasarat-nam (1996), Parthasarathi (2001), Sen (1998), Hossain (1988), and Subramanian (1996).
3 To understand the role of the Company in the development of British legal history, see Harris (2005). Harris recognizes the costs and benefits of state powers embedded in charters. Stern (2011) imagines the seventeenth-century corporation as a form of state.
4 Sultans, subhadars, and rajas were leaders of sultanates, Mughal provinces, and Hindu Princely States respectively. See also Ramusack (2004) for an informed survey of Indian

Princely States and T. Roy (2013) for an analytical treatment of state formation in early modern South Asia.

5 K. N. Chaudhuri's landmark study (1978) of the Company relies partially on systems analysis, a static model of the organization.

6 This definition aligns with Ghosal and Bartlett's (1990) network approach to the multinational corporation. For an overview of business network theory, see Forsgren (2008, Chapter 6).

7 The figure owes to Scott (1910, pp. 92–95) and reflects a paltry commitment compared to the £2 million subscribed for twenty-one years by the Dutch VOC. Throughout the seventeenth and eighteenth centuries the Dutch company was by far the larger enterprise.

8 The Spice Islands here refer to modern Moluku and Banda Islands. Irwin (1991) has characterized the Anglo-Dutch rivalry as a zero-sum game.

9 Prakash (1998, Chapter 4) provides an authoritative summary of imports by type and volume across location.

10 For outstanding recent surveys on Indian and global textile history, see Riello and Roy (2009) and Riello and Parthasarathi (2009), respectively.

11 The list of settlements is not exhaustive. Trade with China took place on a small scale from the 1660s. From 1710, raw silk and tea were purchased consistently in the tens of thousands of pounds. The China trade was conducted on board Company ships by a "Council of Supercargoes." Trade with the ports of Mokha and Gombroon occurred on a much smaller scale.

12 For a fuller discussion of English courts in the early Company settlements, see Fraas (2011) and Fawcett (1934).

13 See Travers (2005) and Metcalf (1998) on ideologies underpinning British expansion.

14 Lincolnshire Record Office, Mon 7–48, Regulations, 16 Feb 1721, paragraph 39.

15 Erikson and Bearman (2006) use ships journals and logs, provided by Farrington (1999), to infer the flow of information along the Company's shipping network. Contrary to their interpretation, the private trade of ships' captains and overseas staff was constructive and designed to benefit the Company.

16 To suggest but a few titles in the copious literature on Indian merchant communities, see Das Gupta and Das Gupta (2001), Brennig (1977), Prakash and Lombard (1999), Prakash (2004), Marshall (1979), and Neild-Basu (1984).

17 British Library, Oriental and India Office Collections (hereafter OIOC), IORL/F/10/1–2, L/F/10/111–112, O/6/37, O/5/29, and O/5/31. The estimate includes covenanted servants, free merchants, seafarers, and European inhabitants of the Company's principal settlements and their dependencies. By contrast, Maddison (2003) reports the Indian subcontinent's population in 1700 at 165 million.

18 Letter dated February 2, 1742, paragraph 43, cited in "A Copy of the Regulations of the East India Company," Lincolnshire Archives Mon 7–48.

19 The figures from Bryant (1975, Appendix I) reflect European infantry only. The Company relied overwhelmingly on its own resources to defend its trade. When Government assistance was sought, the Company was expected to help defray the expenditure.

20 Employees typically spent their careers within the same major region and seldom transferred across trading regions as was the case with the Dutch East India Company. By contrast to the American colonies, governorships in India were not acquired by appeals to ministers, but through internal, seniority-based promotion.

21 A small but concrete example can be found in the Clive of India papers. National Library of Wales, CB6/2 Miscellaneous Correspondence and Papers [c. 1756] contains a letter from the Marathas to Bengal President Roger Drake after the fall of Calcutta. The

Marathas offer to double the compensation for its loss and to expel the French from Bengal, provided the English do not make peace with Bengal's *Nawab*. For an incisive analysis of the transition in Bengal, see Ray (1985–86). For a broader discussion of continuities and change in eighteenth century Indian political history, see Alavi (2007) and Marshall (2005).

22 Geoffrey Parker (1988, pp. 133–134) regards the Adyar River battle "a turning point in Indian history." Sanjay Subrahmanyam (2001, Chapter 1) questions the importance of Adyar River. He suggests instead the sacking of Delhi (1739) by Nadir Shah had widespread repercussions and encouraged French territorial ambitions.

23 OIOC, Cash Journals IOR L/AG/1/5/14–15.

24 OIOC, Committee of Correspondence Minutes IOR D/21.

25 OIOC, Miscellaneous Home Accounts IOR L/AG/18/2/1/p.3.

26 At the request of Company directors, Royal forces appeared episodically in the British settlements in India.

27 The letter was written from Fort St. George before Vansittart's appointment to the head of the presidency of Bengal. Bodleian Library MSS Eng His b. 191 f. 13–20, 2 July 1760.

28 In 1769, the Company had despatched high-powered supervisors to Bengal and confirmed a government appointee, Sir John Lindsay, as plenipotentiary to Madras. Both efforts attempted to reform the civil administrations in India. The Bengal supervisors were lost at sea and the authority of Sir John Lindsay and his successor achieved little. See Nightingale (1985) on the latter.

29 Servants and directors keenly understood the advantages of private from public correspondence. Private correspondence allowed "a freedom not confined by the strict rules of your public character and mine. If anything I mentioned met not with your approbation you should have wrote me [privately] so in answer, but you certainly ought not to have introduced it any manner in the general letter . . . such a proceeding tends to destroy the confidence which I hope would have established in our correspondence." Letter from Vansittart at Ft. William to Sulivan, Bodleian Library MSS Eng his b. 191, f. 99–102, 22 September 1762.

30 See the letter from Clive to Pitt dated 1 January 1759, British Library, OIOC Mss Eur G/37/Box 15/f. 17. As Marshall (1968) describes, others were far more cautious of embracing sovereignty.

31 See for example Vansittart (1766), Bolts (1772), and Verelst (1772).

32 Dudley to Clive, 21 November 1766; cited in Shearer (1976, p. 65). The current pagination is OIOC Mss Eur G37/43/1 ff. 68–71.

33 The £400,000 payment amounted to a considerable empire tax equivalent to 12.5 per cent of the Company's equity base and 15 per cent of gross sales in 1767–1768. The dividend rate was capped at 10 per cent in 1767, but raised to 12.5 per cent in 1769. Bowen (1991) offers a thorough analysis of the Company's role in Britain's political crises.

34 The Company's cashflow problems were amplified by the tax and the insider trading on company stock was fuelled by the cap on dividends, as dissenting peers recognized. See Auber (1826, p. 302).

35 In addition, the Regulating Act of 1773 declared all the possessions in India property of the Crown, established the post of Governor-General and a Supreme Court of Judicature. The law also regulated salaries of senior officials in Bengal as well the election of company directors in London. See Auber (1826, pp. 512–513).

36 British Library Add 29134 ff. 250–251, 8 December 1773.

37 See the classic works by Misra (1959) and Aspinall (1931).

38 In China, tea continued yet as a valuable trade commodity; see Mui and Mui (1984).

References

Alavi, S., ed. (2007). *The Eighteenth Century*, Delhi: Oxford University Press.

Arasaratnam, S. (1996). *Maritime Commerce and English Power: Southeast India, 1750–1800*, Burlington: Variorum.

Aspinall, A. (1931). *Cornwallis in Bengal*, Manchester: Manchester University Press.

Auber, P. (1826). *An Analysis of the Constitution of the East India Company*, New York: Burt Franklin.

Biddulph, J. (1901). *Stringer Lawrence Father of the Indian Army*, London: John Murray.

Bolts, W. (1772). *Considerations on Indian Affairs; Particularly Concerning the Present State of Bengal and Its Dependencies*, London: Printed for J. Alom, P. Elmsly and Brotetherton and Sewell.

Bowen, H.V. (1991). *Revenue and Reform: the Indian Problem in British Politics 1757–1773*, Cambridge: Cambridge University Press.

Bowen, H.V., J. McAleer, and R.J. Blyth (2011). *Monsoon Traders The Maritime World of the East India Company*, London: Scala Publishers Ltd.

Brennig, J.J. (1977). "Chief Merchants and European Enclaves of Seventeenth-Century Coromandel", *Modern Asian Studies*, I, 3: 321–40.

Bruijn, J.R., and F.S. Gaastra (1993). *Ships, Sailors, and Spices*, Amsterdam: NEHA.

Bryant, G.J. (1975). 'East India Company and Its Army, 1600–1778', University of London, PhD Dissertation.

———. (2004). 'Asymmetric Warfare: The British Experience in Eighteenth-Century India', *Journal of Military History 68 (2)*, pp. 431–469.

Chaudhuri, K. N. (1978). *The Trading World of Asia and the English East India Company, 1660–1760*, Cambridge: Cambridge University Press.

Das Gupta, A., and U. Das Gupta (2001). *The World of the Indian Ocean Merchant, 1500–1800. Collected Essays of Ashin Das Gupta*, Oxford: Oxford University Press.

Dodwell, H.H. (1920). *Dupleix and Clive: The Beginning of Empire*, London: Methuen and Co. Ltd.

———. (1929). *The Cambridge History of India, Vol. V, British India*, London: Cambridge University Press.

Erikson, E., and P.S. Bearman (2006). 'Malfeasance and the Foundations for Global Trade: The Structure of English Trade in the East Indies, 1601–1833', *American Journal of Sociology, 112 (1)*, pp. 195–230.

Farrington, A. (1999). *Catalogue of the East India Company Ship's Journals and Logs, 1600–1834*, London: British Library, pp. 1–789.

Fawcett, C. (1934). *The First Century of British Justice in India*, Oxford: Oxford University Press.

Forsgren, M. (2008). *Theories of the Multinational Firm*, Cheltenham: Edward Elgar.

Fraas, A. M. (2011). '"They have travailed into a wrong latitude:" The Laws of England, Indian Settlements, and the British Imperial Constitution 1726–1773', Duke University, PhD Dissertation.

Ghosal, S., and C. Bartlett (1990). 'The Multinational Corporation as an Interorganizational Network', *Academy of Management Review, 15 (4)*, pp. 1603–1625.

Grassby, R. (2004). 'Child, Sir Josiah, first baronet (bap. 1631 d.1699)', in *Oxford Dictionary of National Biography*. Oxford: Oxford University Press.

Harris, R. (2005). 'The English East India Company and the History of Company Law', in E. Gepken-Jager, G. van Solinge, and L. Timmerman, eds., *VOC 1602–2002–400 Years of Company Law, Series Law of Business and Finance, Vol. 6*, Dordrecht: Kluwer Legal Publishers, pp. 219–247.

Hejeebu, S. (2005). 'Contract Enforcement in the English East India Company', *Journal of Economic History 65 (2)*, pp. 496–523.

———. (2009). 'The Demand for Empire: Servants and Directors of the East India Company'. Presented at the Institute for Historical Research, London.

Hilder, H. (1978). 'East India Company's Regulation of Its Servants', *Bengal Past and Present, 97 (1)*, pp. 1–23.

Hill, S. C. (1916). *Catalogue of Manuscripts in European Languages, Vol. II, Part I*, London: Oxford University Press.

Hossain, H. (1988). *The Company Weavers of Bengal: The East India Company and the Organization of Textile Production in Bengal, 1750–1813*, Delhi: Oxford University Press.

Irwin, D. (1991). 'Mercantilism as Strategic Trade Policy: The Anglo-Dutch Rivalry for the East India Trade', *Journal of Political Economy, 99 (6)*, pp. 1296–1314.

Lawson, P. (1993). *East India Company*, London: Orient Longman.

Lenman, B. (2001). *Britain's Colonial Wars, 1688–1783*, Harlow: Pearson Education Limited.

Maddison, A. (2003). *The World Economy: Historical Statistics*, Paris: OECD.

Marshall, P. J. (1968). *Problems of Empire: Britain and India, 1757–1813*, London: Allen & Unwin.

———. (1976). *East Indian Fortunes*, Oxford: Clarendon Press.

———. (1979). 'Masters and Banians in Eighteenth Century Calcutta', in B. B. Kling and M. N. Pearson, eds., *The Age of Partnership: Europeans in Asia Before Dominion*, Honolulu: University Press of Hawaii.

———, ed. (2005). *The Eighteenth Century in Indian History: Revolution or Evolution?* Delhi: Oxford University Press.

Metcalf, T.R. (1998). *The New Cambridge History of India: Vol. III, Part IV, Ideologies of the Raj*, Cambridge: Cambridge University Press.

Misra, B.B. (1959). *The Central Adminstration of the East India Company, 1773–1834*, Manchester: Manchester University Press.

Mui, H. C., and L. H. Mui (1984). *The Management of Monopoly*, Vancouver: University of British Columbia Press.

Nechtman, T.W. (2010). *Nabobs, Empire and Identity in Eighteenth-Century Britain*, Cambridge: Cambridge University Press.

Neild-Basu, S. (1984). 'The Dubashes of Madras', *Modern Asian Studies, 18 (1)*, pp. 1–35.

Nightingale, P. (1985). *Fortune and Integrity: A Study of Moral Attitudes in the Indian Diary of George Paterson, 1769–1774*, Delhi: Oxford University Press.

Osborn, J.R. (1999). 'India, Parliament and the Press under George III: A Study of English Attitudes Towards the East India Company and Empire in the Late Eighteenth and Early Nineteenth Century', Oxford University, PhD Dissertation.

Parker, G. (1988). *The Military Revolution: Military Innovation and the Rise of the West, 1500–1800*, Cambridge: Cambridge University Press.

Parthasarathi, P. (2001). *The Transition to a Colonial Economy*, Cambridge: Cambridge University Press.

Pearson, M.N. (1991). 'Merchants and States', in J.D. Tracy, ed., *The Political Economy of Merchant Empires*, Cambridge: Cambridge University Press, pp. 41–116.

Prakash, O., and D. Lombard (1999). *Commerce and Culture in the Bay of Bengal, 1500–1800*, Delhi: Manohar.

Prakash, O. (1998). *The New Cambridge History of India: Vol II, Part V, European Commercial Enterprise in Pre-Colonial India*, Cambridge: Cambridge University Press.

———. (2004). *Bullion for Goods, European and Indian Merchants in the Indian Ocean Trade, 1500–1800*, New Delhi: Manohar Publishers.

Ramusack, B.N. (2004). *The New Cambridge History of India: Vol III, Part VI, The Indian Princes and Their States*, Cambridge: Cambridge University Press.

Ray, R. (1985–86). 'Colonial Penetration and the Initial Resistance: The Mughal Ruling Class, the English East India Company and the Struggle for Bengal, 1756–1800', *Indian Economic and Social History Review, 12 (1–2)*, pp. 1–105.

Riello, G., and P. Parthasarathi (2009). *The Spinning World: A Global History of Cotton Textiles, 1200–1850*, New York: Oxford University Press.

Riello, G., and T. Roy (2009). *How India Clothed the World: The World of South Asian Textiles, 1500–1850*, Leiden: Brill.

Robins, N. (2006). *The Corporation that Changed the World: How the East India Company Shaped the Modern Multinational*, London: Pluto Press,.

Roy, K. (2005). 'Military Synthesis in South Asia: Armies, warfare, and Indian Society, 1740–1849', *The Journal of Military History, 69 (3)*, pp. 651–690.

Roy, T. (2012). *The East India Company. The World's Most Powerful Corporation*, New Delhi: Allen Lane.

———. (2013). *An Economic History of Early Modern India*, Abingdon: Routledge.

Scott, W. R. (1910). *The Constitution and Finance of English, Scottish, and Irish Joint-Stock Companies to 1720, Vol. II*, Cambridge: Cambridge University Press.

Sen, S. (1998). *Empire of Free Trade: The East India Company and The Making of the Colonial Marketplace*, Philadelphia: University of Pennsylvania Press.

Shearer, T. (1976). 'Crisis and Change in the Development of the East India Company's Affairs, 1760–1773', Oxford University, PhD Dissertation.

Smith, A. (1776). *An Inquiry into the Nature and Causes of the Wealth of Nations*, E. Cannan, ed., University of Chicago Press. Originally published 1904.

Stern, P.J. (2011). *The Company-State: Corporate Sovereignty and the Early Modern Foundations of the British Empire in India*, Oxford: Oxford University Press.

Subramanian, L. (1996). *Indigenous Capital and Imperial Expansion: Bombay, Surat and the West Coast*, Delhi: Oxford University Press.

Subrahmanyam, S. (2001). *Penumbral Visions: Making Polities in Early Modern South India*, Ann Arbor: University of Michigan Press.

Sutherland, L.S. (1952). *The East India Company in Eighteenth Century Politics*, Oxford: The Clarendon Press.

Travers, R. (2005). 'Ideology and British Expansion in Bengal, 1757–72', *Journal of Imperial and Commonwealth History, 33 (1)*, pp. 7–27.

Vansittart, H. (1766). *A Narrative of the Transactions in Bengal from 1760 to 1764*, London: printed for J. Newbery; J. Dodsley; and J. Robson.

Verelst, H. (1772). *A View of the Rise, Progress, and Present State of the English Government in Bengal*, London.

Webster, A. (2009). *Twilight of the East India Company. The Evolution of Anglo-Asian Commerce and Politics, 1790–1860*, Woodbridge: Boydell Press.

4

THE MYTH AND REALITY OF DEINDUSTRIALISATION IN EARLY MODERN INDIA

Indrajit Ray

'Deindustrialisation' – in the general sense of a decline in manufactures – is one of the most debatable and enduring issues in the historiography of economic change in early colonial India. There are two main reasons for this ongoing debate: first, the notion that British colonial policy led to a decline in Indian handicrafts played a role in the nationalist conception of British rule; second, for the student of the field, there remain many unanswered questions about the concept, the measurement, and explanations of the process. This chapter revisits these questions and conducts a comprehensive and critical survey of the related scholarship.

Deindustrialisation was no more than a vague concern in India around the mid-nineteenth century, which subsequently grew into widespread cries and protests during the nationalist movement. It returned to academic discussion thereafter, especially since the 1960s, generating a lively debate (see Morris et al. 1969). Some historians attributed it more than others to colonial discriminations that thwarted the country's economic development in the early modern age (R.P. Dutt 1940). Others questioned this implication or the empirical validity of the issue (Das 1959; Robb 1981). Interestingly, both 'nationalist' as well as 'Marxist' or 'neo-Marxist' writers supported the view that British policy had caused a decline in artisan industry, even though the 'moderate' nationalist leaders in India did not subscribe to the Marxian philosophy. In this chapter, I first ask what evidence, if any, the original hypothesis is based on. My investigation in this respect also helps us understand why the 'nationalist' analysis fell in line with the Marxian. I then review the post-colonial literature to ascertain whether it can adequately justify the occurrence of deindustrialisation in India during the colonial period.

The first section of the paper discusses the alternative definitions of the term, and the origins and antecedents of the hypothesis. I show that its significance in India's 'moderate' nationalism gives a specific connotation to the term. The second section discusses the post-colonial literature on the explanation of deindustrialisation, dividing it into two broad fields: (a) the neo-Marxian school, and (b) the main-stream school. The third section gathers together various empirical studies that seek to prove (or disprove) the occurrence of the event during the colonial period. Although the industry-level case studies in this field concentrate exclusively on cotton textiles, my recent studies broaden the range of examples beyond textiles, and contextualize the deindustrialisation debate within a picture of the regional economy rather than using a stylized picture of India. This work is also discussed in Ray (2011). The last section concludes.

The concept: its origins and antecedents

In the context of British manufacturing industries in the late twentieth century, Kaldor defines deindustrialisation as the continuously declining share of a country in the global trade of manufacturing, which leads to deteriorations in its balance of trade in manufacturing, and hence, in its external balance (Kaldor 1979). Such a scenario arises when the economy's manufacturing activities fail to keep pace with the development in the rest of the world. This is an empirically testable definition. But given the paucity of data and also their questionable quality, an application to nineteenth-century India is not possible. In the Indian context, a number of scholars derive the definition from the concept of industrialization. According to them, the industrialization of an economy consists of (a) a rise in the proportion of national income generated in the secondary sector, (b) a rise in the proportion of popula-tion engaged in the secondary sector, and (c) growing mechanization of industries. Deindustrialisation represents a scenario where one or more of these conditions are reversed. In practice, only employment is usually considered for the empirical verification of the hypothesis (see Ray 2011, pp. 5–6 for discussion). Clingingsmith and Williamson (2008, p. 210), however, define the term on the basis of the employ-ment criterion in their framework of a two-good, three-input model. Assuming an immobile input of land in agriculture and of capital in manufacturing, along with a free mobility of labour across them, they define deindustrialisation as a state of affairs where there is an exodus of labour from the manufacturing sector to agricul-ture. The exodus of labour can either be measured in the absolute numbers (strict deindustrialisation) or as a share of total employment (weak deindustrialisation).

Focusing more on the political antecedent of the term, Roy (2000, pp. 1142–1147) calls deindustrialisation a theory that is constituted of four propositions: (i) traditional industries declined in a colony, (ii) the decline was initiated by technological obso-lescence in the domestic economy, (iii) it was sustained by colonial policies, and (iv) the development of modern industries could not compensate for the economic loss resulting from the decline of traditional industries. This definition poses some prob-lems for empirical application as it does not deal with (a) colonial industry that was not traditional, (b) the decline not being triggered by technological obsolescence but by discriminatory colonial policies, and (c) the decline caused by technological obsolescence but not sustained by discriminatory policies. These alternative events did occur in nineteenth-century India. For example, the shipbuilding industry, which had been developing in Bengal on the basis of European technology since 1780, was destroyed during the colonial period (case a); the decline of the salt industry in Bengal was not initiated by any technological obsolescence (case b); and the decline of the cotton textile industry in Bengal since the mid-1820s was not sustained by any discriminatory colonial policies of Great Britain (case c) (Ray 2011, pp. 171–205, 131–170, 52–87). In view of these issues, I seek to redefine the concept later on.

The genesis of the debate on the Indian experience goes back to Marx's writings (Marx 1853). Not only did he start a debate, but he also bequeathed certain methodological tools to the ensuing debate. In his stylized Indian society, agriculture was totally dependent on the government's public works, especially irrigation, and the industrial economy consisted of the cotton textile industry, which was export-oriented. Textile exports brought in precious metals to satisfy the Indians' great desire for gold and silver jewellery. Marx (1853) believed that the textile industry was so extensive that it defined the contemporary social fabric: 'The hand-loom and the spinning-wheel, producing their regular myriads of spinners and weavers, were the pivots of that society'. In this economy, the decline of textiles would cause a collapse of the entire society. Since the textile industry was export-based, Marx explained its decline with reference to British trade policies. On the basis of trade statistics, he contended that 'England began with driving the Indian cottons from the European market; it then introduced twist into Hindostan, and in the end inundated the very mother country of cotton with cottons' (Marx 1853). Simultaneously, British rule also brought an end to India's agricultural prosperity by neglecting public works and destroying the self-supporting villages that had once combined agriculture with industry, weaving with spinning.

The subsequent debate on India's deindustrialisation inherits three crucial aspects of this analysis. First, the term is defined to imply a state of industrial decline in a country, which resulted from imperial policies. Though this is implicit in the pioneering works in Indian economic history (like R. Dutt 1901), Roy (2000) makes it explicit. We will shortly see that this underlying connection between the decline of industries and the colonial rule anticipated the 'nationalist' version of deindustrialisation. Needless to add, the later debate on deindustrialisation in the UK makes no such political link. Second, the Marxian surmise that the cotton textile industry accounted for industrial activities in India appears to have been implicitly accepted in the literature, since detailed discussion on any other industry is absent in it. Third, the methodological shortcoming of assessing the decline of an industry by trade statistics, which Marx adopted in his analysis for India, is also inherited in the literature (see for example Desai 1971). Morris (1968) raised doubts on the interpretation of textile imports. Higher imports might cater to higher domestic demand – or be re-exported on land routes – without damaging domestic industry. Also, to what extent the decline of exports adversely affected the industry depended on the export share of its output. These methodological issues underline the legacies of Marx's deliberations on the issue.

The conjectural relationship between colonial rule and the decline of industries brought deindustrialisation to the attention of India's nationalist movement during the last three decades of the nineteenth and the early twentieth century. A number of authors such as Digby (1901, pp. 243–285) and R. Dutt (1901) gathered additional data to corroborate the proposition that British trade policies destroyed Indian industries. Some moderate nationalist leaders, Naoroji in particular, gave a further explanation for the hypothesis on the basis of the drain theory (for a discussion, see Ganguli 1965). Naoroji explained how 'the internal drain' mopped up resources from the countryside to the capital city, giving rise to 'the external drain'. According to him, the drain of resources from India stood at more than £500 million for thirty-four years in the second half of the nineteenth century (Naoroji 1901, p. 35). With reference to John Stuart Mill's theory that the stock of capital, rather than the demand for commodities, sets the limit for industrial development of an economy, Naoroji argued that India's deindustrialisation was an outcome of the drain of savings. He further strengthened his argument by another of Mill's dictums that good governance cannot promote industries under the scarcity of capital.

Why were the moderate nationalist leaders so preoccupied with deindustrialisation? It appears that the concern arose out of their worries about mass poverty across the country. In fact, Naoroji points out that there was a vicious circle between deindustrialisation and mass poverty, which was created and perpetuated by the drain of wealth. 'The candle', he writes, 'burns at both ends – capital going on diminishing on the one hand, and labour thereby becoming less capable, on the other, to reproduce as much as before' (Naoroji 1901, p. 56). Growing poverty was its inevitable consequence.

Interestingly, the majority of the moderate nationalist leaders belonged to the urban privileged class and frequently overlooked the plight of the poor. Citing some of these cases, Seth (1999) observes that 'the Congress in these early years was either uninterested in or opposed to government measures purportedly directed at protecting and improving the lot of rural cultivators or urban workers' (p. 105). It is possible that the moderates had a specific agenda. They believed that since deindustrialisation was the cause of mass poverty, its eradication warranted an extensive industrial development in the country, and that such a development necessarily called for the 'Indianisation' of civil services and a responsible government. These latter reforms were the basic agenda of the moderate nationalism in India (see for example Banerjea 1963, p. 126; Karve and Ambekar 1962–1967, p. 178). The Congress also took a resolution at its 1886 session stating the relationship between the introduction of representative institutions and the question of poverty (Zaidi and Zaidi 1976, p. 138).

It is, therefore, clear from this discussion that whereas in industrial economies the origin of the term referred to a decline in the market economy, in the Indian case the term was shaped in a colonial setting and even blurred market forces. This drawback continues in the post-colonial literature, as Robb (1981) notes, 'If the first point about the debate [deindustrialisation] in 1968 is thus its continuity with the past, the second is the obvious one that it called for a methodology that is anti-historical: the threat that certain conclusions are ideologically unacceptable displays more heat than wisdom' (p. 512). These two components of the composite definition – colonial policy and industrial decline – are not conceptually linked. If colonial policies are found oppressive to industries, one should not conclude that there must have been industrial decline; nor should one deduce from an empirical finding on industrial decline that the colonial rule was oppressive. Evidence shows that in nineteenth-century Bengal the silk textile industry survived even under discriminatory policies while the indigo dye industry declined even when the government supported it (Ray 2011, pp. 88–132, 206–244). Thus, an adverse policy is neither a necessary nor a sufficient condition for deindustrialisation to occur. It is not because there could be market forces that ensure survival or decline of industry. Therefore, for the sake of clarity, we should distinguish the causal factors carefully. It is one thing to ask if a decline took place, it is another to ask why the decline took place.

This critique leads me to offer the following definition: deindustrialisation was a state of affairs whereby (a) there was a downfall of an industry, and (b) the industry's downfall was not compensated by the growth of a modern industry in the same line of production. This is empirically easier to test because it is a definition constructed within the framework of industry studies. By contrast, the existing literature seeks to study the question of deindustrialisation within a framework of inter-sectoral job transfers. This is difficult to test because India's nineteenth-century sources are not able to provide support to that end (see also Simmons 1985). It is also a more value-free definition in terms of causal factors. A specific industrial decline may have been caused either by market forces, or technological obsolescence, or by discriminatory colonial policies, or all of them. Studying the problem in this framework would leave least scope for value judgment.

Deindustrialisation: theoretical underpinnings

The post-colonial literature is dominated by attempts to explain India's deindustrialisation, but has not investigated enough whether the event actually took place. This is often acknowledged even explicitly. Thus, Wallerstein (1986) notes, 'The debate over the empirical characterisation will go on for a long time, since we are still very poor in accumulated data on which to base our judgement' (p. PE34). Perlin (1983) also notes 'the remarkable lack of any serious regional monographs on textile industries, in the seventeenth or eighteenth centuries, of a kind long legion in the European historiography' (p. 53).

The post-colonial literature falls broadly under two schools of thought: (a) the neo-Marxist school and (b) the mainstream school. The former regards deindustrialisation as an event in the formation of the capitalist world economy. There is little agreement on how and when the event happened (Brewer 1990; Limqueco and McFarlane 1983). But the majority of the neo-Marxist school acknowledges the drain of wealth in the context of India's incorporation into the world capitalist system. Marx referred to it as the plunder of Bengal, which, according to the neo-Marxists, represented one of the constituents of the primitive accumulation at the 'metropolitan' centres of world capitalism. For peripheral countries, it represented the phase of decapitalisation, which, as Luxemburg (1951, pp. 373–376) points out, might have been ushered in by way of taxation as well. However, in line with Marx's own discourse on India's industrial decline, authors like Frank

(1978) and Wallerstein (1986) believe that British policies motivated the formation of world capitalism. Frank thus points out that capitalism was set in by the successive annulments of various protectionist policies of mercantilism in Great Britain under the philosophy of laissez faire. The process began in 1774 with the withdrawal of import prohibitions on Indian cotton textiles in England, consolidated through the modification of the East India Company monopoly charter in 1793 and the end of the charter on India trade in 1813, and culminated in the repeal of the Corn Laws in 1846 and the Navigation Laws in 1849. Not only did the metropolitan policies thus institute the first stage of capitalism, but they were equally effective in subsequent stages. The following two stages of capitalism witnessed a large-scale world accumulation involving a vast expansion of world trade. With supports from suitable policy designs, the latter brought about deindustrialisation in the periphery and industrialization at the centre, and thus heralded such an international division of labour that a dependent relationship was forged between the core and the periphery.

Wallerstein also points out that deindustrialisation was the starting point of world capitalism. He explains that 'The famous or notorious "general process of deindustrialisation" in India was, of course, very much a part of this qualitative economic change' (Wallerstein 1986, p. PE30). But he does not concur that the free trade policy that Great Britain pursued after its industrial excellence totally explained India's deindustrialisation. A host of restrictive policies, sometimes coercive, are identified instead. In the first place, the monopsonistic power of the East India Company in particular, and that of English traders in general, weakened the bargaining position of Indian artisans and reduced them to 'wage workers'. This destroyed the traditional entrepreneurial skill of society, leaving decision-making at the behest of the English entrepreneurs. Second, contrary to its proclaimed policy of free trade, Great Britain adopted restrictive trade practices regarding the import of Indian textiles, and thus severely curtailed their export outlets in that country. Similar setbacks loomed large in other foreign markets as Great Britain imposed higher tariffs on Indian textiles that were carried on foreign ships and were destined for the markets like the US, Holland, Denmark, Sweden, and Portugal. While these restrictive trade policies crippled the export vents for Indian products, there were also several discriminations from the colonial administration that directly hit domestic industries in India. In sum, Wallerstein also underscores the state policies (though not the free trade policy) as an explanation for India's deindustrialisation.

Since deindustrialisation is not a market-driven outcome in the neo-Marxian analysis but an outcome of various state policies, the motives behind those policies need to be identified. To this end, Wallerstein (1986) mentions 'the elimination of Indian competition, first of all in Britain, second of all in continental Europe and North America, and finally to a significant extent in India itself' (p. PE30) as a secondary goal, and the replacement of the domestic crops like food-grains by cash crops that the world market demanded as the primary one. Deindustrialisation performed two tasks simultaneously: first, it created a vast colonial market for British products; and second, it channelled the colonial supply of raw materials to British industries. The changes in the cropping pattern in Indian agriculture, however, perpetuated the second process, and thus broke down the economic self-sufficiency not only at the village but also at the regional level. Once India was incorporated into the world capitalist system, it became subject to a dependent relationship with the 'core' capitalist country of Great Britain. On the basis of the theory of unequal exchange (Emmanuel 1972), Frank (1984) argues that this core-periphery relationship gave rise to exploitation, which initiated and perpetuated the development of underdevelopment in peripheral countries like India.

Mainstream writers, however, seek to explain deindustrialisation with the contemporary market forces that shifted the terms of trade in favour of agriculture so that the industries were destined to suffer. Such a movement in the sectoral terms of trade could occur under the influence of domestic or international environments, generating alternative hypotheses on this issue. One widely held argument is the hypothesis of globalisation that seeks to explain India's nineteenth-century deindustrialisation with the contemporary wave of the free-trade doctrine in Europe and North America (Morris 1963, pp. 606–608). According to this hypothesis, the industrial revolution generated two effects in the international commodity market. On the one hand, technological and institutional innovations significantly reduced the prices of various manufacturing products. On the other, there were steady multiplications of firms in various industries using more and more raw materials from agriculture leading to soaring prices globally of agricultural raw materials. The movement of international terms of trade in favour of agricultural commodities during the nineteenth century is evident in the British terms of trade between 1801–1810 and 1841–1850, which shows that the ratio of her export prices (representing the prices of manufacturing goods) and the import prices (representing the prices of industrial intermediaries, food, and other primary products) fell by about 40 per cent (Imlah 1952). According to one interpretation, Indian industries could not adequately respond to those changes because of the scarcity of entrepreneurs, the stubborn attitude of the people towards any departure from traditionality, and 'the otherworldliness', signifying deep attachment of the people to spirituality rather than the materialistic world (see Morris 1963, pp. 606–608, for a discussion). Indian industries could not, therefore, reduce costs enough during the phase of globalisation. They gained instead by increasing the supply of industrial raw materials from agriculture such as raw cotton, raw silk, and raw jute. The changing international terms of trade between industries and agriculture was thus reflected in India's domestic terms of trade between them, reallocating her resources to cause deindustrialisation (see also Williamson 2008, p. 374).

To account for adverse domestic factors, Clingingsmith and Williamson (2008) provide two hypotheses, the Mughal collapse hypothesis, and the El Niño hypothesis, belonging broadly to what is known as the hypothesis of negative shocks to agriculture, or 'the dragging-out effect'. Both together suggest that agricultural productivity in India suffered because of historical events during the nineteenth century that reduced the supplies of crops and thus increased their market prices. The resulting movement in the terms of trade in favour of agriculture caused a redistribution of resources away from industries. The Mughal collapse hypothesis draws on the existing literature and emphasizes that as the Mughal authority weakened across northern India from the early eighteenth century, many successor states emerged, which frequently fought wars among them, involving vast public expenditure. Revenue farming became the order of the day. This is evident in Bayly (1983), who reveals that during the ebbing phase of the Mughal hegemony, the burden of rent increased by about 10 per cent. Also, because of frequent wars, cultivation shifted from the insecure areas to newer settlements of inferior land where agricultural productivity should be lower. Simultaneously, the war preparations induced an outflow of human and animal resources from agriculture, drastically increasing the prevailing wage rates and the prices of animals. These historical events elevated agricultural production costs, which in turn pushed up prices.

The El Niño hypothesis seeks to correlate the productivity fluctuation in Indian agriculture with the periodic rise in the surface temperature of the Pacific sea – the El Niño – that caused failures of monsoon rains in India. Clingingsmith and Williamson (2008, pp. 215–216) bring out this relationship empirically on the basis of a fifty-year moving average of droughts during 1550–1900. They pinpoint that the occurrence of droughts per year fell from 0.35 (i.e. one drought every three years) during 1550–1640 to about 0.17 (i.e. one drought every six years) during 1641–1725, and further to 0.10 (i.e. one drought every ten years) in 1735. Infrequent droughts in this period of 1650–1735 corresponded to the Mughal Empire's golden age of Shah Jahan and its overextension and collapse under Aurangzeb. The causation they advance is this: infrequent droughts gave rise to good harvests, which in turn resulted in prosperity in different spheres of the society. To explain the empire's collapse, they argue that the Maratha power, which weakened the Mughal authority, also benefitted from good harvests. For the period 1735–1813, however, Clingingsmith and Williamson suggest that the frequency of droughts steadily increased from once in ten years to once in 2.5 years. Droughts had far-reaching effects. Seeds were eaten up in the year of drought so that production in subsequent years suffered. Moreover, significant depopulation took place across the countryside since famine and epidemics invariably followed droughts. There is evidence that in 1791, the year of the worst El Niño, one half of the inhabitants in the Northern Circars in India died. There are thus two different broad theories regarding the explanation of India's deindustrialisation under the colonial rule. What is the evidence for any of these theories?

Deindustrialisation: empirical evidence

The empirical evidence on India's deindustrialisation broadly falls under two categories: (a) the inter-sectoral studies based on the employment or output criteria, and (b) industry studies (see Appendix 4.1 for a full list of empirical studies). Most works in the former category are based on census data relating to industrial workers. The very first work in this category was Clark (1950), who reconstructs the census data for 1881 and 1911 and reports that the number of workers belonging to manufacturing, mining, and construction as a proportion of the total workforce fell from 28.4 per cent to 12.4 per cent, confirming deindustrialisation. But a number of drawbacks are subsequently noticed in his methodology. In the first place, the 'general labour' category that Clark considers as representing industrial workers in fact included many agricultural labourers. Since the 'general labour' category was dropped afterwards, serious discrepancies cropped up. Second, discrepancies also arose with regard to the definition of 'sellers'. Earlier censuses, particularly those in 1881 and 1891, treated them as industrial workers, but the later ones did not. Third, the enumeration of female workers involved a reporting problem. In many cases, the women working part time in domestic industries, and even in other commercial establishments, were treated as industrial workers. Removing female workers altogether, Thorner and Thorner (1962, pp. 70–71) rework the census data for 1881 and 1931, arriving at a different conclusion from Clark. Though raw data display a fall from 21.1 million in 1881 to 12.9 million in 1931, their filtered data show that the number of manufacturing workers stagnated at around 14.8 million between those periods.

Chattopadhyay (1975) also works on the census data but avoids the earlier censuses because of the disputed data. His study corroborates deindustrialisation on the basis of the following findings: (a) the share of industrial workers in the total population fell from 5.94 per cent in 1901 to 4.50 per cent in 1931, and (b) the share of such workers in the total workforce declined from 8.73 per cent to 6.65 per cent during the same period. In another study, he deals with the presidency of Bengal, and also its three provinces separately (Chattopadhyay 1981). His calculations reveal the occurrence of deindustrialisation in the Bengal presidency as well as in the provinces of Bihar and Orissa, but not in the Bengal province (for 1901–1921). For 1921–1931, a sharp downward trend is noticed in the last series, but Chattopadhyay attributes it to the Great Depression.

The greatest drawback of these census-based studies is that they seek to trace an event in a period when the event might have already finished. If India's deindustrialisation took place in the late eighteenth and the early nineteenth century, as is sometimes suggested, the census, which started only in 1881, would not fully capture these effects. To avoid this problem, Bagchi (1976) compares the census data of 1901 with data collected by the East India Company officer Francis Buchanan Hamilton during his journeys (1809–1813) in Gangetic Bihar (the present-day districts of Patna, Gaya, Shahabad, Monghyr, Bhagalpur, and Purnea). Under the assumption that each spinner supported one other person, Bagchi's study indicates that the share of the population dependent on industry fell from 21.6 per cent to 8.5 per cent, and that the rate of decline was highest for spinners, from 10.3 per cent to 1.3 per cent, as against a fall from 2.3 per cent to 1.3 per cent for weavers, and from 9 per cent to 7.2 per cent for other industrial workers. But it is doubtful to what extent Gangetic Bihar was representative of the presidency of Bengal, let alone India, which housed a number of manufacturing industries at the beginning of the nineteenth century. Further, the census data of 1901 lacked comparability with those of Hamilton concerning the definitions of various working categories, as pointed out by Vicziany (1979). Also, the quality of Hamilton's data is severely questioned in the literature (Roy 2006).

The employment yardstick that these studies have adopted for the measurement of deindustrialisation is also a bone of contention. Krishnamurthy (1976) argues that the falling employment level was not necessarily a phenomenon of deindustrialisation, but that it might represent growing capital intensity under the prevailing technology. Extending this argument, Roy advocates that the capital intensity might have increased owing to the replacement of domestic production by wage labour within the organisation of small scale industries. Referring to Sivasubramonian's data (1997) concerning the rising proportion of income in secondary industries, Roy (2000) observes that 'what we see in census and income statistics is the beginning of a large-scale substitution of labour by machinery within India. . . . We see also strong signs that in fact real incomes increased within small industry as well' (pp. 129–130).

Bairoch (1982, pp. 269–333) follows a different approach based on an estimated time series of world manufacturing output over 1750–1938. His estimation indicates that India's share in the world manufacturing output was as high as 24.8 per cent in 1750, next only to China's (32.8 per cent). While the latter improved its share to 33.3 per cent in 1800, the former was displaced to 19.7 per cent in that year. It fell further to 17.6 per cent in 1830, 2.8 per cent in 1880, and 1.4 per cent in 1913. This study also attracts various criticisms. Apart from the speculative nature of these estimates, in the face of rising manufacturing output in the rest of the world, India's declining share does not necessarily confirm the event of deindustrialisation. Moreover, non-traded manufacturing goods, which the study does not account for, dominated Indian industries in the eighteenth and nineteenth centuries.

Let us now turn to industry-level studies. Clingingsmith and Williamson (2008) evaluate the case of the cotton textile industry in a framework of the sectoral terms of trade. The study is based on a neo-Ricardian model consisting of three sectors – grain, agricultural commodity export, and textiles – with labour as the only mobile input across them costing a nominal wage rate. While grain is not traded, textiles and agricultural commodities are globally traded. The study suggests strong deindustrialisation based on a spectacular rise in the real textile industry wage due to the fall in textile prices and a rise in the nominal wage rate. While the former is explained by contemporary technological innovations, the latter is deduced from the steady upwards surge of grain prices, under the assumption of a constant real wage. These statistics also suggest unfavourable terms of trade for textiles, confirming strong deindustrialisation. A strong deindustrialisation is also evident in the estimated statistics, which show that the inter-sectoral terms of trade between textiles and agricultural commodities moved strongly in favour of the latter. The validity of these conclusions, however, hinges on two crucial assumptions made in the study: first, the Ricardian assumption of constant real wages helps to establish a rising nominal wage rate from an increasing trend of the grain price. Second, it is based on the underlying assumption that adverse terms of trade for industries provide a sufficient condition for deindustrialisation. The latter theoretical construction belongs to the partial equilibrium analysis, which cannot explain a real-world event like deindustrialisation. In a general equilibrium framework, one should recognize, for example, whether the adverse terms of trade for textiles led to price reductions for inputs, especially for raw cotton. The estimation of data, especially the use of some proxy variables, also cast doubt on those conclusions.

For the textile industry, Harnetty (1991) and Twomey (1983) also confirm nineteenth-century deindustrialisation. Harnetty argues that in contrast to its entire share of the domestic market in 1801, the industry could retain only a 23 per cent share in 1900–1901, leaving 66 per cent for imported goods and 11 per cent for mill-made products. For the Central Provinces, where his study concentrates, he notices that the import of those goods shot up from approximately 23 to 105 billion pounds from 1863/4 to 1887/8, whereas the export of country-made cloth moved downwards from approximately 60 to 26 billion pounds in the same period. He also provides evidence for the perpetual decline in the industry's profitability and wage rate. His affirmation of the event is, however, subject to some qualifications (see Frisof 2008, pp. 28–30). Twomey (1983, pp. 49, 52) estimates that the industry's export-related employment in India fell by 300,000 during 1790–1830, of which Bengal shared about 81 per cent, and that the overall reduction of employment in the industry stood at 3.6 million for 1850–1880. But these estimates involve speculations with regards to the output of hand-spun yarn, the growth of population, and per capita income as well as the coefficient relating cloth production to employment.

Guha (1972; discussed in Habib 1985, p. 364) substantiates deindustrialisation in cotton textiles using the consumption of raw materials as a yardstick for the measurement of production. According to his estimates, the net availability of cotton yarns (including the imported and machine-spun varieties) fell from 419 million pounds in 1850 to 240 million pounds in 1870 and further to 184–221 million pounds in 1900. Habib (1985) supports this finding, citing Harnetty's data that British imports of raw cotton from India rose from 145 million pounds in 1855 to 443 million pounds in 1872. He observes, 'Unless the Indian per capita cotton production also increased on such a dramatically high scale, the per capita availability of cotton within the country must have undergone an enormous decline' (Habib 1985, p. 364). But McAlpin (1974, pp. 665–666) denies such an increase in per capita cotton acreage in India during that period. Roy (2012) also points out that, notwithstanding the usefulness of this methodology, cotton acreage estimates suffer from several weaknesses.

Ray (2011) discusses five major manufacturing industries in Bengal during the early colonial rule, namely cotton textiles, silk textiles, indigo dye, salt manufacturing, and shipbuilding. Tracing the pre-colonial root for each of them, the study seeks to assess their performances from 1757–1857, identifying the roles of market forces and state policies therein. The summary statistics on employment are shown in Table 4.1.

The table underscores that far from encountering deindustrialisation, Bengal enjoyed industrial prosperity during 1795–1829, when the level of employment in the five major industries went up overall by almost a million people. This was due to the prosperity of the pre-colonial industries like cotton and silk textiles as well as salt manufacturing on one hand, and the emergence of new industries like shipbuilding and indigo dye on the other. Bengal's industrial decline, however, started in the early 1830s and continued in the following decades. The aggregate fall in the employment level was to the tune of 1.41 million up until 1860, which must have been devastating at the time. This overall industrial decline should, however, be read together with two other findings of the study. First, all these cases of decline cannot be explained by adverse colonial rule; in some cases, market forces initiated and perpetuated the event. Second, it should be noted that all these industries did not totally collapse during the first half of the nineteenth century. For example, while the silk textile industry did not decline at all during this period, the cotton textile industry was reduced only by about 28 per cent. Moreover, certain new industries began to

TABLE 4.1 Change in annual employment in industry in Bengal, 1795–1859

Year	Silk	Cotton[a]	Salt	Ship-building	Indigo	Total employment	Change in employment
1795–9	88,775	179,905	88,020	928	460,080	817,708	–
1800–4	84,040	198,931	90,303	4,508	522,478	900,260	(+) 82,552
1805–9	97,255	141,798	108,567	2,400	833,419	1,183,439	(+) 283,179
1810–4	155,536	126,745	113,639	5,400	868,826	1,270,146	(+) 86,707
1815–9	158,109	210,128	114,655	5,589	994,757	1,483,238	(+) 213,092
1820–4	202,242	145,589	123,785	2,341	1,040,878	1,514,835	(+) 31,597
1825–9	219,267	56,856	121,212	1,429	1,364,060	1,762,824	(+) 599,068
1830–4	188,460	–21,616	149,887	1,074	1,230,295	1,548,100	(-) 565,803
1835–9	237,786	–53,573	93,947	1,626	1,146,199	1,425,985	(-) 122,115
1840–4	232,730	–181,250	98,861	2,443	1,387,171	1,539,955	(+) 113,970
1845–9	227,670	–221,108	90,504	0	1,054,268	1,151,334	(-) 388,621
1850–4	211,227	–317,480	59,044	0	596,865	549,656	(-) 601,678
1855–9	233,271	–468,213	57,289	0	526,861	349,208	(-) 200,448

Source: Ray (2011, p. 252).

a. The figures represent changes in employment opportunities.

emerge in Bengal around the latter part of the study period. They included jute manufacturing, coal mining, paper making, tea plantations, and engineering, which grew rapidly in the second half of the nineteenth century using the latest technology and modern organisation. These industries must have altered the industrial landscape of Bengal; this can already be seen in Chattopadhyay's data on employment for Bengal. Without taking those industries into consideration, one should not jump to any definite conclusions on Bengal's nineteenth-century deindustrialisation.

Conclusion

To sum up, this study identifies the genesis of the debate in the writings of Marx, traces the subsequent debate that largely followed the legacy of Marx, and also followed a link that the nationalists drew between British policy and industrial decline. The chapter further argues that from the standpoint of economic history, it is necessary to distinguish three issues: the definition of the term, the question of its occurrence, and the explanation of the event. The definition needs to be free from any value judgment. It is also proposed that, in light of data constraints, the event should be studied in the framework of industry case studies. The explanation is divided here into the neo-Marxian and the mainstream schools, the former locating deindustrialisation in the context of India's incorporation into the capitalist world system and the latter locating it in nineteenth-century globalisation, eighteenth-century political transition, or in response to an environmental shock. The empirical literature can be divided into inter-sectoral and industry-based studies. The former is largely based on census data of doubtful quality. By contrast, industry studies are more reliable. The most recent study of this type, also quite wide in scope, suggests that deindustrialisation possibly occurred in 1830–1860, but no definite inference should be drawn without taking into account contemporaneously emerging industries in Bengal.

References

Bagchi, A. K. (1976). 'De-industrialisation in India in the Nineteenth Century: Some Theoretical Implications', *Journal of Development Studies, 12 (2)*, pp. 135–164.

Bairoch, P. (1982). 'International Industrialization Levels from 1750–1980', *Journal of European Economic History, 11 (1) and (2)*, pp. 269–333.

Banerjea, S. (1963). *A Nation in Making: Being the Reminiscences of Fifty Years of Public Life*, Bombay: Oxford University Press, reprint of 1925 edition.

Bayly, C. (1983). *Rules, Townsmen, and Bazaars: North Indian Society in the Age of British Expansion, 1770–1880*, Cambridge: Cambridge University Press.

Brewer, A. (1990). *Marxist Theories of Imperialism: A Critical Survey*, London: Routledge.

Chattopadhyay, R. (1975). 'De-industrialisation in India Reconsidered', *Economic and Political Weekly, 10 (12)*, pp. 523–531.

———. (1981). 'Trend of Industrialisation in Bengal, 1901–1931', *Economic and Political Weekly, 16 (35)*, pp. 1425–1432.

Clark, C. (1950). *Conditions of Economic Progress, Second Edition*, London: Macmillan.

Clingingsmith, D., and J.G. Williamson (2008). 'Deindustrialisation in 18th and 19th Century India: Mughal Decline, Climate Change, Climate Shocks and Britain's Industrial Ascent', *Explorations in Economic History, 45 (3)*, pp. 209–234.

Das, M. N. (1959). *Studies in the Economic and Social Development of Modern India, 1848–56*, Calcutta: Government Printing Press.

Desai, M. (1971). 'Demand for Cotton Textiles in Nineteenth Century India', *Indian Economic and Social History Review, 8 (4)*, pp. 337–361.

Digby, W. (1901). *'Prosperous' British India: A Revelation from Official Records*, London: Unwin.

Dutt, R. (1901). *The Economic History of India Under Early British Rule, Vol. 1*, London: Kegan Paul, Trench, Trubner & Co.

Dutt, R.P. (1940). *India Today*, London: Victor Gollancz.

Emmanuel, A. (1972). *Unequal Exchange: A Study of Imperialism of Trade*, New York: Monthly Review Press.

Frank, A. G. (1978). *Dependent Accumulation and Underdevelopment*, London: Macmillan.

———. (1984). *Critique and Anti-Critique: Essays on Dependence and Reformism*, New York: Praeger Publishers.

Frisof, D. (2008). 'Deconstructing De-industrialization: R. C. Dutt, M. D. Morris and Interpreting Nineteenth Century Indian Economic History', *Brown Journal of History, 2 (Spring)*, pp. 21–32.

Ganguli, B. N. (1965). *Dadabhai Naoroji and the Drain Theory*, New York: Asia Publishing House.

Guha, A. (1972). 'Raw Cotton of Western India, 1750–1850', *Indian Economic and Social History Review, 9 (1)*, pp. 1–41.

Habib, I. (1985). 'Studying a Colonial Economy – Without Perceiving Colonialism', *Modern Asian Studies, 19 (3)*, pp. 355–381.

Harnetty, P. (1991). '"Deindustrialization" Revisited: The Handloom Weavers of the Central Provinces of India, c. 1800–1947', *Modern Asian Studies, 25 (3)*, pp. 455–510.

Imlah, A.H. (1952). 'British Balance of Payment and Export of Capital, 1816–1913', *Economic History Review, 5 (2)*, pp. 208–239.

Kaldor, N. (1979). 'Comment', in F. Blackaby, ed., *De-industrialisation*, London: Heinemann.

Karve, D.G., and D.V. Ambekar, eds. (1962–67). *Speeches and Writings of Gopal Krishna Gokhale*, London: Asia Publishing House.

Krishnamurthy, J. (1976). 'De-industrialisation Revisited', *Economic and Political Weekly, 11 (26)*, pp. 964–967.

Kumar, D., and M. Desai, eds. (1983). *The Cambridge Economic History of India, Vol. II, c. 1757–1970*, Cambridge: Cambridge University Press.

Limqueco, P., and B. McFarlane, eds. (1983). *Neo-Marxist Theories of Development*, London and New York: St. Martin's Press.

Luxemburg, R. (1951). *The Accumulation of Capital*, Agnes Schwarzschild, trans. New York: Modern Reader Paperbacks.

Marx, K. (1853). 'The British Rule in India', *New-York Daily Tribune*, 25 June, available at http://www.marxists.org/archive/marx/works/1853/06/25.htm. Accessed 10 August 2014.

McAlpin, M.B. (1974). 'Railroads, Prices and Peasant Rationality: India, 1860–1900'. *Journal of Economic History, 34 (3)*, pp. 662–684.

Morris, M.D. (1963). 'Towards a Reinterpretation of Nineteenth-Century Indian Economic History', *Journal of Economic History, 23 (4)*, pp. 606–618.

———. (1968). 'Toward a Reinterpretation of Nineteenth Century Indian Economic History', *Indian Economic and Social History Review 5 (March)*, pp. 1–15.

Morris, M. D., T. Matsui, C. Bipan, and T. Raychaudhuri, eds. (1969). *Indian Economy in the Nineteenth Century: A Symposium*, Delhi: Indian Economic and Social History Association.

Naoroji, D. (1901). *Poverty and Un-British Rule in India*, London: Swan Sonnenschein.

Perlin, F. (1983). 'Proto-Industrialisation and Pre-Colonial South Asia', *Past and Present, 98 (1)*, pp. 30–95.

Ray, I. (2011). *Bengal Industries and the British Industrial Revolution*, London and New York: Routledge.

Robb, P. (1981). 'British Rule and Indian "Improvement"', *Economic History Review, 34 (3)*, pp. 507–523.

Roy, T. (2000). 'De-Industrialisation: Alternative View', *Economic and Political Weekly, 35 (17)*, pp. 1142–1447.

———. (2006). *The Economic History of India, 1857–1947*, Delhi: Oxford University Press.

———. (2012). 'Consumption of Cotton Cloth in India, 1795–1914', *Australian Economic History Review, 52 (1)*, pp. 61–84.

Seth, S. (1999). 'Rewriting Histories of Nationalism: the Politics of "Moderate Nationalism" in India, 1870–1905', *American Historical Review, 104 (1)*, pp. 95–116.

Simmons, C. (1985). '"De-Industrialisation", Industrialisation, and the Indian Economy, c. 1850–1947', *Modern Asian Studies, 19 (3)*, pp. 593–622.

Sivasubramonian, S. (1997). 'Revised Estimates of the National Income of India, 1900–1 to 1946–7', *Indian Economic and Social History Review, 34 (2)*, pp. 113–168.

Thorner, D., and A. Thorner, eds. (1962). *Land and Labour in India*, Bombay and New York: Asia Publishing House.

Twomey, M.J. (1983). 'Employment in Nineteenth Century Indian Textiles', *Explorations in Economic History, 20*, pp. 37–57.

Vicziany, M. (1979). 'The Deindustrialization of India in the Nineteenth Century: A Methodological Critique of Amiya Kumar Bagchi', *Indian Economic and Social History Review, 16 (2)*, pp. 105–143.

Wallerstein, I. (1986). 'Incorporation of Indian Subcontinent Into Capitalist World-Economy', *Economic and Political Weekly, 21 (4)*, pp. PE28–PE39.

Williamson, J.G. (2008). 'Globalization and the Great Divergence: Terms of Trade Booms, Volatility and the Poor Periphery, 1782–1913', *European Review of Economic History, 12 (3)*, pp. 355–391.

Zaidi, A. M., and S. Zaidi, eds. (1976). *The Encyclopaedia of the Indian National Congress, Vol. 1*, New Delhi: S. Chand.

Appendix 4.1

Various empirical studies on India's deindustrialisation

Author	Nature of study	Year of publication	Reference period	Study area	Measurement yardstick	Evidence of de-industrialisation?
Clark	Inter-sectoral framework	1950	1881–1911	India	Employment level (census data)	Yes
Thorner	Inter-sectoral framework	1962	1881–1931	India	Employment level (census data)	No
Chattopadhyay	Inter-sectoral framework	1975	1901–1931	India	Employment level (census data)	Yes
Chattopadhyay	Inter-sectoral framework	1981	1901–1931	Bengal Presidency	Employment level (census data)	Yes
				Bihar & Orissa	Employment level (census data)	Yes
				Bengal Province	Employment level (census data)	No
Bagchi	Inter-sectoral framework	1976	1808–1901	Gangetic Bihar	Employment level (data of Buchanan & census data)	Yes
Bairoch	Inter-sectoral framework	1982	1750–1938	India	Manufacturing output (own estimation)	Yes
Clingingsmith & Williamson	Industry-level framework	2008	1760–1860	India	Relative prices (secondary source)	Yes
Harnetty	Industry-level framework	1991	1800–1947	Central Provinces of India	Employment level & number of looms (secondary source)	Yes
Twomey	Industry-level framework	1983	1790–1830	India	Trade-induced employment level (own estimation)	Yes
Guha	Industry-level framework	1972	1850–1900	India	Raw material consumption (secondary source)	Yes
Ray	Industry-level framework	2011	1757–1860	Bengal	Employment level (own estimation)	Evidence of industrial growth up to 1829 but deindustrialisation during 1830–60

5

THE RISE OF MODERN INDUSTRY IN COLONIAL INDIA

Bishnupriya Gupta

The nineteenth century saw the emergence of new industries and the modernization of old ones. The handloom industry in India had been the workshop of the world, producing cotton textiles and selling them in the world market before the Industrial Revolution in England. This industry relied on the skills of the weavers and cheapness of labour in a home-based production system using locally produced equipment and age-old technology. Production of jute thread and cloth was also within such an artisanal production system. The use of factory-based methods in production was a new development from the middle of the nineteenth century. The technology was more capital-intensive, generating much higher output per worker. Workers in the new industries were not the owners of capital, and the separation between capital and labour created new types of entrepreneurs and workers. The entrepreneurs needed to raise large amounts of capital to set up production facilities and hire workers in an emerging labour market. The rise of modern industries in colonial India, therefore, relied on new sources of capital and labour that led to the development of modern capital and labour markets. Who were the entrepreneurs and who were the investors in an economy that Max Weber (1916–17) described as lacking in values of capitalism? Who were the new working class?

The literature on industrialization in the nineteenth century has emphasized the negative effect of colonial rule or the inadequacy of the Indian capitalist class. Bagchi's valuable work on private investment constructed an empirical narrative of the rise of modern industry in colonial India while staying within the mould of the nationalist historiography. Morris David Morris's more nuanced view further developed the factual foundation of India's industrial history. This chapter breaks away from these debates and uses insights from informational and institutional economics to trace the development of the modern industrial sector in colonial India and analyze some of the special characteristics of this process. The chapter will have the following themes. First I start with a description of the development of modern industries. I explore the consequences of the specific nature of the capital, product and labour markets in nineteenth-century India for the pattern of industrialization. In particular, I will explore the role of information flows and social networks in product, capital and labour markets. Second, I explore the political economy implications of the pattern of industrialization. This section will bring together literature on interest group activity arising from the pattern of industrial development.

Rise of capitalist production

The inability of the existing handloom-based technology to compete with modern technology in cotton textiles created conditions for the adoption of the technology of factory production. This technology was already in use. Therefore, when restrictions on export of machinery from Britain were lifted in 1843, country after country began to import the new technology to set up domestic production. India was to follow the same path. The challenge was, who were to be the entrepreneurs? The modern textile industry emerged as other sectors also adopted new technologies. Of these, the most prominent were the jute, tea and coal industries. Based on imported technology, the modern industrial sector emerged in India.

The existing industries in the nineteenth century were small scale and based on simple traditional technology from the production of cotton and jute textiles to coal mining and production of iron. Here the need of capital and skilled labour was limited (Morris 1983, pp. 558–563). The problem was that the traditional technology in all sectors could not compete with the technology of the industrial revolution, first in Britain and then in the United States and Germany. The specific prerequisites that led to the industrial revolution in Britain (such as abundance of capital, skilled labour and well-functioning markets) did not exist in India. Nor did India have the substitutes that Germany developed, such as investment banking and apprenticeship of skilled labour (Harley 1992). Indian industrialization therefore relied on borrowed technology and cheap labour.

Accumulation of capital in the industrial sector was more complex. India was a capital-scarce, labour-abundant economy with high interest rates and low wages. In a world without capital controls and low risk against expropriation in a colonial economy, industrialization might have been financed by capital inflows. However, as Lucas argued, long-distance investment in industry was rare and borrowing capital from abroad for industrial development was fraught with informational constraints (Lucas 1990). A new institutional form, "the managing agency system," developed, where a management company invested in and managed firms across different industrial sectors so that both capital and informational constraints could be dealt with.

From the middle of the nineteenth century began a gradual establishment for modern firms in several different industries. Almost simultaneously, the first cotton mill was set up in Bombay by Davar, a Parsi; the first jute mill was set up in Calcutta by George Acland; and the Assam Tea Company established the first tea plantation using modern technology in Assam. The first coal company was also set

TABLE 5.1 Dominant source of capital and entrepreneurship by industry (1914)

Industry	Primary Entrepreneurs	Main Investors	Primary Region
Tea	British	British in Britain	Calcutta
Jute	British	British in India	Calcutta
Coal	British	British in India	Calcutta
Cotton textiles	Indian	Indian	Bombay

Number of joint-stock companies in the city and hinterland

Industry	Calcutta	Bombay	India
Tea	376	0	385
Jute	54	0	55
Coal	225	5	232
Cotton textiles	18	178	227

Source: Gupta (2014) based on Statistical Abstract of British India.

up in Bengal around this time. The early development of corporate business was in railways, banking, insurance, shipping and tea. Railways had the bulk of the investment. This followed the pattern of British investment in other parts of the world. The plantation economy also attracted the interest of British companies. From the mid-nineteenth century, changes in company law allowing the formation of limited liability companies paved the way for the formation of joint-stock companies.

Table 5.1 shows the breakdown of private investment by sectors. Cotton textiles and tea attracted large volumes of investment. However, the investors and entrepreneurs were different. Two major centres of industrial production developed: Bombay and Calcutta. Industries in and around Calcutta such as tea, jute and coal catered to the export market. In Bombay, the cotton textiles industry was mainly an import substituting activity. In eastern India, the companies were set up by British entrepreneurs. In western India, Indian capital dominated the cotton textile industry.[1]

The contribution of large-scale industry to industrial output increased significantly by the early decades of the twentieth century. However, this sector was still a small part of the economy in terms of output and employment. Its share in employment lagged behind that in output reflecting the differences in labour productivity between this sector and traditional industries.

Capital and entrepreneurship: who invested and why?

Lucas (1990) argued that even when returns were high and risk of expropriation low, capital did not flow in large volumes from capital-abundant imperial countries such as Britain to capital-scarce colonies such as India. Volumes of capital flows from Britain to India were relatively small and they were channelled towards infrastructure and export industries. Only a quarter of British capital went to the Empire, of which only 30 per cent went to the colonies under British rule, with India receiving two-thirds (Davis and Huttenback 1985). These flows to the Empire were in sectors different from those to the rest of the world during the period 1865–1914. Davis and Huttenback show that capital flows to manufacturing and trade in the Empire were well below the world average, while in transport they were higher. India's share in agricultural and extractive industries and transport was higher than the world average, but the largest share went to transport. Sectors such as tea, rubber and gold absorbed most of the remainder. Returns were high in India for British entrepreneurs and for Indian entrepreneurs as well. However, British capital flowed into these few sectors. At the same time, Indian investment stayed away from the export sectors and flowed mainly into the cotton textile industry, which was the main import substituting sector.

There are several explanations for this pattern of industrial investment. The first is based on values arising from religion, caste and other social ties (Weber 1916–17, Buchanan 1966). The second arises from the differences in expected rates of return by social groups given the differences in opportunity cost (Gadgil 1971; Morris 1979). The third relates to the discriminatory role of colonial policy, which gave British capital an advantage (Bagchi 1972; Ray 1994). A fourth, less-talked-about explanation will be explored in this chapter: the role of informational asymmetry that gave different social groups different advantages and created a segregated world of industrial investment.

Values as an obstacle

Max Weber saw Hinduism as a hindrance to the development of capitalism in India. To Weber, British capital provided the means of modernization. This view found support in the writings of Anstey (1952) and Buchanan (1966). The caste system and family network were regarded as a hindrance to modernization. By bringing capital and entrepreneurship to colonial India, the British paved the path of industrialization. To Buchanan (1966), the Indians who became entrepreneurs came from the select community of the Parsis, who were distinguished by religion and education from the rest of the India. The Parsis were educated in the Western tradition and many acquired technical and engineering skills of the modern industries in Britain. Morris (1963) questioned the interpretation that Indian cultural values were a hindrance to industrialization. Tripathi (2004), while not convinced by the effect of religious values, sees the contact with Western values and technology by different social groups in India as the reason for their entry into the industrial sector.

Rates of return

This one-sided narrative of India's economic development was disputed by Morris in what he termed the "Rashomon effect" – the value of an industrial activity was perceived differently by different social groups. Morris argued that when conditions were suitable, Indians did not fall behind as entrepreneurs and investors (Morris 1967, 1979). The development of the cotton textile industry is a case in point.

Investment decisions depended on the relative rates of return. The return on capital in this capital-scarce economy was high. But how did it compare with returns on investment in alternative activities? The literature on capital flows from Britain in the late nineteenth century finds the risk-adjusted rates of return on overseas investment to be higher than on domestic investment. The returns on investment for British investors in Indian industries were relative to alternative opportunities available in Britain or elsewhere. Most British investment in this period was in the railways, where the rate of return was guaranteed by the host governments and considered to have a low risk. The guaranteed rates of return on railway investment in India were about 5 per cent. Edelstein's (1976) calculations indicate an average return around 7 per cent. This is the risk-adjusted rate of return as investment decisions would not be guided by the actual rates of return and here the Indian rates had to be adjusted downwards as long-distance investment involved greater risks.

For Indians, the comparable rates of return were in alternative non-industrial economic activities such as trade, where the rates of return were much higher. The estimated rate of return in the cotton trade was 15 per cent. The implied profit rate for jute in Dundee was 10 per cent, while in Calcutta, the lower bound was 20 per cent in 1910 (Clark 1989). Morris (1983, p. 572) suggests that dividend rate proxies the net profit rate, which in jute ranged from 3 to 15 per cent. Estimates of gross profits in cotton textiles before 1914 come up with a figure of 25 per cent and net profits of 10 per cent (Morris 1979). If the rate of return is the explanation, then return on investment in cotton mills and jute mills may not have been that different. It is difficult to see why Indian capital stayed away from jute and not from cotton on the basis of rates of return.

Discrimination

The third explanation focuses on the role of colonial policy. The first is the absence of a favourable tariff policy that characterized industrialization in almost every country that followed Britain. The second is that discrimination against Indian capital was the reason why Indian entrepreneurs could not participate in modern industrial activity. The racially segregated world of European business in Calcutta and the use of the race bar in entry into the main business organizations (such as the Bengal Chamber of Commerce, Indian Tea Association and the Indian Jute Mills Association) support such a contention. In sectors where the British dominated, the Indians found it difficult to enter. In particular, the Indians found it impossible to cross the race bar in the export sector and the formal financial sector. In the eight jute companies owned by the managing agent Bird and Company, less than 15 per cent of the shares were owned by Indians before 1914 (Morris 1983, p. 569). This could be an explanation of the absence of Indian capital in the export-oriented sectors such as tea and jute. But why did the British stay away from cotton textiles? British investment in cotton textiles was only 10–20 per cent of the total investment in this industry (Morris 1983, p. 580). British interests did not face political and social barriers to entry.

Sen (1994) argues that the British entrepreneurs in India did not want to compete with Lancashire and therefore stayed out of the cotton textile industry. Sen also claims that because the cotton textile producers in Britain lobbied against tariffs on British imports of cotton goods, that could have created disincentives for investing in this industry. There are serious flaws in this argument: the capitalist class in Britain was not homogenous. The interests of the textile producers and the machinery exporters were not the same. Machinery producers in Britain collaborated with Indian textile producers. Despite the absence of tariffs, low wages gave Indian producers a big advantage. Indian entrepreneurs were ready to invest in this sector. Why did British capital not follow?

Information and capital flows

This fourth explanation emphasizing the role of information is more persuasive. Morris was the first to discuss the knowledge of markets as a determinant of investment. He argued that it was costly to get commercial information. Economic agents would differ in their information set and assessment of an economic activity and therefore would gravitate towards markets where they had better information. British capital knew the export markets well, but not the import substituting ones (Morris 1983, p. 557). This was the domain of Indian capital. Although British companies controlled the export trade, the purchase of agricultural products for exports and their transport to the ports was in the hands of Indian merchants. So was the distribution of British goods in the Indian markets. Gujarati, Parsi and Muslim merchants operated in caste groups in the city of Bombay as agents of the British mercantile houses. The Marwaris played the same role in the city of Calcutta (Markovits 2002). Indian merchants controlled the trade in raw cotton and the marketing of imported cotton textiles. Marwaris in the East controlled the trade in raw jute. Gupta (2014) discusses the role of social networks in entry. In a world where information flows were limited, community networks filled in the gap. If a member of one community succeeded in an industrial enterprise, others were more likely to undertake the same activity. Information flows were confined to social networks that other parties had limited access to. A firm set up by an entrepreneur of a particular community signalled to other members of the community that this investment was profitable. A successful entrepreneur could also attract further investment from members of the community. However, to outsiders, such signals were noisy, so they did not generate the same response. Therefore, the informational asymmetries and the preference to follow a member of a social group in economic decisions can be important determinants of industrial activity, and investment could be segregated by ethnic groups.

The separate worlds of British and Indian businesses highlight two types of informational asymmetry. The first type relates to informational barriers facing potential entrepreneurs. The second relates to the potential investors drawn from Britain and India, who could invest in new projects. Tea was produced in Asia but sold in the markets in Europe and elsewhere. It was a familiar product to the average British family, and it provided an attractive investment opportunity. Jute (a product used for packaging and for military purposes) was in high demand in international markets, especially during wars. In jute, the firms in Dundee could have been a more attractive investment opportunity, as they were better known in the British market. To British expatriates, the jute industry provided an attractive investment opportunity. Coal was sold to the British railway companies. British entrepreneurs with substantial knowledge of export markets found these industries to be attractive investment opportunities. Because these entrepreneurs were well-known British firms, the industries also attracted British investors in Britain and in India. These companies could soak up the savings of the British expatriates in the army, civil service and trading companies.

The capital and entrepreneurship in the development of the cotton textile industry came from Indian entrepreneurs who raised capital by selling shares to friends and relatives. Neither religion nor education but the knowledge of the trade was the common factor determining entry into a particular sector. Indian entrepreneurs with links to the opium and cotton trade moved to cotton textiles industry when profits in trade declined. Other community members followed. A few British firms that entered production of cotton textiles, such as Crompton Greaves, had been involved in the cotton trade. Most British entrepreneurs, with their involvement in the international tea and jute markets, did not become cotton textile producers. The ethnicity of the entrepreneurs in eastern India may support the Weberian thesis of the Protestant ethic. However, the development of modern industries in western India does not support this idea. Except for the Parsis, who were pioneers in industrial development, no other successful business group enjoyed the advantage of Western education (Ray 1994, p. 4). However, the educated Bengali entrepreneurs[2] did not succeed after their initial success in collaboration with British capital. Desai (1968) argues that the success of the Parsis was not due to a Western education, but because of their involvement in economic activity with the British. The other social and caste groups that succeeded in industrial activity also acted as middlemen and agents for the British firms. Ray (1994) claims that the failure to enter the export trade was a hindrance to becoming entrepreneurs in tea and jute, whereas in the internal trade, the Indians did not face discrimination. Consequently, they could become entrepreneurs in cotton textiles. Gupta (2014) shows that there were no systematic differences in the rates of return between the export and the import substituting industries, which would be the case with barriers to entry. Informational constraints and social network effects are more plausible determinants for the pattern of industrialization.

Informational constraints and organizational structure

Given the informational constraints in long-distance investment, a new form of organization emerged: the managing agency system. These were partnerships of joint-stock companies that started new enterprises and floated shares on the market to raise capital. In many cases existing companies were handed over to the managing agents on the basis of long-term management contracts. The advantage was that the managing agent represented a firm without having a majority control. Consequently, each managing agent could give its name to a large number of new firms in different industries. Each agent had managerial control over firms across a set of industries such as tea, jute and coal. This management structure of British firms provided a reputation mechanism. The potential investors could make their investment decisions on the basis of the reputation of an established managing agent rather than a new firm. A few British managing agents dominated British–owned firms in tea, jute and coal in eastern India. The name was important when selling shares, particularly in London and also for raising loans from banks. What emerged was an oligopolistic control of the industrial sector by a handful of British managing agents. These agents, such as Williamson Magor, Bird and Company, and Andrew Yule, dominated the world of British investment in India.

Indian firms also adopted the structure of the managing agency system and were managed by community and caste-based business groups in cotton textiles in western India. A managerial hierarchy emerged. The financiers were managing agents who had little technical knowledge. The technical expertise was provided by British engineers mainly, but also by Parsi engineers. Indians gradually began to take over these jobs during the interwar years. The labour recruitment and management was left in the hands of a different social group, the *sirdars*, who had social connections with the workers. Each tier of the managerial structure had an informational advantage in an aspect of production. The three–tier managerial structure of different social groups in Indian cotton mills became a source of managerial inefficiency.

Informational constraints and the labour market

India fitted the Lewis model of unlimited supply of labour. Surplus labour in agriculture kept wages low in industry until the surplus ran out. This would allow the industrial sector to grow through reinvestment of profits. Wages would remain low as long as the surplus labour did not run out. In reality, the labour market showed constraints in labour supply for the modern industries. Recruitment of labour for industrial work became an important concern for entrepreneurs. In the long run there was no problem with labour supply, but in the short run there were supply constraints. This reflected the informational asymmetries in different segments of the labour market. The agricultural worker facing seasonal unemployment or "disguised" unemployment did not always know of alternative employment opportunities in the industrial sector. Community ties filled this gap. The *sirdars* or labour contractors would bring workers from rural to urban centres. Despite the differences in ownership across industries, the form of labour recruitment was similar. *Sirdars* were employed by the firms and went to the villages to recruit. These middlemen became important figures in the labour hierarchy.

The industrial labour force was a new social group. Factory labour was a new form of work and the transition was difficult for people used to agricultural and artisanal activities. Factory discipline, which was an important factor in efficiency, developed slowly. Most workers were immigrant single males who moved to Calcutta and Bombay. The tea industry was an exception: workers with families moved to distant plantations. Much has been written about the emergence of a working-class identity in the cotton and jute mills. Workers remained tied to caste and religious identities, and they kept a live connection with their villages (Chakrabarty 1989; Chandavarkar 1994). By the second decade of the twentieth century, wages in large-scale factories were higher than rural wages and showed an upward trend. Real wages of industrial workers were two to three times that of agricultural workers in the interwar period.

The modern industries: cotton, jute, tea and coal

Tea was grown in small holdings in China, but when tea cultivation started as a British enterprise in India, it became a modern plantation industry. Tea companies were set up as joint-stock companies. Tea was cultivated and processed on the plantations, and auctioned in Calcutta and London by tea brokers. Most of the output was sold in the export market. The Indian market was small and it was only in the interwar period, when the British market was saturated, that the companies began a sales campaign for tea in India. The Assam Tea Company was set up in 1837, followed by regular openings of new plantations throughout the nineteenth century, first in Assam and the surrounding regions and then in the hills of Bengal. Some plantations were also located in the elevated region of the Deccan. The British managing agency houses had managerial control of most plantations. The interests of the industry as a whole were represented by the Indian Tea Associations based in London and in Calcutta. The United Planters' Association represented the plantations in southern India. These associations provided the forum through which well-established plantations tried to regulate prices through manipulating output. However, attempts at cartelization were not particularly successful until the Great Depression, as the market was growing and entry was attractive.

Jute is a natural fibre that grows in humid tropical conditions. Raw jute is processed into yarn and woven into jute cloth. Gunny bags made out of this cloth were widely used as packaging material. India was the main supplier of raw jute for the jute mills in Dundee in Scotland. The industry began manufacturing Hessian (superior-quality cloth) and gunny bags in the early years of the twentieth century. In India, production of handspun and woven jute products had been an indigenous enterprise, but factory production was introduced by British companies. Although jute was less important than cotton in terms of industrial investment, the jute industry was the major industrial employer in eastern India. British managing agents dominated the industry; of these Andrew Yule and the Bird Heileger group were the largest. Both controlled about ten companies each, but each company had less than 30 per cent equity. Others such as Begg Dunlop and McLeod had as little as 20 per cent or less equity participation (Lokanathan 1935, p. 187).

The jute industry in India developed as a competitor to the industry in Dundee. Manufacturing in India had two advantages: proximity to raw material and cheap labour. The average Indian wage of 3s.6d. per week compared favourably with the average wage of 10s. per week at Dundee (Goswami 1991, p. 12). The process of jute cultivation and manufacturing remained separate. Jute was cultivated in peasant holdings and sold to the traders who brought the raw material to the jute factories. The factories did not seek to vertically integrate and the trade in raw jute remained in the hands of Indian traders.

George Acland had set up the first jute mill near Calcutta on the banks of the river Hooghly in 1855. The machinery for the mill was brought from Dundee and was used to manufacture yarn. New entry over the next two decades increased capacity from 1,250 looms in 1872 to 3,500 in 1874 and to 6,700 in 1885. There was already an excess capacity in the industry. The Indian Jute Mills Association (IJMA) was set up with the primary objective to coordinate output decisions to keep prices high. For five years from February 1886, the jute mills worked four to four and a half days a week instead of seven days (Rungta 1970, p. 168). During the First World War, the unprecedented increase in the demand for sandbags by the allied governments brought much prosperity to the industry. New companies were started. For the first time two Indian-owned companies – Birla and Hukumchand – entered the industry. The 1920s began with signs of excess production and falling prices, but the mood was optimistic. Entry of new firms continued. A majority of these firms were Indian-owned; the entrepreneurs belonged to the community of Marwaris, who had been involved in the raw jute trade.

Cotton textile production in India was an indigenous enterprise. A Parsi entrepreneur set up the first spinning mill in Bombay in 1854. The next fifty years saw entry of new firms: a few were British, but the majority were Indian. Some went bankrupt within a few years, but many survived and prospered. The main output was yarn for the domestic handloom industry and also for export to the Chinese market. Over time spinning mills bought their own looms and began producing cloth. Unlike in Britain, it was common for cotton mills not to specialize, but to produce both yarn and cloth under one roof. This reflected the fluctuations in demand and the need to make quick changes. While Indian firms catered to the low-count yarn market and the market for coarser varieties of cloth, the imports for Britain were in finer varieties. The industry was first concentrated in Bombay and then spread to Ahmedabad under the entrepreneurship of Guajarati traders. It then spread to other regions of India at the end of the First World War. Bombay mills were struggling to stay competitive against regions that had lower labour costs. The Bombay and Ahmedabad Millowners Association was set up to represent the interests of the cotton mills, but it never played the same economic role in coordinating output decision or lobbying for cartelization as the tea and jute interest groups.

The first coal mine was set up by an Indian firm in the 1830s, but failed. From the 1850s, the British managing agency houses set up joint-stock companies in the coal industry. Most of these were rupee companies. The same British managing agents involved in tea and jute also managed the coal companies. Although these firms used modern technology, they were inefficient compared to British coal mines. The industry relied on cheap labour, but output per worker was lower than in comparable industries in other countries. Demand for coal came from the railways and worked to the advantage of British firms. Indian firms in the industry produced poor-quality coal and catered to local users only.

BOX 5.1   FACTOR PRICES AND CHOICE OF TECHNOLOGY

In a labour-surplus economy with a shortage of capital, each industrial subsector faced the dilemma of what would be the optimal technology. The new factory sector could borrow the technology already in use in another country, where the technology had developed in response to local factor prices. But this technology did not necessarily suit Indian factor endowments. Tasks became more labour-intensive per unit of capital. Each machine was operated by more workers. The machinery was operated as long as possible with repairs and replacement of parts. The lower rate of scrapping and replacement of machinery delayed the introduction of newer technology and machinery of later vintage. The consequence was the lowering of labour productivity in Indian industries.

Nowhere has this issue been as controversial as in cotton textiles. This was an industry that had a base in many countries, including Russia, Brazil and Japan, using machinery imported from the same producers in the UK. The labour-capital ratio in Indian cotton textiles was six times higher in India compared to the United States (Clark 1987). The wages in the United States were ten times higher and in the UK, six times.

A similar comparison of labour per machine can be made in the context of the jute industry, where the machines were the same but the number of workers per machine was higher. Clark (1989) argues that although this difference was much less significant and only to the order of 2.25 : 1, there was a bigger difference in output per worker.

Each task became more labour-intensive even when the machinery was the same. Empirically this translates into lower output per worker and higher inefficiency. Theoretically it reflects a technological choice based on factor prices. In a labour-surplus economy where over 70 per cent of the population was employed in agriculture, wages were determined in agriculture and industry wages paid slightly above agricultural wages.

New industries

Import constraints during the First World War led to increased production in the existing industries, i.e. jute and cotton and the setting up of new import substituting industries. The first steel plant had been set up in 1907 and started to produce steel at the onset of the war. It increased output during the war. Most of these industries faced supply constraints due to limited capacity, and these shortages emphasized the need for local industry. The interwar period marked a change in policy and the need for tariff autonomy was accepted for the first time.

The interwar years saw the growth of new industries. Between 1923 and 1939, fifty-one cases were made for new tariffs and eleven cases for increased tariffs. Local production of chemicals, paper and iron and steel increased. This period also witnessed the entry of multinational corporations. In this sector, the managing agency

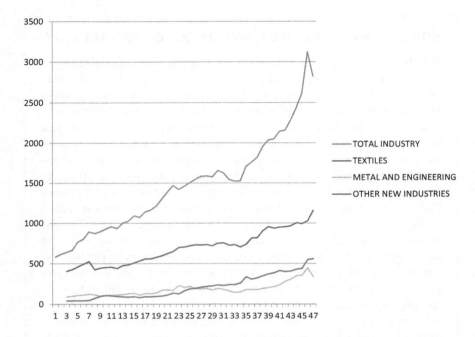

FIGURE 5.1 Changes in employment in large-scale manufacturing industry (thousands), 1900–1901 to 1946–1947.
Source: Sivasubramonian (2000).

houses did not play a role. In 1947, foreign direct investment by multinational corporations accounted for half of the British capital and net portfolio investment of the managing agency houses. Most of this was in chemicals, pharmaceuticals and processed foods (Tomlinson 1978). Indian business groups proved more dynamic as they became entrepreneurs in the new industries. Tata Steel is a case in point. The Tata family was involved in cotton textiles in Bombay, and also in the iron and steel trade. They became the pioneers in steel production. However, despite the extensive railway network, the linkage effects to other sectors were limited as the sector relied on imports from Britain. The Second World War highlighted the absence of local production of machinery and intermediate goods. This became the core of India's industrial policy after independence.

The political economy of industrialization

India's policy towards industrialization differed sharply from that followed by the countries of the second industrial revolution, such as the United States and Germany and other late industrializers. Tariffs were used extensively to build new industries substituting imports. India's colonial status prevented an autonomous tariff policy. Industries that received government support were those that catered

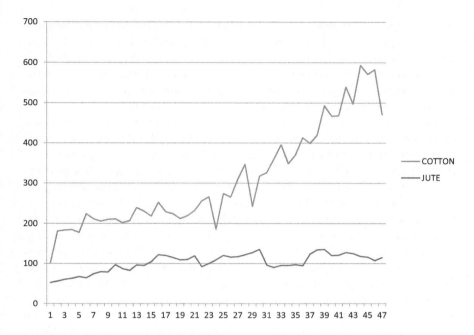

FIGURE 5.2 Changes in output in large-scale manufacturing industry (million rupees in 1938–1938 prices), 1900–1901 to 1946–1947.

Source: Sivasubramonian (2000).

to the British market. Generous land grants were given to the tea companies. Laws to assist indentured migration of labour to the remote tea plantations in eastern India were put in place in response to the demand of British industrial interests. The import substituting cotton textiles industry received little protection. When the Government of India imposed a tariff of 5 per cent on cotton textiles imports to generate revenue in the 1880s, Lancashire lobbied to get a countervailing duty excise tax on the local producers.

After the First World War, demands for government intervention were voiced by both Indian and British interests. The export industries had faced buoyant markets and expanded capacity, making high profits as prices remained high. The import substituting industries also did well due to the natural protection offered by the war. Therefore, as prices and profits began to decline and industries faced excess capacity, the industrial interests began to articulate their demands.

The demand for policy protecting the industrial sector followed different patterns in Calcutta and Bombay. The export industries lobbied the state for support towards forming cartels to reduce output and increase prices. Both in tea and jute, there were efforts to cartelize from the early 1920s. The jute cartel under the initiative of the Indian Jute Mills Association took shape in 1919. Jute firms were to operate a significantly reduced number of hours, stop expansion of capacity and if necessary make part of the existing capacity redundant. The conditions of output reduction became more stringent as prices fell further after the onset of the Great Depression in 1929. Efforts of cartelization in the tea industry began in 1929 as the world economy went into recession. The control of output by a handful of managing agency firms made cartelization feasible in both industries.

Of the two cartels, the tea cartel was an international effort involving the major producing countries: India, Ceylon and the Dutch East Indies. As prices plummeted in 1929, an international agreement was signed by the tea producer associations in India, Ceylon and the Dutch East Indies in 1930, whereby the signatories agreed to reduce output by a certain percentage of past production. Enforcement of this agreement was entirely voluntary. The tea associations asked their members to restrict output, but there was no official regulatory mechanism to ensure compliance. Attempts to renew the agreement in 1931 and 1932 failed, but as prices continued to fall in all markets, the International Tea Agreement was signed in 1933. This time the governments of the tea-producing countries passed legislation to enforce export quotas, which remained in place until the beginning of the Second World War. The legislation also regulated expansion in acreage. The industry in India adopted a voluntary agreement to limit sales in the large domestic market. The tea cartel had succeeded in stopping a sharp decline in prices. In addition, it made new entry more difficult, ensuring that tea prices and profits were maintained (Gupta 2001).

The case of jute turned out to be different. As a response to the declining prices after the First World War, cartelization became a permanent feature of the industry. Throughout the IJMA's history, excess capacity had recurred in the industry; the cartel had dealt with the problem through regulation of output. However, in the 1920s, two developments created a new challenge for the smooth functioning of the cartel. First, other centres of jute production in Europe could seriously affect India's market share if prices were high. Countries in Eastern Europe such as Poland and Czechoslovakia also enjoyed the advantage of relatively cheap labour. The second and more important development was the emergence of a fringe group of smaller firms that were quite different in terms of ownership and management. Many of the new firms were Indian owned, yet they were less enthusiastic about the cartel and remained outside. Despite the move towards increased regulation within the IJMA, outside mills had long working hours. Unlike in tea, this large fringe of outsiders stayed out of the cartel and increased market share. This made the jute cartel inherently unstable (Gupta 2005). The jute industry lobbied unsuccessfully for state support for cartelization as the state government of Bengal was unwilling to side with the industry against the jute growers (Goswami 1991). The cartel was finally abandoned in 1937.

The response of the cotton textile industry was very different. Early attempts in the cotton industry at cartelization had failed due to the large number of firms dispersed throughout the country and the absence of oligopolistic control as in tea and jute. The Indian business class was regionally and socially fragmented, which hindered the creation of a homogeneous interest group (Markovits 2002, pp. 19–23).

However, as profits began to decline with the end of the war, the industry's demand for tariffs became vocal. The need for tariff autonomy was accepted for the first time. The setting up of the Fiscal Commission opened the door to lobbying by economic interest groups. The textile industry made representations to the Commission and argued for preserving the Indian market for the domestic industry. British interest had changed too. Japan had emerged as a competitor for British textiles in several markets and had made big inroads into the Indian market. British cotton textiles faced a shrinking market share in different parts of the world. A tariff policy formulated by the British government took the form of Imperial preference in the 1930s, which gave British goods easier access to the Indian market and penalized Japanese goods. The new industries that emerged in the interwar years also lobbied successfully for protection.

The political economy of the industrial development changed forever in a direction that would lead to the Nehruvian policy of state-led industrialization. The genesis of this could be seen in the "Bombay Plan" of 1944, when the industry leaders laid down their vision of industrialization in an independent India. The political movement towards independence had the support of several Indian business groups.

Conclusion

This chapter summarized the debates on the pattern of industrialization in colonial India using three well-researched strands of the literature. British capital dominated the industries that were complementary to the imperial economy such as tea and jute. Import substituting industries, such as cotton textiles, were developed by interest entrepreneurs. First, the chapter explored competing explanations of the separation of activities by ethnicity. Was this caused by discriminatory British policies or social network effects arising from informational asymmetries? Second, it provided explanations for the more intensive use of labour for a given technology in the industrial sector. Did this reflect inefficiency or rational choice of technology based on factor endowments? Last, it discussed the political economy of industrialization in colonial India and the role of interest groups in lobbying for state intervention. Here too, the distinction between British and Indian interests was highlighted.

Notes

1 See Gupta (2014) for a discussion of the segregated world of Indian and British investment.
2 Bengal had one of the highest literacy levels in English in the 1901 Census.

References

Anstey, V. (1952). *Economic Development of India*, London: Longmans, Green & Co.
Bagchi, A. K. (1972). *Private Investment in India*, Cambridge: Cambridge University Press.
Buchanan, D. (1966). *The Development of Capitalist Enterprise in India*, London: Frank Cass.

Chakrabarty, D. (1989). *Rethinking Working-class History: Bengal, 1890–1940*, Princeton: Princeton University Press.

Chandavarkar, R. (1994). *Origins of Industrial Capitalism in India*, Cambridge: Cambridge University Press.

Clark, G. (1987). 'Why Isn't the Whole World Developed?' *Journal of Economic History, 47 (1)*, pp. 141–173.

———. (1989). 'Why Isn't the Whole World Developed? A Reply to Hanson', *Journal of Economic History, 49 (3)*, pp. 707–714.

Davis, L. E., and R.A. Huttenback (1985). 'The Export of British Finance', *The Journal of Imperial and Commonwealth History, 13 (3)*, pp. 28–76.

Desai, A. (1968). 'Origins of Parsi Enterprise', *Indian Economic & Social History Review, 5 (4)*, pp. 307–317.

Edelstein, M. (1976). 'Realized Rates of Return on UK Home and Overseas Portfolio Investment in the Age of High Imperialism', *Explorations in Economic History, 13 (3)*, pp. 283–329.

Gadgil, D. R. (1971). *Industrial Evolution of India in Recent Times*, Bombay and London: Oxford University Press.

Goswami, O. (1991). *Industry, Trade and Peasant Society: The Jute Economy of Eastern India, 1900–1947*, Delhi: Oxford University Press.

Gupta, B. (2001). 'The International Tea Cartel in the Great Depression', *Journal of Economic History, 61 (1)*, pp. 144–159.

———. (2005). 'Why Did Collusion Fail? The Indian Jute Industry in the Inter-War Years', *Business History, 47 (4)*, pp. 532–552.

———. (2014). 'Discrimination or Social Networks: Industrial Investment on Colonial India', *Journal of Economic History, 74 (1)*, pp. 141–168.

Harley, C. K. (1992). 'Substitutes for Prerequisites: Endogenous Institutions and Comparative Economic History', in R. Sylla and G. Toniolo, eds., *Patterns of European Industrialization: The Nineteenth Century*, London and New York: Routledge.

Lokanathan, P. S. (1935). *Industrial Organization in India*, London: G. Allen & Unwin.

Lucas, R. E. (1990). 'Why Doesn't Capital Flow From Rich to Poor Countries?', *American Economic Review, 80 (22)*, pp. 91–96.

Markovits, C. (2002). *Indian Business and Nationalist Politics 1931–39*, Cambridge: Cambridge University Press.

Morris, M. D. (1963). 'Towards a Reinterpretation of Nineteenth Century Indian Economic History', *Journal of Economic History, 23 (4)*, pp. 606–618.

———. (1967). 'Values as an Obstacle to Economic Growth in South Asia: An Historical Survey', *Journal of Economic History, 27 (4)*, pp. 588–607.

———. (1979). 'The South Asian Entrepreneurship and the Rashomon Effect', *Explorations in Economic History, 16 (3)*, pp. 341–361.

———. (1983). 'The Growth of Large Scale Industry to 1947', in D. Kumar and M. Desai, eds., *The Cambridge Economic History of India, Vol. II*, Delhi: Cambridge University Press, pp. 553–676.

Ray, R. (1994). *Entrepreneurship and Industry in India, 1800–1947*, New Delhi: Oxford University Press.

Rungta, R. S. (1970). *The Rise of Business Corporations in India, 1850–1900*, Cambridge: Cambridge University Press.

Sen, A. K. (1994). 'The Pattern of British Enterprise in India 1854–1914: A Causal Analysis', in R. Ray, *Entrepreneurship and Industry in India, 1800–1947*, New Delhi: Oxford University Press.

Sivasubramonian, S. (2000). *The National Income of India in the Twentieth Century*, New Delhi: Oxford University Press.

Tomlinson, B. R. (1978). 'Foreign Private Investment in India, 1920–1960', *Modern Asian Studies, 15 (3)*, pp. 655–677.

Tripathi, D. (2004). *The Oxford History of Indian Business*. New Delhi: Oxford University Press.

Weber, M. (1916–17/1958). *The Religion of India: The Sociology of Hinduism and Buddhism*, Glencoe, IL: Free Press.

6

COLONIAL INDIA AND THE WORLD ECONOMY, C. 1850–1940

Gopalan Balachandran

For a subject so formative to India's anti-colonial nationalism, its external economic relations under colonial rule has not been a major field of research. For many decades the critiques made by late nineteenth century economic nationalists such as Dadabhai Naoroji and Romesh Dutt shaped a "common sense" about these relations, which independent India's economic choices and policies reflected and reinforced. Many of these policies have been overturned since the 1980s without, however, doing much to disturb the historical wisdom.

Early nationalist critiques of British economic policies focused on their impact on the colony and its population. This meant emphasising bilateral links between India and Britain to the relative neglect of India's links with its wider region and Britain's evolving web of multilateral links. Restoring these contexts aids in providing a more rounded view of India's changing locations and roles as the world economy formed in the middle of the nineteenth century and evolved through to the Second World War. A focus on the impact of external policies and environments can help clarify economic and related connections and pathways between India and the rest of the world.

Dense networks of commerce have been a historical feature of the Indian subcontinent. Linking culturally, economically, and politically diverse places, these networks were distinguished by recognized markets, intermediaries, normative codes, and regulatory usages. They also spilled beyond this landmass into an extensive frontier arc spanning inland western, central, and south-eastern regions of Asia, southern and eastern Africa stretching northwards to the Horn, and the hinterlands served by the gulf and Red Sea ports.

It is often supposed that a dominant north Atlantic capitalism, turbo-charged by colonialism, imposed itself on established patterns of Asian commerce in the nineteenth century. Reality was more complex. The Indian subcontinent witnessed dramatic transformations in the nineteenth century, among them the expansion of the British Empire. As the former became politically and administrative more enclosed, frontiers and linkages across the wider region were reshaped; the barriers dividing territories under British-Indian sovereignty, other sovereignties, and the areas in between grew more marked. The subcontinent turned simultaneously toward remoter shores, i.e. a northern Atlantic region indisputably growing as a hub of power and imperial ambition by the late nineteenth century. These transformations did not sweep aside subcontinental commerce. Rather, it re-layered them in three rough folds – within the subcontinent, across its frontiers and the wider region, and the north Atlantic region – with differentiable (though hybridizing) normative, regulatory, and cultural frameworks. By the last decade of the nineteenth century, political and commercial rivalries were beginning to spawn or intensify competing hubs, including notably in Asia beyond the Indian Ocean and west across the Atlantic.

This chapter develops the story of colonial India's external economic relations against these broad backdrops. It is organized in seven sections. The next section relates broad trends in India's external accounts. The following, 'Trade, capital transfers, and the domestic economy', deals with the vexed issue of the 'drain', (i.e. India's unrequited current account transfers) and its impact. Next, 'Currency, banking, and the external sector', relates changes in the institutional arrangements, principally of trade, currency, and banking, through which the subcontinent's external transactions flowed and its effects transmitted. The following section, 'Money, multilateralism, and the world economy', places these arrangements in the multilateral framework of the late-nineteenth-century world economy. Contemporary patterns of commerce and entrepreneurship linking India to inland Asia and the Indian Ocean rim are the focus of the section entitled 'Regional commerce and entrepreneurship'. The last section is devoted to labour, mobility, and migrations from colonial India.

Trends in external trade and balance of payments

India's external trade underwent dramatic change during the nineteenth century. At the start of the century, it was still a leading exporter of manufactures, notably cotton cloth, which accounted for a third of its exports. By its halfway mark, India was transformed predominantly into an exporter of agricultural products and unprocessed raw materials. The share of cotton cloth was now about 4 per cent. There was an uptick in the share of yarn and cotton piece good exports from the 1880s. Jute manufactures shortly followed. But on the eve of the First World War, India remained very much an exporter of primary products. Not much had changed in this structure on the eve of the Second World War despite an increase in the share of jute manufactures (Chaudhuri 1983, pp. 842–844).

Estimates of the share of foreign trade in national income vary. According to K. N. Chaudhuri's calculations based on V.K.R.V. Rao's national income estimates, exports (9.54 per cent) and imports (7.73 per cent) accounted for about 17.3 per cent of national income in 1931–1932 (Chaudhuri 1983, pp. 804–805). This figure almost certainly increased during the half-century preceding 1914, perhaps stabilizing near the 20 per cent mark in the 1920s and declining in the 1930s. Nabendu Sen esti-mated the share of foreign trade rising from less than 12 per cent of national income in the 1860s to about 14 per cent by the 1890s, and averaging about 18 per cent of *gross* national product thereafter until the First World War, with a peak of 22 per cent in 1912–1913 (Sen 1992, pp. 34–37). Assuming incomes grew 1 per cent annually, this would suggest trade growing at around 2 per cent. Tirthankar Roy estimates a faster rate of increase, from 4 per cent in 1857 to over 20 per cent in 1913, or annu-ally at 4 per cent at similar rates of income growth (Roy 2000, pp. 34–35).

K. N. Chaudhuri also estimated that Indian foreign trade 'more than quadrupled in value and volume' between 1814 and 1858 (Chaudhuri 1971, p. 1). If incomes grew at 1 per cent during this period, we are left with a share of trade to income in 1814 of about 1.5 per cent (Chaudhuri 1971, pp. 110–111). Since this appears too low, it is likely that Sen understates the growth of Indian foreign trade between 1858 and 1913. Roy probably overstates it. What seems indisputable, however, is India's growing exposure to world trade from the mid-nineteenth century.

As noted earlier, Indian foreign trade had turned distinctly 'colonial' by 1850 and remained so throughout our period. India is estimated to have run a trade surplus (excluding treasure) of 2–4 per cent of GNP between c. 1860 and 1913, and 0.5 to 2 per cent between 1921 and 1946. Imports of precious metals and the so-called 'home charges' left little room for other service payments, and together with invest-ment, necessitated capital imports (Goldsmith 1983, pp. 16–17, 76–77).

Foreign investment appears to have been small before 1857 and consisted pri-marily of East India stock. Goldsmith estimates investment inflows at 1 per cent of national income between 1860 and 1913, doubling however from 0.7 per cent over 1860–1898 to 1.5 per cent over 1899–1913. 'Moderate and irregular' after 1913, foreign investment probably averaged 1 per cent of income between 1921 and 1929. India made net capital *exports* of 0.5 per cent of GNP annually in the 1930s and nearly 5 per cent during the Second World War. For the period 1921–1946 as a whole, Indian capital exports are estimated at 1.6 per cent of GNP (Goldsmith 1983, pp. 17–18, 76–78). Capital imports perhaps represented about a fifth of gross capital formation and a quarter of net capital formation between 1860 and 1913. Gross and net capital formation rates averaged 6–8 per cent and 4–6 per cent respectively of GNP for 1901–1913, and 7 per cent and 2.25 per cent respectively over 1914–1946 (Goldsmith 1983, p. 19, 79).

Trade, capital transfers, and the domestic economy

Its colonial status primarily determined India's external macro-institutional artic-ulations. London-based exchange banks began to claim a bigger role in financ-ing Indian trade from about the 1860s. As the management of Indian currency also passed gradually into the hands of London-based officials and institutions, by the end of the century the India Office in London and the colonial government instituted monetary and banking arrangements that magnified the impact of trade fluctuations on the colony. Consequently, despite its relatively small size, the trade sector exerted a disproportionately large influence on the Indian economy and its peoples' livelihoods.

In latter-day neo-classical parlance, successive generations of officials imagined and managed India as a 'small open economy'. This meant a passive macro-economic stance and pro-cyclical behaviour that intensified the impact of external influences on the Indian economy. The commitment to preserving an open economy (including not interfering with destabilizing short-term capital movements so long as they did not threaten the pound sterling) and discharging external obligations was more tenaciously pursued in India than in any other major non-industrial country. This, more than the intrinsic exposure of its economy to foreign trade, explains why colonial India was always a passive victim of trade and economic shocks originating overseas.

It is useful at this stage to separate two aspects of this tenacious openness: short-term capital movements and the discharge of *current* account obligations. The latter have attracted attention in the context of the 'drain' and are discussed later. But the importance of the former has been less well recognized.

Banking or trading capital represented the principal component of short-term capital movements to India. As its exports became more agricultural in character, Indian trade acquired a pronounced seasonal character, with a 'busy season' coinciding with the harvesting calendar from October through to April. The resulting demand for working capital increased seasonal interest rates, which, since the colony's monetary system was now run from London, declined only when London-based exchange banks remitted funds to finance it. These funds returned to London at the end of the busy season. In addition, the British-owned commercial banks that mobilized deposits in India deployed a large proportion of them in London. While financing trade, short-term flows accentuated India's economic and institutional weakness in several directions, including the persistent underdevelopment of the banking system and the centralization of banking resources in London. While the latter helped consolidate London's position as an international financial centre, both factors reinforced India's dependence on overseas capital to finance trade, as well as on foreign loans for investment. The former was extremely sensitive to conditions in commodity and money markets in London. Prone also to 'herd' effects (if not to actual oligopolistic collusion), fluctuations in the availability of overseas trading capital caused external shocks to be transmitted almost directly to the Indian producer.

India's dependence on overseas banks for short-term capital did not affect foreign trade only. Trade financing was the safest segment of banking in India. Its pre-emption by exchange banks increased the overall risk profile of domestic commercial banking. Without developed commercial banks, the Indian monetary system (comprised almost wholly of currency and coin until the 1920s) remained inelastic and dependent for currency expansion on the inflow of funds to finance trade (Goldsmith 1983, p. 9; Chaudhuri 1983, p. 805). Fluctuations in short-term capital flows thus exerted a direct impact on the colony's monetary and macro-economic environment.

The second aspect of India's openness was its tenacious discharge of external current account obligations. There are two issues here: the 'quality' of these obligations and the effects on the economy of servicing them. In assessing the latter we may distinguish between secular (or long-term) effects and short-term effects (i.e. the aggravated effects of the transfer in the presence of economic or financial instability). Besides, since tracing these effects also involves establishing the intermediary processes, it is useful to keep in mind the overall impact of the transfer process on the institutional features of the colonial Indian economy.

Indian nationalist critiques of the colony's current account liabilities have been a subject of frequent debate in the century or more since they were made, though in the last few decades, the stronger passion seems to come from critics of the critiques rather than the latter's protagonists (Davis and Huttenback 1986; Foreman-Peck 1989). This is an irresolvable debate because partisans on rival sides might share similar normative frameworks, but not the same perspectives or counterfactual assumptions. For instance while most historians would agree that colonial India's military charges to Britain were excessive and unjustified, Davis and Huttenback insist that even here, India did not quite pay its way. Naoroji and Dutt believed the employment of European civil servants and professionals represented a 'moral and material drain' from India. For their British contemporary Alfred Marshall, the drain ran in the other direction because of Britain's 'unreckoned exports . . . [of] a great number of . . . young men . . . in the prime' of their lives, who returned home 'more or less shrivelled and worn out' by their colonial careers (Indian Currency Committee 1899, question 11,818). It is well known British shipping and insurance firms colluded to fix freight and premiums and could wage aggressive price wars to deter competition. Yet whether over-reliance on one power or set of entities for such services produced efficiency gains or monopoly (or sovereignty) rents would also depend on counterfactual assumptions.

Their contextual nature underlines the importance of sovereignty in assessments of the quality of colonial India's transfers of current incomes to Britain. This point was not lost on Dadabhai Naoroji, who told the Herschell Committee that though Brazil (an independent country) and Australia (a self-governing dominion) paid 'large sums to foreigners' every year, these obligations had their 'people's consent'. India, by contrast, was 'helpless and voiceless in all burdens put upon her' (Indian Currency Committee 1893, questions 2,346–2,353).

The processes by which India's current account transfers impinged on the domestic economy have not been investigated in equal detail outside the literature on 'forced commercialization'. It seems highly plausible, a priori, that annual transfers of the order of 1–2 per cent of national income (or some 25–40 per cent of estimated domestic savings) would have had a depressive effect on growth (Maddison 1972, pp. 63–64). Of equal significance is the manner in which these transfers were effected. The economic literature on unilateral transfers identifies two mechanisms, operating via terms of trade and incomes. To put it starkly, as a country's external liability translates into a domestic liability for its population, the latter has to sell (i.e. export) more of what it produces and/or consume/invest a smaller proportion of income in order to meet the liability. The former mechanism could depress export prices and the terms of trade, while the latter depresses incomes and growth to finance the external transfer.

If on one hand India is assumed to be a 'small' country – i.e. it faced parametric prices for its principal exports – the former mechanism is unlikely to have been important, and India's transfers may have been financed mainly through income adjustments. On the other hand, it is not unlikely under some domestic market conditions that the compulsion on producers (say, peasant households) to finance fixed revenue obligations (which were the domestic counterpart of India's external obligations) weakened their bargaining power and depressed the prices at which they could sell their crop to traders. Given parametric world prices (and fixed exchange rates), this would have led to a transfer of incomes from peasant households to traders and other market intermediaries, and it would have had a depressive effect on domestic incomes and consumption. We may complicate this story by introducing non-peasant agents: say, agricultural wage-workers whose services also represented the non-traded good, and who consumed the exportable good, i.e. the food sold by peasant households (their employers) and exported by trading companies. In this situation, wages (being the price of the non-traded good) may be expected to fall relative to that of the traded good (food) and workers would experience a decline in real incomes. The aggregate fiscal burden and its distribution between traders, peasants, and wage-workers would also depend on the relative imperfections of the two markets.

India's external current account obligations were at least in principle not more inflexible than those of other non-industrial countries – many of which defaulted, some repeatedly, on their overseas loans and lived to borrow another day. As is well known, countries that defaulted during the Depression performed better than those that did not (O'Connell 1984; Jorgensen and Sachs 1989, pp. 57–68). Britain's grim determination and India's subordinate political position, however, ensured that servicing its external obligations became the overriding concern of economic policy and the key measure of India's economic health and its institutional development (Balachandran 2002). The priority accorded to servicing external obligations in turn dictated the need for 'efficient' domestic revenue collection. It seems plausible that, together, these priorities distorted markets, contributed to more regressive tax incidence, and also skewed incentives, the secular rate and pattern of investment, and the rate and quality of economic growth. They could also greatly accentuate the impact of a trade shock (such as a fall in the price of India's exports) on incomes and consumption, and dictate pro-cyclical policies (such as expenditure cuts and tax increases), magnifying the impact of the original shock.

Currency, banking, and the external sector

We may now elaborate on the domestic impact of India's external transfers via its monetary and banking systems. From the early 1860s, when the British Indian currency system acquired some uniformity, monetary and banking arrangements were mainly oriented to financing India's external trade and transfers.

While local marketing networks remained in place, by the late nineteenth century, European trading houses had largely taken over the business of moving India's produce to overseas markets. Indigenous trading firms and networks were now relegated to 'maintain[ing] . . . [export] supply lines' for European trading houses, and 'marketing channels in the interior' for the foreign goods the latter imported (Ray 1995, pp. 485, 493–494; Yang 1998). The monetary media for these transactions – mainly silver and gold – depended on their availability and relative profitability before the late nineteenth century when the India Office began expanding its sale of 'council bills' (i.e. rupee remittances) in London as a substitute for precious metal flows.

Instituted with the limited aim of enabling the colonial government to meet its London liabilities without the expense of reshipping metal back from the colony, rupee remittances became the principal means of financing Indian trade after they began to be sold to pre-empt gold shipments from Britain, or if British monetary conditions warranted, intercept and divert to London the Egyptian and Australian gold shipments destined to India. Auctioned at regular intervals or placed on tap for limited periods, these remittances were available to only a small clutch of London-based exchange banks with a handful of branches in India's main port cities, tightly bound to a London-centred financial, shipping, insurance, and information network. Japanese, US, and other countries' banks and firms were also now obliged to remit funds to India through these means. Indian banks were shut out of the business, Indian trading firms also having recourse only to the 'retail' distribution of its proceeds, or to more costly banking remittances.

The ascendancy of British trading houses and banks was not inevitable. Much remains to be known about how it came about or how the accompanying processes affected incentive structures and institutional arrangements. Indian bankers were closely involved in financing the East India Company. Subcontinental entrepreneurs traded, lent, brokered, and cultivated extensive business links in the region and beyond. But their relatively decentralized operations were less amenable to control and regulation by a colonial apparatus intent not merely on financing exports and monetizing export surpluses (which Indian bankers did with renowned efficiency), but also in their smooth remittance to London. Centralizing the surplus in London ensured India's external obligations became by default the first charge on it. In due course, it would also facilitate London's emergence as an international monetary centre. These re-centred monetary and banking arrangements hastened the decline of indigenous bankers and their financing networks.

An important development during the last quarter of the nineteenth century was the depreciation of silver and consequently of the rupee and other Asian currencies. Currency depreciation would have stimulated import substitution in India and other parts of silver-using Asia vis-à-vis countries with gold currencies. Depreciation would have also boosted the profitability of producing for European markets relative to non-traded goods (Nugent 1973).

Which of these effects would have dominated or how colonial era changes in monetary and institutional arrangements for trade and financing would have played out remain open questions. What seems evident is that credit markets developed a dual character: one market looking out to European trading houses and the London-based banks financing them, and the other to smaller traders and traditional bankers restricted now to financing domestic and regional trade. We are accustomed to regarding the latter as niche players, for their activities rarely received the official attention devoted to institutions for securing the imperial financial interest in India. Yet the former operated over a large region and was also in terms of volume the larger of the two (Balachandran 1998). It comprised innumerable agents of various sizes working with low overheads and community-based networks of information and credit appraisal, far more adept at developing new markets and lines of business than in resisting the predatory entry of deep-pocketed European banks backed by colonial governments.

If left to itself, how this dual market would have evolved remains a matter of speculation. The colonial authorities struck another blow in 1893 against indigenous banking by closing India's mints to free coinage of silver. Thereafter, Indian reserves were rapidly centralized in London, and its monetary system hitched more tightly to council bills and monetary conditions in London. Unable any longer to import silver for coinage, indigenous bankers were reduced to being intermediaries for British banks in India. Besides accentuating the market's duality, these changes are likely to have led to some financial disintermediation, and distortions and inefficiencies in the use of financial resources in its more distant reaches. For the next several decades, commercial banks were largely confined to major ports and urban centres. The European banks operated at some remove from the bazaar and faced little competition from fledgling Indian-owned banks whose growth was slowed by unsound practices and poor regulation (Balachandran 1998).

Money, multilateralism, and the world economy

Before the late nineteenth century, when a recognizable 'world economy' began to form, long-distance trade mainly involved bilateral pairs, or triangular patterns such as the Asian junk trade, the Indian Ocean spice trade, or more notoriously, the transatlantic slave trade and the opium trade with China. Less palpable even to participants, multilateral trading patterns emerged from retrospective reconstructions of trade accounts (Hilgerdt 1943, pp. 393–394). Especially where it was dominated by monopolies or entrenched companies, trade tended to follow discrete bilateral nodes and triangular networks that might also long outlive such monopolies (Fichter 2010). Thus, even for late-nineteenth-century Britain, bilateral, triangular, and multilateral trading patterns coexisted in layered arrangements (Saul 1960, pp. 44, 171). Multilateral trade grew more discernible as tropical raw materials and agricultural commodities became pivotal to world trade, its role in this trade enabling Britain to emerge as a key multilateral hub. London also emerged as an international commercial banking centre where overseas banks and trading firms were obliged to maintain liquid balances and sterling consequently as a reserve currency. Modern international money, multilateralism, and the world economy as we know it were, in short, 'joint' products of a particular late-nineteenth-century conjuncture. India was crucial to this conjuncture.

With its surpluses financing Britain's trade imbalances with the rest of the world, India became a crucial pillar of late-nineteenth-century multilateral trade (Saul 1960, pp. 56–63). The firms, agency houses, and banks involved in Indian trade already banked their balances and working capital in London. With its monetary reserves also invested in London, by 1900 the colony had become an unwitting pioneer of a sterling-based gold exchange standard. As London became India's de facto central bank, rupee remittances became the instrument for regulating money supply, credit, exchange rate, and economic conditions in the colony.

The rupee was a silver currency until 1893. Between 1871 and 1892, silver slid from 61 pence per ounce to 39 pence, and the rupee from 2 shillings (24 old pence) to 14 pence. A falling rupee hurt British producers of tradables (notably cotton goods and wheat) and raised the rupee cost of the Indian government's external obligations. In 1893 Indian mints were closed to free silver coinage, following which the United States discontinued government silver purchases. The resulting drop in silver prices aggravated British exporters' anxieties in Asia, particularly China and Japan, which were still on silver. Consequently the future of Indian currency became a lever for those agitating to put Britain on a bimetallic standard and restore its international competitiveness.

London's 1898 decision to put the rupee on a gold-sterling basis was thus pivotal to Britain's own political economy, and to whether its future global role lay in manufacturing or finance. However, shortly afterwards, Britain confronted a series of external financial shocks starting with the South African war (1899–1902), which made an Indian gold standard distinctly ill-suited to its interests. From 1901 the colony's currency and exchange reserves were transferred to London and held predominantly in the form of sterling securities (Balachandran 2008, pp. 317–319). India's role as a linchpin grew as Britain's external finances weakened, and France and the United States began drawing gold away from London. Thanks to booming world trade, India's trade surplus tripled from £19 million to £57 million between 1898 and 1913. Anxious to finance this surplus without undue gold losses to the colony, Britain steered the rupee firmly toward a sterling basis, expanding council bill sales and banking the proceeds in London, where they helped ease interest rates and monetary conditions. By 1913, India had also emerged as the largest holder of British government securities, accounting for nearly 30 per cent of currency and 'official' holdings of sterling (Lindert 1969, pp. 18–19; Balachandran 2008, pp. 318–320; De Cecco 1975, pp. 62–75).

Metropolitan concerns also affected the use of the rupee as currency in other parts of the empire. In the wake of the 1907 sterling crisis, the gold reserves of the Straits Settlements were transferred to London to insulate them from Indian market pressures, and the colony's currency was reorganized (Nelson 1987, pp. 53, 68–69). Britain replaced the rupee as currency in East Africa with a new shilling linked to and backed by sterling reserves in London. This move in the midst of pronounced sterling instability to affirm Britain as East Africa's 'primary economic and political referent' deprived the protectorate of the 'flexibility of the . . . rupee trade' and resulted in prolonged instability (Mwangi 2001, pp. 781–784). The effects of currency reorganization on trade in the region await investigation.

Regulating gold flows to India became a more pressing concern in the 1920s when Britain – confronting chronic economic weakness in the form of persistently high unemployment, capital volatility, and weak sterling – sought an expansionary world economy to ease its own recovery. Britain now intensified efforts to eliminate any residual use of gold as money in the colony (Balachandran 2008). Further, as Keynes had observed, gold flows to India were counter-cyclical to the world economy, rising during booms to moderate them and falling or reversing during a slump (Keynes 1913). Britain used its control over monetary and exchange rate policies in the 1920s to generate deflationary expectations and depress Indian gold imports, and in the 1930s, when the Depression forced Indian households to liquidate their gold holdings, to deepen deflationary pressures to boost this outflow. Thus Indian gold exports eased Britain's external liquidity pressures and exerted an expansionary influence on the world economy during the Depression (Balachandran 2002).

Regional commerce and entrepreneurship

Shut out of some trades and subordinated in others, subcontinental entrepreneurs nonetheless found or developed new niches and opportunities. Losses for some also meant opportunities for others. By the 1840s even a large, well-connected opium trader like Jamsetjee Jeejeebhoy could not withstand competition from British agency houses with better access to markets in London and political support in India (Siddiqi 1982). Yet Jeejeebhoy's misfortunes also arose from new, more nimble Indian entrants with leaner business models. Consequently, when it ended, the opium trade involved a more diverse group of subcontinental traders than it had half a century before (Siddiqi 1982, pp. 323–324).

New and established entrepreneurs competed to take advantage of late-nineteenth-century changes in trade and shipping by opening new avenues for business and expanding or consolidating existing ones. For example, traders from Hyderabad (Sind) exploited the growth of maritime transport and tourism to create a world-wide market for curios and souvenirs. Beginning modestly as pedlars, they grew into a string of trading emporia along the world's main shipping arteries to gird the globe from Kobe to Panama. Complexly held together by connections of kinship, cross-holdings, and multi-branch proprietorships and quickly outgrowing Sind's own craft industry, these emporia developed standardized product lines, long-distance supply chains, and dispersed distribution networks linked through *entrepots* including Singapore, Surabaya, Cairo, and Gibraltar. They supplied tastes for Oriental curios, Asian silks, and fashions such as *Japonisme*, sourcing 'authentic' craft items from Japan and China and in the process pioneering a mass market for tourist curios and souvenirs (Markovits 2000, pp. 119–121).

In reverse, communities of overseas traders were to be found in many Indian towns and cities. Besides Armenian, Baghdadi, and Chinese traders in the major port towns, traders from Central Asia and Iran were a frequent presence, especially in India's northern and north-western regions.

Some entrepreneurial communities specialized in banking more than trade. Prominent among them were the Nattukottai Chettiars from Chettinad in Tamil Nadu, and Shikaripuri from Sind.

Originally a community of salt traders, the Nattukottai Chettiars (or *Nakarattars*) had expanded into inland and coastal trade in rice, cotton, and credit by the late eighteenth century. In the nineteenth century they opened agency offices in Calcutta, and following in the footsteps of the British army had offices in Singapore and Penang by 1825, and in Burma by the middle of the century. Translating colonial conquest into commercial opportunity, they financed the production and export of tea from Ceylon, rubber and tin from Malaya, and rice from Burma. Forced to cede trade financing to British banks, Nakarattar bankers became their agents in the interior, still however oiling the wheels of trade by lending to farmers and moving their produce to ports. Growing loan defaults blocked a high proportion of their funds in land in the 1920s and 1930s before the rise of peasant-nationalist protest in the region led to a sharp contraction of the Nakarattar network (Rudner 1994).

Shikaripuri bankers (or *shroffs*) financed commerce between India and Central Asia. At various times since the eighteenth century, the Shikaripuri network extended northwards into Afghanistan, Russian Central Asia, the southern regions of Sinkiang, and westwards into Persia. The *hundis* they issued circulated widely between Nijni-Novgorod and Calcutta (Markovits 2000, pp. 186). As the caravan trade declined, Shikaripuris in Central Asia turned to local trade and to lending money on their own account or as intermediaries for Russian banks, the biggest among them lending to kinsfolk arrayed in a hierarchy whose lowest rungs comprised small rural moneylenders. Expelled from Russia after 1917, they redeployed to India, Burma, and Malaya, and they intensified their presence in Iran as auxiliaries of British power (Markovits 2000, Chapter 3, pp. 57–109).

India's coastal and regional trade received a fillip in the nineteenth century. The western Indian Ocean attracted Gujarati and Kachhi merchant communities like the Banias, Bhatias, Khojas, and Memons. Operating triangular networks linking Mandvi with Muscat and Zanzibar, they branched out to Bombay and Karachi as well as to trading centres in the Gulf and along the East African coast, trading pearls from Oman; cloves from Zanzibar; cashews from Mozambique; and rice, sugar, spices, and cloth from India. Said to finance the reciprocal Arab trade in guns and slaves, thanks to revenues from their trade, they also became the mainstay of the finances of the Imam of Muscat. Attracted by the 'unrivalled commercial capabilities of the coast', they cooperated with British campaigns to suppress the slave trade and followed them into the interior (Bose 2006, pp. 99–102; Goswami 2010; Mehta 2001; Ray 1995, pp. 540–542, 544–545). Gujarati merchants also ran the trade in popular sheeting cloth (called *merekani*) from Salem, Massachusetts. During the American Civil War they had British cloth 'remade' to imitate *merekani* before substituting it with cheaper sheeting manufactured in Bombay. Pre-colonial East Africa consequently became the first large overseas market for Bombay cotton manufactures (Presthold 2008, pp. 78–85).

An ubiquitous presence along the East African coast and numbering in the thousands in ports like Zanzibar and Mombasa, by the late nineteenth century Gujarati traders and money-changers had, according to Bartle Frere, become 'the one invariable and most important link of all' in trade between coast and interior (Ray 1995, p. 544; Bose 2006, p. 102). They were as indispensable to supplying the East African caravan trade as they were to supplying European settlers (Rockel 2006, p. 90). Transacting across diverse environments, Indian traders' operations spanned commodities, currency, and finance. While the largest firms operated as diversified businesses, smaller merchants specialized in individual commodity or business lines, and the humblest of them all – the proverbial *dukawallas* – extended the networks deep inland, where they became the versatile mainstay of an emerging retail economy (Mwangi 2001, pp. 770–772, 774–777, 779–782). From the early 1920s onwards, these networks were stunted by a succession of developments, including the consolidation of colonial rule, competition with British settlers, discrimination at the hands of settler-dominated colonial government, and the Depression.

Neeladri Bhattacharya (2003) has drawn attention to another layer of trading relationships made up of 'small rivulets of traders' from among settled and nomadic trading communities or peasants taking to trade in the fallow season. Dismissed as pedlars or criminals, their networks spanned the north-eastern, northern, and north-western regions of the subcontinent, extending into central and north-central Asia. Traversing vast plains and high passes and linking agrarian, pastoral, and urban ecosystems, these networks transacted a wide portfolio of goods ranging from cattle reared or bought along the way to cloth from urban wholesale markets such as Delhi.

Some subcontinental pedlar networks spread further afield – scores of East Bengal traders operating along emerging circuits of leisure travel between North America, Central America, and the Caribbean. Some lived, cohabited, or married into African-American and Hispanic communities. Still, the subcontinent remained the main source of stock-in-trade and personnel, such mobility being dictated by the need to cultivate and sustain markets, and renew supplies, cultural capital, and kinship ties (Bald 2013). While not much is known about US networks after the First World War, by the 1920s, the subcontinental trading presence had expanded sufficiently in Britain for wholesalers to pay or advance passage fares for retail tradesmen from India. However these networks that supplied the bottom of the retail hierarchy appear to have sourced their wares from other parts of Europe rather than India (Visram 2002, pp. 259–263). Last but not least, hundreds of peasant cultivators from Punjab and north-west India travelled to Australia, Canada, Latin America, and the United States in the hope of buying their own farms. Most failed because of restrictions on land ownership or on the entry of family labour. A few succeeded by renting farms or marrying into local Hispanic families.

Labour and mobility

Pedlars, peasants aspiring to own land, and even Shikaripuri moneylenders scrabbling together a hard existence in Central Asia illustrate the intimate relationship between trade, entrepreneurship, labour, capital, and community in the nineteenth century. Peddling and itinerant wage employment often financed mobility including for leisure or pilgrimage, many poor pilgrims combining them with the Hajj and serendipitous sight-seeing tours through the Gulf. Peddling also overlapped with wage employment, serving as a fallback in the event of need or, as in Africa and the Caribbean, a tentative first shot at escape from wage labour.

The idea of a subcontinent historically frozen into immobility commands little support today. The subcontinent and its regions had always known eddying flows. Circular, linear, or indeterminate, these comprised mercenaries, peasants, soldiers, and literati, besides merchants, pilgrims, displaced cultivators, and other working people. The *radius* of the eddies and the nature of circulation could also vary with means, opportunity, and risk (Markovits, Pouchepadass, and Subrahmanyam 2003, Introduction).

Two mid-nineteenth century changes exerted an enduring impact over the following decades. First, improved transport – notably thanks to railways, steamships, and shorter and more predictable voyages – increased mobility. Many more people took to the road, in doing so improvising new associations between wage employment, peddling, trade, itinerant work, mendicancy, pilgrimage, proselytization, travel for knowledge, and so on. Historians have distinguished in these flows markings of a 'religious economy' in the Indian Ocean (Green 2011). Even religious pilgrimage could take a 'bazaar' form, or embrace corporate and governmental forms and logics (Miller 2006).

Second, improved transport and communications intensified spatial patterns of specialization and the social division of labour. For instance, the post-abolition reinvigoration of Caribbean plantations and the spread of the plantation economy in the Indian Ocean rim helped reconcile rising working-class expectations in Europe and the profitability of its businesses. Neither could have been sustained without subcontinental (and Asian) labour.

An estimated 29 million people left India for Southeast Asia and lands around the Indian Ocean and South Pacific between c.1840 and 1930. More than half went to Burma, over 8 million to Ceylon, 4 million to the Straits Settlements and Southeast Asia, and about a million to Africa and Indian Ocean and Pacific Islands (McKeown 2004, pp. 157–158). They worked in coffee, tea, rubber, and sugar plantations; tin mines; road, railway, and public construction projects; ports, harbours, workshops, and railways; as well as shops and offices and in the lower rungs of the colonial and business bureaucracy. In addition, 2 million Indians are also estimated to have gone abroad for business rather than employment (Markovits 2000, p. 17).

Some of these movements took place on short-term indenture contracts (Kaur 2004, pp. 638–639). Slavery in the Caribbean began to be abolished from the 1830s, only to be replaced until 1917 by the import of indentured labour from the subcontinent – more than half a million were shipped on renewable five-year indenture contracts, mostly to work on sugar plantations. Indian labourers were also recruited for indenture in Natal and in East Africa. Overall in this period, India exported some 1.5 million indentured labourers to the Caribbean, Indian Ocean and Pacific islands, the Straits Colonies, Natal, and East Africa (Tinker 1974). Indenture was also used to mobilize labour for Assam's tea plantations (Behal and Mohapatra 1992).

A large proportion of the labour for Southeast Asia passed through intermediaries, generically termed *kanganis*, who recruited against wage advances. Kangani-based recruitment is distinguished from indenture because a breach of contract was a criminal offence under the latter and a civil liability under the former. This may have been a distinction without a difference if kangani was merely a looser contractual system of debt and advances than indenture for 'tying down labourers to particular employers' (Mohapatra 2007, p. 111; Mazumdar 2007, pp. 130–131).

The subcontinent also emerged as a hub of large-scale 'offshoring' in the late nineteenth century for employment on deep-sea Western merchant vessels. Indian crews were most prominent in British shipping, where their numbers grew from a few thousand in the 1870s to 24,000 in 1891 and 52,000 in 1914. They made up 10 per cent of the employment on British vessels in 1891, nearly 18 per cent by 1914, and 25 per cent in 1937. Indian crews meant lower wage costs and, in addition to ships trading with Britain, were employed on ships plying the Atlantic, Pacific, and Indian oceans, not to mention thousands of *dhows, bagallas*, and other 'native' vessels carrying freight and passengers between ports in the Indian Ocean rim. Hundreds of African, Arab, Chinese, and European sailors also often crowded Indian ports. Seafarers emblematized the circular nature of labour flows from the subcontinent. Until the 1920s, only a notable few made homes ashore at the Western ports they frequented during their voyages. Linear patterns became more discernible thereafter, coinciding also with intensified restrictions in many Western countries on employment and residence of seafarers from the subcontinent and other regions of Asia (Balachandran 2012).

Conclusion

Colonial India's economic links with its immediate region were complex, variegated, changing, and changeable. Speaking historically, they involved both tracing external transactions that were palpably economic in nature, such as trade and capital flows, and uncovering the significant economic dimensions of transactions less overtly economic at the time, such as peddling, pilgrimage, etc. This distinction, and the split-screen approach it necessitates, is useful and necessary because as the world economy as we know it was coming into existence in the late nineteenth and early twentieth centuries, so too were many of the forms of regulation associated with it that are now taken for granted. Imagining anew the complexity of the subcontinent's external economic relationships without reducing them to conventional measures of commodity trade and capital flows also helps to shed light on neglected dimensions that may grow in significance with further research.

References

Balachandran, G. (1998). *The Reserve Bank of India, 1951–1967*, Delhi: Oxford University Press.
———. (2002). 'The Interwar Slump in India: The Periphery in a Crisis of Empire', in Theo Balderston, ed., *The World Economy and National Economies in the Interwar Slump*, Basingstoke: Palgrave Macmillan, pp. 143–171.

————. (2008). 'Power and Markets in Global Finance: The Gold Standard, 1890–1926', *Journal of Global History, 3 (3)*, pp. 313–335.

————. (2012). *Globalizing Labour? Indian Seafarers in World Shipping, c. 1870–1945*, Delhi: Oxford University Press.

Bald, V. (2013). *Bengali Harlem and the Lost Histories of South Asian America*, Cambridge, MA: Harvard University Press.

Behal, R., and P. Mohapatra (1992). 'Tea and Money versus Human Lives: The Rise and Fall of Indentured system in Assam's Tea Plantations 1840–1908', *Journal of Peasant Studies, 19 (3–4)*, pp. 142–172.

Bhattacharya, N. (2003). 'Predicaments of Mobility: Peddlers and Itinerants in Nineteenth-century Northwestern India', in C. Markovits, J. Pouchepadass, and S. Subrahmanyam, eds., *Society and Circulation: Mobile Peoples and Itinerant Cultures in South Asia, 1750–1950*, Delhi: Permanent Black.

Bose, S. (2006). *A Hundred Horizons: The Indian Ocean in the Age of Global Empire*, Delhi: Permanent Black.

Chaudhuri, K. N. (1971). *Economic Development of India Under the East India Company, 1814–1858: A Selection of Contemporary Writings*, Cambridge: Cambridge University Press.

————. (1983). 'Foreign Trade and Balance of Payments (1757–1947)', in Dharma Kumar, ed., *The Cambridge Economic History of India, Vol. II: c. 1757–1970*, Cambridge: Cambridge University Press, pp. 804–877.

Davis, L. E., and R. A. Huttenback (1986). *Mammon and Pursuit of Empire: The Political Economy of British Imperialism, 1860–1912*, Cambridge: Cambridge University Press.

De Cecco, M. (1975). *Money and Empire: International Gold Standard, 1890–1914*, Oxford: Blackwell.

Fichter, J. R. (2010). *So Great a Proffit: How the East Indies Trade Transformed Anglo-American Capitalism*, Cambridge, MA: Harvard University Press.

Foreman-Peck, J. (1989). 'Foreign Investment and Imperial Exploitation: Balance of Payments Reconstruction for Nineteenth Century Britain and India,' *Economic History Review, 42 (3)*, pp. 354–374.

Goldsmith, R. (1983). *The Financial Development of India, 1860–1977*, Delhi: Oxford University Press.

Goswami, C. (2010). *The Call of the Sea: Kachchhi Traders in Muscat and Zanzibar, c. 1800–1880*, Hyderabad: Orient Blackswan.

Green, N. (2011). *Bombay Islam: The Religious Economy of the West Indian Ocean, 1840–1915*, Cambridge: Cambridge University Press.

Hilgerdt, F. (1943). 'The Case for Multilateral Trade', *American Economic Review, 33 (1)*, pp. 397–407.

Indian Currency Committee (1893). *Minutes of Evidence, Part II*, London: Her Majesty's Stationery Office.

Indian Currency Committee (Fowler Committee) (1899). *Minutes of Evidence, Part II*, London: Her Majesty's Stationery Office.

Jorgensen, E., and J. Sachs (1989). 'Default and Renegotiation of Latin American Foreign Bonds in the Interwar Period', in B. Eichengreen and P. H. Lindert, eds., *The International Debt Crisis in Historical Perspective*, Cambridge, MA: MIT Press.

Kaur, A. (2004). 'Indian Immigrants (Nineteenth and Twentieth Centuries)', in O. K. Gin, ed., *Southeast Asia: A Historical Encyclopedia from Angkor Wat to East Timor, Vol. 1*, Greenwood, CT: ABC Clio.

Keynes, J. M. (1913). *Indian Currency and Finance*, London: Macmillan.

Lindert, P. H. (1969). *Princeton Studies in International Finance: No. 24, Key Currencies and Gold, 1900–30*, Princeton: Princeton University Press.

Maddison, A. (1972). *Class Structure and Economic Growth: India & Pakistan Since the Moghuls*, New York: W. W. Norton.

Markovits, C. (2000). *The Global World of Indian Merchants: Traders of Sind from Bukhara to Panama*, Cambridge: Cambridge University Press.

Markovits, C., J. Pouchepadass, and S. Subrahmanyam, eds. (2003). *Society and Circulation: Mobile Peoples and Itinerant Cultures in South Asia, 1750–1950*, Delhi: Permanent Black.

Mazumdar, S. (2007). 'Localities of the Global: Asian Migrations Between Slavery and Citizenship', *International Review of Social History, 52 (1)*, pp. 124–133.

McKeown, A. (2004). 'Global Migration, 1846–1940', *Journal of World History, 15 (4)*, pp. 155–189.

Mehta, M. (2001). 'Gujarati Business Communities in East African Diaspora: Major Historical Trends', *Economic and Political Weekly, 36 (20)*, pp. 1738–1747.

Miller, M. B. (2006). '"Pilgrims" Progress: The Business of the *Hajj*', *Past and Present, 191 (1)*, pp. 189–228.

Mohapatra, P. (2007). 'Eurocentrism, Forced Labour, and Global Migration: A Critical Assessment', *International Review of Social History, 52 (1)*, pp. 110–115.

Mwangi, W. (2001). 'Of Coins and Conquest: African Currency Board, the Rupee Crisis, and the Problem of Colonialism in the East African Protectorate', *Comparative Studies in Society and History, 43 (4)*, pp. 763–787.

Nelson, W. E. (1987). 'The Gold Standard in Mauritius and the Straits Settlements between 1850–1914', *Journal of Imperial and Commonwealth History, 16 (1)*, pp. 48–76.

Nugent, J. B. (1973). 'Exchange-Rate Movements and Economic Development in the Late Nineteenth Century', *Journal of Political Economy, 81 (5)*, pp. 1110–1135.

O'Connell, A. (1984). 'Argentina into the Depression: Problems of an Open Economy', in R. Thorp, ed., *Latin America in the 1930s: The Role of the Periphery in the World Crisis*, London: Macmillan and St Martin's Press.

Presthold, J. (2008). *Domesticating the World: African Consumerism and the Genealogies of Globalization*, Berkeley: University of California Press.

Ray, R. (1995). 'Asian Capital in the Age of European Domination: The Rise of the Bazaar, 1800–1914', *Modern Asian Studies, 29 (3)*, pp. 449–554.

Rockel, S. J. (2006). *Carriers of Culture: Labor on the Road in Nineteenth-Century East Africa*, Portsmouth, NH: Heinemann.

Roy, T. (2000). *Economic History of India, 1857–1947*, Delhi: Oxford University Press.

Rudner, D. W. (1994). *Caste and Colonialism in Colonial India: The Nattukottai Chettiars*, Berkeley: University of California Press.

Saul, S. B. (1960). *Studies in British Overseas Trade*, Liverpool: Liverpool University Press.

Sen, N. (1992). *India in the International Economy, 1858–1913: Some Aspects of Trade and Finance*, Calcutta: Orient Blackswan.

Siddiqi, A. (1982). 'The Business World of Jamsetjee Jejeebhoy', *Indian Economic and Social History Review, 19 (3–4)*, pp. 301–323.

Tinker, H. (1974). *A New System of Slavery: The Export of Indian Labour Overseas, 1830–1920*, London: Oxford University Press.

Visram, R. (2002). *Asians in Britain: 400 Years of History*, London: Pluto Press.

Yang, A. (1998). *Bazaar India: Markets, Society, and the Colonial State in Gangetic Bihar*, Berkeley: California University Press.

7

AGRICULTURE IN COLONIAL INDIA

Latika Chaudhary, Bishnupriya Gupta,
Tirthankar Roy, and Anand V. Swamy

Agriculture in colonial India produced more than half of the GDP and employed more than half the labour force – the latter is true to the present day. Its fortunes were, therefore, central to the growth of the economy and the welfare of its citizens. It is fair to say, however, that, especially in the twentieth century, it did not flourish: output failed to keep up with the population.[1] Another obvious failure was the occurrence of devastating famines, the last major one in Bengal in 1943. Therefore, this chapter aims to answer, sequentially, two questions: Why was growth so slow? And what accounts for the famines? Our purpose is not to provide a definitive answer, but to offer the reader a menu of hypotheses.

What were the potential sources of growth? Many contemporary economists argue that the 'deep' determinants of growth are 'institutional', in particular, the nature of property rights and enforcement of contracts (see for example North 1990). Even from the very early days of conquest, British administrators defended their rule in these terms: they had brought Pax Britannica to warring regions and India would flourish under their good governance, central to which was the creation of secure property rights and the rule of law. The second section of this chapter discusses this issue briefly, in part because this is the main subject of Iyer's chapter (Chapter 8 in this volume).

Trade was another potential spur to growth. India became more integrated with the global economy during the nineteenth century, a phenomenon often referred to as *commercialization*. Standard trade models would suggest that India could exploit its comparative advantage in the production of labour-intensive agricultural products; this could lead not only to gains from specialization, but also allow hitherto unused factors of production (land in particular) to be brought into use. However, in the context of colonial India, many scholars have argued that trade under colonial conditions had some special features, so the standard predictions of trade models did not apply. This class of issues is considered in the third section.

Another potential source of growth is public investment – irrigation being the strongest candidate. Indeed the post-independence literature suggests that public and private investments have been complementary (Bardhan 1984). In the fourth section we consider how the colonial state performed in this dimension.

Finally, we turn to the issue of famines. At first glance one might wonder why this issue needs special attention. Is it not fairly obvious that famines will occur in an economy that does not produce enough food? Closer examination suggests that while low food production might lead to an undernourished population, it does not automatically lead to large-scale mortality crises – short-run governmental policy can play a critical role. We consider the relative importance of food production versus crisis management in determining the incidence and severity of famines.

The institutional framework

The beginning of formal British rule in India is often dated to 1765 when the East India Company became *Diwan* (roughly, finance minister) of Bengal, a huge and rich region corresponding to present-day Indian states of West Bengal, Bihar, a portion of Orissa, and present-day Bangladesh. The central task of the *Diwan* was the collection of land taxes. This was especially important for the East India Company because it was a corporation, a profit-seeking entity. The taxes it collected could partly be used to buy textiles, which it would then sell in Europe. But the task was complicated. A small group of British officials was administering an enormous area with a great variety of land tenure arrangements: the various rights associated with a piece of land did not necessarily belong to a single individual. One might have the right to collect taxes from the village for the state (and keep a portion), another might be a 'landlord' within the village, a third might have the right to continuous occupation and cultivation of the land, and so on. Faced with a daunting task, the Company settled on a simple solution: a diverse group of former tax collectors were declared 'proprietors' and their taxes were fixed, in nominal terms, in perpetuity. If they could not pay the tax, the land would be sold. Though this arrangement, famously known as the Permanent Settlement of 1793, was introduced with considerable rhetorical flourish, its biggest virtue was its administrative ease: the Company had 'outsourced' revenue collection to the owners/tax collectors, known as *zamindars*, and had sidestepped the issue of the rights of others lower in the hierarchy.[2]

As time went by, and the Company became more secure, it became more willing to take on more administrative burden. In some regions it contracted with *zamindars*, but the tax was not fixed in perpetuity – it could be raised after regular intervals. This, of course, required more detailed knowledge concerning land rights and productivity. Even more administration-intensive was the approach (*raiyatwari*) that it introduced in large parts of western and southern India, where, in principle, the actual cultivator was the owner (Kumar 1965, S. Guha 1985). Now the government had to identify the holdings of individual peasants and indeed individual fields. Variants of *raiyatwari* and *zamindari* involving joint responsibility for payment of taxes were introduced in some portions of the United Provinces and in Punjab.

Whatever the choice of land tenure, a key issue was the level of taxation. When the Permanent Settlement was introduced, the tax rate was set at a high level because it was to be fixed in perpetuity. According to Islam, rates were 'unbearably high', i.e. beyond the capacity of the *zamindar* (Islam 1979, p. 25). Even Marshall, while not taking such a strong view, suggests that taxes were 12.5 per cent higher in 1793 compared to 1757 (Marshall 1987, p. 144). However, as inflation and growth occurred over the nineteenth century, the tax became less significant (because it was fixed in nominal terms in perpetuity). Nevertheless, in the *raiyatwari* regions, high land taxes remained a concern for a much longer period, especially in the Madras Presidency (Kumar 1965, pp. 92–95). Kumar's (1983, p. 918) best guess is that for British India as a whole, land taxes were around 10 per cent of agricultural output in the 1860s. By the end of the colonial period this figure was down to 2 per cent.

From the late nineteenth century, agrarian unrest forced the Company to revisit the *zamindari* regions and consider the rights of people lower in the agrarian hierarchy: it passed a series of legislations to protect tenants, the most prominent of which was the Bengal Tenancy Act of 1885. It also became increasingly concerned with the problem of land transfer, usually after defaulting on a loan, from peasants to non-cultivating moneylenders. It passed several legislations to limit these transfers, the most prominent of which was the Punjab Land Alienation Act of 1900. Various laws prohibiting usury were also passed. By the end of the colonial period there was a large body of land and credit legislation.

Were these institutions conducive to growth? Banerjee and Iyer (2005, pp. 1190–1213) and Iyer (Chapter 8 in this volume) have focused on institutional overhang, presenting statistical evidence that *zamindari*-type arrangements had adverse consequences in post-colonial India. While there is an extensive qualitative literature on these topics for the colonial period itself, there is little rigorous statistical work establishing the impact of various institutional choices made by the Company or the Raj. To some extent this is because systematic data collection on output and acreage really began only in the late nineteenth century. It is also true, of course, that it is not easy to isolate the impact of a single institutional innovation. Still, this remains an open area for research.

The Company was (originally) primarily a trader, so it was inevitable that its conquest of India would lead to greater integration of the Indian economy with the global economy. The next section considers the consequences.

Trade and commercialization

Commercialization of agriculture usually means a process whereby peasants produce primarily for sale in distant markets. The process can be voluntary, a rational response to relative price changes, or involuntary, being compelled by distressing circumstances such as famines or excessive taxation. International specialization that accompanied nineteenth-century world trade expansion turned India and other tropical countries into a producer and exporter of primary goods and minerals. Did peasants everywhere commercialize to an equal extent? Did commercialization improve their standard of living? Such questions have often motivated empirical research on commercialization.[3]

Similar to that in other tropical states, the demand for Indian primary products increased during the globalization of the nineteenth century. The commercialization was led by indigo, opium, and cotton from the early nineteenth century, and wheat, rice, cotton, jute, groundnut, and sugarcane from the last quarter of the century. The value of exports increased at 4 per cent per year between 1876 and 1913. The share of primary products was well over half throughout, and agricultural exports in real terms doubled in this period. If we include processed primary goods such as tea or hides, the scale of expansion would be even larger. Agricultural prices went through pronounced cycles in the first half of the nineteenth century, but from the third quarter began to rise steadily, and at a faster rate than the prices of manufactured exports from the industrial countries. The average export price of Indian wheat in 1920 was three times what it had been in 1870.

Agricultural production expanded from 1870 to 1900 at an average rate of about 1 per cent per year and cultivated land area expanded by 30–40 per cent between 1870 and 1946. Table 7.1 summarizes agricultural expansion in the twentieth century.[4] The net area under cultivation increased by 13 per cent between 1895 and 1936, accompanied by an increase in the proportion of non-food grains from 9 to 13 per cent. This was largely driven by cotton that went from just under 5 per cent of net area sown in 1895 to 7 per cent in 1936. Rice and wheat were the main food grains, accounting for around 35 and 11 per cent respectively of the net area sown. Bengal specialized in rice production (90 per cent of net area sown) while Punjab specialized in wheat (35 per cent of net area). Cotton was grown primarily in Bombay and the Central Provinces.

How was this expansion achieved? Adjusting for land quality, India was not exactly a land-abundant region in the middle of the nineteenth century. Much of the fertile Gangetic plains had run out of an open land frontier by 1870 and had little room to expand cultivation. The important examples of acreage expansion in response to commercialization, therefore, were few. The five core zones were Punjab, Sind, Narmada Valley, the western part of the United Provinces (UP), and coastal Andhra Pradesh. Water or the presence of irrigation was vital in all five regions, supplying sufficient moisture for winter crops and thus enabling extra production for trade. Irrigation canals thus contributed directly to production for trade.

By 1936, almost one fifth or 51 million acres of the total area sown was irrigated, with government canals being the main source of irrigation. They accounted for 46 per cent of the total irrigated area, followed by wells at 25 per cent (mostly private and common in the United Province), tanks at 12 per cent (common in Madras), private canals at 8 per cent, and other sources such as field embankments accounting for the rest (see Table 7.2). British India had one of the largest irrigated areas compared to other parts of the world, but a relatively small proportion of total land under cultivation was irrigated.

Punjab and Sind were the main beneficiaries of government canals. In the early nineteenth century, Sind was an arid desert and western Punjab was mainly a dry savannah that supported pastoralist populations but little cultivation. The region,

TABLE 7.1 Agriculture acreage summary

	Total area* (acres)	Net area sown (as %)	per net area sown (%)					
			Food grains total	Rice	Wheat	Oilseeds	Non food total	Cotton
British India 1895	539,093,648	36.5	92.4	35.2	11.6	7.1	9.1	4.9
British India 1904	554,234,736	37.6	89.7	33.4	11.3	7.0	10.2	5.7
British India 1913	618,927,145	36.2	89.8	35.1	10.6	6.7	11.3	6.3
British India 1920	667,361,372	34.1	87.9	35.1	11.0	6.9	13.4	6.9
British India 1936	625,149,442	35.6	89.6	35.3	10.6	5.6	12.8	6.9
(1936–37)								
Madras	80,104,239	39.6	81.8	31.2	0.0	16.5	10.9	7.8
Bombay	48,721,608	57.8	70.8	6.5	5.9	7.6	23.3	13.2
Bengal	49,254,596	49.7	97.0	89.9	0.6	4.5	10.9	0.2
UP	67,848,920	53.3	105.4	18.7	21.1	2.8	7.0	1.9
Punjab	61,001,600	45.7	80.2	3.7	33.7	4.1	28.8	10.4
Bihar	44,324,194	44.9	101.4	50.0	5.7	7.7	2.0	0.2
CP and Berar	63,004,800	39.0	82.7	23.1	12.8	9.4	18.8	16.1
Assam	35,484,800	18.6	85.9	82.3	0.0	6.5	3.1	0.5
Sind	30,027,932	15.7	84.2	25.1	19.8	4.3	21.8	19.0
Orissa	20,594,776	31.5	95.2	79.4	0.1	4.8	1.2	0.1

Sources: The year 1895 refers to 1894–95 and so forth. Data sources for individual British India (BI) years – 1895: Statistical Abstract 1894–95 to 1903–04, Table 117 (India 1905); 1904: Statistical Abstract 1903–04 to 1912–13, Table 119 (India 1915); 1920: Statistical Abstract 1910–11 to 1919–20, Table 117 (India 1922); 1936: Statistical Abstract, new series, 1927–28 to 1936–37, Table 197, East India (India 1939). The province data refers to 1936–1937 and is from Table 200 (same source as BI data for 1936). Non-food is the area under cotton, jute, other fibres, indigo, other dyes, opium, tobacco, and fodder crops.

*According to survey.

however, was located on the upper Indus plains, and the five tributaries of the Indus carried the potential for canal irrigation on a large scale. Especially between 1870 and 1920, engineers built a system of inundation and perennial canals tapping the waters of these rivers, turning vast tracts in the *doabs* (interfluvial tracts) into arable land. Nine 'Canal Colonies' were created out of these irrigation projects, and collectively irrigated more than 10 million acres (Ali 1987, p. 114). By 1936, 47 and 79 per cent respectively of the total area sown in Punjab and Sind was irrigated.

The canals raised output, cultivated area, trade, and revenue, and induced a shift towards higher-valued crops.[5] Commercialization gave rise to towns populated by merchants, artisans, and service workers. After 1921, when the conversion of wastelands was reaching its limits, Punjab peasants benefited also from successful plant

TABLE 7.2 Area under irrigation

	Area irrigated (acres)	Area irrigated / area sown	Proportion of area irrigated by (%)				
			Govt canals	Private canals	Tanks	Wells	Other sources
British India-1886	23,098,822	16.5	29.9	4.0	19.0	37.8	9.3
British India-1904	34,244,590	14.3	41.3	6.2	16.7	31.4	4.3
British India-1913	45,539,074	17.8	39.0	5.5	15.0	27.1	13.4
British India-1920	48,963,033	19.2	42.0	5.4	15.0	25.9	11.7
British India-1936 (1935–36)	51,317,373	19.7	46.1	7.5	11.7	24.8	9.9
Madras	8,620,443	24.2	43.2	1.7	36.0	16.2	2.9
Bombay	1,061,316	3.6	20.0	8.2	10.7	58.6	2.4
Bengal	1,594,155	5.8	12.9	12.9	44.5	3.7	26.0
UP	10,765,157	24.7	32.6	0.3	0.6	49.2	17.3
Punjab	15,018,851	47.2	67.5	2.8	0.2	28.6	0.9
Bihar	4,469,085	18.8	16.0	18.1	32.9	12.9	20.2
CP and Berar	1,317,639	4.9	0.0	82.7	0.0	12.3	4.9
Assam	643,433	9.0	0.1	53.1	0.2	0.0	46.6
Sind	4,141,876	78.7	90.0	0.3	0.0	0.5	9.3
Orissa	1,046,546	15.2	28.0	4.6	30.4	7.5	29.5

Sources: Data sources for individual years – 1886: Statistical Abstract 1876–77 to 1885–86, Table 27 (India 1887); 1904: Statistical Abstract 1894–95 to 1903–04, Table 119 (India 1905); 1913: Statistical Abstract 1903–04 to 1912–13, 1915, Table 121 (India 1915); 1920: Statistical Abstract 1910–11 to 1919–20, 1922, Table 119 (India 1922); 1936: Statistical abstract 1926–27 to 1935–36, new series, Table 198 (India 1938).

breeding experiments in wheat and cotton. Coastal Andhra and western UP were the other regions endowed with canals, whereas the Narmada Valley had its own moisture-retention system connected with its distinctive ecology.

If canal construction was limited to certain regions, another infrastructure project – railways – came up everywhere, bringing down transportation cost in overland trade. This effect was especially strong in peninsular India, where wheeled traffic had very limited reach. Better market access because of the railways sometimes induced peasants outside the core zones to expand export production by reducing fallow and adopting more intensive cultivation methods when possible. The railways were partly a result of lobbying by Lancashire textile interests that wanted cheap ways to transport cotton. But the drive to build infrastructure also owed to a modernization ideology dating to the 1850s. Other projects that further reduced the cost of trade were the Suez Canal (1869), steamships, and telegraphic communication.

Given the weight of agriculture in the economy of South Asia, it is unsurprising that the subject has inspired considerable research. By far the biggest cluster of archival research in Indian economic history concerns the commercialization process and its effects on peasant standard of living.[6] While these myriad studies hail from different backgrounds and styles of analysis, they hone in on one stylized fact − rather paradox − of great significance. Agricultural productivity, which was low to begin with, remained low for most of the colonial period despite an increase in market growth. This had far-reaching consequences because trends in agricultural productivity directly influenced GDP, real wages, and standard of living. Indeed, low agricultural productivity was the fundamental proximate cause of underdevelopment in India. Low land yield was not only the root of poverty, stagnation, and small tax receipts, but probably also of frequent and destructive famines.

Although the non-agricultural sectors never fell into deep crisis (notwithstanding some decline in artisanal activity), GDP growth responded to non-agricultural income marginally because agriculture carried a much larger weight. National income estimates based on official statistics are available consistently from 1900 onward and more unevenly between 1865 and 1900. These estimates establish that GDP (total and per capita) increased at modest rates between 1865 and 1914, and at rates close to zero between 1914 and 1947 (Table 7.3). Agricultural income imparted the strongest effect on GDP. Agricultural output grew between 1865 and 1914 because land area apparently rose between these dates. But after 1914, acreage and income growth slowed together. Labour productivity growth was small throughout, and especially so in agriculture. To cite Broadberry and Gupta, 'labour productivity growth in the economy as a whole was held back by stagnation in agriculture' (Chapter 2 in this volume, p. 27). Commercialization imparted no more than a ripple on the agricultural wage.

Why did commercialization have no efficiency effects? Why were trade profits not invested in land improvement?

An older qualitative literature has argued that the non-agricultural classes captured the gains. Neither this group nor the cultivators invested in agriculture. Since taxes, interest rates, and rents increased at the expense of the income earned by the

TABLE 7.3 Average annual growth rates of GDP by sector of origin, 1865–2007

	GDP at factor cost, constant prices				*Population*	*GDP per head*
	Primary sector	*Secondary sector*	*Tertiary sector*	*Total*		
1865–1910	1.1			1.5	0.5	1.0
1910–1940	0.0	2.3	2.2	1.1	1.1	0.0
1950–1964	3.0	6.8	3.8	4.1	1.9	2.1
1965–1985	2.5	4.3	4.4	3.6	2.3	1.4
1986–2007	3.4	6.8	7.1	6.3	1.7	4.6

Source: Indian Union from 1950, British India for periods before. The primary sector consists of agriculture, forestry, and fishing; secondary sector of manufacturing, mining, electricity, gas, and construction; and the tertiary sector of trade, hotels and transportation, financial and business services, administration, and defence. For more details and sources, see Roy (2012).

cultivator, he had no incentive to invest in land improvement. Older nationalist readings that directly blame tax policy such as Bagchi (1983) rely on this argument, as do models of 'forced' commercialization in Bhaduri (1973, pp. 120–137) and in Marxian class analyses.

BOX 7.1   INTERLINKED CONTRACTS, DEBT, AND INVESTMENT

In the literature on Indian agriculture, critics of colonial policy have linked three specific features of agrarian markets – market power, interlinked markets, and debt traps – to investment failures. *Market power* is the ability to fix price as a monopolist or via collusion with other sellers. The contrast is with a competitive market in which the lender, landlord, or employer is a 'price-taker'. A small group of landlords in a village might, for instance, be able to set rents.

In economics textbooks, we are usually introduced to markets one at a time: supply and demand determine the rental price of land, the interest rate, and so on. But, in principle, two people can simultaneously interact in more than one market. For example, a trader could lend money to a farmer at the beginning of the agricultural season and buy his crop from him at a reduced price – now the interest rate is embedded in the lower price. This is the idea of *interlinked markets*. Peasants often fall into a *debt trap* when having once borrowed – high interest payments keep them in debt. It is a 'trap' because they are borrowing today only because they borrowed in the past.

If all these features are part of an agricultural economy, the powerful players – especially landlord-lenders – may profit so much from lending that they have little incentive to invest to raise productivity. The general point that markets do not necessarily treat all equally and can yield inefficient and inequality-enhancing outcomes also emerges from models of *asymmetric information* in which wealthier participants have an advantage because they have more collateral (D. Ray 1998).

Producing for trade clearly needed finance because cash crops were traded over long distances under ex-ante contracts that involved more investment in time and money. The extended monetization of rent and tax (combined with the disparity between seasons of tax collection and harvests) required credit, which clearly increased in the course of commercialization. There is also qualitative evidence of an increase in inequality (Ludden 1988, pp. 493–519; Roberts 1985, pp. 281–306). For example, in nineteenth-century Tamil Nadu, Ludden (1988) finds that 'Mahajan *mirasidars* and headmen used their control of land, labour, and various commercial assets to accumulate . . . financial resources' (p. 506). Similar stories apply to the core zones of commercialization, whether it be new frontiers such as the Canal Colonies, or old ones in the Gangetic plains.

But these inequalities among cultivators do not easily explain the absence of land-augmenting investment. Likewise, the evidence on rent and interest rates is difficult to read because gains in the form of these payments often accrued to richer peasants. More importantly, land tax as a proportion of agricultural income had been falling since the late nineteenth century and is not a credible explanation for low productivity.

If the gains made by peasants did not translate into commensurate efficiency gains, several other candidates exist to explain the low productivity of agriculture. First, peasants were irrational; they did not invest but spent their earnings on consumption. Second, peasants did invest, but they could not acquire land from less-efficient cultivators because of legal barriers to land transfer. Third, across all zones, structures of tenancy or user rights created adverse incentives for investment. Fourth, peasants did invest but their numbers were too small because commercialization occurred on a very limited scale.

Many British administrators believed in a variant of the first hypothesis, attributing the lack of saving and investment to cultural propensities like the desire for conspicuous consumption on weddings or a fascination with gold jewellery. But peasant irrationality raises more questions than it answers. Peasant irrationality is only an assumption. Acquisition of gold can be read as a precautionary saving. There is evidence that peasants did invest if they had extra money – but when they could, they acquired more land rather than improving existing land.

The second and third hypotheses cannot be ruled out. New legislation from the 1870s onwards increasingly erected obstacles to land transfers, which increased the transaction cost of land acquisition. Tenancy legislation also strengthened the rights of occupancy tenants. Measuring the aggregate effect of these obstacles is difficult because most of them were provincial laws that made the operation of the land market dissimilar between major regions. An aggregate assessment of their impact remains to be done.

The fourth hypothesis is not disputable, though it does not explain why productivity was relatively unchanged even in the core zones. The scale of commercialization was undoubtedly limited. Production for long-distance trade was small in the aggregate relative to peasant production for local sale or subsistence. As seen in Table 7.1, cotton accounted for a mere 7 per cent of net area sown by 1936 compared to 35 per cent under rice. Non-food crops were less than 15 per cent of net area sown at their peak.[7] Exportable goods came from very few districts. Canal-endowed districts were exceptions rather than the rule. Outside coastal Madras, Punjab, and UP, the proportion of irrigated area to total area sown was under 15 per cent (see Table 7.2). Almost none of the rain-fed zones participated deeply in the export boom. In 1914, the agricultural export to agricultural value-added ratio was about 14 per cent (excluding tea export), and the agricultural export to agricultural production ratio was about 7–10 per cent. Thus, exports had a small influence on peasant agriculture as a whole.

Why was the geographical spread of commercialization limited? Roy (2007, pp. 239–250; 2012) suggests that the quality of land was generally too poor to sustain agricultural expansion or a risk-free diversification away from the main subsistence. Water scarcity and poor soil characterized most of the regions outside the major river deltas. This in turn limited the possibilities of fertilizer application. The difference in yield between rain-fed and irrigated agriculture varied in the nineteenth century by as much as a factor of four. With 20 per cent of the cultivated area under irrigation in 1936, rainfall overwhelmingly influenced average yield, making it one of the smallest yields in the contemporary world. With such stark differences in yields, why did the public and private sector not invest more in irrigation? We turn to this subject next.

Irrigation

In spite of the importance of government canals, a majority of irrigation works in India came under the private sector. For example, state works provided water to 42 per cent of the total irrigated area, with canals at 35 per cent and tanks at 7 per cent in 1901. Wells were the most common private form of irrigation, accounting for 29 per cent of irrigated area (Great Britain 1932, p. 11). The 1904 Irrigation Commission created in the wake of the 1896–1897 and 1899–1900 famines heavily shaped colonial irrigation policy and advocated for new state projects while also urging the Government of India (hereafter GOI) to offer more subsidies for private projects. It is very likely the public-private breakdown remained similar up until independence.[8]

Both canals and tanks required coordination across multiple jurisdictions and groups that may have been difficult for private parties to achieve. Hence the public sector should and could have played a bigger role. The GOI borrowed to finance state irrigation works if the project was expected to yield sufficient net revenues to cover interest charges (such as most of the canal schemes in UP and Punjab).[9] Some projects were also financed from GOI revenues. This was particularly relevant for 'protective works' that could protect areas from famine. A separate famine fund was used to finance protective irrigation projects and railways.[10]

While the GOI was active in developing railways, irrigation was short-changed in the colonial budget. Table 7.4 shows the proportion of expenditure charged against revenue in India for railways and irrigation. In almost every decade, irrigation received less than 5 per cent of the total budget. Although railway expenditures decreased over time from 23 per cent in 1894 to 15 per cent in 1935, there was no reallocation of that money to irrigation. In terms of productive projects for which the GOI borrowed money, the picture was the same. Of the total expenditure on railways and irrigation works that was expected to cover their borrowing costs ('productive works'), more than 85 per cent was devoted to railways between 1894 and 1919.

Historians have long recognized these patterns, and many of the nationalist persuasion have argued that the disproportionate colonial emphasis on railways was socially inefficient because of the link between irrigation and economic development (see Chandra 1968, pp. 35–75; Sweeney 2011). According to this view, railways better served the strategic interests of the Raj and the differential expenditures were yet another example of colonial exploitation. The returns (net profits as a proportion of capital outlay) on irrigation were comparable to or sometimes even

TABLE 7.4 Irrigation expenditures under GOI budget

| | Proportion of Gross Expenditures Charged against Revenues | | Proportion of Expenditures Charged against Capital | |
	Railways	Irrigation	Railways	Irrigation
1894–95	23.0	3.1	87.2	12.8
1900–01	24.4	3.2	93.7	6.3
1910–11	15.5	4.1	90.3	9.7
1919–20	10.2	2.9	94.4	5.6
1935–36	15.2	3.2		

Source: Statistical Abstracts of India. *Gross expenditures* are calculated from General Statement of the Gross Expenditure charged against Revenue in India and England. Expenditures charged against capital are calculated from Expenditure on State Railways and Irrigation Works in India chargeable against Capital.

higher than railways.[11] Higher railway profits cannot account for the higher public investment on railways. This lends support to the nationalist critique. However, the more relevant question is whether the positive impact of irrigation on the economy was higher than the positive impact of railways. A rigorous cost-benefit analysis of public investment in railways versus irrigation still remains to be done.

Most studies suggest railways lead to price convergence, more trade, and an increase in agricultural incomes. Hurd (1984) calculates social savings from railways of around 9 per cent of national income by 1900. We know much less about the economic impact of irrigation. In a study of UP, Whitcombe (1972) describes the government canal schemes as a 'costly experiment' that selectively increased the acreage of commercial export crops such as wheat, sugarcane, indigo, and cotton at the expense of staples such as millet and pulses, making peasants more vulnerable to famines. Moreover, the canals imposed tremendous environmental costs by increasing the salinity in the soil, causing more waterlogging, and contributing to higher incidences of malaria.

The study by Stone (1984) of the same region offers a different and more balanced assessment. While recognizing the unequal distribution of the canal schemes across districts and their negative impact on malaria, he argues that many of the other negative externalities of canals were greatly exaggerated. Canals led to higher productivity, an increase in agricultural income, and a positive cycle of growth and development in the western UP canal districts. Unfortunately, neither of these studies offers a quantitative assessment of the net gains to society.

While colonial officials like Malcolm Darling (1928) celebrated the Canal Colonies of Punjab, some modern scholars such as Agnihotri (1996) have raised ecological concerns similar to those discussed. Taking a different tack, Ali (1987) has questioned the nature of growth generated by the Canal Colonies, arguing that land grants were used to reward and generate support from the landed classes of Punjab, who were also hugely represented in the British Indian army. The connection between land and military thereby generated may have been to the long-term detriment of the political economy of Pakistan. The politics of post-independence Pakistan are beyond the scope of this chapter. For the colonial period itself though, there appears to be a prima facie case for viewing the addition of more than 10 million acres of cultivable land in a positive light. However, we still need systematic examination of its impact on the standard of living.

By 1920, public investment in canals had fallen as the GOI ran out of money. The fall in investment partly explains the slowdown in extensive agricultural growth. But the particular technological model of irrigation expansion had also reached a limit. The solution that had been tried successfully by the British Indian engineers was redistribution of surface water. If that solution worked for Punjab and Sind, it was not feasible in the peninsular regions where the rivers did not carry enough water for distribution. Eventually, there was substantial expansion of irrigation in independent India, using different technologies. Gross irrigated area increased by 16 million hectares (close to 40 million acres) between 1950–1951 and 1971–1972, one dimension of the activity of a far more interventionist state Vaidyanathan 1983.

The rationale for expanding irrigation came, in part, as we have seen, from the desire to combat famine, which is the subject of the next section.

Famines

The performance of an economy and the standard of living are often difficult to judge because of issues of measurement: GDP, inequality, poverty, malnutrition, all are difficult to measure to the present day. But famines are highly visible, usually leading to intense criticism and questioning of governmental policy. Colonial India was no exception. Indeed, at the very beginning, in 1771, a massive famine in Bengal cast a shadow on the quality of governance of the East India Company, and was one of the factors contributing to greater oversight by the Crown and Parliament (see Hejeebu, Chapter 3 in this volume). However, the story of famine policy really begins in the second half of the nineteenth century when a series of famines embarrassed the Raj. Famines were read, on the one hand, as evidence of the shortcomings of British rule, broadly construed. But, on the other hand, it was evident in some cases that a commitment to laissez-faire – non-intervention even in the face of crisis – and budgetary stringency contributed to the disaster (Klein 1984, pp. 185–214).

How could famines be prevented? As one might expect from the Raj, a series of Famine Commissions were set up that examined a range of issues, from land tenure to debt to famine relief. After the Famine Commission of 1880, a set of Famine Codes was formulated in 1885 (Drèze 1995, p. 82). These codes recommended vigilance towards early warning signs of famine. The key policy was that the government would provide employment (and, hence, access to food) to villagers within some reasonable distance of their villages. This was visualized as a method of self-selection where only the truly needy would avail of the opportunity. Some 'gratuitous relief' was also provided to those who could not work.

In addition to the Famine Codes, there was hope that the spread of railways could bring food into vulnerable regions. McAlpin (1983) and, more recently,

Burgess and Donaldson (2010, pp. 449–453) suggest that railways reduced the severity of famines. By the 1940s there was reason to think famines were a thing of the past.[12] But this was not to be: in 1943, in the middle of the Second World War, Bengal suffered a famine leading to possibly as many as 3 million deaths. The Bengal Famine has been heavily analysed and is central to a highly influential approach to famines formulated by Amartya Sen.

Sen's general point, presented in a series of works, is that a famine occurs when there is a breakdown of 'entitlement' to food. The breakdown can occur for many reasons: an agricultural labourer who does not find work might not be able to buy the food that is actually available; hoarders and speculators might keep food supplies off the market, anticipating a rise in food (this will make prices rise right away); if purchasing power dries up in the distressed region, food can even travel away towards places where there is more effective demand;[13] and governments might fail to act to procure food from abroad or distribute the food on hand. Sen's framework does not deny the importance of increasing agricultural productivity, but the thrust of his work is to counter explanations based on the sheer physical availability of food, which he labelled FAD (Food Availability Decline). Famines, he argued, whether in Ireland in 1848 or Bengal in 1943, reflected a political problem: the alienation of the rulers from the ruled. A memorable conclusion of his various analyses is the following observation (Sen 1999): 'Famines are, in fact, so easy to prevent that it is amazing that they are allowed to occur at all' (p. 175).

Though Sen's contribution to our understanding of famines is widely respected, subsequent studies of the West Bengal Famine, in particular, suggest that he may have swung the pendulum too far away from FAD (Sen 1977). Goswami (1990, pp. 445–463) has re-examined the physical availability of stocks of food grain in Bengal and concluded that there was indeed a decline in the physical availability of food during the Bengal Famine. Tauger (2003, p. 64) buttresses this point with a discussion of evidence of fungal disease from Rice Research Stations. He finds that in 1942, yields of the *aman* crop (planted in June-July and harvested in December-January), which usually yielded two-thirds of the total rice output, was typically down 70–90 per cent compared to 1941. The *aus* crop (planted in March-April and harvested in August-September), which usually contributed a quarter of rice output, fell by 40 per cent or more in several areas. O'Grada (2008, pp. 5–37) has argued that the occupational distribution of distress is consistent with a supply shock rather than just price manipulation by speculators or demand factors. Absent a supply shock, producers of rice should not have been hurt – only net buyers should have been. The evidence is to the contrary: a survey of destitute migrants in Calcutta in 1943 for instance found that one in five was a cultivator. O'Grada's examination of correspondence within British officialdom also indicates considerable scepticism, even anguish, regarding official claims of adequacy of food availability. He also points out that the search for hoards of food grains amassed by speculators carried out by the government yielded very little.[14]

Famines would have been less likely had agriculture in colonial India been more productive. For instance, cultivators would have had more to subsist on and agricultural labourers would have earned more money with which to buy food. Still, even given the levels and trends in output, the nature of governance surely affected the incidence of famines. Sen (1999) has noted that 'there has never been a famine in a functioning multiparty democracy' (p. 178). And indeed there has never been a famine in independent India, even though per capita physical availability of food has been very low at times, especially before the Green Revolution.[15]

Conclusion

This chapter examined explanations for agricultural performance that are internal to agriculture. But agriculture is also linked to other sectors, and in principle, explanations can come from elsewhere. Faster industrial growth could have led to increased demand for agricultural products as well as outmigration. On the other hand, if India was 'deindustrialised' in the late eighteenth and the nineteenth centuries, as has often been argued, it would mean more people would remain within the agricultural sector. Once the land frontier had been reached, diminishing returns would set in and reduce output per person.

Arguments about deindustrialization usually pertain to the decline of India's traditional industries, especially textiles, given international competition from cheaper machine-made products. An alternative explanation could focus on the growth or lack thereof of 'modern', i.e. factory-based, production. The performance of both 'traditional' and 'modern' industry have been extensively studied and debated, and the reader will find useful material on these topics in the chapters in this volume by Gupta (Chapter 5) and Ray (Chapter 4).

The rate of growth of the international economy, the consequent demand for Indian exports, and exchange rate policies are other potential areas of interest. The Great Depression and the overvaluation of India's exchange rate in that period significantly hurt Indian agriculture.[16]

Finally, in thinking about governmental investments in infrastructure in the twentieth century, it is worth remembering that the Raj was a conservative state: it did not tax much, due to political concerns, and it did not spend much. Public expenditure at the beginning of the twentieth century was 10 per cent of national income and it remained roughly the same except during the World Wars. By contrast, public expenditure increased from 10 per cent of GNP in Japan in 1879–1883 to 25 per cent in 1905–1913. In England the figure rose from 9 per cent of GNP in 1890 to 39 per cent by 1950 (Kumar 1983, p. 927). The Raj was not an actively developmental state, neither in agriculture nor elsewhere.

Notes

1 Agricultural productivity, which was low to begin with, remained low for most of the colonial period despite an increase in market growth (Kurosaki 1999).
2 The literature on the Permanent Settlement in Bengal is enormous: see for instance R. Guha (1963), Bose (1993), and Ray (1979).

3 We define *commercialization* in a narrower sense than the literature by focusing on trade in distant markets. The literature sometimes regards this as production for the market, not just for long-distance trade.

4 We focus on acreage for which the data are considered more reliable. See Blyn (1962) for details on acreage and productivity in this period by region.

5 That said, the composition of irrigated crops remained relatively stable with food crops, rice, and wheat primarily, accounting for 80 per cent of total irrigated acreage compared to 15 per cent for non-food crops.

6 We direct the interested reader to the editorial introductions and essays collected in the following volumes to learn more about this literature: Ludden (1994); Bhattacharya et al (1991); Robb, Sugihara and Yanagisawa (1996); Robb (1996); and Raj et al. (1985). Connected readings on capital and credit, institutions, agricultural labour, and agricultural production statistics can be found in Bose (1994); Stein (1992); Prakash (1992); and S. Guha (1992). For two detailed and recent surveys, see Roy (2012) and Tomlinson (2013).

7 Food crops could also be commercial crops, for example wheat. This suggests a higher proportion of acreage under commercial crops.

8 Unfortunately, the Statistical Abstracts of British India do not report acreage irrigated by tanks, wells, and other sources disaggregated by public and private funding.

9 Another type of classification was major works with capital and revenue accounts, minor works with revenue accounts, and minor works with no revenue accounts. See Great Britain, East India (irrigation) (1904) for more details.

10 The Famine Fund was financed from general revenues, so effectively, the irrigation works in this category also were financed from revenue as opposed to loans. The allocation of expenditures within the Famine Fund varied from year to year between famine relief, protective railways, protective irrigation works, and programmes to reduce debt. Yet irrigation never accounted for a large share of the budget. For example, protective irrigation works averaged 5 per cent of the Famine Relief and Insurance Fund between 1893–1894 and 1903–1904 (calculations based on Statistical Abstracts, India 1905).

11 Bogart and Chaudhary show that net returns as a per cent of capital outlay never exceeded 10 per cent for railways (Chapter 9 in this volume). But many canals in Punjab generated net returns in excess of 15 per cent (Paustian 1930).

12 Discussing the period up to 1907, Klein (1984) argues persuasively that while 'modernization' (e.g. improvements in transportation) increased the capacity of the state to counter famines, ideological changes lagged this process: Malthusian and Social Darwinist concerns, not to mention budgetary worries, inhibited effective governmental intervention. A more financially liberal response to famines, including a greater willingness to offer 'gratuitous relief', emerged in parallel with the growth of liberalism in Britain.

13 See Sen's discussion of the Irish Famine of 1848 and the Wollo Famine in Ethiopia in 1973 (Sen 1999, p. 172).

14 Most authors also agree on the importance of the war: food would not be imported into Bengal because it was needed for the war effort. The fear of a Japanese invasion had also led to the impounding of boats, which prevented the movement of rice from surplus to deficit regions (Goswami 1990, p. 449).

15 Using 1961 as the base year of 100, per capita food grain production was usually higher than 100 in the period 1893–1894 to 1945–1946 (it was 99 from 1936–1937 to 1945–1946). In independent India, the figures could decrease to 79 and 80 in 1966 and 1967 without famines occurring (Drèze 1995, p. 92).

16 The interested reader might follow up the sources cited by Roy (2012, p. 322).

References

Agnihotri, I. (1996). 'Ecology, Land Use and Colonization: The Canal Colonies of Punjab', *Indian Economic and Social History Review, 33 (1)*, pp. 37–58.

Ali, I. (1987). 'Malign Growth? Agricultural Colonialism and the Roots of Backwardness in Punjab', *Past and Present, 114 (1)*, pp. 110–132.

Bagchi, A. (1983). *The Political Economy of Underdevelopment*, Cambridge: Cambridge University Press.

Banerjee, A., and L. Iyer (2005). 'History, Institutions, and Economic Performance: The Legacy of Colonial Land Tenure Systems in India', *American Economic Review, 95 (4)*, pp. 1190–1213.

Bardhan, P. (1984). *The Political Economy of Development in India*, Delhi: Oxford University Press.

Bhaduri, A. (1973). 'A Study in Agricultural Backwardness Under Semi-Feudalism', *Economic Journal, 83 (329)*, pp. 120–137.

Bhattacharya, S., S. Guha, R. Mahadevan, S. Padhi, and G. N. Rao, eds. (1991). *The South Indian Economy: Agrarian Change, Industrial Structure, and State Policy, c.1914–1947*, Delhi: Oxford University Press.

Blyn, G. (1962). *Agricultural Trends in India, 1891–1947: Output, Availability, and Productivity*, Philadelphia: University of Pennsylvania Press.

Bose, S. (1993). *Peasant Labour and Colonial Capital: Rural Bengal Since 1770*, Cambridge: Cambridge University Press.

———, ed. (1994). *Credit, Markets and the Agrarian Economy*, Delhi: Oxford University Press.

Burgess, R., and D. Donaldson (2010). 'Can Openness Mitigate the Effects of Weather Shocks? Evidence From India's Famine Era', *American Economic Review, 100 (2)*, pp. 449–453.

Chandra, B. (1968). 'Reinterpretation of Nineteenth Century Indian Economic History', *Indian Economic and Social History Review, 5 (1)*, pp. 35–75.

Darling, M. (1928). *Punjab Peasant in Prosperity and Debt*, London: Oxford University Press.

Drèze, J. (1995). 'Famine Prevention in India', in J. Drèze, A. Sen, and A. Hussain, eds., *The Political Economy of Hunger: Selected Essays*, Oxford: Clarendon Press.

Goswami, O. (1990). 'The Bengal Famine of 1943: Re-Examining the Data', *Indian Economic and Social History Review, 27 (4)*, pp. 445–463.

Great Britain, East India (irrigation) (1904). *Report of the Indian irrigation commission, 1901 1903. Part I.—General*, Parliament, House of Commons.

Great Britain (1932). *Statement Exhibiting the Moral and Material Progress and Condition of India During the Year 1931–32*, London: His Majesty's Stationery Office.

Guha, R. (1963). *A Rule for Property in Bengal: An Essay on the Idea of the Permanent Settlement*, Paris: Moulton and Co.

Guha, S. (1985). *The Agrarian Economy of the Bombay–Deccan 1818–1941*, Delhi: Oxford University Press.

———, ed. (1992). *Growth, Stagnation or Decline? Agricultural Productivity in British India*, Delhi: Oxford University Press.

Hurd, J.M. II (1984). 'Railways', in D. Kumar and M. Desai, eds., *The Cambridge Economic History of India: Vol. II, c.1757–c.1970*, New Delhi: Orient Longman, pp. 737–761.

India (1905). *Statistical Abstract Relating to British India From 1894–95 to 1903–04*, London: Her Majesty's Stationary Office.

Islam, S. (1979). *The Permanent Settlement in Bengal: A Study of Its Operation 1790–1819*, Dacca: Bangla Academy.

Klein, I. (1984). 'When the Rains Failed: Famine, Relief, and Mortality in British India', *Indian Economic and Social History Review, 21 (2)*, pp. 185–214.

Kumar, D. (1965). *Land and Caste in South India: Agricultural Labour in the Madras Presidency in the Nineteenth Century*, New York: Cambridge University Press.

————. (1983). 'The Fiscal System', in D. Kumar and M. Desai, eds., *The Cambridge Economic History of India: Vol. II*, New Delhi: Orient Longman, pp. 905–944.

Kurosaki, T. (1999). 'Agriculture in India and Pakistan 1900-1995', *Economic and Political Weekly, 34 (52, December, 25–31)*, pp. 160–168.

Ludden, D. (1988). 'Agrarian Commercialism in Eighteenth Century South India: Evidence From the 1823 Tirunelveli Census', *Indian Economic and Social History Review, 25 (4)*, pp. 493–519.

————, ed. (1994). *Agricultural Production and Indian History*, Delhi: Oxford University Press.

Marshall, P.J. (1987). *The New Cambridge Economic History of India: Vol. 2*, Cambridge: Cambridge University Press.

McAlpin, M. (1983). *Subject to Famine: Food Crises and Economic Change in Western India, 1860–1920*, Princeton, NJ: Princeton University Press.

North, D. (1990). *Institutions, Institutional Change, and Economic Development*, Cambridge: Cambridge University Press.

O'Grada, C. (2008). 'The Ripple That Drowns? Twentieth-Century Famines in China and India as Economic History', *The Economic History Review, 61 (S1)*, pp. 5–37.

Paustian, P. W. (1930). *Canal Irrigation in the Punjab; An Economic Inquiry Relating to Certain Aspects of the Development of Canal Irrigation By the British in the Punjab*, New York: Columbia University Press.

Prakash, G. (1992). *The World of the Rural Labourer in Colonial India*, Delhi: Oxford University Press.

Raj, K. N., N. Bhattacharya, S. Guha, and S. Padhi, eds. (1985). *Essays on the Commercialization of Indian agriculture*, Delhi: Oxford University Press.

Ray, D. (1998). *Development Economics*, Princeton, NJ: Princeton University Press.

Ray, R. (1979). *Change in Bengal Agrarian Society, c. 1760–1870*, Delhi: Manohar.

Robb, P., ed. (1996). *Meanings of Agriculture*, Delhi: Oxford University Press.

Robb, P., K. Sugihara, and H. Yanagisawa, eds. (1996). *Local Agrarian Societies in Colonial India*, Richmond, UK: Curzon Press.

Roberts, B. (1985). 'Structural Change in Indian Agriculture: Land and Labour in Bellary District, 1890–1980', *Indian Economic and Social History Review, 22 (4)*, pp. 281–306.

Roy, T. (2007). 'A Delayed Revolution: Environment and Agrarian Change in India', *Oxford Review of Economic Policy, 23 (2)*, pp. 239–250.

————. (2012). *The Economic History of India 1857–1947*, 3rd ed., Delhi: Oxford University Press.

Sen, A. (1977). 'Starvation and Exchange Entitlements: A General Approach and Its Application to the Great Bengal Famine', *Cambridge Journal of Economics, 1 (1)*, pp. 33–59.

————. (1999). *Development as Freedom*, New York: Alfred A. Knopf.

Stein, B., ed. (1992). *The Making of Agrarian Policy in British India, 1770–1900*, Delhi: Oxford University Press.

Stone, I. (1984). *Canal Irrigation in British India: Perspectives on Technological Change in a Peasant Economy*, Cambridge: Cambridge University Press.

Sweeney, S. (2011). *Financing India's Imperial Railway, 1875–1914*, London: Pickering & Chatto.

Tauger, M. (2003). 'Entitlement, Shortage, and the 1943 Bengal Famine: Another Look', *Journal of Peasant Studies, 31 (1)*, pp. 45–72.

Tomlinson, B. R. (2013). *The Economy of Modern India*, 2nd ed., Cambridge: Cambridge University Press.

Vaidyanathan, A. (1983). 'The Indian Economy Since Independence (1947–70)', in D. Kumar and M. Desai, eds., *The Cambridge Economic History of India: Vol. II*, New Delhi: Orient Longman, pp. 949–990.

Whitcombe, E. (1972). *Agrarian Conditions in Northern India, Vol. 1: The United Provinces Under British rule 1860–1900*, Berkeley: University of California Press.

8

THE LONG-RUN CONSEQUENCES OF COLONIAL INSTITUTIONS

Lakshmi Iyer

India is a land of disparities. Economic and human development outcomes vary considerably across the regions of India. In 2004, annual per capita incomes ranged from 32,000 rupees in the state of Haryana to 6,000 rupees in the state of Bihar. The 1991 census recorded 95 per cent of villages in Kerala as having a primary school, but only 39 per cent of villages in Bihar had one. Similarly, the percentage of villages supplied with paved roads varies across districts from 10 to 100 per cent. These differences persist despite explicit commitments by the Indian state to equalize access to infrastructure.

These large and persistent disparities mirror the large disparities observed across countries. In 2004, GDP per capita varied from $40,000 in the United States to $780 in Niger. The differences were equally large two decades ago, suggesting a lack of convergence in economic outcomes.[1] Over the past two decades, a substantial body of research has linked such persistent disparities to the long-run effects of historical institutions, often instituted by colonial powers.[2]

This chapter explores the historical roots of India's regional inequalities. Which colonial institutions are likely to be important in explaining the wide variation in development outcomes in post-colonial India? Ferguson (2002) identifies several distinctive features that the British Empire tended to disseminate, which set it apart from other colonial powers. His list includes English forms of land tenure, the English language, Scottish and English banking, the common law, Protestantism, team sports, the limited state, representative assemblies, and the idea of liberty. This chapter focuses on two important ones: land tenure institutions (which determine the distribution of economic wealth) and the degree of accountability of administrators (which representative assemblies might help to establish).

Both these factors are related to substantial bodies of empirical work over the past decade. In the cross-country literature, the work of Engerman and Sokoloff (2001; 2005) has generated a substantial literature tracing out the long-run effects of an unequal distribution of wealth. Acemoglu, Johnson and Robinson (2001) document the persistence of colonial institutions, which limit the power of the executive and protect private property, and their long-run effects on economic development. This has also generated a large stream of empirical research on historical institutions.

In the case of India, historical land inequality plays a substantial role in determining economic and human development outcomes several decades after the end of the colonial rule. Places with landlord-based land tenure systems, which had higher inequality in the distribution of assets during the colonial period, are less likely to adopt new agricultural technologies and to invest in public goods like education and health facilities. As a consequence, these places have lower agricultural yields, lower levels of literacy and higher levels of infant mortality.

India provides an excellent venue for comparing the long-run consequences of direct versus indirect colonial rule, which generate very different incentives for ruler accountability. Of course, comparisons of places with different types of colonial rule are likely to yield biased results because there might be many characteristics that make an area more likely to be administered directly by a colonial power (such as a location on the coast, or the production of particularly desirable commodities), and these characteristics might also determine long-term outcomes for the area, irrespective of what kind of colonial rule was imposed. This problem of disentangling correlation from causation is a common one, faced by most cross-sectional empirical studies. The next section reviews the strategies used by some cross-country studies to avoid such biased inferences. In the case of India, specific historical episodes can be used to control for such selectivity of colonial rule. For instance, Governor-General Lord Dalhousie's 'Doctrine of Lapse' annexed Native States where the ruler died without a natural-born heir, which provides a plausibly exogenous determinant of direct colonial rule. Neither Dalhousie's predecessors nor his successors followed such a policy, which enables us to check whether such deaths would change long-term outcomes in the absence of direct colonial rule.

The nature of indirect colonial rule meant that Indian rulers were liable to be deposed by the British if their states were badly misgoverned; no such penalty was incumbent on colonial administrators in directly ruled areas. After controlling for the selectivity of British colonial rule, I find that areas under indirect colonial rule have substantially better provision of public goods and better human development outcomes in the long term, a finding consistent with the results from other colonial settings. Post-colonial policies of equal access to public goods help to erase some of these differences, but they are still apparent more than three decades after the end of colonial rule.

The chapter begins by briefly reviewing the persistence of investments made in colonial times, and the cross-country literature on the long-run effects of specific colonial institutions. The next section conducts an in-depth analysis of historical land tenure systems in India. The following section compares outcomes across areas under direct and indirect colonial rule in India, after controlling for the highly selective nature of the British annexation policy. The chapter closes with a summary of the conclusions.

Long-run effects of colonial institutions: cross-country evidence

How much do historical circumstances affect later economic outcomes? One obvious channel of influence is the physical persistence of historical investments. Huillery (2009) conducts a regional study of West African countries and finds that areas where the French colonial administrators built more schools, health centres and roads in the early twentieth century continue to have better health and education outcomes at the end of the millennium. These investments are correlated according to their nature. In other words, places that had more schools or more teachers in 1925 have better education outcomes in 1995, places with more health facilities in 1925 have better health outcomes and so on. She is unable to distinguish whether this reflects simple long-term persistence of such facilities, or whether the presence of such facilities reflects the quality of local institutions, which then persist until the present day.

The clearest illustration of persistence in India is through the presence of railways: the current railway map of India (Figure 8.1A) is remarkably close to the railway map of India in the colonial period (Figure 8.1B). The British laid the foundations of India's rail network, and India had the fourth largest railway network in the world by 1870. In fact, the only major line to be built in the post-independence period is the Konkan Railway, which extends all the way down the west coast. Donaldson (2010) shows that the establishment of the railway network led to significant reductions in regional price differentials during the colonial period and a 16 per cent increase in real incomes for districts with access to the rail network. Other types of development outcomes can also be highly persistent. For instance, Kerala continues to be the state with the highest literacy rate in India, reflecting at least in part the policies put in place by the enlightened rulers of Travancore and Cochin in the nineteenth and early twentieth centuries, such as building schools in every district.

While the importance of institutions for economic development has been recognized for a long time (see North and Thomas 1973), a substantial empirical literature over the past few years has focused on institutions put in place by colonial powers. One reason for focusing on former colonies is the assumption that the institutions put in place by colonial powers are somewhat independent of the exact characteristics of the colonies themselves. The colonial experience can thus be used to construct causal estimates of the effects of institutions. I will describe briefly some of the key institutions highlighted by the cross-country literature, which are likely to be relevant in explaining the variation in development outcomes across the regions of India.

The seminal work of Engerman and Sokoloff (2001; 2005) drew attention to the fact that colonial rule often brought institutions such as forced labour or slavery, and extreme inequalities in the distribution of economic and political power. Examining the paths of development of colonies in North and South America, they document the fact that countries that were more suitable for large-scale plantation agriculture were more likely to have institutions of forced labour and slavery, and also to have worse outcomes in the post-colonial period. Interestingly, these were also the places that had the best economic outcomes in the early colonial period.

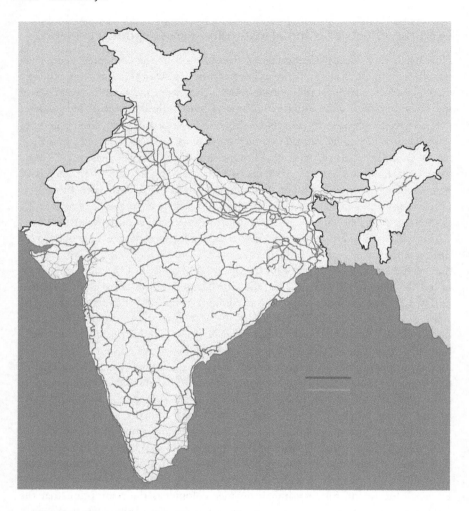

FIGURE 8.1A India railway map 2009

Source: http://commons.wikimedia.org/wiki/File:Indianrailways-gauges-blank.png and the author.

Barbados and Cuba for example were among the richest colonies in the sixteenth century, when sugar was a highly valuable commodity.

The work of Engerman and Sokoloff has generated a substantial literature, both on extending the results to a within-country context, and on testing specific mechanisms through which initial inequalities might affect subsequent development. The results have been mixed. Several studies have confirmed the original hypothesis that places with coercive labour institutions have lower levels of development in the long run. Bruhn and Gallego (2012) use regional data from Latin American colonies to find that places that were suitable for plantation crops (and therefore more likely to use slave labour) are worse off today. They also find evidence for lower political representation of such areas. Nunn (2008b) compares states and counties

FIGURE 8.1B India railway map 1909

Source: http://commons.wikimedia.org/wiki/File:Indianrailways-gauges-blank.png and the author.

within the United States and also finds that areas that had greater slave use have poorer economic development outcomes in the long run. But the intervening channel does not appear to be economic inequality. Acemoglu, Bautista, Querubin and Robinson (2008), in their study of the region of Cundinamarca in Colombia, find that initial *political* inequality is much more predictive of later economic outcomes than initial economic inequality.

A related set of papers has considered the effects of slavery on the originating communities (i.e. places from which slaves or forced labourers were taken). Nunn (2008a) finds that communities in Africa that exported a greater number of slaves have significantly worse economic outcomes in the post-colonial period. These effects are attributed to the poorer quality of institutions in places where slavery was more rampant, and to lower levels of trust in communities more exposed to the slave trade (Nunn and Wantchekon 2011). Dell (2010) finds a similar result for the long-run effects of the *mita*, a Spanish colonial system of forced labour in Bolivia and Peru. Areas that were more exposed to the *mita* have significantly lower levels of public-goods provision and worse development outcomes in the post-colonial period. In the case of India, the long-run consequences of slavery or bonded labour have not been studied systematically (see Fukazawa 1991 for some estimates of the number of slaves in India during the colonial period).

A second stream of literature on historical institutions focuses on the protection of private property, which requires certain limits on the executive power of the state and incentives for good governance. Several papers have documented a strong relationship between measures of good governance and economic growth (see, among others, Knack and Keefer 1995; Mauro 1995; Hall and Jones 1999). Acemoglu et al. (2001) made a significant advance on this literature by using the colonial experience to convincingly identify the effects of property right institutions on income per capita. Better property rights are associated with higher levels of per capita GDP in 2000, but what determines the quality of property rights institutions? Acemoglu et al. (2001) hypothesize that colonial powers were more likely to establish 'good' institutions (i.e. those that protect private property more effectively) in their colonies if they expected to settle there in large numbers. They then use data on the initial mortality rates of early settlers as a proxy for the likelihood of colonial settlement. This settler mortality is found to be highly correlated with initial quality of institutions (such as constraints on the executive) and with measures of property rights protection in 2000.

While institutions appear to be highly persistent, the introduction of new institutions by colonial powers often results in a reversal of fortune compared to the pre-colonial levels of development. In a follow-up paper, Acemoglu, Johnson and Robinson (2002) show that places that were highly developed before the introduction of colonial rule (as proxied by urbanization or population density) are less developed later. Such a reversal does not occur in countries that never became colonies. They attribute this to the fact that colonial powers were more likely to implement extractive institutions in initially richer or densely populated places, leaving them unable to fully utilize the new opportunities provided by the Industrial Revolution in the nineteenth century. In a similar vein, Nunn and Puga (2012) find that places in Africa that were protected from the slave trade due to natural barriers such as rugged terrain are likely to do better in the long run, despite their original geographic disadvantage.

Some recent papers have documented the highly persistent effects of initial governance quality. Most of these studies find that 'indirect' colonial rule, under which native rulers retain a substantial degree of autonomy, results in better long-run outcomes. Bertocchi and Canova (2002) compare colonies across Africa and find that post-independence economic performance is better in colonies that were 'dependencies' and had a greater degree of autonomy in the colonial period. But these dependencies are all British colonies, so it is not clear whether the effect they capture is in fact a 'British colonial rule' effect. Lange (2004) obtained historical court records from thirty-three former British colonies and computed the

fraction of cases presided over by a local chief as a measure of pre-colonial autonomy. This measure is highly correlated with measures of institutional quality and
good governance.

Gennaioli and Rainer (2007) constructed measures of pre-colonial state
centralization in different African countries as a proxy for local autonomy and
accountability of local rulers. They find that this measure of pre-colonial local
accountability is highly correlated with better provision of public goods such as
health, education and infrastructure. The effects of these institutions are greatest in
the immediate post-independence period and become more muted in the 1970s
as post-colonial states develop. In a similar vein, Berger (2009) studied different
regions of Nigeria in detail, and finds that places that developed greater bureaucratic capabilities during the colonial period continue to be better governed in the
post-colonial period, and they do a better job of providing public goods such as
immunization.

It is interesting to note that the strong cross-country relationship between property rights protection and income per capita (documented by Acemoglu et al. 2001)
does not fit the Indian case very well. For instance, we can see that India's level of per
capita GDP is far below the level predicted for its institutional quality (Figure 8.2).

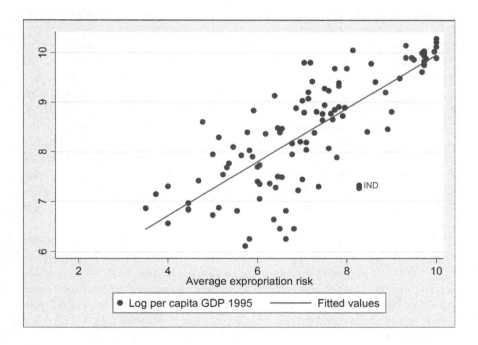

FIGURE 8.2 Property rights protection and income per capita (cross-country relationship)

Notes: Average expropriation risk is an index of protection against expropriation obtained from Political
Risk Services. The index ranges from 0 to 10, with 0 corresponding to the lowest degree of protection
and 10 to the highest.

One possible reason for this seeming anomaly is that important institutions, such as land tenure systems, varied considerably across different parts of British India, generating different degrees of initial economic inequality. Further, nearly a quarter of the population of India was under the rule of native rulers and therefore experienced only an indirect version of colonial rule. As we shall see, such variation in institutional quality did have an impact on long-run development outcomes across the regions of India.

Initial land inequality in India: the impact of land tenure systems

We use the terms *land revenue systems* or *land tenure systems* to refer to the arrangements the British colonial administration made to collect the land revenue from cultivators of the land. Up to a first approximation, all cultivable land in British India fell under one of three alternative systems: landlord-based systems (also known as *zamindari* or *malguzari*), individual cultivator-based systems (*raiyatwari*) and village-based systems (*mahalwari*). In landlord-based systems, the British delegated revenue collection authority to landlords with authority over large areas. In village-based systems, the revenue collection was delegated to village bodies consisting of several people. In individual cultivator systems, the British collected land revenue directly from the cultivator. The map in Figure 8.3 illustrates the geographic distribution of these systems.

As one might expect, places with landlord-based land tenure systems had a substantially higher degree of inequality in the distribution of land during colonial times. Similar to the work of Engerman and Sokoloff (2001), we find that comparing areas with different land tenure systems shows an interesting reversal of fortune. As an illustration, let us compare the district of Madura in Madras Presidency, which was under landlord-based (*zamindari*) land tenure, with the district of Tanjore, which was under the cultivator-based (*raiyatwari*) system. In 1901, Madura had higher rice yields than Tanjore. Indeed, it is usually the case that only highly fertile areas could support a hierarchy of claimants on the soil and thereby facilitate a landlord-based system. By 1982, though both districts had made substantial gains in productivity, the relative ranking was reversed and Tanjore had higher rice yields (see Figure 8.4).

We see a similar reversal when we look across the districts of Uttar Pradesh. Figure 8.5A shows that wheat yields were lower in districts where a larger proportion of land was not under the control of landlords. This 'non-landlord proportion' is computed by Banerjee and Iyer (2005), using data from district level settlement reports compiled by British administrators in the 1870s. Again, we see that this pattern is not persistent: by 1987, landlord-based areas (areas with a lower value for non-landlord proportion) are lagging behind in terms of wheat yields.

Why do landlord areas lag behind non-landlord areas? Banerjee and Iyer (2005) consider several possible explanations. They show that this cannot be attributed to geographic differences: landlord areas on average are more fertile, have higher rainfall and, as shown earlier, actually were more productive in colonial times. It is also

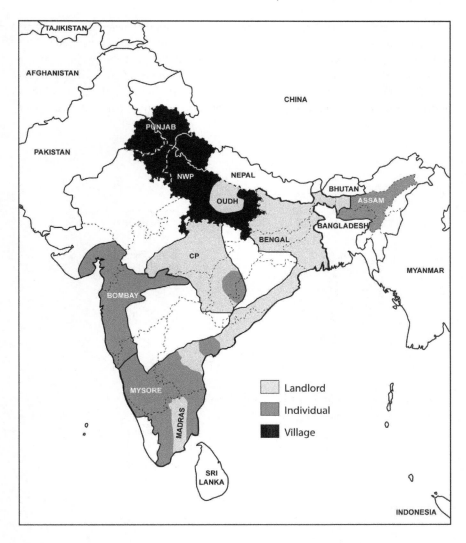

FIGURE 8.3 Geographic distribution of colonial land tenure systems in India
Source: Banerjee and Iyer (2005).

not the case that the British systematically implemented landlord-based systems in areas with slower growth potential, which would confound any inference we tried to draw from this comparison. Banerjee and Iyer (2005) document the substantial role played by ideology and historical events in the establishment of these systems. In particular, areas conquered by the British after 1820 were particularly likely to have non-landlord systems due to changing ideology in England and the establishment of important policy changing precedents in Madras Presidency and the North-Western Provinces. There was a subsequent reversal of policy to favour landlords after the 1857 mutiny. Therefore, being conquered between 1820 and 1856 is a relatively exogenous determinant of the probability of getting a non-landlord tenure system. Using this exogenous source of institutional variation also yields the result that non-landlord systems do better in the post-colonial period. A final check is to examine the outcomes for neighbouring districts, which

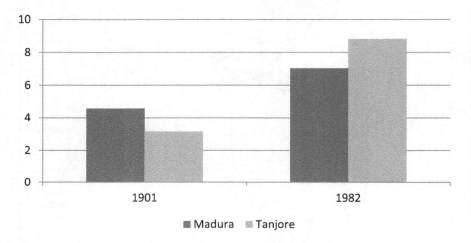

FIGURE 8.4 Rice yields (tons per hectare) in Madura and Tanjore
Source: Data on rice yields from Yanagisawa (1996).

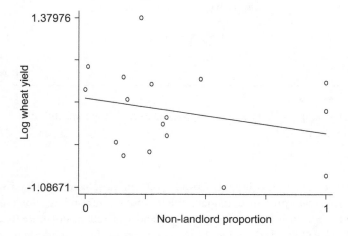

FIGURE 8.5A Wheat yields across Uttar Pradesh districts in the 1870s
Source: Banerjee and Iyer (2005).

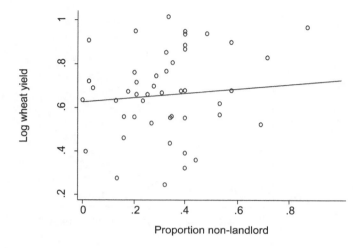

FIGURE 8.5B Wheat yields across Uttar Pradesh districts in 1987
Source: Banerjee and Iyer (2005).

we might expect to be very similar in terms of geographical, demographic and cultural characteristics, but were nevertheless subject to different land tenure systems (see map in Figure 8.3). Restricting the comparison to such neighbouring districts also yields the result that landlord areas perform worse than non-landlord areas in the post-colonial period.

One interesting observation is that the gap between landlord and non-landlord areas widens during the late 1960s, especially in agricultural investments such as irrigation and fertilizer usage (Figure 8.6). This was the time when the new agricultural technologies of the Green Revolution were entering India, primarily in the form of high-yielding varieties of seeds, which needed these additional investments to be really effective. Indeed, Banerjee and Iyer (2005) find that landlord areas were much slower to adopt these new technologies. The slower adoption of high-yielding varieties, and the complementary investments in irrigation and fertilizer usage, is enough to explain the yield differential between landlord and non-landlord areas.[3]

This raises the interesting question why the landlord areas were slower to adopt the new technology. One possible explanation is that the policy priorities were very different in the two types of areas. States that had a greater proportion of land under landlord tenure devoted greater efforts to the passage of land reform legislation, passing six pieces of land reform legislation on average between 1957–1992 compared to an average of three for non-landlord states. More importantly, they

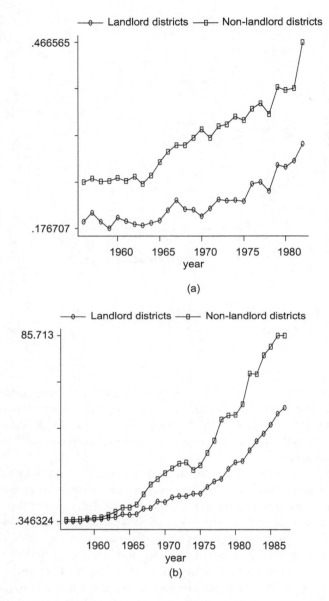

FIGURE 8.6 Non-landlord areas invest more in irrigation and fertilizer after 1965

Source: Banerjee and Iyer (2005).

also spent considerably less on development expenditure, averaging 29 rupees per person per year 1966–1992 compared to 49 rupees for non-landlord states. This suggests that these states were devoting more attention to the demands for land reform at the cost of adopting productivity-enhancing technology.

This difference in development spending also shows up in other outcomes, such as the provision of public goods. We see striking differences in public goods provision between landlord-based areas and areas with individual cultivator systems. For instance, only 77 per cent of villages in landlord areas were provided with primary schools in 1991, compared to 91 per cent of villages in individual cultivator areas (Table 8.1). The differences in other public goods are even bigger: in landlord-based areas, only 8 per cent of villages had high schools, 31 per cent had paved roads, and 3 per cent had a primary health centre. In contrast, 22 per cent of villages in the individual cultivator areas had access to a high school, 58 per cent had paved roads, and 9 per cent had a primary health centre.

The difference in access to public goods has significant consequences for human development outcomes. In particular, we see that literacy rates are significantly lower in *zamindari* areas as late as 1991, which is more than three decades after the end of colonial rule. Further, because the differences in development spending arise in the post-colonial period, we see that the development gaps between these areas do not narrow over time. Literacy rates in *raiyatwari* districts were 38 per cent higher in 1961 (29 compared to 21 per cent), and remained 37 per cent higher in 1991 (55 compared to 40 per cent). A similarly large differential is observed in infant mortality rates in 1991.

Another important fact is that this historical variable explains a substantial fraction of the variation in access to public goods across the districts of India. For instance, a sizeable 27 per cent of the variation in access to primary schools is explained simply by the historical fact of having had a *raiyatwari* land tenure system rather than a *zamindari* one. This variable accounts for 22 per cent, 28 per cent and 12 per cent of the variation in access to high school, paved roads and primary health centres respectively. Historical land tenure also accounts for a quarter of the variation in literacy rates and a fifth of the variation in infant mortality rates across *zamindari* and *raiyatwari* areas.[4]

TABLE 8.1 Historical land tenure, access to public goods and human development outcomes

	Zamindari areas	Raiyatwari areas	Variation explained by historical land tenure
Access to public goods (fraction of villages with access in 1991)			
Primary school	0.77	0.91	27%
High school	0.08	0.22	22%
Primary health centre	0.03	0.09	12%
Paved roads	0.31	0.58	28%
Human development outcomes			
1991 literacy rate (%)	40	55	25%
1961 literacy rate (%)	21	29	20%
1991 infant mortality rate (number of deaths per 1,000 live births)	94	65	24%

Sources: Census of India, census village directories, Banerjee and Iyer (2005).

Banerjee and Iyer (2005) show that these relationships are robust to the inclusion of the village-based (*mahalwari*) areas, to the introduction of geographic controls, and can be mostly explained by the differences in development spending per capita. Banerjee, Iyer and Somanathan (2005) examine the same relationship for a much wider range of goods, and find that landlord-based areas lag behind in almost all types of public infrastructure: education and medical facilities, transport infrastructure, water and electricity provision.

An important related question in this regard is whether political institutions function differently in landlord areas. Engerman and Sokoloff (2005) suggest that unequal areas invest less in education because the elites in these areas feared that such investments might end up undermining their authority. They demonstrate that areas with higher inequality extended suffrage to a smaller proportion of their population and that the extension of the franchise to larger sections of society came later in these places. Thus, historical patterns of inequality continue to affect long-term outcomes by changing the nature of the political system and the pattern of democratization.

In the case of India, the land tenure systems do not exist in their original form in the post-colonial period. Landlord-based systems have been formally abolished and there are almost no taxes on agricultural income. A series of land reforms has also significantly reduced land inequality in those areas. It is, however, possible that those who are still the elites retain power by restricting access to the political system or by capturing the democratic process. Banerjee and Iyer (2009) find that non-landlord areas have slightly higher electoral participation rates than landlord areas; however, the differences in public goods provision cannot be explained by the differences in electoral participation. In terms of electoral competition, landlord areas look very similar to non-landlord areas using measures such as the number of people contesting the election or average vote margins. The difference thus is not in explicit measures of political participation, but in the policy choices made by elected governments.

Historical governance arrangements in India: direct versus indirect colonial rule

In the case of India, about 45 per cent of the total area of British India (excluding Burma and Sind) and 23 per cent of the population was not under direct British colonial rule. They were ruled by Indian kings, who had considerable autonomy over most internal matters, including administration and revenue collection systems, land tenure, legal codes, currency, education policy and health initiatives.[5] These places were called *Native States* or *Princely States* by the British (only England could officially have a king).

The map in Figure 8.7 shows the geographical distribution of Native States. We see that Native States were present in all parts of India, with somewhat higher concentrations in the western and central parts of the country. Native States varied considerably in size: some consisted of only a few villages, while the largest Native State, Hyderabad, had an area of 98,000 square miles. The majority of rulers were Hindu rulers, though there were several Muslim and Sikh rulers as well.

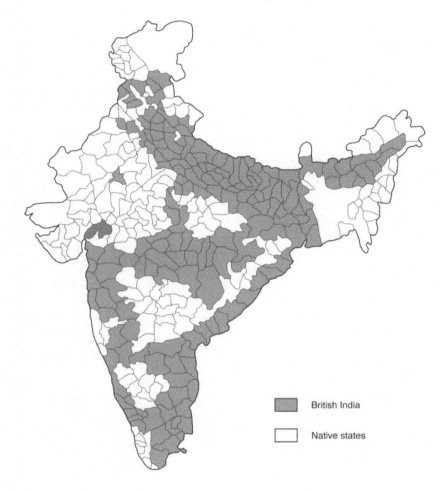

FIGURE 8.7 Geographical distribution of Native States in India
Source: Iyer (2010).

These native rulers had all accepted the 'paramountcy' of British power in the subcontinent, and most of them had signed explicit treaties with the British. In practice, this meant that the foreign and defence policies of these states were controlled by the British: Native States could not declare war and peace or even communicate with other states without British permission, and they were limited in the size of the armies they could maintain. Most Native States also had tribute obligations to the British.

Why did these Native States exist in the first place (i.e. why did the British not annex the whole of India into the British Empire)? Obviously, the British chose to focus their attention on more attractive areas first (such as those with high agricultural potential or rulers who would be easy to defeat militarily). Over the period

1757–1857, the British East India Company annexed many areas of the Indian subcontinent. The usual means of annexation was by means of conquest, but many areas were also annexed for non-payment of treaty dues, or on the basis of preventing misrule by native rulers. Lord Dalhousie, Governor-General from 1848–1856, also annexed several Native States when their native rulers died without a naturally born son. This was in contrast to the practices of earlier Governors-General, who usually recognized adoptions by Indian rulers.

In 1857, Indian soldiers in the British army mutinied against their officers. After some initial losses, the British rallied and were able to suppress the mutiny by the end of 1858. Many Native States aided the British during the mutiny by supplying troops and equipment or by defending the Europeans within their territory. Conversely, several erstwhile rulers of recently annexed states had been at the forefront of opposing the British during the mutiny. After this major shock to British power, the administration of India was taken over by the British Crown from the East India Company in 1858. Plans of further annexation were given up, with the Queen's proclamation of 1858 stating specifically, 'We desire no extension of our present territorial possessions'.[6] Thus, the areas that had not been annexed until 1858 continued to be Native States until the end of British rule in 1947.

Although the British gave up outright annexation of territory, they reserved the right to intervene in the internal affairs of Native States 'to set right such serious abuses in a Native Government as may threaten any part of the country with anarchy or disturbance'.[7] They exercised this right in several Native States, often by deposing the ruler and installing another in his place (usually a son, brother, cousin or adopted heir) or by appointing a British administrator or council of regency for some time before allowing the ruler to take up ruling powers again. Different viceroys used this power to intervene in different degrees. One of the most vigorous in this regard was Lord Curzon, viceroy 1899–1905, during whose tenure fifteen rulers were either forced to abdicate or were temporarily deprived of their powers (Ashton 1982).

When the British left India in 1947, all Native States signed treaties of accession to the newly independent nations of India or Pakistan. By 1950, all of the Native States within the borders of India had been integrated into independent India and were subject to the same administrative, legal and political systems as those of the erstwhile British Indian areas. The rulers of these states were no longer sovereign rulers, but many of them continued to play an active role in the politics of post-colonial India. They were granted annual incomes, referred to as *privy purses*, by the Indian government as partial compensation for their loss of state revenue, but this privilege, along with all other princely honours, was discontinued in 1971.

Does having a history of indirect colonial rule, as opposed to direct colonial rule, make a difference to post-colonial outcomes? Using data from the census of 1991, I compare the extent of public goods provision in the two types of areas by computing the fraction of villages in each district having access to schools, medical facilities and paved roads. A simple comparison indicates that the areas under direct and indirect colonial rule look very similar using these measures (Table 8.2).

TABLE 8.2 Indirect colonial rule, public goods and development outcomes

	British India	Native States
1991 fraction of villages having		
Primary school	0.78	0.82
Middle school	0.25	0.30
Primary health sub-centre	0.10	0.09
Paved roads	0.47	0.45
Human development outcomes		
Literacy rate 1991 (%)	42.5	39.6
Infant mortality 1991	80	80

Sources: Census of India, census village directories, Iyer (2010).

However, we should note that the comparison does not account for the fact that the British decided to annex only certain areas. A look at the map in Figure 8.7 reveals a strong preference for places with better agricultural potential: the desert areas of Rajasthan and the forested areas of central India were not annexed, while almost all areas of the fertile Gangetic plains were. So the comparison in Table 8.2 confounds the long-run effects of direct British rule (if any) with the effects of the specific area characteristics that made annexation attractive.

To disentangle these two effects, I use the fact that Lord Dalhousie's Doctrine of Lapse proposed to annex states in which native rulers died without a natural heir. Therefore, if a Native State was unlucky enough to suffer this circumstance *during Lord Dalhousie's tenure* (1848–1856), it had a high probability of being annexed. In eight Native States, the ruler died without an heir in 1848–1856: four of these were annexed (Satara, Jhansi, Nagpur and Sambalpur). Of the sixty-five states where such a death did not occur, only three were annexed in the same period. Since other Governors-General recognized adopted heirs and did not follow this policy, the Doctrine of Lapse constitutes a purely circumstantial means of being subjected to direct colonial rule, *independent of the characteristics of the local area.* This means that comparing states that experienced 'lapse' (death of a ruler without a natural heir in 1848–1856) to those that did not will give us a causal estimate of the impact of direct British rule. Of course, this entails restricting our sample of districts to those that were not already annexed by 1848. This is one example of an 'instrumental variables' strategy that uses such uncorrelated variation in the explanatory variable to compute causal effects of specific changes (see Box 8.1 for details).

BOX 8.1 INSTRUMENTAL VARIABLES

Many comparative studies examine the relationship between institutional quality and future outcomes. Figure 8.2 shows a strong relationship between the extent of property rights protection and income per capita. But this leaves open the question of causality: perhaps countries that have better property rights are inherently different in some way from those that have poor property rights. For instance, they may have systematically different geographic characteristics, or have systematic differences in other institutional variables as well. One way to overcome these concerns is to control statistically for *all* the other things that might matter, which can be difficult.

Another solution is to find instances where the adoption of a specific institution was determined by specific historical circumstances, uncorrelated with other factors that might determine income levels in the present day. Acemoglu et al. (2001) use *initial settler mortality* as one such instrumental variable, on the grounds that it satisfies the two requirements of a good instrument. First, they show that this is indeed a significant determinant of current institutional quality because colonial powers instituted better protections for property rights in places where initial settler mortality was lower. Second, this variable does not affect present-day outcomes through channels other than historical institutional quality (the 'exclusion' restriction), since the authors are able to control directly for the current prevalence of specific diseases such as malaria. Angrist and Pischke (2009) provide further details on instrumental variables.

When I perform this comparison, we see that areas where 'lapse' happened (and that therefore went on to have direct colonial rule) have significantly worse access to public goods outcomes as late as 1991. We see this particularly for middle schools and paved roads, as well as for infant mortality. In Iyer (2010), I show that these differences are statistically significant, and continue to hold even after controlling for geographic characteristics of the areas.[8]

Can we be sure that these differences are purely because of direct colonial rule, and not because of other circumstances that are typical of 'lapsed' areas? Perhaps areas where rulers were more likely to die childless are particularly unhealthy areas or have royal families with weak health. A particularly useful way to assess such potential confounding factors is to use the fact that the Doctrine of Lapse (and indeed all annexations) was stopped in 1858. So if rulers died without heirs after this date, the states would not get annexed. When I compare areas where rulers died without heirs in 1858–1884 with other Native States, we do not see any large differences in access to middle schools, health facilities or roads – thus lending greater credibility to the argument that it is actually the institution of direct colonial rule that makes these areas lag behind (Table 8.4).

Do these differences in access to public goods and development outcomes diminish over time, or are they magnified by post-colonial policies? We should note that the Indian state had explicit policies of equalizing access to public goods. For instance, the Minimum Needs Program of the 1970s envisioned a norm of having a primary school and safe water within a mile of every village, paved roads to

TABLE 8.3 The Doctrine of Lapse, public goods and human development outcomes

	Lapse happened	Lapse did not happen
1991 fraction of villages having		
Primary school	0.81	0.81
Middle school	0.21	0.29
Primary health sub-centre	0.04	0.10
Paved roads	0.29	0.45
Human development outcomes		
Literacy rate 1991 (%)	41.0	39.5
Infant mortality 1991	106	82

Sources: Census of India, census village directories, Iyer (2010).

TABLE 8.4 What if 'lapse' did not lead to direct colonial rule?

	Ruler died without heir in 1858–1884	Ruler did not die without heir in 1858–1884
1991 fraction of villages having		
Primary school	0.76	0.84
Middle school	0.28	0.31
Primary health sub-centre	0.06	0.10
Paved roads	0.43	0.45

Sources: Census of India, census village directories, Iyer (2010).

villages with populations over 1,000 and electricity to at least 40 per cent of villages in every state (Banerjee and Somanathan 2007). Indeed, we see that post-colonial policies have been successful in erasing the differences between Native State and British Empire areas. Table 8.5 shows that the differences in access to public goods between direct and indirect rule areas was greater (in percentage terms) in the 1960s than in the 1990s. We also see a significant difference in access to primary schools (39 per cent of villages in directly ruled areas had access compared to 46 per cent in indirectly ruled areas), which did not exist any longer in 1991 (Tables 8.2 and 8.3). Similarly, we see a literacy advantage in indirectly ruled areas in the 1911 Census, which disappeared by the 1961 Census. Post-colonial policies in this case have been able to gradually erase the impact of history, though the effects can be discerned more than three decades after the end of colonial rule.

Which aspect of indirect rule leads to these areas having a long-run advantage? Iyer (2010) finds that Native States where the ruler had been deposed for misrule by the British tend to have public goods outcomes similar to directly ruled British areas. In other words, areas that were poorly governed in colonial times tend to have worse public service delivery in post-colonial times as well. This is consistent with the fact that British administrators typically had much shorter tenures than native Indian rulers (the average tenure for a Native State ruler was twenty years, while British administrators held a given post for only about a year) and that they did not

TABLE 8.5 Indirect colonial rule, public goods and development outcomes in earlier periods

	Lapse happened	Lapse did not happen
1961 fraction of villages having		
Primary school	0.39	0.46
Middle school	0.04	0.09
Dispensary	0.02	0.08
Paved roads	0.11	0.18
1961 literacy rates (%)	19.7	20.2
1911 literacy rates (%)	2.8	5.8

Sources: Census of India, census village directories, Iyer (2010).

face any significant penalty for delivering poor outcomes (Indian rulers could be deposed while British administrators were at best transferred to different areas). In this sense, it may be unfortunate that independent India has opted for the British system of administration, with most policy implementation under the control of career bureaucrats with very short tenures in specific posts.[9] Other explanations, such as different levels of taxation, political participation or land tenure systems, are unable to explain the gap between directly and indirectly ruled areas.

Conclusions

A large literature has examined the long-run effects of colonial institutions on economic outcomes. I show that the Indian case fits cross-country patterns in several respects: initial inequality in the wealth distribution leads to poorer long-run outcomes and places with initially better governance appear to derive long-run advantages. Institutions and incentive structures put in place during the colonial period are able to explain a significant fraction of the high variation in economic and human development outcomes across regions of independent India.

The detailed study of India contributes to the larger literature on historical institutions in three ways. First, the historical record provides exogenous policy changes, by means of which we are able to obtain causal estimates of the long-run effects of historical institutions. This is not always feasible in cross-country comparisons. Comparison of different areas of the same country also has the advantages of limiting the range of potential omitted variables, and of comparing areas that have similar political and administrative arrangements in the post-colonial period. Second, the results suggest that some hypotheses proposed in the cross-country literature are not generalizable to all areas. For instance, the result that places with greater initial inequality have different patterns of political participation (as found by Engerman and Sokoloff 2005 for American colonies) does not appear to be true in India. Finally, the Indian case study highlights the fact that historical and modern factors interact in complex ways, and that current policy choices can exacerbate or diminish historical differences.

Many aspects of India's historical institutions remain to be explored in a systematic empirical way. The nature of credit and labour markets, the impact of internal and external trade barriers, and the role of different social and cultural norms are specific topics of considerable interest. While there has been some recent work related to these topics (see Donaldson 2010 and Chaudhary 2009), much more remains to be done. Finally, a detailed exploration of how historical institutions evolve over time, and the factors related to their persistence or change, would add greatly to our understanding of India's economic history.

Notes

1 The lack of unconditional convergence across countries is documented in Lopez and Serven (2009), while Caselli, Esquivel and Lefort (1996) find some evidence of conditional convergence. Ghani, Iyer and Mishra (2010) find no evidence of income convergence across the regions of South Asia.
2 This is not meant to be a comprehensive review of the literature on historical institutions and their long-run effects. See Nunn (2009) for a survey of the effects of history on development.
3 These computations are based on data from the India Agriculture and Climate Data Set, available for download from http://ipl.econ.duke.edu/dthomas/dev_data/datafiles/ WB_India_Agric_Data.zip. Documentation for these data are available at http://ipl.econ. duke.edu/dthomas/dev_data/datafiles/india_agric_climate.htm. The data for Banerjee and Iyer (2005) can be obtained at http://www.aeaweb.org/aer/data/sept05_data_banerjee.zip.
4 I obtain these figures by comparing the R-squared across regressions with and without the land tenure variable.
5 Over time, some states adopted the legal codes and currency prevailing in British India. The British usually did not force them to do so but waited instead for native princes to cooperate with them.
6 'Proclamation by the Queen in Council to the Princes, Chiefs and People of India', published by the Governor-General at Allahabad, November 1, 1858. Full text available at http://www.csas.ed.ac.uk/mutiny/confpapers/Queen'sProclamation.pdf.
7 Lord Canning, Government of India Foreign Department Despatch No. 43A to S/S, April 30, 1860.
8 See Iyer (2010) for a series of other robustness checks for the results in Table 8.3, including propensity score matching, adjusting standard errors through resampling, and including state fixed effects. The results are also robust to the exclusion of specific Native States known for their progressive policies, such as Mysore or Travancore.
9 See Iyer and Mani (2012) for an analysis of bureaucrats' career progression and relationship with politicians in post-colonial India.

References

Acemoglu, D., S. Johnson, and J. Robinson (2001). 'The Colonial Origins of Comparative Development: An Empirical Investigation', *American Economic Review*, *91 (5)*, pp. 1369–1401.
———. (2002). 'Reversal of Fortune: Geography and Institutions in the Making of the Modern World Income Distribution', *Quarterly Journal of Economics*, *117 (4)*, pp. 1231–1294.

Acemoglu, D., M.A. Bautista, P. Querubin, and J. Robinson (2008). 'Economic and Political Inequality in Development: the Case of Cundinamarca, Colombia', in E. Helpman, ed., *Institutions and Economic Performance*, Cambridge: Harvard University Press.

Angrist, J., and J.-S. Pischke (2009). *Mostly Harmless Econometrics: An Empiricist's Companion*, Princeton: Princeton University Press.

Ashton, S.R. (1982). *British Policy Towards the Indian States, 1905–1939*, London: Curzon Press.

Banerjee, A., and L. Iyer, (2005). 'History, Institutions and Economic Performance: The Legacy of Colonial Land Tenure Systems in India', *American Economic Review, 95 (4)*, pp. 1190–1213.

———. (2009). 'Colonial Land Tenure, Electoral Competition and Public Goods in India', in J. Diamond and J. Robinson, eds., *Natural Experiments in History*, Cambridge, MA: Harvard University Press.

Banerjee, A., L. Iyer, and R. Somanathan (2005). 'History, Social Divisions and Public Goods in Rural India', *Journal of the European Economic Association, 3 (2–3)*, pp. 639–647.

Banerjee, A., and R. Somanathan (2007). 'The Political Economy of Public Goods: Some Evidence from India', *Journal of Development Economics, 82 (2)*, pp. 287–314.

Berger, D. (2009). 'Taxes, Institutions and Local Governance: Evidence from a Natural Experiment in Colonial Nigeria'. Working Paper, New York University.

Bertocchi, G., and F. Canova (2002). 'Did Colonization Matter for Growth? An Empirical Exploration into the Historical Causes of Africa's Underdevelopment', *European Economic Review, 46 (10)*, pp. 1851–1871.

Bruhn, M., and F. Gallego (2012). 'Good, Bad, and Ugly Colonial Activities: Do They Matter for Economic Development?' *Review of Economics and Statistics, 94 (2)*, pp. 433–461.

Caselli, F., G. Esquivel, and F. Lefort (1996). 'Reopening the Convergence Debate: A New Look at Cross-Country Growth Empirics', *Journal of Economic Growth, 1 (3)*, pp. 363–389.

Chaudhary, L. (2009). 'Determinants of Primary Schooling in British India', *Journal of Economic History, 69 (1)*, pp. 269–302.

Dell, M. (2010). 'The Persistent Effects of Peru's Mining Mita', *Econometrica, 78 (6)*, pp. 1863–1903.

Donaldson, D. (2010). 'Railroads of the Raj: Estimating the Impact of Transportation Infrastructure', Working Paper, Massachusetts Institute of Technology.

Engerman, S.L., and K.L. Sokoloff (2001). 'The Evolution of Suffrage Institutions in the New World,' NBER Working Paper no. 8512.

———. (2005). 'Colonialism, Inequality and Long-Run Paths of Development', NBER Working Paper no. 11057.

Ferguson, N. (2002). *Empire: The Rise and Demise of the British World Order and the Lessons for Global Power*, New York: Basic Books.

Fukazawa, H. (1991). *The Medieval Deccan: Peasants, Social Systems and States, Sixteenth to Eighteenth Centuries*, Delhi, New York: Oxford University Press.

Gennaioli, N., and I. Rainer (2007). 'The Modern Impact of Pre-colonial Centralization in Africa', *Journal of Economic Growth, 12 (3)*, pp. 185–234.

Ghani, E., L. Iyer, and S. Mishra (2010). 'Are Lagging Regions Catching Up with Leading Regions?' in E. Ghani, ed., *The Poor Half Billion in South Asia*, Oxford: Oxford University Press.

Hall, R., and C. Jones (1999). 'Why Do Some Countries Produce So Much More Output Per Worker Than Others?' *Quarterly Journal of Economics, 114 (1)*, pp. 83–116.

Huillery, E. (2009). 'History Matters: The Long Term Impact of Colonial Public Investments in French West Africa', *American Economic Journal – Applied Economics, 1 (2)*, pp. 176–215.

Iyer, L. (2010). 'Direct versus Indirect Colonial Rule in India: Long-term Consequences', *Review of Economics and Statistics 92 (4)*, pp. 693–713.

Iyer, L., and A. Mani (2012). 'Traveling Agents: Political Change and Bureaucratic Turnover in India', *Review of Economics and Statistics, 94 (3)*, pp. 723–739.

Knack, S., and P. Keefer (1995). 'Institutions And Economic Performance: Cross-Country Tests using Alternative Institutional Measures', *Economics and Politics, 7 (3)*, pp. 207–227.

Lange, M. (2004). 'British Colonial Legacies and Political Development', *World Development 32 (6)*, pp. 905–922.

Lopez, H., and L. Serven (2009). 'Too Poor to Grow', World Bank Policy Research Working Paper 5012.

Mauro, P. (1995). 'Corruption and Growth', *Quarterly Journal of Economics, 110 (3)*, pp. 681–712.

North, D. C., and R. P. Thomas (1973). *The Rise of the Western World: A New Economic History*, Cambridge: Cambridge University Press.

Nunn, N. (2008a). 'The Long Term Effects of Africa's Slave Trades', *Quarterly Journal of Economics, 123 (1)*, pp. 139–176.

———. (2008b). 'Slavery, Inequality, and Economic Development in the Americas: An Examination of the Engerman-Sokoloff Hypothesis', in E. Helpman, ed., *Institutions and Economic Performance*, Cambridge: Harvard University Press, pp. 148–180.

———. (2009). 'The Importance of History for Economic Development', *Annual Review of Economics, 1 (1)*, pp. 65–92.

Nunn, N., and D. Puga (2012). 'Ruggedness: The Blessing of Bad Geography in Africa', *Review of Economics and Statistics, 94 (1)*, pp. 20–36.

Nunn, N., and L. Wantchekon (2011). 'The Slave Trade and the Origins of Mistrust in Africa', *American Economic Review, 101 (7)*, pp. 3221–3252.

Yanagisawa, H. (1996). *A Century of Change: Caste and Irrigated Lands in Tamil Nadu 1860s–1870s*, Delhi: Manohar.

9

RAILWAYS IN COLONIAL INDIA

An economic achievement?

Dan Bogart and Latika Chaudhary

Railways were the biggest infrastructure investment of the British Raj, and they were interconnected with many aspects of the Indian economy. This chapter reviews the organization of railways, describes the major trends in performance, assesses the effect of regulation and ownership on railway performance, and discusses the impact of railways on the economy.

Both economists and historians have long been interested in Indian railways (see Hurd and Kerr 2012; Kerr 2007 for reviews). One strand of the literature has focused on colonial policy and in particular the role of dividend guarantees to private British companies that built the main network. A key policy shift occurred from the 1880s to the 1900s when the Government of India (GOI) took a majority ownership stake in the main trunk line railways and began financing new railway construction. This transition led to changes in railway performance and operations that were generally beneficial to the Indian economy. In fact, the overall productivity growth of Indian railways was high up until the First World War and far exceeded the productivity growth in other sectors (Bogart and Chaudhary 2012; 2013). But other accounts are more critical, arguing for example that the GOI subsidized the construction of many wasteful lines (see Sweeney 2011 for a recent view of this argument). The literature generally paints a nuanced picture of colonial policy with many questions still unanswered.

Another strand of the literature has studied the effect of railways on market integration, famines and national income. Despite disagreement on the precise mechanisms, the evidence overwhelmingly suggests that Indian railways increased market integration and raised incomes (see Donaldson 2012 for example). Railways also appear to have ameliorated the effects of famines despite nationalist arguments to the contrary. But an important puzzle still remains: why did railways fail to generate economic growth and development?

Organization

The initial impetus for railway construction in India came from British mercantile firms with trading interests in India (Thorner 1955). Since existing transportation was poor, British firms hoped railways would lower transport costs, allowing easier access to raw cotton from India while opening Indian markets to British manufactured goods.

The first passenger line measuring twenty miles opened in 1853 connecting the port of Bombay to Thana. Figures 9.1 to 9.3 illustrate the spread of the network from 1870 to 1930. While the four major ports were well connected to the interior, there were few interior-to-interior connections. Moreover, less developed parts of the country, like the southeast, had few lines even as late as 1930. The GOI determined route placement and commercial viability appears to have dictated routes up until the 1870s. However, military and famine concerns influenced the construction of lines after the 1870s.

The trunk lines connecting the ports to the interior were constructed on the standard gauge of 5 feet 6 inches, wider than the standard 4 feet 8 inches employed in the United States and Britain. The British engineering community favoured the broad gauge because they believed it would lower the cost of operating high volume railways (Puffert 2009). However, opinions changed by the 1870s and cheaper metre gauge systems (3 feet 3¾ inches) were constructed. By 1900, the metre gauge lines comprised 41 per cent of the network compared to 56 per cent on the standard gauge. In yet another break of gauge, small branch lines were constructed on narrow gauges (i.e. less than 3 feet) in the twentieth century.

As seen in Figure 9.4, which graphs total route miles from 1854 to 1940, the network grew rapidly in the 1880s and 1890s with mileage increasing from 9,308 in 1880 to 24,752 in 1900. However, the rapid pace of development slowed in the twentieth century.[1] Although India had the fourth largest rail network in the world by the early 1900s, the scale was not as impressive after accounting for population. For example, Brazil's rail network had six times as many miles per person as India by 1910 and Russia had almost three times the rail miles per capita.[2]

The construction and management of colonial railways involved private British companies, the GOI and Indian Princely States. In the first phase up to 1869, private British companies constructed and managed the trunk lines under a public guarantee. In the second phase, the GOI began constructing and managing railways in the 1870s. The third phase, beginning in the early 1880s, involved hybrid public-private partnerships between the GOI as majority owner of the line and private companies. Finally in the fourth phase, the GOI began taking over railway operations in 1924.

Private companies incorporated in Britain constructed the trunk lines. They were organized as joint-stock companies set up via contracts with the Secretary of State for India seated in London. The contracts were enforced and administered by the GOI. More than 90 per cent of the shareholders were British and most of the

FIGURE 9.1 Map of railways in 1870

Source: Digitized from Great Britian (1871). Report to the Secretary of State for India in council on railways in India, for the year 1870–71. London: Her Majesty's Stationery Office.

capital was raised through equity. The companies hired an 'agent' resident in India, who acted as a liaison to the board of directors in London. The agent hired subcontractors to carry out the construction (Kerr 1995).

These early contracts shared many features. The GOI determined route and gauge. They also had the authority to supervise construction and subsequent operations. Companies received free land from the GOI and a 5 per cent guarantee on the capital at a fixed exchange rate of 1s.10d. to the rupee. The contracts were valid for ninety-nine years. While the company could hand over the railways to the GOI at any time, the GOI could only purchase the company at twenty-five or fifty years from the date of the original contract.

The guarantee was perhaps the most important feature of the contracts. If net earnings (i.e. gross earnings minus working expenses) as a proportion of capital

FIGURE 9.2 Map of railways in 1909

Source: Digitized from Great Britian (1909). Administration Report on the Railways in India for the calendar year 1909 (East India: Railways). London: Her Majesty's Stationery Office.

outlay yielded less than the guaranteed return of 5 per cent in any year, the GOI compensated the company the difference up to 5 per cent. Such guarantee payments were treated as debt. When annual net earnings exceeded the guaranteed level, the company was required to repay any past guarantee payments by transferring half of their surplus profits over 5 per cent to the GOI. After past guarantee payments were paid off, the company received the entire surplus profits (Bell 1894).

The guarantees proved to be costly. Construction costs on the early lines exceeded expectations at almost £20,000 per mile compared to initial estimates of £12,000. These lines were also unprofitable for many decades (i.e. they earned less than 5 per cent) because traffic developed slowly. Hence, the GOI was forced to honour the 5 per cent guarantee to shareholders and had made interest payments

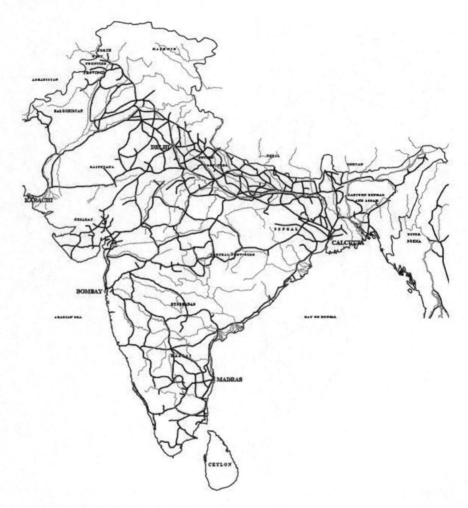

FIGURE 9.3 Map of railways in 1931

Source: Digitized from Government of India (1932). Report by the railway board on indian railways for 1930–31. Calcutta: Government of India Central Publication Branch.

of almost £30 million by 1869 (Hurd 1983). In addition, the GOI incurred losses on account of the fixed exchange rate set in the contracts. In the 1860s and 1870s, the rupee was worth no more than 1s.8d., while the contract rate for guarantee payments was 1s.10d. to the rupee.

Guarantees were not the only form of public intervention. According to the contracts, a GOI representative, appointed by the Secretary of State, sat on company boards. In principle he had the authority to veto any decision. The GOI also appointed a consulting engineer to approve construction and operational work. While strong in theory, GOI representatives found it difficult to implement their preferred policies, at least in the early decades of railway construction (Thorner

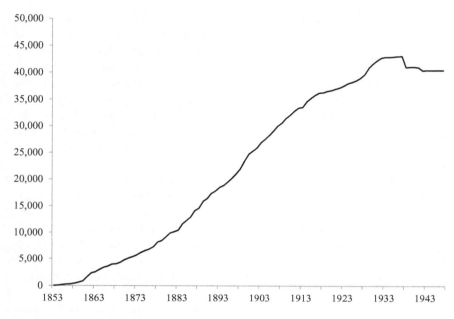

FIGURE 9.4 Total route miles, 1854–1947

Source: Government of India (1955).

1955). Part of this was due to early inexperience among GOI representatives and part was due to the subordinate authority of the GOI to the Secretary of State. Both these constraints eased over time and the situation turned in favour of the GOI by the early 1900s.

Worried about paying interest guarantees into the indefinite future, the GOI turned against private provision in the 1860s, ushering in a phase of public ownership in the 1870s (second phase). The GOI constructed and operated railway lines using borrowed capital. No new major contracts were signed with private companies. Private companies continued to own and operate trunk lines, while the GOI now owned and operated what might be termed *secondary lines*. Notably, many GOI railways opted for the metre gauge instead of the standard gauge because of their lower construction costs.

However, the GOI construction of railways was short-lived. The 1870s economic depression coupled with the war in Afghanistan increased the GOI's fiscal burden, turning the tide against state provision. Severe famines in 1877 further hurt its cause. The subsequent Famine Commission recommended a rapid extension of railways, which the GOI was unable to achieve because of its annual constraints on borrowing. Advocates of private provision capitalized on the GOI's economic woes and won their battle in 1879 when the Secretary of State called for an end to the era of GOI owned and operated railways.

In the third phase between 1880 and 1924, the GOI assumed greater ownership of railways. Among the former guaranteed companies, the East Indian was the first whose contract reached its twenty-fifth anniversary in 1879. A new public-private partnership replaced the old contract. The GOI purchased four-fifths of the shares in the East Indian, and a reconstituted private company controlling the remaining one-fifth of the shares managed operations under a new contract for a minimum term of twenty-five years. Any profits would be split between the GOI and the reconstituted company in proportion to their respective capital shares. The purchase price was based on the mean market value of the company's stock in the preceding three years and payments were made in the form of annuities (Bell 1894, pp. 66–72). The guarantee was retained on the remaining capital stock of the East Indian railway company, but it was lowered to 4 per cent.

The GOI negotiated similar contracts and purchased all the original private companies constituted in the 1850s and 1860s. Upon taking ownership, the GOI undertook mergers of several lines operating in the same region. In all but three cases, the GOI chose to outsource the operations to private companies. However, the GOI chose to operate three railways directly via the colonial Public Works Department.[3] Profits in these cases were paid into the treasury and annual appropriations from the GOI budget provided the capital. Guarantees were completely eliminated on these railways.

Beginning in the 1880s, most new railways were also organized as GOI owned and privately operated. But, there was more variation in their contractual terms. One company for example, the Bengal Central, received free land and a 5 per cent guarantee for five years, while another, the Rohilkhand and Kumaon Railway, received a 4 per cent guarantee during the construction phase and an annual subsidy of Rs. 40,000 for ten years after construction.[4] Under these schemes, the GOI generally owned a majority of the capital while the companies constructed the lines and managed subsequent operations. In exchange, the companies shared net profits with the GOI in proportion to their respective capital shares. Companies raised the necessary capital, which was guaranteed at lower rates and often for shorter periods.

As the GOI became the majority owner of railways, new changes were introduced in operations and management. The GOI began to organize regular railway conferences and introduced a code of general rules for the working of all railways (Bell 1894, p. 114). Railways were separated from Public Works in 1905 and placed under the direct authority of a newly constituted Railway Board. The board set future policy, including extensions of the network and construction of new lines, and it managed operations on existing lines. An important goal of this re-organization was 'the improvement of railway management with regard both to economy and public convenience' (House of Commons 1906, p. 132).

By the 1920s, Indians grew increasingly dissatisfied with private British operations of railways owned by the GOI. They were unhappy about the quality of third-class passenger facilities, the treatment of third-class passengers (the most important category of passenger revenues) and the under-representation of Indians in upper management positions. As the operations contract of the East Indian came up for renewal, the GOI set up a committee to assess the relative advantages and disadvantages of state versus private management of railways.

While the committee was unanimous in recommending increases and improve-ments to railway finances, it did not reach an agreement on the appropriate orga-nization of management. Half the members recommended a complete transfer of railway management to the GOI and the other half recommended transferring the management of the East Indian to Indian-domiciled private companies. The GOI opted for the former strategy and in 1925 the management of the East Indian was transferred to the GOI. Over the next two decades, the GOI took over operations from all the privately operated railway lines as their contracts came up for renewal. The nationalization of Indian railways was complete by it's independence.

Performance of Indian railways

British authorities collected a wealth of data on Indian railways, which was published in annual reports from 1859 to 1947.[5] We use series compiled by the Government of India (1955), Hurd (2007), and Bogart and Chaudhary (2013) to review broad trends.

Trends in inputs and outputs

The annual reports give figures on capital outlay for all Indian railways. We plot this series per mile adjusted to 1873 prices in Figure 9.5.[6] The relatively high capital per mile of the 1860s suggests private companies receiving guarantees were not overly concerned with construction costs as one would expect. But the wider standard gauge and technically sophisticated bridges constructed during the 1860s and 1870s also contributed to higher costs. As the GOI became the majority owner, there was a trend towards lower capital outlays in the late nineteenth and early twentieth century. It would appear that the incentives to keep construction costs low were higher under GOI ownership.

The reported series is likely to underestimate the growth of the capital stock because it does not account for a change in prices. Wages and the price of railway capital imports were lower in nominal terms in the 1850s and 1860s when the first trunk lines were built. In Bogart and Chaudhary (2013), we calculate the capital stock for major railways from 1860–1912 using a real investment series and find that nominal capital outlay is understated in the 1860s.

Turning to labour inputs, Figure 9.6 documents the trends in railway employ-ment relative to mileage.[7] The large decline in relative employment in the 1860s is due to the expansion of the trunk lines. Employment increased in the 1870s rela-tive to mileage before declining in the 1880s and 1890s. The second decline can be explained by the GOI takeover of the guaranteed companies in this period. In Bogart and Chaudhary (2012), we show the shift to GOI ownership reduced labour inputs relative to capital. The reduction in labour intensity is one of the surprising effects of state ownership in India. Labour per mile increased again in the 1900s and 1910s before another stark reduction in the late 1920s. Most of the 1920s decline was due to cuts in labour rather than an increase in route mileage. While total employ-ment fluctuated, the proportion of non-Indians (largely Europeans) continuously

FIGURE 9.5 Capital per mile (1873 rupees) 1861–1941

Source: Government of India (1955).

declined, falling to just over 2 per cent in 1939 after peaking at 8 per cent in 1869. Despite the decline, Europeans occupied most of the upper-management positions. This was extremely unpopular in India for obvious reasons. In response, the GOI finally began to hire and promote more Indians in the 1920s (Kerr 2007).

The third key input, fuel, is not reported in any of the published series compiled by historians. Although fuel is reported in official publications, it is a challenging series because fuel inputs changed from the 1860s to the 1910s. Initially, British coal and Indian wood were the main fuel sources. However, the Indian coal industry expanded over time and by the First World War Indian coal had supplanted British coal as the primary fuel source. We have constructed a quality-adjusted fuel consumption series for most railways between 1874 and 1912 (Bogart and Chaudhary 2013), which shows a substantial growth in fuel especially in the 1900s. For example, the East Indian's fuel consumption increased by a factor of four or at an average annual growth rate of 3.7 per cent. Fuel consumption also grew relative to labour inputs. Between 1874 and 1912, the ratio of fuel consumption to employment grew by 1.15 per cent per year. The more intensive use of coal fuel might have implications for the Indian climate, although the effects have not been studied thus far.

Similar to inputs, outputs grew tremendously on Indian railways. The standard measure of output for freight traffic is the *ton mile* and similarly the *passenger mile* for passenger traffic. Hurd's (2007) series for 1884–1939 indicates that freight output increased by a factor of 9.6 and passenger output by a factor of 6.5. The average

FIGURE 9.6 Labour per 1,000 miles

Sources: Morris and Dudley (1975) for labour and Government of India (1955) for miles.

annual growth rate was 4.2 and 3.5 per cent respectively. Freight and passenger traffic grew at the same rate until the 1930s when freight traffic began to exceed passenger traffic. However, the proportion of passenger and freight revenues remained constant, with freight revenues averaging 66 per cent of total revenues between 1884 and 1939 (Hurd 2007).

When outputs grow faster than inputs, productivity must increase. This was indeed the case for Indian railways, at least before the 1920s. Passenger and freight output grew by 3.5 and 4.2 per cent annually respectively between 1881 and 1939. By comparison, route miles and employment increased by approximately 2.5 per cent per year over the same period. Figure 9.7 shows the trends in freight and passenger output divided by route miles. Output per mile more than doubled from the early 1880s to the 1920s and fluctuated around the same level for twenty-five years after that. The trends are similar for output per worker. Ton miles or passenger miles per unit of fuel consumption grew less. Between 1874 and 1912, each measure increased by only 1 per cent per year (Bogart and Chaudhary 2013).

Based on these series, Indian railways experienced high labour and capital productivity growth from the 1880s to the 1910s, but lower fuel productivity growth. A composite productivity measure is known as *total factor productivity*, or TFP. A definition of TFP is given in Box 9.1. Many studies in economics estimate TFP growth because it provides a key metric of economic performance. In Bogart and Chaudhary (2013) we estimate TFP for the pre-1913 period and find a healthy growth rate

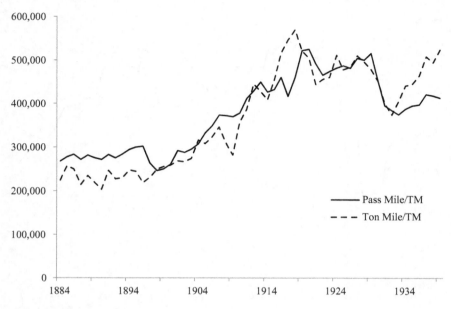

FIGURE 9.7 Passenger and freight traffic

Source: Figure taken from Hurd (2007).

of 2.3 per cent per year. This is in stark contrast to the rest of the Indian economy such as agriculture, which saw close to no productivity growth in the late nineteenth and early twentieth century. India's TFP growth rate in railways also exceeded that of Britain in the nineteenth century. Even more remarkable is that only a small part of the TFP growth was due to capacity utilization, such as running trains more frequently. It seems that Indian railways successfully adopted new technologies.

BOX 9.1 TFP GROWTH

Consider a production process where output is produced using labour and capital. Total factor productivity (TFP) also affects output by augmenting labour and capital. More formally, let *Y* represent output and *L, K* and *A* represent labour, capital and productivity respectively.

A standard formulation of the production process is defined by $Y = AK^{\alpha}L^{1-\alpha}$.

Taking logs and differentiating with respect to time yields an expression $\Delta Y = \Delta TFP + \alpha * \Delta K + (1-\alpha) * \Delta L$.

Rearranging terms gives $\Delta TFP = \Delta Y - \alpha * \Delta K - (1-\alpha) * \Delta L$.

The term α can be estimated using econometrics. It is sometimes assumed to equal the share of labour payments in total costs. TFP growth can be calculated with estimates of labour, capital and output growth.

Less is known about the causes of the productivity slowdown after the First World War. The collapse of world trade in the 1920s is probably the most immediate explanation. The productivity of railway tracks closely aligns with demand, which dropped substantially as international markets got into trouble. More research is needed on the interwar period to get a complete picture of the performance of colonial Indian railways.

Trends in fares, revenues and profits

We examine the trends in fares using Hurd's (2007) series on real average revenue per ton mile and real average revenue per passenger mile from 1884 to 1939. Average revenue per unit provides a reasonable proxy for prices, with the caveat that fares and freight charges often differ by time of purchase and commodity. Thus, there is no single market price even for the same trip.

As seen in Figure 9.8, which plots the average revenue per ton mile and passenger mile, the decline in rates is remarkable. Freight charges in 1919 are 21 per cent of their level in 1884. Fares in 1919 are 43 per cent of their level in 1884 – but this trend reversed after 1919. Freight charges and fares rose, and by 1939 they had returned to 1900 levels. The trends in productivity are similar to those for fares and freight charges. Railways could charge lower prices and still earn decent profits because their productivity was rising.

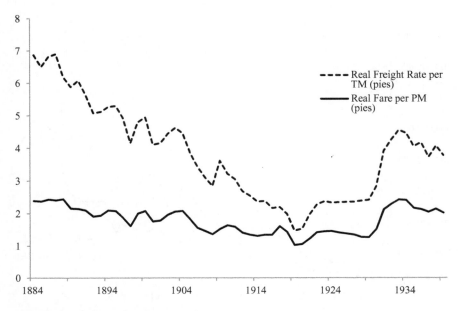

FIGURE 9.8 Real passenger and freight rates

Source: Hurd (2007).

The fall in railway fares and freight charges prior to 1919 decreased international and interregional trade costs, leading to higher exports and domestic trade. While the literature has emphasized the gains achieved by the eve of the First World War, less attention has been paid to the reversal in freight charges and fares by 1930, and the implications for Indian economic development.

Profits were arguably the most important economic indicator for railway investors and the colonial treasury. Profits are the difference between gross earnings and working expenses. The latter measure the operational costs of railways, including the wage bill for train staff and station staff; spending on fuel; spending on maintenance of the track, plant and equipment; and traffic and administration expenses. Figure 9.9 plots real working expenses and gross earnings (expressed in 1873 rupees). It is clear that the value of railway services grew rapidly, as did the cost of providing railway services. Revenues increased by a factor of 128 over the eighty-year period, implying an annual average growth rate of 6.2 per cent. The revenue figures can be used to assess the value of railways services to the Indian economy. In 1901 railway revenues were approximately 2.6 per cent of national income using Sivasubramonian's (1997) estimates. By 1919, they represented 3.2 per cent of national income, and by 1939, revenues accounted for 4.9 per cent of income.

Revenues peaked in years with good harvests and sharply declined in bad years, such as the decline in 1908. Earnings also decreased following the end of the First World War. That combined with the steep rise in working expenses on account

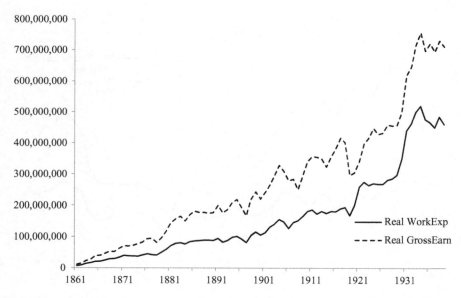

FIGURE 9.9 Working expenses and gross earnings (Rs.)

Source: Government of India (1955).

of long-overdue repairs and renewals, caused a sharp decline in net earnings after 1921. Prior to the 1920s, the difference between revenues and working expenses was growing and railways were enjoying high profits. Net earnings peaked towards the end of the First World War at 7–8 per cent and dropped thereafter to 4–5 per cent. Railways initially did not pay large returns to investors and the GOI, but eventually they yielded a good return. In fact, one might argue that the profits were too large and reflect some monopoly pricing.

Government ownership, policy and performance

Colonial railways underwent various organizational changes over the course of their history. They began under private ownership with public guarantees. Then, in the late nineteenth century, the GOI purchased a majority ownership stake in the original private railways. The private sector was not eliminated, however, as companies continued to operate railways, albeit with lower guarantees. After the 1920s, the GOI assumed control over operations as well. How did these ownership changes influence performance?

The guarantees have been heavily criticized by researchers (Sanyal 1930; Thorner 1955; Hurd 1983; Derbyshire 2007; Sweeney 2011) and by GOI administrators (such as Lord Lawrence in the 1860s). According to their critics, guarantees were responsible for the high construction costs of the 1860s, agency problems within companies, the poor performance of the initial lines, the related interest costs imposed on the GOI (and, hence, Indian tax payers) and the inability of railways to transform the traditional agricultural economy into a modern industrial one. In this view, guarantees were yet another example of colonial policy stifling Indian economic development at the expense of British interests.

Guarantees clearly weakened private incentives to improve efficiency, but critics often overlook that such schemes may have also allowed for the construction of the first Indian railways. Infrastructure investments – be it in roads, gas, electricity or railways – are notoriously difficult to administer, contract and regulate, especially in developing economies (Laffont 2005; Estache and Wren-Lewis 2009). Unlike rich countries with well-developed domestic capital markets, developing economies have to borrow money on international capital markets or attract foreign capital. Such capital is not forthcoming without an implicit subsidy or guarantee, which serves as insurance for risk-averse private providers because of demand uncertainty (see for example Engel, Fischer, and Galetovic 2013). Though necessary, such guarantees and related government inducements may weaken incentives to decrease costs. Thus, governments have to strike the right balance between attracting private capital and minimizing moral hazard by private firms.

The experience of Indian railways highlights the problem. Rich countries like Britain raised domestic capital to finance railways, but Indian capital markets were too weak to raise money for such a large infrastructure project. Colonial India had two options: the GOI (or the East India Company in the early 1850s) could directly borrow money on international capital markets or the GOI had to attract foreign direct investment, which required a public guarantee. GOI attempts to raise private capital without guarantees were unsuccessful for most of the colonial period. Since the GOI was unable to borrow large sums on favourable terms in the 1850s, guarantees were likely necessary to attract foreign capital.

Figure 9.10 illustrates the issue by plotting the guarantees and the GOI's borrowing costs over time. The guarantee is 5 per cent up to 1880 and 3.5 per cent from 1881–1940.[8] We also plot the net earnings divided by capital outlay. In the 1860s, railway earnings were far below the 5 per cent guarantee, averaging just over 2 per cent. The low earnings may have been influenced by the guarantees, but it is likely that rates of return would have been less than 5 per cent absent any government intervention. The GOI could have borrowed money to finance railways, but it is unclear if this was a better policy. The public cost of borrowing averaged 4.6 per cent in the 1860s, not substantially below the 5 per cent guarantee. In the 1870s, the opportunities for public financing improved. Public borrowing costs fell below 4 per cent. Unsurprisingly, the GOI started to finance and construct state-owned railways precisely at this time. As GOI bond yields continued to decline, the GOI could have publicly financed the next phase of railway development in the 1880s. Yet it made a decision to continue with private financing and to lower the guarantees to match their borrowing cost. Here lobbying may have influenced policy making. According to Sweeney (2011), London financial and commercial interests (including the Rothschilds) successfully pushed for new guaranteed companies. Many retired GOI officials also became active investors in private railways, using their former influence to advocate projects.

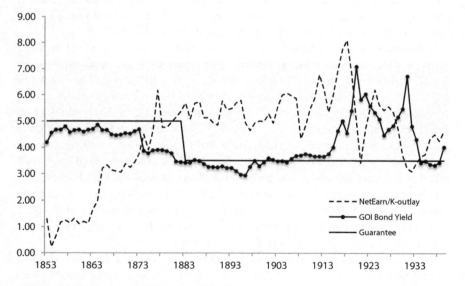

FIGURE 9.10 Net earnings, GOI bond yields and guarantees

Sources: Data on net earnings are from Government of India (1955) and GOI bond yields are from Global Financial Data.

The shift to majority GOI ownership was the other major policy change. State ownership is generally viewed as detrimental for performance in the economics literature (Megginson and Netter 2001), but our analysis of Indian railways suggests otherwise. Using a rich railway-level panel, which exploits changes in ownership within railways, we find operating expenses were 13 per cent lower on average following a change to GOI ownership. Most of these declines were driven by lower labour costs. Controlling for total route miles, total employment decreased by 25 per cent on average, including both Indians and Europeans (Bogart and Chaudhary 2012). On the capital side, we find no evidence of a decline in capital productivity or TFP following the switch to GOI ownership. Unlike many contemporary state-owned enterprises, the transition to GOI ownership did not negatively impact performance and in fact had some positive effects.

Overall, we believe colonial policy played a more neutral role than has been previously argued. First, the maligned guarantees were necessary to finance Indian railways. Second, the GOI ownership of railways did not lead to any significant decline in productivity. Aggregate TFP increased as the GOI became a majority owner. The GOI gained financially from an efficient railways sector. Although railways contributed a small share to tax revenues in the 1870s, by 1916 almost 37 per cent of total tax revenues came from railways.[9] Even after accounting for working expenses, net railway revenues accounted for 12 per cent of GOI revenues in the 1920s and 1930s. Railway profits were intertwined with the GOI's revenue goals and increasing profits became a key policy objective in the early twentieth century. Still, the GOI's profit motives may have hurt social goals, like development.

Railways and Indian economic development

A large body of literature has examined the economic effects of railways, focusing on two major themes: first, whether the introduction of railways increased market integration and price convergence, and second, whether railways increased national income. These themes address a larger question: Did railways spur economic growth and development in India?

Railways and markets

A large literature has examined the effects of railways on price convergence by studying crop price variation across districts (Hurd 1975; Mukherjee 1980; McAlpin 1974; Derbyshire 2007). Hurd (1975) compared average prices and the standard deviation of prices across railway and non-railway districts. In railway districts, prices were less dispersed and closer to the mean compared to non-railway districts. McAlpin (1974) found that prices of both food and non-food crops converged as railways expanded. Collins (1999) extended the analysis to wages and found limited evidence of wage convergence. This is perhaps less surprising since labour is less mobile than products like grain or cotton.

Two recent studies have re-examined the impact of railways on market integration using more sophisticated econometric techniques. Andrabi and Kuehlwein (2010) regress the price gap for wheat and rice between major Indian cities on an indicator variable for whether a railway connected the two cities in each year. The focus is on changes in price gaps over time (that is, before and after railways link a market pair). Their estimates imply that railways can explain only 20 per cent of the overall 60 per cent decrease in price dispersion between the 1860s and 1900s. Hence, they conclude the effects of railways on market integration are overstated.

Donaldson (2012) arrives at a different conclusion using variation in salt prices. His approach is novel because salt was produced in certain parts of India and then distributed to different districts. Using a theoretical model, Donaldson shows that inter-district price differences in salt are equal to trade costs because salt is produced in one district and consumed in many other districts. He then empirically measures trade costs and finds that the arrival of railways significantly reduced trade costs. His empirical exercise controls for alternate modes of transportation. Road transport increased price gaps in salt markets by a factor of eight relative to rail, implying that railways could lower trade costs by as much as 87 per cent in markets that were served by roads only. The estimated effects of river or coastal transport relative to rail are smaller in magnitude (price gaps are nearly four times larger), but still substantial. Using the estimated trade costs parameter, he finds that railroads significantly increased trade flows.

The literature on market integration yields somewhat contradictory conclusions. Andrabi and Kuehlwein (2010) find a small effect of railways and Donaldson (2012) finds a large effect. In our view, Donaldson's finding is more convincing. Andrabi and Kuehlwein do not take into account that two districts may not be directly connected but connected via a third district. By construction, their estimates understate the effect of railways. The conclusions may also differ because there is a missing variable in both analyses: the freight rates charged by railways in each market. Average freight rates differed across railways and across commodities, with special rates sometimes offered for grain or coal.

Railways and famines

After the devastating famines in the late nineteenth century, the GOI pushed for new protective railways that could potentially reduce the burden of famines. Contemporaries and subsequent researchers alike have since debated how railways interacted with famines. One view argues railways contributed to famines because they allowed food grains to leave drought-stricken areas during times of famine (Sen 1980). Researchers also argue that protective railways constructed in the 1880s and 1890s did not mitigate the effects of the 1896 or 1901 famine (Sweeney 2011). These studies rely largely on qualitative accounts. In contrast, Burgess and Donaldson (2010) find famines were less devastating in districts connected to a rail network using detailed district-level data. In fact, rainfall shocks no longer caused famines once a district was connected to the railways.

Railways and income

Starting with Fogel (1970) and Fishlow (1965), economic historians have used the 'social savings' methodology to examine how much railways increased national income. The goal is to measure how much consumer surplus was gained from railways at some benchmark date, say 1900. The reasoning is that railway customers would have relied on alternative transport modes, like wagons and boats, in the absence of railways. A simple approximation of the gain in consumer surplus is the difference between freight rates for wagons and railroads multiplied by the quantity of rail traffic in the benchmark year. Prices are meant to capture the marginal costs of each technology under perfect competition and the quantity of traffic proxies for consumer demand.

Hurd (1983) was the first to make a social savings calculation for Indian railways. He assumed that freight rates would have been between 80 and 90 per cent higher without railways, based on the observed differences between rail freight rates and those for bullock carts during the mid-nineteenth century. Using the volume of freight traffic in 1900, he estimated social savings to be Rs. 1.2 billion, or 9 per cent of national income. The social savings of Indian railways look large compared to the United States and western European countries, where the social savings of railways rarely exceed 5 per cent of national income. However, compared to other less developed countries, Indian railways look less impressive. Summerhill (2005), for example, finds that social savings from railways in Brazil were at least 18 per cent of national income around 1913.

The social savings methodology provides a powerful and simple tool, but it has some problems. First, it is not clear what the price of road or water transport would have been in the absence of railways. Congestion would have increased on roads and rivers with the increased traffic volume. The cost of using alternative transport modes is arguably underestimated in most cases as a result (McClelland 1968, p. 114). Second, the social savings calculation omits spillovers. In theory, railways should increase demand for iron and steel and increase competition in manufacturing. They also contribute to agglomeration of economic activity, like the emergence of cities.

In spite of these critiques, there are reasons to doubt the importance of spillovers in the Indian case. Most iron and steel imports came from Britain and thus backward linkages of this kind had a limited effect. The manufacturing sector was small as well, so forward linkages were weaker. Indian cities also remained quite small well into the twentieth century. The urbanization rate barely moved upward from 10 per cent in 1870. Donaldson (2012) has explored this issue further by developing a theoretical model where the railways' only impact is to increase farm gate prices via lower trade costs. He then finds that the estimated effect of railways on agricultural income is very close to what would be predicted by the model, a 16 per cent increase in agricultural income.

The primary impact of railways in the Indian economy was to increase interregional and international trade. But this raises a different question: Why did railways not do more, such as spurring a higher rate of economic growth? Some scholars blame colonial policy. The GOI paid a lot of attention to profits, and freight rates were perhaps not set at the socially optimal level. Fares were quite high considering income levels in India. For example, the Robertson Report (1903) argued that Indian fares and rates should be one-sixth of English fares when in fact they averaged between one-third to two-thirds. Had fares been lower, the growth of the Indian economy might have been higher. Still, low productivity in agriculture was the main drag on the Indian economy. It is perhaps too much to expect railways to compensate for the poor performance of agriculture.

Conclusion

This chapter reviewed the development and organization of the Indian rail network, the trends in railway performance, the effects of ownership and the impact of railways on the Indian economy. The major conclusions are that the GOI had a strong influence on railways from the beginning, but the GOI's role increased with time culminating in nationalization. The performance of Indian railways was quite different before and after 1920. There was a trend towards higher output, productivity and profits between 1850 and 1919, followed by stagnation after 1920. Unlike other settings, government ownership of railways did not undermine efficiency or performance. Lastly, railways increased market integration and national income, but it appears that railways could have done more to aid Indian economic development. Despite the large body of literature, several issues still remain, such as the reversal in performance after 1920, the interaction between Princely States and railway operations, and the GOI's shifting priorities and goals vis-à-vis railways. We hope future research will address these questions in more detail.

Notes

1 The series is constructed using data from Government of India (1955).
2 Cross-country data on rail network development is from Bogart (2009) and Mitchell (2003).
3 One was the Sind, Punjab and Delhi railway, which was merged with neighbouring state railways to create the Northwestern Railways. The GOI chose to manage this railway for military reasons. The other two state operated railways were Eastern Bengal, and Oudh and Rohilkhand.
4 See Sweeney (2011) for more details on the Bengal Central.
5 See Hurd and Kerr (2012) for the different railway report series. As is common with any series, the data are not without problems. We encourage researchers to read the reports accompanying the statistical series when using these data.
6 Morris and Dudley (1975) have many concerns with these data. They argue the capital series is problematic because it includes construction costs but not land costs. Companies were given the land for free. In the early decades of railway construction, there was some ambiguity about the types of expenses charged against capital versus working expenses. This led to an official minute in 1864 clarifying the specific expenses to be enumerated in each account. Another accounting change in 1923–1924 created a separate depreciation fund to better account for wear-and-tear in the capital numbers.

7 The data are from Morris and Dudley (1975).
8 The guarantees in the third phase varied across companies, but we use 3.5 just as an average.
9 Calculations are based on total gross public revenues of British India and total public revenues derived from railways. Both series are reported in the Statistical Abstracts of British India (1915).

References

Andrabi, T., and M. Kuehlwein (2010). 'Railways and Price Convergence in British India', *Journal of Economic History, 70 (2)*, pp. 351–377.

Bell, H. (1894). *Railway Policy of India: With Map of Indian Railway System*, Rivington: Percival.

Bogart, D. (2009). 'Nationalizations and the Development of Transport Systems: Cross-Country Evidence from Railroad Networks, 1860–1912', *Journal of Economic History, 69 (2)*, pp. 202–237.

Bogart, D., and L. Chaudhary (2012). 'Regulation, Ownership and Costs: A Historical Perspective from Indian Railways', *American Economic Journal: Economic Policy, 4 (1)*, pp. 28–57.

———. (2013). 'Engines of Growth: The Productivity Advance of Indian Railways Before World War I', *Journal of Economic History, 73 (2)*, pp. 340–371.

Burgess, R., and D. Donaldson (2010). 'Can Openness Mitigate the Effects of Weather Fluctuations? Evidence from India's Famine Era', *American Economic Review: Papers and Proceedings, 100 (2)*, pp. 449–453.

Collins, W. (1999). 'Labor Mobility, Market Integration, and Wage Convergence in Late 19th century India', *Explorations in Economic History, 36 (3)*, pp. 246–277.

Derbyshire, I. (2007). 'Private and State Enterprise: Financing and Managing the Railways of Colonial North India, 1859–1914', in I. Kerr, ed., *27 Down: New Departures in Indian Railway Studies*, Delhi: Orient Longman, pp. 276–313.

Donaldson, D. (2012). 'Railways and the Raj: The Economic Impact of Transportation Infrastructure', *American Economic Review*, forthcoming.

Engel, E., R. Fischer, and A. Galetovic (2013). 'The Basic Public Finance of Public-Private Partnerships', *Journal of the European Economic Association, 11 (1)*, pp. 83–111.

Estache, A., and L. Wren-Lewis (2009). 'Toward a Theory of Regulation for Developing Countries: Following Jean-Jacques Laffont's Lead', *Journal of Economic Literature, 47 (3)*, pp. 729–770.

Fishlow, A. (1965). *American Railroads and the Transformation of the Antebellum Economy*, Cambridge: Harvard University Press.

Fogel, R. (1970). *Railroads and American Economic Growth: Essays in Econometric History*, London: John Hopkins Press.

Government of India (1955). *History of Indian Railways, Constructed and in Progress Corrected up to 31 March 1955*, Delhi: Government of India Press.

House of Commons (1906). 'Statement exhibiting the Moral and Material Progress and Condition of India during 1904–05; Thirty-fifth number', London: British Parliamentary Papers.

Hurd, J. II (1975). 'Railways and the Expansion of Markets in India 1861–1921', *Explorations in Economic History, 12 (3)*, pp. 263–288.

———. (1983). 'Railways', in D. Kumar and M. Desai, eds., *Cambridge Economic History of India: Vol. II, c. 1757 – c. 1970*, Cambridge: Cambridge University Press, pp. 37–761.

———. (2007). 'A Huge Railway System But No Sustained Economic Development: The Company Perspective, 1884–1939: Some Hypotheses', in I. Kerr, ed., *27 Down: New Departures in Indian Railway Studies*, Delhi: Orient Longman, pp. 314–346.

Hurd, J., II, and I. Kerr (2012). *India's Railway History: A Research Handbook*, Leiden: Brill.

India (1915). *Statistical abstract relating to British India from 1903–04 to 1912–13*, London: His Majesty's Stationary Office.

Kerr, I. (1995). *Building the Railways of the Raj, 1850–1900*, Oxford: Oxford University Press.

———. (2007). *Engines of Change: The Railroads that Made India*, Westport: Praeger.

Laffont, Jean-Jacques. (2005). Regulation and Development. New York: Cambridge University Press.

McAlpin, M.B. (1974). 'Railroads, Prices and Peasant Rationality: India, 1860–1900', *Journal of Economic History, 34 (3)*, pp. 662–684.

McClelland, P. D. (1968). 'Railroads, American Growth, and the New Economic History: A critique', *Journal of Economic History, 28 (1)*, pp. 102–123.

Megginson, W., and J.M. Netter (2001). 'From State to Market: A Survey of Empirical Studies on Privatization', *Journal of Economic Literature, 39 (2)*, pp. 321–389.

Mitchell, Brian R. (2003). International Historical Statistics: The Americas, 1750–2000. Palgrave MacMillan, London.

Mitchell, Brian R. (2003). International Historical Statistics: Europe, 1750–2000. Palgrave MacMillan, London.

Morris, D.M., and C.B. Dudley (1975). 'Selected Railway Statistics for the Indian Subcontinent', *Artha Vijñana, 15 (3)*, pp. 1–128.

Mukherjee, M. (1980). 'Railways and Their Impact on Bengal's Economy, 1870–1920', *Indian Economic and Social History Review, 17 (2)*, pp. 191–209.

Puffert, D. (2009). *Tracks Across Continents, Paths through History: The Economic Dynamics of Standardization in Railway Gauge*, Chicago: Chicago University Press.

Robertson, T. (1903). *Report on the Administration and Working of Indian Railways*, London: Darling & Son.

Sanyal, N. (1930). *Development of Indian Railways*, Calcutta: University of Calcutta.

Sen, A. (1980). 'Famines', *World Development, 8 (9)*, pp. 613–621.

Sivasubramonian, S. (1997). 'Revised Estimates of the National Income of India, 1900–1901 to 1946–1947', *Indian Economic and Social History Review, 34 (2)*, pp. 113–168.

Summerhill, W.R. (2005). 'Big Social Savings in a Small Laggard Economy: Railroad-Led Growth in Brazil', *Journal of Economic History, 65 (1)*, pp. 72–102.

Sweeney, S. (2011). *Financing India's Imperial Railway, 1875–1914*, London: Pickering & Chatto.

Thorner, D. (1955). 'The Pattern of Railway Development in India', *Far Eastern Quarterly, 14 (2)*, pp. 201–206.

10

CASTE, COLONIALISM AND SCHOOLING

Education in British India

Latika Chaudhary

The subject of education is among the most neglected in Indian economic history. Few economics articles have been published on the topic and even the extremely detailed *Cambridge Economic History of India* (Kumar and Desai 1983) has no chapter on education. The few historical studies are of a qualitative nature. For example, Nurullah and Naik (1951) offer a dated but excellent review of colonial policies and their impact on education development. Scholars like Bellenoit (2007) have studied the influence of missionaries on education and Basu (1974) has explored the relationship between the rise in secondary education, political nationalism and colonial policies. The general consensus holds British policy responsible for the many defects of the colonial education system and the low rates of schooling.

Within Indian economic history, the neglect of education dates to an older era when economists studied physical investments and the idea of education as a human capital investment was new. Since then, many studies have shown that education has a positive impact on economic growth (for example, Schultz 1962, 1971; Becker 1964; Mincer 1974; Easterlin 1981; and Benhabib and Spiegel 1994). An educated labour force has been linked to greater worker productivity, a faster ability to adopt new technologies and lower crime. Schultz (1983) has linked education to development even in agricultural economies. Literate farmers may be quicker to adopt superior inputs and engage in more information sharing, contributing to higher productivity. Nonetheless, one needs to examine whether and how demand for education in India – a low-income society – impacted schooling.

This chapter briefly reviews colonial policy, describes the broad patterns on enrolment and literacy, and discusses how policy interacted with local conditions to influence the trajectory of Indian education.[1] The main goal is to identify specific factors that hurt the cause of mass education in the colonial era. Although primary school enrolment was low in British India, secondary school enrolment was comparable to developed countries. A strong private demand for secondary education was partially responsible, but colonial policies exacerbated the problem by allocating a large share of public resources to secondary schools and colleges. Finally, the caste and religious divisions within Indian society compounded the problem of scarce public and private resources.

Colonial policies

Over the nineteenth century, the indigenous system of schooling in British India was replaced by a new state system of education. After the British Crown took control from the East India Company in 1858, the Government of India (GOI) under the authority of the India Office in London became the relevant decision-making body. Beginning in the 1870s, the GOI decentralized public services, including education to provincial governments, followed by another wave of decentralization to district and municipal boards in the 1880s. Indians served on these boards in an elected and nominated capacity. The Montagu-Chelmsford reforms ushered in a limited form of self-government in 1919. Education was placed under the purview of provincial legislative councils composed of elected Indian representatives. A more comprehensive form of self-government was introduced in 1935 under Provincial Autonomy. Despite these political changes, enrolment and literacy remained stable and disappointingly low up to independence.

Under the former indigenous system, schools were of two types: elite religious schools for students interested in a lifetime of higher learning and local elementary schools where village boys were introduced to the 3 R's in the vernacular medium.[2] Due to a lack of official patronage, both elite schools and local indigenous schools declined. Wood's *Education Despatch* of 1854 was the first official document akin to a national education policy, which outlined the Company's role in the provision of schooling. While earlier policies had promoted 'a very high degree of education for a small number of natives' in the English medium,[3] the Company now emphasized the importance of expanding vernacular primary education to the rural population. Given the high costs of building such a system, the Despatch introduced public subsidies known as *grant-in-aids* to partially support privately managed schools. Under this system, grants were available to schools that followed a secular curriculum (religious neutrality), were under private management and were open to public inspection. By encouraging grant-in-aids, the East India Company created an important role for private actors in the education sector.

Beginning in the 1860s, a new system emerged whereby publicly financed and managed schools (provincial government and local board schools) functioned alongside privately managed aided and unaided schools. Provincial governments were more active in setting up secondary schools and colleges, while rural district and urban boards focused on primary schools. These boards managed public primary schools and gave grants to private aided schools. Aided and unaided schools were privately managed by Indians and by various mission societies. Although missionaries controlled a large number of private schools in the early nineteenth century, their share declined over the second half of the century as private Indian participation increased.[4] Many of the former indigenous schools disappeared in this period. Some were successfully converted into aided schools and the rest were classified as private unrecognized schools because they did not conform to official standards.[5]

Spurred by a strong private demand for English education, the late nineteenth century saw a sharp increase in the number of private English secondary schools and colleges. This was driven by Indian elites hoping to secure lucrative government jobs after graduation.[6] British administrators recognized the growth of secondary education was outpacing primary education, and subsequent policy reports highlighted the need to expand primary schooling. Local boards were encouraged to build new schools or offer more public grants to aided schools. Specific schemes were adopted to increase education in groups with below average literacy. Public revenues were targeted to primary education in the early twentieth century, with a new focus on quality and greater state control. These positive measures notwithstanding, the GOI resisted adopting a policy of free primary education and delayed the introduction of compulsory schooling.[7] Beginning in 1918, a mild form of compulsory schooling was introduced just as education was transferred to the control of provincial governments under elected Indian ministers.

Under dyarchy provincial governments dramatically increased public spending on education. By 1931–1932, public expenditures were more than three times the 1911–1912 level, a significant increase in real terms because price levels decreased in these decades. Many villages now had at least one primary school, if not multiple. Unfortunately, this increase in public schools did not translate into literacy gains: 1931 literacy was only marginally above that in 1921. In reviewing the progress of education, the Hartog Committee in 1929 (Great Britain 1929) attributed the discrepancy to the rapid expansion of poor quality, single-teacher schools. Consequently, there was a consolidation of schools in the 1930s and many poor-quality schools were shut down. While the subject of education enjoyed popular and political support in the 1920s and 1930s, it gave way to other pressing concerns after Provincial Autonomy was introduced in 1937.

Enrolment and literacy

The numerous commissions, official acts and policy recommendations of the colonial era translated into a mixed picture of lopsided progress. While the goal of extending basic education to the larger population was unrealized, huge gains of perhaps uncertain quality were made at the secondary and post-secondary level.

Total enrolment as a percentage of the population increased from an extremely low 0.014 per cent in 1853 to 4 per cent in 1940. While the Statistical Abstracts document the total number of students in the mid-nineteenth century, a systematic enumeration began after the Hunter Education Commission highlighted the need for better data collection (India 1883). The first *Quinquennial Report on the Progress of Education in India* was released in 1886–1887 and subsequent Quinquennial

Reports were published up until 1947. Table 10.1 uses these series to illustrate enrolment rates by level and province from 1891 to 1941 (House of Commons 1899, 1909, 1914, 1919; India 1948). The Quinquennial Reports do not report the age breakdown of the population, but suggest that the primary school age population (ages 5 to 10) accounted for 15 per cent of the total population. I use this figure to construct the school-age population in each province. Students enrolled in unrecognized indigenous schools such as *maktabs* and *tols* are not counted in these rates.

As late as 1891 only one out of ten primary school-age children were enrolled in any type of school. The number of students steadily increased in the twentieth century, but even by 1941 only one-third of school-age children (35 per cent) were enrolled in school, with sharp regional differences. While primary school enrolment clearly increased, the gains at the secondary and collegiate level were more remarkable. Secondary school enrolment more than quadrupled between 1891 and 1941, with more than 6 per cent of school-age children attending secondary school by 1941.[8] The gains at the post-secondary level were even more dramatic: college enrolment increased more than sevenfold, with most of the gains accruing to arts colleges. These statistical patterns match qualitative accounts of urban Indians flocking to post-secondary institutions in large numbers.

The enrolment rates are striking when placed in an international context. Using information in Lindert (2004), Table 10.2 documents primary and secondary enrolment rates in India compared to more advanced economies (such as France and the United States) and countries at comparable levels of development (Mexico and Brazil). Lindert's series for British India excludes private unaided schools. He also defines the school-age population as ages 5 to 14 across countries. The 15 per cent school-age population is useful in the Indian context to evaluate the number of primary school-age children attending school, but to generate comparable statistics Table 10.2 uses enrolment rates from Table 10.1 adjusted for the school-age population ages 5 to 14.[9]

Table 10.2 reports data from the Quinquennial Reviews and Lindert's series for British India. Since Lindert excludes private unaided schools, his series underestimates Indian enrolment. Despite the difference, both series highlight India's poor performance at the primary level. British India had one of the lowest primary school enrolment rates in every decade, averaging 9 per cent and far below the 80 per cent enrolment rate in advanced parts of Europe. Among the set of less-developed economies, Indian primary school enrolment (14 per cent in 1930) is lower than Brazil (22 per cent), Japan (61 per cent), Mexico (37 per cent) and Chile (56 per cent). In comparison, secondary school enrolment in British India is comparable to France and even exceeds the UK in the 1890s and 1900s. In 1910, the percentage of the school-age population enrolled in secondary schools was 1.4 per cent for India, 1.4 per cent for France and 2.1 per cent for the UK. While secondary school enrolment in British India was comparable to developed countries, primary education was far below average.

TABLE 10.1 Enrolment rate (pupils/school-age population)

	1891–92	1901–02	1911–12	1921–22	1931–32	1941–42
All Recognized Institutions:						
BRITISH INDIA	**9.6%**	**10.8%**	**16.0%**	**20.9%**	**30.2%**	**34.8%**
Bengal	12.7%	13.5%	24.4%	26.2%	36.2%	43.7%
Bihar & Orissa			15.5%	15.0%	18.4%	22.3%
Bombay (inc. Sind)	14.0%	14.9%	20.7%	30.9%	39.7%	54.1%
Central Provinces & Berar	7.0%	8.9%	13.4%	15.8%	19.4%	21.4%
Madras	11.8%	12.9%	18.6%	27.5%	41.0%	46.7%
Punjab	4.8%	6.0%	10.6%	17.8%	33.9%	29.8%
United Provinces	3.1%	5.2%	8.8%	14.2%	20.1%	21.9%
Primary Schools:						
BRITISH INDIA	**8.1%**	**8.9%**	**13.0%**	**17.0%**	**23.6%**	**27.1%**
Bengal	10.7%	11.0%	17.7%	20.5%	28.2%	34.2%
Bihar & Orissa			13.0%	13.5%	15.6%	17.6%
Bombay (inc. Sind)	12.8%	13.4%	18.6%	27.5%	34.9%	46.2%
Central Provinces & Berar	5.7%	7.4%	10.9%	12.5%	14.3%	15.4%
Madras	10.3%	10.9%	16.6%	24.4%	37.4%	42.2%
Punjab	3.2%	3.7%	7.0%	10.3%	13.6%	12.9%
United Provinces	2.2%	4.1%	7.2%	12.2%	16.5%	16.6%
Secondary Schools:						
BRITISH INDIA	**1.4%**	**1.7%**	**2.4%**	**3.3%**	**5.7%**	**6.3%**
Bengal	1.8%	2.2%	5.1%	4.7%	6.0%	6.6%
Bihar & Orissa			1.2%	1.2%	2.3%	4.1%
Bombay (inc. Sind)	1.1%	1.3%	1.8%	2.7%	3.8%	5.8%
Central Provinces & Berar	1.2%	1.4%	2.4%	3.2%	4.8%	5.7%
Madras	1.4%	1.8%	1.8%	2.7%	2.9%	3.7%
Punjab	1.6%	2.1%	3.3%	7.2%	19.2%	16.1%
United Provinces	0.8%	1.0%	1.4%	1.6%	3.0%	4.1%
Arts and Professional Colleges:						
BRITISH INDIA	**0.05%**	**0.06%**	**0.09%**	**0.16%**	**0.23%**	**0.35%**
Bengal	0.06%	0.09%	0.23%	0.31%	0.33%	0.47%
Bihar & Orissa			0.04%	0.05%	0.08%	0.13%
Bombay (inc. Sind)	0.05%	0.08%	0.12%	0.26%	0.38%	0.57%
Central Provinces & Berar	0.01%	0.01%	0.03%	0.05%	0.10%	0.16%
Madras	0.08%	0.08%	0.09%	0.17%	0.21%	0.29%
Punjab	0.02%	0.06%	0.12%	0.20%	0.43%	0.46%
United Provinces	0.04%	0.04%	0.08%	0.10%	0.16%	0.32%

Source: Progress of Education in India, Quinquennial Reviews (1891–1947). Data are not shown individually for the smaller provinces. Up to 1911/12, the data include some native states of Bombay, Bengal, Central Provinces and United Provinces but they represent 5% of the population. Secondary schools include high schools, middle English and middle vernacular schools. However, primary schools include middle vernacular schools for Bombay (all years) and for Madras from 1911–1912. Bihar and Orissa are included in Bengal for 1891–1901. Enrolment and population data for Bengal, Bihar and Orissa are from the Statistical Abstracts for 1911/12. School-Age Population is defined as 15% of the province population reported in the Quinquennial Review.

TABLE 10.2 Comparative enrolment rates (number enrolled per 1,000 of the school-age population)

	India	India-Lindert	Mexico	Brazil	Chile	Japan	France	Prussia	UK	USA
Primary School										
1880	.	42	187	70	111	306	816	711	549	906
1890	49	44	181	69	192	370	832	742	646	971
1900	53	47	185	102	245	507	859	732	720	939
1910	78	65	186	123	431	599	857	720	729	975
1920	102	80	231	147	422	602	704	758	701	924
1930	142	113	374	215	556	609	803	699	745	921
Secondary School										
1880	.	4	.	.	5	2	12	31	3	9
1890	8	8	1	.	3	3	11	32	3	20
1900	10	9	.	0	7	13	11	40	7	37
1910	14	12	2	5	12	74	14	44	21	55
1920	20	16	.	6	56	108	16/24	92	44	110
1930	34	28	5	8	52	165	19/32	94	58	193

Source: The India series in column 1 uses 25% of the total population to define the population aged 5 to 14, similar to the population age group used by Lindert. The Lindert series are drawn from Lindert (2004, vol. 2, appendix tables C1 and C3).

Apart from the low national rate, enrolment varied tremendously within India. At every level, the more advanced coastal provinces of Bengal, Bombay and Madras outperformed the interior provinces of Bihar and United Provinces (hereafter UP). Differential returns and the related private demand for primary education clearly influenced these regional patterns, as did land revenue policies (Chaudhary 2010b). Primary school enrolment in Bombay and Madras averaged 15 per cent (adjusted for population ages 5 to 14), and was higher than Brazil (12 per cent), but still below Mexico, Chile and Japan (22, 33 and 50 per cent respectively). Even the top performers of British India were unable to match the average educational attainment in the other developing economies of this era.

An examination of Indian literacy paints an equally, if not more, dismal picture. The Census began enumerating literacy in the late nineteenth century, but these early Censuses classified the population into individuals learning at a school, college or home; individuals who were literate but not under instruction; and individuals who were illiterate and not under instruction. Subsequent Censuses found problems with this classification. Hence, in 1901 individuals were categorized as literate or not, but there was no consistent standard and local officials used their own standards to determine literacy. Beginning in 1911, a uniform standard was adopted: an individual who could read and write a short letter was enumerated as literate.

The top panel of Table 10.3 illustrates the evolution of literacy by gender and province. Male literacy increased by 5 percentage points between 1901 and 1931, but it averaged only 17.8 per cent in 1931. Female literacy was incredibly low at

TABLE 10.3 Literacy (in percentages)

| | Ages 10 & over | | | | | | | | English Literacy | |
| | Male | | | | Female | | | | 1931 | |
	1901	1911	1921	1931	1901	1911	1921	1931	M	F
BRITISH INDIA	12.9	14.0	16.1	17.8	0.9	1.4	2.2	3.0	2.24	0.29
Assam	8.9	11.7	14.4	16.9	0.6	0.8	1.5	2.3	2.20	0.15
Bengal	13.8	18.7	21.0	20.1	0.7	1.5	2.3	3.4	4.27	0.48
Bihar & Orissa		10.4	11.4	10.8		0.5	0.7	0.8	0.92	0.07
Bombay	14.8	15.8	18.1	18.6	1.1	1.7	3.0	3.0	2.86	0.56
CP & Berar	7.9	8.7	10.3	12.2	0.3	0.4	1.0	1.1	1.11	0.13
Madras	16.0	18.3	19.9	21.1	1.2	1.7	2.6	3.2	2.57	0.35
Punjab	8.6	8.4	9.0	11.2	0.4	0.8	1.1	1.8	1.88	0.19
United Provinces	7.5	7.8	8.5	10.4	0.3	0.6	0.8	1.2	1.09	0.13

| | 1931 Literacy | | | | | | | | | |
	All	Hindu	Muslim	Christian	Jain	Tribal	Brahman	Depressed Castes	Highest Literacy	Caste w/Highest Literacy
BRITISH INDIA	8.3	8.4	6.4	27.9	35.3	0.7	33.4	1.6		
Assam	9.3	10.6	6.6	21.1	38.5	1.8	.	3.1	25.6	Ahom
Bengal	11.1	15.7	6.7	43.8	42.4	0.9	43.1	5.0	62.7	Baidya
Bihar & Orissa	5.3	5.5	5.6	12.0	38.3	0.7	19.2	0.6	36.2	Kayastha
Bombay	10.8	10.2	6.9	37.1	32.4	0.5	51.0	2.8	51.0	Brahman
CP & Berar	6.6	6.4	15.0	56.4	36.3	0.7	35.2	1.5	35.2	Brahman, Baniya
Madras	10.8	10.4	12.5	21.3	35.5	0.3	54.3	1.5	54.3	Brahman
Punjab	6.3	9.6	3.3	9.8	29.5	0.0	15.1	0.8	27.6	Khatri
United Provinces	5.5	5.0	5.7	28.4	35.9	0.0	15.9	0.5	44.65	Kayastha

Source: Census of India 1931, Volume 1, Part 1 – Report, Chapter IX, Subsidiary Tables I, II, III and V. Individual data are not presented for the smaller provinces. Madras includes Cochin and Travancore States for Brahman. The all India Brahman literacy is the average across provinces and princely states included in this table.

3 per cent in 1931. Even the limited gains in primary school enrolment seen in Table 10.1 did not translate into comparable literacy gains. While primary school enrolment almost doubled between 1901 and 1931, literacy increased merely from 13 to 18 per cent for males and 1 to 3 per cent for females. Colonial officials were well aware of this discrepancy and numerous reports bemoaned the tremendous waste in the education sector. The main problem was insufficient attendance. For

example, out of 100 students beginning primary school in 1922–1923, only 18 were in class four by 1925–1926. The remaining had either dropped out or in a few cases stagnated to a lower grade. If we assume it takes at least four years of regular attendance from class one to class four to acquire functional literacy, only 18 per cent of primary school students were becoming literate. The wastage was even worse in female schools, where girls were regularly pulled out of school for early marriage among other reasons (Hartog Committee, Great Britain 1929). Although the significant and persistent gender divide in education was recognized historically, no effective solutions emerged in the colonial period.

Although average literacy was low, the small numbers of literates were highly educated: 13 per cent of male literates could read and write in English, and 10 per cent of female literates also possessed English literacy. Instruction in the English medium was more common at the secondary level, and these patterns further reinforce India's high level of secondary education. Since wastage was less common here, the secondary system was also more successful at increasing literacy.

The bottom panel of Table 10.3 reports literacy by religion and caste in 1931. Certain religious groups such as Christians and Jains were among the most literate in colonial India. Jains were predominately an affluent trading community and education was almost an economic necessity. At the other end of the spectrum, tribal groups living in geographically remote parts of the country had the lowest literacy: less than 1 per cent. Average Muslim literacy (6.4 per cent) was below Hindu literacy (8.4 per cent), but again there were regional differences.

Literacy also varied by caste. Brahmans at the upper end of the caste hierarchy averaged 33 per cent, while depressed castes averaged 1.6 per cent. Despite the regional differences, the inter-caste patterns are visible across provinces. In 1931, in Bombay and Madras, 80 per cent of Brahman males could read and write, while lower-caste literacy ranged from a high of 5 per cent in Bengal to a low of 0.5 per cent in UP. Brahmans were not the only upper caste with above-average literacy. They were the most literate Hindu caste in Bombay, Central Provinces and Madras, but were substantially below the Kayasthas in UP (45 compared to 16 per cent) and the Baidyas in Bengal (63 compared to 42 per cent). Broadberry and Gupta (2010) also highlight the high levels of literacy in the different trading castes, which in many provinces matched or exceeded Brahman literacy. Still, these differences among the educated castes were small compared to the differences between the upper castes and the depressed castes. The inter-caste patterns reflect a combination of economic, political and social differences. For example, the depressed castes were poorer on average and at least until the 1920s had no real political voice. Thus, it is difficult to isolate the effect of caste from the economic and political differences between these groups.

This overview highlights three features of India's education development. First, it illustrates the low rates of primary school enrolment and literacy. Second, secondary and collegiate education fared much better in comparison. Third, there were large differences by caste, gender, region and religion. The next section proposes explanations to account for these patterns.

Returns, colonial policies or caste?

Returns to schooling

In standard economic models, rational individuals invest in schooling when returns (i.e. wages) exceed the direct costs of school fees and the opportunity costs in terms of foregone wages. Applying this model to India suggests low returns to primary education are perhaps one explanation for low literacy. India's large agricultural sector and relatively low GDP per capita in the nineteenth and early twentieth century probably weakened the demand for basic education. A heavy reliance on child labour during the agricultural season also increased the opportunity costs of sending children to school. Such economic hardships were often noted in official reports. For example, the Hartog Committee (Great Britain 1929) had the follow-ing to say on the subject of mass education: 'In India the great majority of parents who live on the land are poor, and their poverty is aggravated by improvidence and debt. Being illiterate and having an outlook confined almost entirely to their own surroundings and the daily routine of life, much persuasion is needed to convince them of the advantage of sending their children to school and keeping them there long enough to receive effective education, however, rudimentary. Even if school-ing is free or school fees are small, the temptation to take a child away from school as soon as he is old enough to mind cattle or goats (which in an unfenced country has to be done by somebody) is great' (p. 37).

The opportunity cost of sending a child to school may have been high in colo-nial India, but was it higher than in other rural economies? As shown earlier, pri-mary enrolment in India was low even relative to countries at comparable levels of development that presumably faced similar opportunity costs. Moreover, the low level of education would suggest the returns to any schooling should be high because of the scarcity of skilled labour. Many of the statements on the perceived low returns are based on qualitative evidence, but what is needed is a quantitative assessment of the returns to education. Sadly, there are no such estimates. To accu-rately estimate returns, one needs individual or group information on wages by education and age. Such data do not exist for the colonial period. The Price and Wage series (India 1886) offer wages for skilled (common mason, carpenter and blacksmith) and unskilled workers (agricultural labour). These are not the same as literate and illiterate workers. But we can use other sources to get wages for post-men and teachers, occupations that require basic literacy.

Table 10.4 generates crude estimates of the rate of return to literacy for a sample year, 1900. To assess returns without individual data, we begin with wages of post-men and primary school teachers as post-literacy wages. The return is calculated using the formula:

$$(Y_1 - Y_0) / (S * (Fees + Y_0))$$

Here, Y_1 represents the wages for literate workers such as postmen and primary school teachers. Y_0 represents the wages for unskilled or skilled labour. S is the number of years in school: 10 by assumption (four years of primary and six years of secondary school). When we calculate the returns relative to skilled labour, we assume the opportunity cost is half the skilled wage when these individuals are in school. We calculate these returns for individuals working as postmen relative to unskilled or skilled labour, reported under Returns (1) and (2). Since primary school teachers commonly worked as postmen, we also calculate returns to the joint primary school teacher and postman wage in Returns (3) and (4).

These calculations are subject to many assumptions and caveats. First, the sources report a range of teacher salaries and we use the average of the range reported for each province. Second, many teachers received gifts in kind that are not included in the salary (House of Commons 1904).[10] Third, the assumption of ten years in school is ad hoc. Most primary schools hired teachers with at least a secondary school certificate; ten years is perhaps a lower bound. Fourth, in the case of Bengal, the different pieces of data are not reported for the exact region. In view of these problems, the estimates on returns should be viewed as more suggestive than definitive.

Despite their shortcomings, the estimates suggest high returns to literacy relative to unskilled labour. Postmen could expect returns ranging from 8 to 13 per cent (1) and doubling up as a primary school teacher increased the range to 15–40 per cent (3). In comparison, the returns relative to skilled labour are more nuanced. Working just as a postman in the colonial period was not economically superior to working as skilled labour (2), but the joint postman and primary school teacher combination generated high returns ranging from 4 to 29 per cent (4). The returns relative to skilled labour should be interpreted with caution because skilled workers may have been functionally literate (for example, carpenters). This would negatively bias the return calculations.

While this crude and simple exercise misses many factors (e.g. probability of employment, discount rates and wages in other educated jobs), the returns are similar to estimates calculated for the post-independence period using better data. For example, Nalla Gounden (1967) estimates returns on the order of 16 per cent to becoming literate. The returns to primary schooling average 20 per cent across several studies from the 1960s and 1970s, although more recent studies suggest lower returns to primary schooling (Psacharopoulos and Patrinos 2004). Overall the estimates in Table 10.4 are higher, but they do suggest non-trivial returns to education.

Low returns may be unable to completely account for India's poor performance in the primary sector, but there was low demand for basic education in many segments of the population. What then was driving this low demand? Market failures along different fronts come to mind. Due to high illiteracy in the general population, parents were probably unaware of the costs and benefits of schooling. Even if they were aware of the benefits, the poor may have been unable to borrow to finance their children's education because of weak capital markets. Intergenerational commitment problems may have worsened both the credit market and information failures. The high level of social fragmentation may have contributed to low demand and impeded the ability to develop public solutions. These are just potential hypotheses and more research is necessary to identify the exact role of such forces.

TABLE 10.4 Returns to education

Province	Annual Wages in 1900 (Rs.)					Returns			
	Unskilled	Skilled	Postmen	Primary School Teacher	Annual Primary School Fees (Rs.)	Postman relative to unskilled labour (1)	Postman relative to skilled labour (2)	Postman + PS teacher relative to unskilled labour (3)	Postman + PS teacher relative to skilled labour (4)
Bengal	71	149	126	55	1.65	8%	−3%	15%	4%
Punjab	87	231	117	290	0.73	3%	−10%	36%	15%
Bombay	81	242	134	340	0.75	6%	−9%	48%	19%
Central Provinces	50	145	115	130	0.24	13%	−4%	39%	14%
Madras	51	175	120	135	1.02	13%	−6%	40%	9%
UP	48	98	108	135	0.23	12%	2%	40%	29%

Source: Annual wages for unskilled and skilled workers are from the Price and Wage Reports for 1900. These series often report a range for the monthly wage, which was converted into the annual wage by using the average of the range and multiplying by 12. The wage for Bengal does not include Eastern Bengal and Assam, the wage for Punjab is the average for Punjab and North-West Frontier Province (NWFP) and UP is the average for Agra and Oudh. Wages for postmen are from the Statistical Abstracts relating to British India from 1894–1895 to 1903–1904, Table 199 (1905). Monthly wages are converted to annual wages by multiplying by 12. The wage for UP is the average for United Provinces of Agra and Oudh. Primary school teacher salary and school fees are from the Progress of Education in India, Quinquennial (1901–1902), Volume II, Table 102 for primary school teacher salaries and Table 112 for primary school fees (expenditures from fees in boys primary schools, per pupil and per annum). These data are for 1901–1902. The primary school teacher salary is the average of the minimum and maximum reported for each province. The average monthly salary was multiplied by 10 to obtain the annual salary assuming teachers work for ten months of the year.

Returns to education also fail to explain the differences between the primary and secondary sector. Private returns to secondary education may have been high in the nineteenth century because well-paying jobs such as GOI clerks and inspectors required matriculation certificates. But anecdotal evidence suggests private returns fell in the early twentieth century as public jobs became harder to find and graduate unemployment increased (see Nurullah and Naik 1951, Basu 1974 and Quinquennial Reviews of the period). Moreover, estimates of private and social returns for the decades following Indian independence suggest returns to primary education were higher than secondary education (see Nalla Gounden 1967; Blaug, Laylard and Woodhall 1969; Psacharopoulos 1973; and Heyneman 1980). Nonetheless, differential returns offer a compelling explanation for the regional variation. School enrolment and literacy were higher in the coastal provinces because they offered more economic opportunities for literate workers. The private demand for education was probably related to the size of the GOI bureaucracy in urban cities and the opportunity for non-traditional employment in law and state offices.

Colonial policies

There are many dimensions to education policy such as spending, the choice of public versus private schools, questions of curriculum and teacher training. This section focuses exclusively on spending and evaluates whether public spending was adequate to the needs of mass education.

Although the British created a new system of education, public investments in education were small. Table 10.5 reports total public expenditures on education from 1881–1931. Public spending accounted for over 50 per cent of total spending on education, increasing to 60 per cent in the 1930s as the GOI increased grants to expand mass schooling. Despite the absolute increase, education accounted for a small share of the total budget, averaging 3.5 per cent. As late as 1931 the GOI allocated less than 1 rupee per person to education and public spending accounted for 0.74 per cent of national income. In comparison, public investments on education increased to 1.2 per cent of national income in 1950–1951 and then doubled to 2.4 per cent by 1960–1961 (Nalla Gounden 1967).

These numbers are especially low when placed in an international context. Government expenditures on human capital in British India were among the lowest in the world from 1860 to 1912 (Davis and Huttenback 1986). Government

TABLE 10.5 Public expenditures on education

	Public Expenditures	Real Public Expenditures (1881 Rupees)	Real Public Expenditures per capita	As a % of		
				Total Education Spending	Total GOI Budget	National Income
1881–82	10,602,683	10,602,683	0.05	56.18%	1.50%	.
1891–92	15,618,184	11,595,318	0.05	51.17%	1.76%	.
1901–02	17,703,968	13,554,601	0.06	44.13%	1.68%	0.14%
1911–12	40,523,072	22,823,339	0.09	51.56%	3.47%	0.21%
1921–22	114,961,178	42,354,118	0.17	62.56%	5.18%	0.33%
1931–32	168,419,016	110,772,239	0.41	61.95%	7.65%	0.74%

Sources: Public expenditures include spending by all levels of government, e.g. government grants, provincial revenues, and district and municipal funds. These data for 1881–1882 are from Table 147, Statistical abstract relating to British India from 1876–77 to 1885–86 (1887). The data for 1891–92 to 1921–22 are from Progress of Education in India 1917–1922, Volume II-Statistics, Part III – Supplemental Tables, Table 4 – p. 74. The data for 1931–32 are from Progress of Education in India 1927–1932, Volume II – Statistical Tables and Appendices, Part II – Supplemental Tables, Table 5 – p. 60. The GOI budget used in the calculations for 1881–1882 is from Table 43, Statistical abstract relating to British India from 1876–77 to 1885–86 (1887); 1891–92 is from Table 39, Statistical abstract relating to British India from 1885–86 to 1894–95 (1896); 1901–02 is from Table 46, Statistical abstract relating to British India from 1894–95 to 1903–04 (1905); 1911–12 is from Table 46, Statistical abstract relating to British India from 1903–04 to 1912–13. (1915); for 1921–22 from Table 60, East India (statistical abstract). Statistical abstract for British India with statistics, where available, relating to certain Indian States from 1912–13 to 1921–22 fifty-seventh number (second number of new series, 1925); for 1931–32 is from Table 112, East India (statistical abstract). Statistical abstract 1926–27 to 1935–36, sixty-ninth number (fourteenth number of new series, 1938). The national income figures are from Sivasubramonian (1997).

expenditures in British India were lower than in the Indian Princely States, other less-developed countries like Brazil and Mexico, and British dependent colonies. This is true in absolute terms and as a proportion of the total budget. For example, the Indian Princely States allocated 10 per cent of their budget to human capital and foreign underdeveloped countries averaged 6 per cent.

Official reports recognize that public spending was inadequate to meet the needs of mass education, but the same reports were critical of more spending leading to better outcomes. In policy circles low demand was viewed as the primary constraint on educational development. On the other hand, Congress leaders and Indian nationalists bemoaned the low public spending and advocated higher spending as the key to better outcomes. The two positions mirror contemporary debates on the causal effect of public spending on educational outcomes (Glewwe 2002).

Chaudhary (2010a) offers the first credible estimates of the causal effect of local public expenditures on literacy. The findings suggest public investments on primary education had a positive and significant effect on male literacy, but no significant effect on female literacy. The British and Indian views were both partially correct: higher public spending would have increased male literacy, but building more public schools was not the answer to the severe and persistent problem of female illiteracy.

While low public spending cannot explain the poor absolute or relative performance of Indian women, differential economic returns are not a convincing explanation either. Low female literacy combined with a growing need for female teachers in the colonial period suggests returns to female education must have been significant. At the very least, it is hard to believe returns by gender were that far apart to account for the wide gender gap. The divergence between men and women in education also parallels the divergence in labour market performance; for example, men replaced women in higher-paying industrial jobs over the colonial period. Whether a difference in education contributed to differences in labour market performance, or vice versa, is unclear. Still, the problem of female illiteracy does appear to be policy-invariant because female literacy lags behind male literacy even today (65 per cent compared to 82 per cent in 2011).

Public spending would certainly have increased male literacy. However, the GOI may have been reluctant to increase spending because it was not cost effective. The estimates in Chaudhary (2010a) suggest a reallocation of the entire public education budget to primary education was insufficient to make a serious dent in the high level of illiteracy.[11] The GOI needed to substantially increase public funding. Some policy reports made crude calculations of the potential costs of a large-scale expansion of the primary sector. For example, in 1929 the Hartog Committee (Great Britain 1929) estimated a total cost of rupees 19.5 crores (1 crore = 10 million) on a recurring basis to introduce compulsory education covering more than 80 per cent of the school-age population. However, even as late as 1941 public expenditures on education were 18 crores, of which less than 50 per cent were allocated to primary education. It would appear the schemes to expand mass education were never seriously implemented.

Thus, the most significant policy failure was inadequate public spending in absolute terms and as a proportion of the budget. Why did the GOI not spend more on education? Perhaps the rate of return to education investments was lower than other public investments, or perhaps the GOI was hesitant to promote mass education because of the potential political implications for colonial rule. Or perhaps the cost-benefit calculations did not work in the government's favour because India lacked the necessary tax institutions to extract the surplus from an educated work force. Personal incomes were subject to taxation, but the institutional set-up to either increase the rates or extend them to a larger share of the population was perhaps politically infeasible in the twentieth century. These are potential questions – a systematic economic investigation of the GOI's motives and constraints remains to be done.

Caste, religion and fragmented societies

By underinvesting in public education, colonial rule constrained the development of primary education. But this does not imply that India would have enjoyed better outcomes as an independent state. If anything, the slow progress after 1947 demonstrates that inadequate funding was not the only problem. The presence of numerous castes and religions combined with the hierarchal divisions in Indian society seriously undermined private and public attempts to expand basic education.

Indian elites – defined by caste, wealth and occupation – were among the chief beneficiaries of English education. But many of these same elites actively blocked schemes to expand public primary education (Mandal 1975; Mukhopadhyay 1984). Landed elites were reluctant to support public education because they bore a disproportionate cost in terms of land taxes, the main revenues for public primary schools.

In principle, public schools were open to all members of the community, but in practice it was difficult for the lower castes to attend these schools. Schools in Madras were often located either in temples or parts of the village where these groups were not allowed. On account of such problems, special schools were opened for the lower castes either by the GOI or by private missionaries – but it was difficult to find qualified teachers to staff the schools. Such school segregation increased public costs because villages could not exploit the economies of scale in school provision.

The effects of caste and religious heterogeneity were even worse in the private sector. Using district-level data on schools and local conditions, Chaudhary (2009) finds that characteristics of the local elite strongly influenced the provision of primary schools. Brahmans and other educated upper castes successfully directed private and, to a smaller extent, public resources to secondary schools for their children. Districts with a greater share of Brahmans had more public and private secondary schools, plus a smaller ratio of primary to secondary schools. Districts with high levels of caste and religious diversity had fewer private primary schools and a smaller ratio of primary to secondary schools. However, upper castes were unable to completely co-opt the public policy making process: districts with larger proportions of lower castes and Muslims also had more public secondary schools. But these official attempts to circumvent the local politics of school provision were not particularly effective in increasing literacy.

Apart from caste, a heavy reliance on religious schools hurt the progress of Muslim literacy. Muslim literacy rates in heavily Muslim dominant districts were particularly low because they had experienced a more recent collapse of Muslim political authority and hence had more powerful and better-funded religious authorities. The religious authorities established religious schools, which were less effective at promoting literacy on the margin than public schools (Chaudhary and Rubin 2011).

Colonial policies did not do much to ameliorate these longstanding inequalities between groups. Public spending was too low and susceptible to elite capture at many levels. Since official policy could not override the local opposition to members of the lower caste attending public schools, separate schools were created for these groups. But these public secondary schools were not as effective in increasing literacy as the primary schools (Chaudhary 2009). More adequate primary school provision would have been more successful.

Conclusion

This chapter reviewed the basic education patterns in British India and placed the poor Indian performance in a comparative perspective. Despite the small gains in enrolment, literacy was stagnant for most of the period. Simple calculations illustrate that returns to literacy were perhaps not as low as qualitative accounts argue. Rather, inadequate public spending and social divisions within Indian society jointly hurt the progress of basic education.

The disadvantages of heterogeneous societies for public goods provision are not unique to India. Many studies have found similar negative effects of heterogeneity in countries ranging from the United States to Kenya (Alesina, Baqir and Easterly 1999; Miguel and Gugerty 2005). In the Indian case, the inequality between castes further heightened these social divisions.

India's poor schooling record also has important implications for her trajectory of growth. In an influential paper, Acemoglu, Johnson and Robinson (2001) argue that non-settler colonies such as India fell behind because of poor-quality institutions, i.e. extractive institutions, set up by the colonizers. In this view, weak property rights are a key example of extractive institutions. However, Glaeser, La Porta, Lopez-De-Silanes and Shleifer (2004) argue for the primacy of human capital over institutions. By the early twentieth century, the colonial Indian state was not very extractive: tax rates were low by international standards and property rights by most accounts were decent. However, human capital development was severely deemphasized and almost ignored completely. It would appear then that education was an important constraint on economic growth. But before we draw definitive conclusions, future research needs to better explore the links between human capital, the rate of public and private investment, and technological adoption in the Indian context. I hope this chapter spurs research on the general relationship between human capital and growth in India, as well as the specific constraints on education development outlined throughout the chapter.

Notes

1 The chapter focuses exclusively on British India due to data and space constraints.
2 For details see Adam (1838), Nurullah and Naik (1951) and Basu (1982).
3 See Despatch to Government of India on the Subject of General Education in India, House of Commons (1854).
4 After the Despatch, colonial officials did not treat missionary efforts favourably. Mission schools had to compete with newly established government schools, and upper-caste Indians preferred the secular nature of government schools. In 1883, the government explicitly stated their preferences for promoting Indians in the field of private education relative to missionaries.
5 See the Hunter Indian Education Commission Report, House of Commons (India 1883). By 1917, less than 10 per cent of pupils were enrolled in private indigenous schools. Since private indigenous schools were uninspected, and frequently opening and closing, their data are not very accurate.
6 For example, the number of English secondary schools and arts colleges more than doubled from 1881/82 to 1921/22 from 2,133 to 4,904, while the number of pupils more than quintupled from 149,233 to 823,416 (Basu 1974, p. 105).
7 Gokhale, a champion of primary education, introduced a private bill in 1911 that out-lined a modest system of compulsory education for boys between the ages of 6 and 10. The bill was rejected on the grounds that there was no popular demand for such a measure.
8 Secondary schools include middle schools and high schools, both of which had attached primary classes offering higher quality instruction compared to vernacular primary schools. On average, less than 10 per cent of total primary level pupils were enrolled in primary departments of secondary schools. For example, 8.9 per cent and 9.5 per cent of total primary level pupils were in secondary schools in 1907 and 1912 respectively. See *Progress of Education in India: Quinquennial Review*, House of Commons (1914).
9 The Quinquennial Reviews report total population for each province, which in a few cases includes information on the neighbouring Princely States. Since they are unclear about which Princely States are included, I cannot use the Census data by age to gener-ate an exact count of the population aged 5 to 14. Based on the Census of 1911 (India 1913), the 5-to-14 age category appears to be around 25 per cent of the population on average. So, I used 25 per cent of the population as reported for each province in the Quinquennial Reviews to generate the enrolment rates in Table 10.2.
10 The wages are reported as the average monthly salary of primary school teachers in schools for boys and girls. The wages are presumably also averaged over the different types of schools (public, aided and unaided), but the sources are unclear whether this is the case or not.
11 Expenditures on primary schools averaged only 34.3 per cent of public education expen-ditures from 1891/92 to 1916/17. The share was fairly stable over this period – it was 32 per cent in 1891/92, went up to 42 per cent in 1901/02 but came back down to 31 per cent in 1911/12 (Progress of Education in India: Quinquennial Review, Richey 1924, vol. II, p. 125).

References

Acemoglu, D., S. Johnson, and J. Robinson (2001). 'Colonial Origins of Comparative Development: An Empirical Investigation', *American Economic Review, 91 (5)*, pp. 1369–1401.

Adam, W. (1838). *Third Report on The State of Education in Bengal Including Some Account of the State of Education in Behar*, Calcutta: G.H. Huttmann, Bengal Military Orphan Press.

Alesina, A., R. Baqir, and W. Easterly (1999). 'Public Goods and Ethnic Divisions', *Quarterly Journal of Economics, 114 (4)*, pp. 1243–1284.

Basu, A. (1974). *The Growth of Education and Political Development in India 1898–1920*, Delhi: Oxford University Press.

———. (1982). *Essays in the History of Indian Education*, New Delhi: Concept.

Becker, G.S. (1964). *Human Capital: A Theoretical and Empirical Analysis with Special Reference to Education*, New York: National Bureau of Economic Research.

Bellenoit, H.J.A. (2007). *Missionary Education and Empire in Late Colonial India, 1860–1920*, London: Pickering & Chatto.

Benhabib, J., and M.M. Spiegel (1994). 'The Role of Human Capital in Economic Development: Evidence from Aggregate Cross-Country Data', *Journal of Monetary Economics, 34 (2)*, pp. 143–174.

Blaug, M., P.R.G. Layard, and M. Woodhall (1969). *The Causes of Graduate Unemployment in India*, London: Allen Lane.

Broadberry, S., and B. Gupta (2010). 'The Historical Roots of India's Service-led Development: A Sectoral Analysis of Anglo-Indian Productivity Differences, 1870–2000', *Explorations in Economic History, 47 (3)*, pp. 264–278.

Chaudhary, L. (2009). 'Determinants of Primary Schooling in British India', *Journal of Economic History, 69 (1)*, pp. 269–302.

———. (2010a). 'Taxation and Educational Development: Evidence from British India', *Explorations in Economic History, 47 (3)*, pp. 279–293.

———. (2010b). 'Land Revenues, Schools and Literacy: A Historical Examination of Public and Private Funding of Education', *Indian Economic and Social History Review, 47 (2)*, pp. 179–204.

Chaudhary, L., and J. Rubin (2011). 'Reading, Writing and Religion: Institutions and Human Capital Formation', *Journal of Comparative Economics, 39 (1)*, pp. 17–33.

Davis, L.E., and R.A. Huttenback (1986). *Mammon and the Pursuit of Empire: The Political Economy of British Imperialism, 1860–1912*, New York: Cambridge University Press.

Easterlin, R. (1981). 'Why Isn't the Whole World Developed?' *Journal of Economic History, 41 (1)*, pp. 1–19.

Glaeser, E.L., R. La Porta, F. Lopez-De-Silanes, and A. Shleifer (2004). 'Do Institutions Cause Growth?' *Journal of Economic Growth, 9 (3)*, pp. 271–303.

Glewwe, P. (2002). 'Schools and skills in developing countries: education policies and socio-economic outcomes', *Journal of Economic Literature, 40 (2)*, pp. 436–482.

Great Britain (1929). *Indian Statutory Commission. Interim report of the Indian Statutory Commission (Review of growth of education in British India by the Auxiliary committee appointed by the commission)*. London: His Majesty's Stationery Office.

Heyneman, S.P. (1980). 'Investment in Indian Education: Uneconomic?' *World Development, 8 (2)*, pp. 145–163.

House of Commons (1854). 'Despatch to Government of India on General Education in India', *Sessional Papers (393), XLVII. 155*.

———. (1899). 'Progress of Education in India, 1892–97 (Third Quinquennial Review)', *Sessional Papers, (Cd. 9190), LXV. 501*.

————. (1904). 'Review of Progress of Education in India, 1897–98 to 1901–02. Fourth Quinquennial Review (East India: Education)', *Sessional Papers (Cd. 2181, 2182), LXV.1*.

————. (1909). 'Progress of Education in India, 1902–1907. Fifth Quinquennial Review (East India: Education)', *Sessional Papers (Cd. 4635, 4636), LXIII.1*.

————. (1914). 'Progress of Education in India, 1907–12. Sixth Quinquennial Review (East India: Education)', *Sessional Papers (Cd. 7485, 7486), LXII.1*.

————. (1919). 'Seventh Quinquennial Review, 1912–1917 (East India: Education)', *Sessional Papers (Cd. 256, 257), XXVIII.1*.

India (1883). *Report of the Indian Education Commission Appointed by the Resolution of the Government of India Dated 3rd February 1882*, Calcutta: Superintendent of Government Printing.

————. (1886). *Prices and wages in India*, Calcutta: Superintendent of Government Printing.

————. (1913). *Census of India, 1911*, Calcutta: Office of the Superintendent of Government Printing.

————. (1948). *Progress of education in India, 1937-1947: Decennial review*, Delhi: Government Press.

Kumar, D., and M. Desai, eds. (1983). *Cambridge Economic History of India: Vol. II, c.1757 to c.1970*, Cambridge: Cambridge University Press.

Lindert, P. (2004). *Growing Public: Social Spending and Economic Growth since the Eighteenth Century*, Cambridge: Cambridge University Press.

Mandal, A. (1975). 'The Ideology and the Interests of the Bengali Intelligentsia: Sir George Campbell's Education Policy (1871–74)', *Indian Economic and Social History Review, 12 (1)*, pp. 81–98.

Miguel, T. and M.K. Gugerty (2005). 'Ethnic Diversity, Social Sanctions and Public Goods in Kenya', *Journal of Public Economics, 89 (11–12)*, pp. 2325–2368.

Mincer, J. (1974). *Schooling, Experience and Earnings*, New York: Columbia University Press.

Mukhopadhyay, G. (1984). *Mass Education in Bengal (1882–1914)*, Calcutta: National Publishers.

Nalla Gounden, A. M. (1967). 'Investment in Education in India', *Journal of Human Resources, 2 (3)*, pp. 347–358.

Nurullah, S., and J. P. Naik (1951). *A History of Education in India (During the British Period)*, London: Macmillan.

Psacharopoulos, G. (1973). *Returns to Education: An International Comparison*, Amsterdam: Elsevier.

Psacharopoulos, G., and H.A. Patrinos (2004). 'Returns to investment in education: A further update', *Education Economics, 12 (2)*, pp. 111–134.

Richey, J. A. (1924). *Progress of education in India, 1917-1922*. Calcutta: Superintendent of Government Press.

Schultz, T.W. (1962). 'Reflections on Investment in Man', *Journal of Political Economy, 70 (5)*, pp. 1–8.

————. (1971). *Investment in Human Capital*, New York: Free Press and Macmillan.

————. (1983). *Transforming Traditional Agriculture*, Chicago: University of Chicago Press.

Sivasubramonian, S. (1997). 'Revised estimates of the national income of India, 1900–1901 to 1946–47', *Indian Economic and Social History Review, 34 (2)*, pp. 113–168.

11

THE GROWTH OF A LABOUR MARKET IN THE TWENTIETH CENTURY

Tirthankar Roy

From the middle of the nineteenth century until the present times, wage employment increased in all major occupational categories in India, and the scale of self-employment reduced. For some well-known examples of the forms that this assumed, over a million people migrated as labourers to the tropical colonies between 1840 and 1920; a million or more left home to work in tea estates and the industrial cities; a large field of self-employment (artisanal industry) shrank in scale; famines pushed people into wage labour; and the demographic transition from the 1920s began adding an ever larger flow of job seekers even as self-employment opportunities were shrinking.

Using Census statistics, we can construct a broad profile of the long-term trend. Between 1901 and 2001, dependency on wage work increased (Table 11.1). The exact numbers depend on the definition of a worker, which is a murky issue, but the general trend is robust. To some extent, the shift towards wage work had its origin in industrialization. Manufacturing employment increased from 8 per cent in 1901 to 13 per cent in 2001, and agricultural employment fell from 71 to 58 per cent. However, industrialization cannot explain it all because there was change even within a livelihood class. For example, the relative share of wage workers increased within industry from 11 per cent in 1901 to 16 per cent in 1961, to 67 per cent in 2001. Similarly, the share of the government, which is a large employer, increased in tertiary-sector employment from 7 per cent in 1901 to 16 per cent in 2001. This chapter, however, will ignore the role of the government and focus on market-led changes in employment structure.

India was not unique in experiencing such a transformation, which swept through much of the world during the last 200 years. The emergence of wage employment is a central problem for the economic history of the modern world. It forms part of what Karl Polanyi called 'the great transformation', meaning the emergence of market relations from a transactional milieu characterized by reciprocity

TABLE 11.1 Wage and non-wage workers, 1901–2001 (numbers in millions, ratios in %)

	1901 (UI)	1961 (IU)	2001 (IU)
Population	294.4	438.9	1,028.7
Workers	138.9	188.7	402.2
1. Wage Workers	30.4	46.6	170.4
2. Government employees	2.2	7.3	19.1
3. Indentured Emigrants	2.0	0.0	0.0
4. Total of 1–3	36.7	53.9	189.5
5. Self-employed	80.0	134.8	210.0
Self-employed/Total Workers	75.1	71.4	52.2
Wage Workers (1+3)/Total Workers (excluding government)	21.9	24.7	42.3
Wage Workers (4)/Total Workers (including government)	23.4	28.6	47.1

Notes: Categories included in wage workers in 1901 are farm servants, field-labourers, general labour, 'operatives' in brickworks, stoneware, railways, presses, cotton gins and mills, jute mills, clothing units, silk factories, and mines. Categories of wage workers for 1961 and 2001 are agricultural labour, mining, non-household industry, and construction. Figures for 2001 include main and marginal workers.

Source: Census of India, various years. UI: Undivided India; IU: Indian Union.

and redistribution (Polanyi 2001). It figures in John Hicks' *Theory of Economic History* as an illustration of how factor markets emerged from the bed of a command economy (Hicks 1969). The formation of a *proletariat* – or workers divorced from the instruments of production and dependent on wages – is a key element in the Marxist theory of capitalism. The prehistory of the proletariat developed through the work of Friedrich Engels, who first studied how the proletariat lived, and the studies of the German activist Karl Kautsky, who discussed the mechanisms of proletariat formation, and received its fullest development in Maurice Dobb (Engels 1987, Kautsky 1971, Dobb 1946). Later, the process came to be called *pauperization*, which would include the dispossession of peasants of land and small businesses and artisans of markets.

We are, then, dealing with a process of change that is a defining characteristic of modern world history. Does world history offer useful insights about India? Parallels between the two have been drawn in the scholarship known as *labour history* in India, mainly using Marxist categories and concepts. The next section discusses the received framework and suggests why a different conceptual framework is necessary.

The received view

Although labour history is an established field in Indian academia, much of it is about politics rather than markets. The scholarship originated in a Marxist debate of the 1970s on the prospect of a popular revolution in India, and why it was late in coming. It moved later towards 'Gramscian' issues of the 'hegemony' of the capitalist class, and incorporated 'Foucauldian' ideas about means of social control. Antonio Gramsci was an Italian Marxist, and Michel Foucault a French philosopher. In the process of incorporating influences from global Marxism and post-Marxist radicalism, two broad arguments on labour emerged, which can be called the Marxist and the postcolonial arguments (for discussion on and examples of the older version, see essays in Prakash 1992 and Haynes and Prakash 1992; on the newer version, see essays in Van der Linden and Mohapatra 2009).

The common point of reference between them is the nineteenth-century globalization, consisting of an enormous rise in trade, migration, and investment throughout the world, or the development of capitalism in an Indian setting. The British Empire supplied indirect and direct support to the process. Indians took part in it in a variety of roles, peasants exported commodities, consumers purchased imported textiles, merchants profited from these trades and reinvested the profit back into factories, which were run with imported technology. Further, European capitalists set up plantations and mills, and a large number of people left India to work abroad. Did this process of modernization and globalization benefit the Indian worker?

The Marxist model answers that it did not, and it offers an economic history narrative showing how the emergence of wage work was caused by increasing distress and dislocation. The story follows the pauperization thesis illustrated with reference to the adverse effects of colonialism and nineteenth-century free trade upon the peasants and the artisans. Owing to deindustrialization and forced commerce, peasants and artisans lost access to their means of production and joined the proletariat, while workers lost control over their labour. Their traditional livelihoods were destroyed – and in the new world of wage employment, they were exploited by employers who had acquired more political power in the colonial regime. In short, wage work emerged because of a dislocation and crisis that beset self-employment. Growth in the number of labourers represented 'a marked increase in the pace of pauperization' (Jha 1997, p. 6). The original statement of the thesis with Indian data goes to the credit of Patel (1952) and Patnaik (1972).

The postcolonial argument shares the same conclusion, but stresses a different dynamic. It makes social control the object of interest and examines techniques of control by studying colonial discourses. It turns labour history into a story of a colonial type of subjugation, often circumscribed by formal law introduced to favour expatriate capitalists. New forms of wage employment appearing in the mills, plantations, and indentured labour markets in this story made workers victims of exploitation because the colonial rulers perfected modern techniques of controlling the subjects (see essays in Van der Linden and Mohapatra 2009). The state also changed the discourse of freedom and bondage (Prakash 1990). The advantage of the second paradigm over the first is that it avoids the need to make a sharp polarization between capitalists and workers as necessitated in Marxist narratives. It explains better why class polarization did not lead to popular revolution. In its turn, the second paradigm prefers to work with a new bipolar construct, the poles represented by the colonial state and the Indian subjects.

Both these arguments were revised marginally in works in labour history. It was shown how class formation was shaped by indigenous cultures (Chakrabarty 1989). It was argued, in the style of the British 'new left' historian E. P. Thompson, that the workers were less victims of circumstances, but tried by various means to control and reshape their situation. These contextual elements, such as relationships forged in the city neighbourhoods influenced their class consciousness (Chandavarkar 1994; see also Basu 2004). The Subaltern Studies Collective explored the distinct character of working-class consciousness that took shape through resisting colonial power (Ludden 2001; Roy 2002b).

While relevant and useful in parts as conceptual models of livelihood experiences, these paradigms are limited. They either caricaturize or overlook economic factors. Specifically, they encounter five problems. First, this literature in its origin is an offshoot of the Marxist engagement with political activism by workers. Therefore, labour historians have tended to restrict themselves to contexts that easily lend themselves to the study of organized politics. The city factory suits that project; self-employment in agriculture or handicrafts does not. These fields are not only under-researched, but also under-theorized, since they cannot be conceptualized with the help of 'class', but require dealing with other kinds of collectivities. The fixation with organized politics led labour historians to underplay the agency of the family, gender, or community in shaping work and well-being.

Second, both arguments are caught up in a view of the world made up of binaries – two classes in the Marxist case, and rulers and subjects in the postcolonial case. But the huge diversity that characterized the labourers in India renders any binary model impractical. A differentiation also needs to be made in the political sphere. The postcolonial argument is founded on the tenet that British colonialism wrought all the important transformations in India in the nineteenth century – but the British Empire ruled only over half the space of South Asia. Even within the half that it governed, it had limited powers to regulate anything. It was an unusually weak state in fiscal terms. There were many economic forces of change that the Empire merely adapted to, including demography, migration, and industrialization.

Third, because they ignore institutional and contractual variety, both variants of labour history shut out the possibility of workers being able to choose between alternatives. *Choice* is a taboo word in the Marxist and postcolonial labour history. But the absence of choice flattens out a whole range of institutional differences that the worker may have perceived and compared. In the late nineteenth century, manual workers were not ignorant about the implications of joining the indenture as opposed to staying home as agricultural labourers. Both were wage work and both involved the threat of coercion by the employer. A worker could still choose between disciplinary mechanisms depending on what one would earn in each site, what prospects of mobility there were in each case, and how intrusive discipline was upon the social lives of workers. By discarding choice, the framework remains incapable of discussing how workers compared and perceived these alternatives, and therefore produces an incomplete history of wage labour.

Fourth, the roles of colonialism, colonial law, and colonial power are overstated in postcolonial history. Wage employment has been on the rise not only in colonial times, but also in postcolonial times. It has been on the rise not only in India but throughout the world. A conceptual model of wage employment that tends to read it as a relationship engineered by colonialism and free trade is too restrictive to be extended to the present times and for studying comparative history. We need explanations of wage employment that are not tied to colonialism.

Fifth, the two arguments cannot explain the selectivity and bias in the wage employment process in India. All who were affected by conditions leading to wage work did not necessarily join wage work or join it in the same fashion. Of particular importance in this regard was a systematic difference between men and women.

It is not being suggested that forced wage employment did not occur. But there were many cases of volitional or wilful entry into the labour market as well, which the received labour history cannot account for easily. It is necessary to clarify what is meant by *voluntary entry*.

A rational choice approach

The Marxist pauperization thesis attributes the rise of wage employment to adverse forces pushing people to leave traditional livelihoods in the nineteenth century. An additional framework favoured here would see idle labour as a structural condition present from long before the nineteenth century and wage employment as a response to new opportunities of exchanging idle labour for a market wage. This is a distinct view from another non-Marxist framework known in the literature, which argues that conditions of labouring were present before, but recorded better in the Censuses (Kumar 1965). The additional model in this chapter is necessary because it can distinguish between different patterns of response to new opportunities, whereas none of the other models can do this. The pauperization thesis, for example, cannot easily distinguish between different types of pauperized people.

Idle labour, or surplus labour, had always been present in the agricultural system because of the low productivity and pronounced seasonality of tropical monsoon agriculture. Any rural worker would find it rational to offer services outside agriculture and in an urban market. But such idle labour was not sufficiently mobile before because of high transaction costs in the labour market, especially the high costs of moving from one institutional set-up to another, and the costs in terms of time and money of accessing wage opportunities located far away from home. These obstacles became weaker from the nineteenth century onwards. Transportation, relocation, and transaction costs in the labour market fell, so that more people joined wage employment. Taken together, these propositions form a rational choice alternative to the Marxist narrative.

A rational choice model does not imply that the workers joined wage employment because they earned higher wages than before. At least in rural labour circulation, labour supply increased without a significant rise in wages. We know that labour supply increased from the fact that agricultural production expanded on a more or less unchanging technology. There are several explanations available to explain this feature, and all implicitly or explicitly assume surplus labour. For example, in a 'classical' approach, wages would follow customs and institutional constraints, departing only temporarily from its 'natural' long-term levels to sink back to it. The underlying assumption is that of flexible supplies of labour at the ruling wage. Alternatively, in a neoclassical model, labour supply reflects the labour–leisure choice at different levels of wage. If there is surplus labour in the economy, leisure is abundant and valued little, and wage labour is scarce and valued more, so that a small increase in wage is likely to lead to a large supply of effort. In both cases, high transaction cost would limit the choices.

I have shown elsewhere that the force of custom was strong in the eighteenth century employment arrangements, and it weakened from the nineteenth century onwards, suggesting a shift in the institutional conditions underlying labour supply from a classical pattern towards a neoclassical one (Roy 2007). The prospect that there were deep changes in the institutions of the labour market builds a new bridge between Indian history and global history. 'The problem faced in earlier . . . times', writes one historian, '[was] to find a mechanism to shift from a "backward bending" to a "forward sloping" labour supply curve', a problem that demands attention to 'those institutions that influenced or determined the nature and limits of collective behaviour' (Engerman 1997, pp. 97, 102). This chapter suggests that a similar question can be asked for India.

Combining both Marxist pauperization theory and an institutional approach, we can outline three distinct types of shift in work that could translate into an increase in the proportion of wage workers.

First, there was a decline in self-employment. Self-employment declined because certain forms of it ceased to be competitive. For example, many artisans who once made and sold goods at the same time specialized in making rather than selling. They did this because markets tended to be located further away, so that trade needed more capital. Second, wage employment shifted from institutional arrangements that were less likely to be recorded as wage work towards institutional arrangements that were explicitly recognized in the Censuses as wage work. Third, wage employment and self-employment increased in an interdependent fashion, and the joint increase was sustained by longer working hours on average. These three processes, this chapter will suggest, characterized particularly the experiences of artisans, labourers, and peasants respectively.

The third process has received attention in a recent scholarship on industrialization in Europe and Japan (Berg, Hudson, and Sonenscher 1983; Saito 2005). In these regions in the eighteenth century, peasant families that had earlier been supplying some artisanal goods experienced an increase in demand for artisanal goods, and responded by working harder and devoting more time than before to wage work. A relative shift in favour of wage work occurred because entire families devoted extra hours to the labour market. Similar to this third argument, the industrious revolution thesis claims that the desire to consume a wider variety of market-purchased goods (some of which were coming in from the tropics) induced self-employed European peasants to increase their work effort in non-farm activities in the eighteenth and the early nineteenth centuries, usually under putting-out contracts (De Vries 1994). For women, whether urban or rural, pre-industrial or industrial, the margin between wage work and intra-family work was a thin one. One recent contribution on pre-industrial Holland shows that this characteristic owed in part to the employers' strategies to contain the core urban workforce by shifting work to the part-timers (Van Nederveen Meerkerk 2006). For many people, who were caught up in structural changes like those seen in the earlier examples, combining self-employment and wage employment made sense. Self-employment reduced the risks of market participation whereas wage employment provided access to a wider basket of consumer goods and services.

I will now show how these three mechanisms illustrate the growth of a labour market in India.

Route 1: from self-employment to wage employment

Marxists have argued that one of the pathways that led to wage work is 'forced commercialization', especially in those regions of western and southern India where the *ryotwari* settlement was instituted (see Patnaik 1972, 1983; Prakash 1992). According to this mechanism, landholding peasants mortgaged their title to borrow money at a high rate of interest, in order to either meet the risks of export market fluctuations or revenue demands. Unable to repay these loans, they lost access to land. Some landowning and tenant farmers did perform labour on the side or even became full-time workers, but the scale was probably not very large. According to the best measures available, inequality in landholding was relatively low and did not change. Furthermore, the extent of land transfer remained small (for more discussion on numbers to back up these claims, see Kumar 1975; Roy 2009).

A second mechanism was deindustrialization, which decreased the demand for artisanal labour and increased the supply of agricultural labour (see Ray, Chapter 4 in this volume, for a fuller discussion of the process). Many artisans did lose their livelihoods – but we need to be cautious about who they were, and what they did to compensate for the loss. Deindustrialization concentrated among groups that produced intermediate goods of generic quality such as cotton yarn or pig iron. These goods were more easily mass produced and mechanized. But artisans making finished consumer articles were often highly skilled and able to produce design or quality that could not be reproduced with machines (Roy 1999). These groups did not face mass unemployment and were rarely known to take up agricultural labour. Furthermore, certain generic skills such as carpentry or joinery, smithy, and construction work were valued in a range of new livelihoods, and experienced a rise in wages (Sivasubramonian 2000).

While some of the skilled groups did not suffer large scale job losses, they nevertheless needed to be more willing to experiment. They could still face changing consumer preference for lighter and cheaper craft goods. Large urban markets offered scope to earn more money and demanded innovative ability. In order to meet the demands of new markets, they needed to move closer to the cities (for example, handloom weavers moved to the spinning mill towns), sometimes to work in larger factory-type workshops and to make use of new tools and processes. When these changes happened, old institutions of work like the family firm weakened. The men among artisan families had better prospects of earning wages in factories and workshops than had the women, who were left behind and turned agricultural or became unemployed (Roy 1999, 2010).

On the other side of the economic spectrum, a category of workers who lived wholly on the income of assets, and who were quite prominent in 1901, disappeared by the end of the century. These were the people who lived on the income of property, mainly landed property. Rent receivers formed 20 per cent of the non-wage workers according to the 1901 Census, and were a small enough group to be ignored in the late twentieth century. Rents generally increased in the twentieth century, in some cases by an enormous extent. But living on rent became difficult partly because legal procedures had made realization of the rise in rents difficult, and partly due to the demographic transition, which led to a subdivision of property. The beginning of this change probably went back to the nineteenth century, when many landlords and *talukdars* of northern India experienced declining fortunes because of regulations over rent, and left the village for urban service. On the many occasions when such classes of people joined government service, the move showed up in the Census data as a net increase in wage employment.

Route 2: from wage employment to wage employment

Jan Breman's well-known work illustrating the transformation of one form of labour ties to another in two South Gujarat villages; notwithstanding, this class of shifts remains under-researched in labour history (Breman 1974).[1]

Early Census officials puzzled over the existence of a large group of people in central and western India whose employers were not individuals but whole collective bodies. This category, which figured in the early colonial Censuses and disappeared later, was called *general labour*. Some of these workers were possibly engaged in customary service contracts such as *balute* in Maharashtra. Investigations suggest that the category also included rural labourers who performed diverse services for the village or the peasants (for a discussion, see Thorner and Thorner 1962).

What general labour might mean in reality is illustrated in this 1817 description of members of a Gujarat village:

> The duties of the Dhers are well-known to be as follows: to carry the baggage of all travellers as far as the next village on the road . . . to be the village scavengers . . . to act occasionally, too, as watchmen . . . to convey letters from the public functionaries and Patells to the next village . . . Money also, or other valuables, is sent in this manner with perfect safety; and they are intelligencers,

and know well how to shew boundaries . . . Spinning and weaving are principal occupations of the Dhers.

(Williams 1825, p. 98)

These groups were maintained by means of *inam* or rent-free land as well as standard fees collected from the cultivators. A remark that figures in an 1827 report
on the Deccan suggests that the nature of their right on land was ambiguous. 'The
Mahrs conceive that they have the right to mortgage or otherwise dispose of lands
held for the performance of specific duties to the village and the government'. It
probably mattered little as 'they *cannot* absolve themselves and their descendants
from their duties' (Sykes 1838, p. 290, emphasis in original). The mention of caste
names in these discussions on labour suggests that general labour was more closely
associated with social position than contractual status in the labour market.

During the second half of the nineteenth century, obligatory services for the
villages declined due to the exit of some of the members to the city, specialization
of some in specific trades such as leather work, and specialization of others in casual
agricultural wage labour, and social reform movements. The trend was a general
one, but it took several decades before the Census decided to drop the category
altogether (the 1951 Census retained it, the 1961 Census did not). While general
labour disappeared, few among the group seemed to specialize in trade and manufactures, even though some of them were reported as part-time artisans as in one
of the earlier citations. Such movements were not unknown, but there were many
more movements from 'general' labour to specialized labour, or from labour for a
group to labour for single employers. Huge construction projects, railways, roads,
and canals, drew in hundreds and thousands of rural workers, who would formerly
be classified as general labour.

Furthermore, from the late nineteenth century, the circulation of workers within
agriculture increased in scale and in terms of the average distance covered. One
effect was that the average duration of employment contracts came down in rural
India. For example, the farm servant contract had been common in southern India,
and sporadically elsewhere, before the Census period; but these contracts began
to end. Debt bondage may have increased at the same time, but it is impossible to
determine the scale at which this was happening. In Madras, the fall in farm servant
contracts was dramatic. The farm servants may have been a reflection of caste hierarchy. They may represent a form of labour tying or labour hoarding in response
to the high seasonal fluctuations in demand for labour. From the workers' point of
view, farm servant arrangements earlier made sense as an insurance against famines.
In any case, increased migration weakened both caste hierarchy and these insurance
schemes. Circulation was gainful because the commercialization of agriculture in
some regions had raised wages there.

Several prominent streams of seasonal circulation of agricultural labourers
emerged from the late nineteenth century onwards (Roy 2005). Large numbers of
workers migrated every season from the uplands of the Godavari, Krishna, Guntur,
and Visakhapatnam districts to the Krishna–Godavari deltas for farm work. Many

people from Chhattisgarh went every cotton season to the Berar cotton fields and gins. The wheat fields of Narmada Valley – that is, Jabalpur, Sagar, and Damoh – received migrants from the United Provinces in the north and from Rewa, wherein the Gonds descended from the hills during the harvests. Workers from Bihar migrated to Bengal in the jute harvest season, while workers from Azamgarh were recruited for large-scale earthwork in Bengal. From Ratnagiri, many people went to work in the cotton fields of Broach. The Punjab Canal Colonies received migrants from Rajputana. Agricultural labourers also went to take up work in the plantations, urban services, railways, and other public works, and (only rarely) in the mills. These shifts, which elsewhere I have called *reallocation*, were not just transfers of population between locations and jobs, but also involved transfers between institutions (Roy 2002a). When rural workers left their villages, they left long-term arrangements to take part in casual-cum-seasonal arrangements. Therefore, migration also hastened the breakup of customary terms of employment. Earlier in this chapter, I referred to the same transition as a move from a classical labour supply situation to a neoclassical one.

Route 3: combining self-employment and wage employment

Because of the high seasonality of monsoon agriculture, there was extensive under-employment among the peasantry. Agriculture rarely offered full-time work for more than 200 days in a year, and much less than that in the dry regions. Year-round work was available in mills, mines, and plantations. Even the relatively well-off peasant families could afford to send their adult males to non-agricultural wage work, while recalling them to meet the peak season labour demand.

A good example of this strategy was the mill worker of Bombay and Calcutta. Unlike in England, where artisans joined the factory labour force on a large scale, the entry of artisans in the Indian textile mills on the factory floor happened on a small scale and selectively. The mill workforce mainly consisted of peasants. Unlike in Japan, where peasant households themselves engaged in making handicrafts, in India, the skilled artisan and the peasant formed discrete occupational groups. Artisans did take up factory work in Bombay and Calcutta, but in small batches and in specialized departments. By and large, the Indian mill workers came from the agricultural village.

Another distinctiveness of the Indian factory workforce was that migration was (and continues to be) unusually biased towards males. Women married early – the average age in 1901 was 13 – and families started early. Consequently, women were less mobile and tended to work more in households and farms, rather than in wage employment, let alone urban factories (Table 11.2) (Roy 2005). Compared to the cotton textile mills of New England, England, and Japan, Indian factories employed very few women. The proportion of women in the workforce in the Lancashire cotton textiles was about 50 per cent in 1819. In 1920, 70 per cent of the workers in the spinning and weaving shops in Japanese cotton mills were women. Among New England textile workers, 90 per cent were female in 1828, with the figure declining to about 60 per cent by the middle of the nineteenth century. By contrast,

TABLE 11.2 Women workers, 1901–2001 (numbers in millions, ratios in %)

	1901 (UI)	2001 (IU)
Workers	43.0	127.2
Agriculture	27.5	91.1
Manufacturing	4.9	25.0
Wage Workers	14.8	66.2
Agriculture	9.4	49.4
Manufacturing	0.1	16.8
General labour	3.9	0.0
Ratios		
Women Wage Workers/Wage Workers	46.3	38.9[a]
Women Workers/Workers	30.9	31.6
Women/Agricultural labourers	46.0	46.3
Women/Manufacturing workers	7.1	32.9

a: Agriculture and Manufacturing

Notes: Categories included in wage workers in 1901 are farm servants, field-labourers, general labour, 'operatives' in brickworks, stoneware, railways, presses, cotton gins and mills, jute mills, clothing units, silk factories, and mines. Categories of wage workers for 1961 and 2001 are agricultural labour, mining, non-household industry, and construction. Figures for 2001 include main and marginal workers. *Source:* Census of India, various years. UI: Undivided India; IU: Indian Union.

in 1926, women formed only 23 per cent of Mumbai's textile workforce, which was the highest proportion among major Indian factory cities – and even this figure was falling. In Kanpur, the corresponding percentage was 5, and in South India 10. In the jute industry of Calcutta, the proportion of female workers was 20 per cent at the end of the interwar period.

These patterns arose because few peasants migrated as families to the big city. The cost of living in the big city surely was a deterrent. But there were two other reasons constraining women's entry into the urban labour market: most women of working age needed to mind young children, and they needed to look after land. Even if the family did not own sufficient land, it made sense to retain a foothold in the village. In effect, the decision of the women to stay behind would imply a higher intensity of work for all members of the household, for women in self-employment and for men in wage employment. All this would mean that for quite a large proportion of the factory workers in the nineteenth century, the urban factory offered the chance of a reallocation of family labour between agricultural and non-agricultural work.

What did these transformations mean for wages?

Trends in wages: stagnation in rural wage, divergence overall

Any general account of labour supply needs to be consistent with two stylized facts on wages: the long-term constancy in rural real wage, and a tendency of divergence between the rural agricultural wage and the urban non-agricultural wage.

Interest in trends in real wages nowadays derives from an interest in standard of living. Given that manual wage workers in general, and agricultural workers in particular, are often among the poorest people in the Indian society, wages constitute a robust measure of poverty. A recent work has used the ratio between GDP and wage per head as a proxy for economy-wide inequality (O'Rourke and Williamson 1999). By both these measures, colonial India may have seen a growth of measurable poverty (an increase in the number of poor, not the depth of poverty), and a mild rise in inequality. I stress *measurable* because poverty is hard to define and harder to measure if a large part of labour supply remains outside market relations as was the case in pre-colonial India and during much of the colonial period as well.

Agricultural real wages changed little on average, while fluctuating a great deal from year to year, between 1900 and the mid-1960s. The inertia dates back at least to the end of the eighteenth century (Table 11.3). Real agricultural wages in the 1960s were only 20 per cent higher than those in the 1780s, and even that trend is not a robust one. From the 1970s onwards, the trend in real agricultural wages turned upward. Thereafter, the acceleration may have fallen somewhat,

TABLE 11.3 Agricultural wage, average annual in Rs., 1785–1968

	Money Wage	Real Wage (1873 Prices)
1784–88	14	27
1810	18	35
1830	24	32
1857	24	29
1870–75	35	35
1882–25	38	27
1899–1900	48	37
1920	73	29
1929	100–110	47
1931	59	38
1936	53	28
1941	41	15–18
1946	205	31
1951	241	48
1960		42
1968		42

Notes: The data in this table were constructed by using a variety of sources. For details, see Roy (2007, 2009). Most wages relate to eastern and southern India until the 1870s and to all-India averages thereafter. The former dataset is collated from British Parliamentary Papers and contemporary surveys. The dataset for the period 1870s–1920s was gathered from two official sources: that relating to the interwar period from published or unpublished provincial surveys; and that relating to the post-1950s, mainly from Mukherjee (1995) and Jose (1988). Typically, the eighteenth and nineteenth century numbers are available in the form of annual or monthly wages, whereas the later numbers are reported as daily wages. These were converted into annual wages, assuming a year of 220 working days. For the eighteenth and nineteenth centuries, the deflator used is the price of rice in Bengal, available in the Global Price and Income History Group website. For the later periods, the weighted commodity prices index or the agricultural GDP deflator was used. The wartime prices and wages are not reliable because of fluctuations during the year.

but no actual reversal occurred – which, when seen against the historical pattern, is nothing short of a revolution. The average real wage has approximately doubled between 1983 and 2004. A recent paper argues that the upward trend reflects a rise in the average productivity of land more than intersectoral shifts of workers (Eswaran et al. 2009). Research that makes careful distinctions between sub-periods and regions also observes that in the 1990s, as the successive waves of 'Green Revolutions' exhausted their respective potentials, the growth rate in rural wages slowed and variations increased (Chavan and Bedamatta 2006; Srivastava and Singh 2006).

There is something to be said for a classical approach to labour supply when we look at the eighteenth and early nineteenth century labour history. Custom and tradition played a big role in determining remuneration in pre-colonial and early colonial India. The extensive use of general labour and farm servant arrangements points in that direction. Direct evidence on wage setting also suggests a bias towards the status quo. These arrangements made labour relatively immobile. It was easy to move from a customary arrangement to casual labour, but it was not easy to move from one customary arrangement into another because the force of custom depended on the identity of the subjects. With the availability of a casual labour market on the margin, older arrangements decayed quickly. In the twentieth century, custom was much less a force in wage setting. But wages did not necessarily respond because labour supply had become more flexible. In Europe and Japan too, real wages did not necessarily respond to proto-industrial production. The obvious interpretation is that the supply of effort increased. The models of institutional change discussed before do imply a highly elastic labour supply. India was an example of the same process; the difference was in the details.

A major part of the reallocation was confined to unskilled and rural labour. No matter where the agricultural labourers went, the long-term demand for rural labour – and therefore wages – was rigidly set by the yield of agricultural land. There was no significant and sustained increase in average yield in India between 1700 and 1970 (on the statistical foundations of this proposition, see Roy 2013). Population growth further depressed wages in the mid-twentieth century. Where possible, rural labour left agriculture altogether – the most visible outlets in the nineteenth and early twentieth centuries being indentured labour – but the proportion of exit was too small to make much difference to wages (Table 11.1).

In contrast to rural wages, the wages of skilled artisans and manufacturers were historically higher than agricultural wages, and they tended to rise faster (Roy 2007). Non-agricultural wages in the late twentieth century had also risen somewhat faster than rural wages. The artisans were, no doubt, subjected to a decline in livelihood. Yet, national income statistics show that the average wage of skilled artisans rose in the early twentieth century (Sivasubramonian 2000). The rise reflected, in part, an increased demand for artisanal skills of certain types (mainly textiles) and, in part, the adoption of better tools and processes. But as we have seen earlier, these changes could entail better prospects for the men among artisan households than for the women. Increased labour circulation did not eliminate all wage differentials.

Barriers to labour mobility between the high and the low wage sectors persisted because of differences in skills and because of market failure in skill acquisition. Much circulation stayed confined to low wage and low earning segments instead.

Conclusion

This chapter tried to offer a more differentiated, and therefore more realistic, picture of the rise of wage employment than available from the received account. The latter attributes the process to distress of various kinds. The present account does not dispute distress, but adds to it another dynamic: the prospect that rural surplus labour could more easily seek alternative and supplementary earning opportunities. Combining the distress-led and volitional processes, we can see that different groups participated in wage work differently.

Three patterns are identified: decline in self-employment, which mainly characterized the artisans; shifts between forms of labour, which characterized the rural labourers; and combining self-employment with wage employment, which characterized many peasant groups. Whenever there were movements between sites of work, women tended to remain behind; this was especially true of peasants and skilled artisans, less true of rural labourers.

One general effect of the change was an increase in the supply of effort overall, so that wages remained stagnant in the long run. The wage depression was not necessarily a welfare loss, for the supply of effort also enabled many families to utilize surplus labour gainfully.

Note

1 In an appreciative review article, Charlesworth (1979) argued that Breman supplied an insufficient and overly stylized account of the economic history of institutional change.

References

Basu, S. (2004). *Does Class Matter? Colonial Capital and Workers' Resistance in Bengal, 1890–1937*, Delhi: Oxford University Press.

Berg, M., P. Hudson, and M. Sonenscher, eds. (1983). *Manufacture in Town and Country before the Factory*, Cambridge: Cambridge University Press.

Breman, J. (1974). *Patronage and Exploitation. Changing Agrarian Relations in South Gujarat, India*, Berkeley: University of California Press.

Chakrabarty, D. (1989). *Rethinking Working-Class History: Bengal 1890–1940*, Princeton: Princeton University Press.

Chandavarkar, R. (1994). *The Origins of Industrial Capitalism in India: Business Strategies and the Working Classes in Bombay, 1900–1940*, Cambridge: Cambridge University Press.

Charlesworth, N. (1979). 'Review of Breman (1974)', *Modern Asian Studies, 13 (1)*, pp. 152–157.

Chavan, P., and R. Bedamatta (2006). 'Trends in Agricultural Wages in India: 1964–65 to 1999–2000', *Economic and Political Weekly, 41 (38)*, pp. 4041–4051.

De Vries, J. (1994). 'The Industrial Revolution and the Industrious Revolution', *Journal of Economic History, 54 (2)*, pp. 249–270.

Dobb, M. (1946). *Studies in the Development of Capitalism*, London: Routledge and Kegan Paul.

Engerman, S. (1997). 'Cultural Values, Ideological Beliefs, and Changing Labor Institutions: Notes on their Interactions', in J.N. Drobak and J.V.C. Nye, eds., *The Frontiers of the New Institutional Economics*, San Diego: Academic Press, pp. 95–119.

Engels, F. (1987). *The Condition of the Working Class in England*, London: Penguin.

Eswaran, M., A. Kotwal, B. Ramaswami, and W. Wadhwa (2009). 'Sectoral Labour Flows and Agricultural Wages in India, 1983–2004: Has Growth Trickled Down?' *Economic and Political Weekly, 44 (2)*, pp. 46–55.

Global Price and Income History Group. Retrieved from http://gpih.ucdavis.edu/. Accessed 10 December 2012.

Haynes, D., and G. Prakash, eds. (1992). *Contesting Power: Everyday Resistance in South Asian Society and History*, Berkeley: University of California Press.

Hicks, J. (1969). *A Theory of Economic History*, Oxford: Oxford University Press.

Jha, P. (1997). *Agricultural Labour in India*, Delhi: Vikas Publishing.

Jose, A. V. (1988). 'Agricultural Wages in India', *Economic and Political Weekly, 23 (26)*, pp. A46–A58.

Kautsky, K. (1971). *The Class Struggle*, New York: Norton.

Kumar, D. (1965). *Land and Caste in South India*, Cambridge: Cambridge University Press.

———. (1975). 'Landownership and Inequality in Madras Presidency: 1853–54 to 1946–47', *Indian Economic and Social History Review, 12 (3)*, pp. 229–261.

Ludden, D., ed. (2001). *Reading Subaltern Studies*, Delhi: Permanent Black.

Mukherjee, M. (1995). *Selected Papers on National Income*, Calcutta: Firma KLM.

O'Rourke, K., and J. Williamson (1999). *Globalization in History*, Cambridge, MA: MIT Press.

Patel, S. (1952). *Agricultural Labourers in Modern India and Pakistan*, Bombay: Current Book House.

Patnaik, U. (1972). 'Development of Capitalism in Agriculture – I', *Social Scientist, 1 (2)*, pp. 15–31.

———. (1983). 'On the Evolution of the Class of Agricultural Labourers in India', *Social Scientist, 11 (1)*, pp. 3–24.

Polanyi, K. (2001). *The Great Transformation: The Political and Economic Origins of Our Time*, Boston: Beacon Press. Originally published 1944.

Prakash, G. (1990). *Bonded Histories: Genealogies of Labour Servitude in Colonial India*, Cambridge: Cambridge University Press.

———, ed. (1992). *World of the Rural Labourer in Colonial India*, Delhi: Oxford University Press.

Roy, T. (1999). *Traditional Industry in the Economy of Colonial India*, Cambridge: Cambridge University Press.

———. (2002a). 'Economic History and Modern India: Redefining the Link', *Journal of Economic Perspectives, 16 (3)*, pp. 109–130.

———. (2002b). 'Subaltern Studies: Questioning the Basics', in *Economic and Political Weekly, 37 (23)*, pp. 2223–2228.

———. (2005). *Rethinking Economic Change in India: Labour and Livelihood*, London: Routledge.

———. (2007). 'Globalization, Factor Prices, and Poverty in Colonial India', *Australian Economic History Review, 47 (1)*, pp. 73–94.

———. (2009). 'Factor Markets and the Narrative of Economic Change in South Asia', *Continuity and Change, 24 (1)*, pp. 137–167.

———. (2010). 'The Long Globalization and Textile Producers in India', in Heerma van Voss, L., E. Hiemstra-Kuperus, and E. Van Nederveen Meerkerk, eds., *The Ashgate Companion to the History of Textile Workers*, Aldershot: Ashgate, pp. 253–274.

————. (2013). *An Economic History of Early Modern India*, London: Routledge.

Saito, O. (2005). 'Pre-Modern Economic Growth Revisited: Japan and the West', Working Paper, London School of Economics. Retrieved from http://eprints.lse.ac.uk/22475/1/wp16.pdf. Accessed 15 December 2012.

Sivasubramonian, S. (2000). *National Income of India in the Twentieth Century*, Delhi: Oxford University Press.

Srivastava, R., and R. Singh (2006). 'Rural Wages during the 1990s: A Re-estimation', *Economic and Political Weekly, 41 (38)*, pp. 4053–4062.

Sykes, W. H. (1838). *Special Report on the Statistics of the four Collectorates of Dukhun under the British Government*, London: British Association for the Advancement of Science.

Thorner, D., and A. Thorner (1962). *Land and Labour in India*, Bombay: Asia Publishing House.

Van der Linden, M., and P.P. Mohapatra, eds. (2009). *Labour Matters: Towards Global Histories (Studies in Honour of Sabyasachi Bhattacharya)*, Delhi: Tulika Books.

Van Nederveen Meerkerk, E. (2006). 'Segmentation in the Pre-Industrial Labour Market: Women's Work in the Dutch Textile Industry, 1581–1810', *International Review of Social History, 51 (2)*, pp. 189–216.

Williams, M. (1825). *Memoir on the Zilla of Baroche*, London: Cox and Baylis.

12

INDUSTRIAL LABOUR IN LATE COLONIAL INDIA

Susan Wolcott

Sivasubramonian's (2000) data on the productivity of Indian industrial labour indicate only an 11 to 15 per cent improvement over the period 1900–1938 (depending on the method of calculation). A detailed examination of these data shows that most of even this small measured productivity growth in organized industry can be attributed to the enormous gains made by the Tata Iron and Steel Company (TISCO). Since – with the notable exception of TISCO – virtually all organized industries in India experienced stagnant labour productivity from 1900 to Independence, there may be an economy-wide explanation.

Indian industry had a very promising beginning. The first modern manufacturing mills were erected in India in the 1850s. By the 1870s, there were profitable cotton textile mills in Bombay City and profitable jute textile mills in Calcutta. In the years before the First World War, the Indian cotton industry had a significant share of the yarn market of China, and the Indian jute industry came to dominate world markets (Morris 1983). Bengal Iron and Steel was producing pig iron at competitive prices by the turn of the twentieth century, and exporting to Japan among other countries (Yonekura 1994, p. 69).

The situation was less promising by the late 1930s. The Indian cotton industry was slowly expanding, but behind significant trade barriers. Exports were insignificant. India remained dominant in jute textiles, but the industry was in long-term decline due to changing international transportation technologies. India had developed a steel industry under the guidance of Ratan Tata, though his remained the only steel-producing firm in the country until the very late 1930s. And while TISCO was profitable throughout the period, it relied heavily on trade protection from the late 1920s (Spiegelman 1960).

While there were many aspects of Indian industries' failure to become internationally competitive under the Raj, low labour productivity must surely have played a significant part. The chapter begins with an examination of the available industrial labour data to give an overview of Indian industrial labour markets. I next discuss potential explanations given in the literature for the observed pattern of limited productivity growth. Then I move to a more in-depth examination of patterns of productivity, profits and wages for India's four largest industries: cotton textiles, jute textiles, coal mining and iron and steel.

Overview of the Indian labour market

Table 12.1 gives percentage shares for all occupations in British India 1901–1931. Across these years, the labour force grew very slightly from 131.6 million workers to 139.1 million workers (Roy 2005, p. 33). The structure of the workforce did not change much over these years. The vast majority, 70 to 75 per cent, were cultivators or agricultural labourers. Manufacturing labour was just under 10 per cent of the workforce. Plantation labour was less than 5 per cent, and mining and quarrying not quite 2 per cent. These data define manufacturing to include both modern industries and traditional artisanal production. The latter was significantly larger. Roy (2005, p. 33) gives an estimate of 0.6 million, or 0.4 per cent of the labour force engaged in modern mill industries in 1901, growing to 1.6 million, or 1.2 per cent of the labour force in 1931. As an example of the importance of artisanal employment, Krishnamurty (1983, Table 6.5) reports 2.9 million workers in cotton textiles in 1921. However, the Industrial Census of 1921 reports only 350,679 workers in modern cotton-weaving firms (see Table 12.2).

Despite this, I concentrate here on the formal sector. First, there is so much more known about the formal sector. It was subject to a minimum degree of government oversight, so we have basic figures on production and employment. There were also frequent ad hoc government reports with additional information. Commodities were standardized and so there is fairly abundant price information. A more salient point is that these industries are ones that are typically important in modernization. It may be that India took a unique, labour-intensive path to modernization, as Roy (2005) argues. Still, the organized sectors are those that can be most usefully compared across the developed and developing world and thus are important

TABLE 12.1 The industrial distribution of the workforce in undivided India, 1901–1931 (%)

	1901	1911	1921	1931
Cultivators	50.3	49.6	53.5	44.3
Agricultural labourers	19.1	20.8	18.6	26.3
Livestock, forestry, fishing, hunting & plantations, orchards & allied activities	3.8	4.4	4.0	4.6
Mining & quarrying	0.1	0.2	0.2	0.2
Manufacturing	10.1	9.6	8.8	8.5
Services	16.5	15.4	14.9	16.0

Source: Adapted from Krishnamurty (1982, Table 6.2).

TABLE 12.2 Main results of the industrial census in India, taken in 1921

	Total employment	Number of females per 100 males	Share of Europeans & Anglo-Europeans among supervisors	Ratio of supervisors to all employees	Ratio of skilled workers to unskilled
I. Growing of Special Products	820,868	89	0.24	0.02	0.02
tea plantations	*747,661*	*94*	0.22	0.01	0.02
II. Mines	266,743	36	0.13	0.04	0.36
collieries	*181,594*	*39*	0.10	0.04	0.41
III. Quarries of Hard Rocks	27,234	33	0.04	0.04	0.24
IV. Textiles and Connected Industries	773,065	25	0.07	0.04	0.82
cotton weaving	*350,679*	*26*	0.04	0.04	1.06
jute mills	*287,336*	*20*	0.20	0.02	0.79
V. Metal Industries	169,693	6	0.18	0.07	0.94
iron and steel works	*39,449*	*16*	*0.09*	*0.08*	*0.72*
TOTAL INDIA	2,681,125	36	0.12	0.05	0.40

Source: Statistical Abstract for British India, India (1932).

indicators of how effectively a developing country's markets functioned relative to developed-world standards.

Table 12.3 presents data on output per labourer in each of the major divisions in India from 1900 to 1938 (Sivasubramonian 2000). The primary sector was composed of four subsectors: agriculture, livestock, forestry and fishing. The lowest values per labourer as well as the lowest growth rates can be observed in the primary sector. The secondary and tertiary sectors, in contrast, have much higher levels of output per person, and show substantial and consistent growth over the four decades. The tertiary sector consists of the government, government commercial services including the railways and communications, other services and house property. The secondary sector, the focus of this chapter, has three subcategories: mining, organized manufacturing and artisan production. The sector's overall productivity growth across the four decades was an impressive 61.26 per cent, but none of the three subcategories had such rapid productivity growth. The overall growth is primarily due to the large shift in employment within the sector away from artisanal production and towards the much higher value per worker category of manufacturing. Sivasubramonian estimates that average factory employment 1930–1938 was roughly double the average in 1900–1913, while average artisanal employment

TABLE 12.3 Real product per worker (Rs.) by sectors at 1937–1938 prices

Years	Primary	Components of secondary			Secondary	Tertiary	All
		Mining	manufac-turing	Artisan			
1900–01 to 1904–05	102	537	661	144	172	271	138
1905–06 to 1909–10	102	478	645	141	178	291	140
1910–11 to 1914–15	107	428	594	160	198	324	150
1915–16 to 1919–20	109	462	550	129	174	322	149
1920–21 to 1924–25	107	422	484	152	196	350	152
1925–26 to 1929–30	109	493	581	214	267	401	167
1930–31 to 1934–35	112	404	647	239	293	406	174
1935–36 to 1939–40	111	355	760	196	278	406	173
per cent change 1900–01 to 1939–40	8.22	−33.79	14.98	36.20	61.26	50.00	25.78

Source: Sivasubramonian (2000, Table 7.19, p. 479, and Appendix Table 6g, pp. 437–438).

TABLE 12.4 Average net value added per worker in eight industries, 1937–1938 prices

	Cotton textiles	Jute textiles	TISCO	Other 5 industries	All 8 industries	8 industries less TISCO
1900–01 to 1913–14	920.24	455.65		916.62	725.36	725.47
1914–15 to 1919–20	798.52	432.28	880.11	995.70	641.88	637.30
1920–21 to 1929–30	747.30	355.78	1,226.00	1,022.98	604.88	587.54
1930–31 to 1938–39	947.04	375.37	3,403.88	966.53	802.19	744.54
per cent change over period	2.912	-17.62	286.76	5.44	10.59	2.63

Source: Sivasubramonian (2000, Tables 4.8, 4.10, 4.25 and 4.27). Note: The industries covered here are cotton textiles, jute textiles, TISCO, sugar, paper, cement, wool and matches.

declined 21 per cent across those periods. Mining employment was fairly stable over the four decades, though productivity fell fairly dramatically.

Sivasubramonian estimates growth in labour productivity over the four decades in organized manufacturing at 15 per cent. This is only an estimate as systematic data for output and employment were not available for all modern factory industries.[1] Table 12.4 presents a decomposition of growth in the net value added per worker in the eight industries for which there are fairly complete data, and which provided the backbone of Sivasubramonian's estimate. The table has separate series for cotton textiles, jute textiles, and iron and steel. The other five industries are aggregated.[2] The table indicates that the lion's share of growth of net value added per worker in the eight covered industries can be attributed to Tata Iron and Steel. With TISCO, net value added rises 10.59 per cent 1900–1938, but without TISCO, the increase is only 2.63 per cent. TISCO began to operate during the First World War. As a relatively high value added industry, just its creation exerted some compositional upward pull to the value per worker series for the eight covered industries. Much more importantly, however, TISCO managers achieved a 287 per cent increase in value added per worker 1920–1938.

The labour forces across these large industries varied from one another, and even more from agriculture. Table 12.2 gives the main employment results of the Industrial Census of 1921. For the most part, these data cover modern industries, but the data included 'Growing of Special Products' even though it was actually plantation agriculture. I have included the information as it presents a useful contrast to the other, more typical industries. First note the relative size of each category. The largest category, 'Growing of Special Products', is dominated by tea plantations. The textiles category is nearly as large in terms of employment. Within the textiles category, cotton is the larger industry, but jute is nearly as large. Mining is next to textiles in terms of importance. Employment in collieries (the dominant category) is roughly half the size of cotton textile employment, while iron and steel has a labour force of about one-tenth the size of the cotton industry. Another noteworthy feature is that the industrial labour force was predominantly male. On the tea plantations, 94 women were employed for every 100 males. Collieries had the next largest share of female workers, and yet only 39 women were employed for every 100 males. Modern factory industries, such as textiles and metals, had even fewer female workers. The table also shows that the majority of supervisors were Indian – but Europeans and Anglo-Europeans were also important on the tea plantations and in the jute mills. Finally, there was much greater need for supervision and skilled workers in industry, and to a lesser extent in mining, relative to agriculture, here proxied by tea plantations.

Though the industrial workforce differed in measurable ways from the agricultural workforce, industrial labour was not too far removed from agriculture in this period. Most contemporary observers believed, in fact, that the main purpose of factory labour was to add to the families' land holdings in the village, and consequently, workers had only a weak attachment to industry.[3] The strong version of the non-attachment argument is that workers were agriculturists first and factory workers second. Morris (1965) argues that this strong view is almost certainly wrong. Colonial India was an agricultural economy, and so it is not surprising that the bulk of Indian workers came from agricultural villages. In the case of Bombay, the workers were predominantly from the Konkan and Deccan plateau in the southern part of the Presidency, within 200 miles of Bombay City. The jute mill workers were also from agricultural villages, in their case from villages in Bihar, Orissa and the United Provinces, 300–500 miles east of Calcutta. There is only limited evidence, however, that mill hands in either cotton or jute came from families with landholdings (Morris 1965, pp. 85–86 for cotton; Das Gupta 1976, pp. 312–317 for jute). Further, in cotton, where there is monthly data on absenteeism and production, there is no evidence that either was affected by the agricultural calendar. What evidence is available suggests that while the majority of mill hands did go for extended stays to their native place, these visits were not typically an annual occurrence. Even Myers (1958), who was quite critical of Indian labourers' long absences from industrial work, suggested that Indian workers 'are partially committed to factory jobs in that they regard them as more or less permanent jobs which can be interrupted (but not lost) by periodic visits to the village' (p. 45). While the strong version of the 'agriculturist first' argument is too strong for cotton and jute, the evidence suggests that the mill hands did maintain their village ties. In fact, while established workers in cotton textiles, at least in Bombay, were likely to have brought their wives to the city, even though employment for these women was limited (Mazumdar 1973), jute workers' wives were typically left in the village where they continued to be engaged in agricultural work (Sen 1999). Also, there is at least anecdotal evidence that both cotton and jute workers did retire to their native villages, and were replaced in the mills by their own sons and nephews. This 'circular migration' created multigenerational links between rural villages and urban mills (see Patel 1963, for cotton; De Haan 1997, for jute).

The 'agriculturist first' depiction of labour was accurate in the mining industry. The poorest coal miners were landless. Some miners were given land nearby to supplement their mining wages and to tie them to firms (Simmons 1976), but not all. The Jharia coal field produced almost 70 per cent of India's coal. Only 25 per cent of its workers were permanently settled; the rest were migrants. The settled workers' wives and daughters worked alongside the males. The transient workers' wives remained in the village (Seth 1941). While managers may have complained of absenteeism in the cotton mills, absenteeism was a well-documented phenomenon in coal. Monthly coal production varied inversely with the need for labour in agriculture. Coal production peaked in February, was fairly strong until April, but then fell off sharply during the harvesting and sowing period. In Jharia, between 1929 and 1936, the average fall between February and May was 15 per cent. Labour supply varied year-to-year based on the quality of the harvest. 'The better the harvest the smaller the labour supply and vice versa. In other words, the adversity of agriculture is the opportunity of mining, as the coal-fields get sufficient labourers in the case of crop failure' (Seth 1941, p. 34).

TISCO may have been different. There are no complaints of absenteeism in the historical accounts, which may be one reason why TISCO would have had the most productive workforce in India by Independence. Tata was careful in recruitment for TISCO. He had a deliberate strategy of recruiting from a wide area 'to make the threat of combination and dear wages less likely . . . and to prevent large strikes' (Wacha quoted in Simeon 1993, p. 138). Tata established a labour bureau in 1923 at TISCO. Two cards were kept for each employee: one listing among other things any punishments the employee had incurred; the second listed the employee's dependents, if any. For many years, TISCO was able to get almost all necessary recruits from the 'dependent card' of workers with good records (S.B. Datta 1986, p. 88).

Potential explanations of low and stagnant labour productivity

The previous section established that no Indian industry for which we have detailed production data experienced significant labour productivity growth over the four decades 1900–1938 other than TISCO. The next point we should address is why.

The academic literature on colonial Indian labour productivity has concentrated almost entirely on the cotton industry. There are actually two issues that are of interest: low initial labour productivity and labour productivity stagnancy. In a widely cited article focusing on cotton textile production across many countries circa 1910, Clark (1987) pointed out that though wages varied greatly across countries, labour costs were much more tightly distributed as, internationally, labour productivity and wages were strongly negatively correlated. Clark included both India and Japan in his analysis. He estimates that Indian and Japanese labour costs were approximately the same, and both Indian and Japanese labourers were only 25 per cent as efficient as British labourers. Clark argues that differences in productivity reflect differences in effort levels across countries and suggests that these differences might have been due to cultural norms. Wolcott and Clark (1999) and Wolcott (1994) suggest that labourers' resistance to increased effort also played a role in the stagnation of Indian labour productivity in the years between the two World Wars.

Recently, Gupta (2011) has offered a different explanation for the low productivity in cotton textiles in the early twentieth century. She points out that the Indian economy was dominated by agriculture, and argues that the tiny manufacturing sector would have taken the wage as given and adjusted machine-manning levels to the going market wage. Thus, the low wage led to low effort, not the reverse as Clark argued.

BOX 12.1 MANAGEMENT IN THE COTTON MILLS

Scholars at Stanford University in California spent millions of dollars on management consultant fees to see if better management could improve production at modern cotton-weaving mills near the city of Mumbai (Bloom et al. 2013). The management consultants introduced 'lean manufacturing' techniques, such as meeting daily with the production team to monitor efficiency goals. The mills increased output by 9 per cent without adding capital or labour.

Why did firms allow inefficiencies before the consultants' intervention? 'The equilibrium appears to be that with Indian wage rates being extremely low, firms can survive with poor management practices' (Bloom et al. 2013, p. 41). Gupta (2011) makes an almost identical claim for the colonial mills: 'Low wages reduced managerial incentives to make productivity-enhancing changes' (p. 97). Clark (1987) argues that management is not the culprit, at least not historically. The local labour force determines the extent to which management can effect changes. The question becomes, do low wages cause low efficiency? Or is low efficiency causing low wages?

Zeitz's (2013) research on Chinese cotton textile mills in the 1920s and 1930s provides a useful perspective. Britain was the technological leader in cotton textiles in this period, but British-managed mills in China had much lower productivity than Japanese-managed mills in China. The secret to the Japanese success was that their labour discipline practices had evolved in a culture similar to China's, where corruption was the norm. Britain's labour recruitment and training was delegated to foremen with direct shop-floor contact with the workers. This led to efficient production in Britain. In China, labour recruitment was controlled by criminal gangs. Delegation to criminals was inefficient. The Japanese recognized that efficiency required mitigating the power of the gangs, and did so.

In China in the 1920s and 1930s, and in the modern mills of Mumbai, efficiency improvements required management to develop techniques to control labour. Low wages lessen the urgency to develop those techniques.

Yet another possibility is that workers did resist managements' efforts to increase effort levels, but not because of *individual* preferences. In earlier articles (Wolcott 1994, 1997) I argued that workers were acting *collectively* to maintain employment levels, by comparing the successful labour reorganization in the Japanese cotton textile industry in the 1920s to the contemporaneous failed attempts at labour 'rationalization' among the Indian cotton textile mills. These efforts were most prominent in Bombay City, but there was a significant movement towards rationalization in Ahmedabad, and similar trials took place in many other individual mills throughout India. Workers were collectively opposed to rationalization even when it promised higher wages for some individuals because it would decrease total employment.[4]

There is a substantial literature suggesting mill workers were able to exert some control over their wages and effort levels in cotton textiles. Labour recruitment in cotton textiles was entirely in the hands of native foremen. *Jobbers*, as they were called in cotton textiles, relied on village and caste ties to secure workers. The links through the jobbers caused each mill to effectively be a separate labour market, facilitating and enforcing cohesion among the workforce of each mill (Newman 1979, 1981). As early as 1892, J.N. Tata suggested expanding recruitment beyond the Bombay Presidency to dilute this cohesion. 'A judicious admixture of Bombay men with men from the Upper Provinces would have a most wholesome effect' (Tata quoted in Morris 1965, p. 54). Chandavarkar (1994, 1998) argues that what began with caste and village ties and work gang links then expanded to co-workers and other tenement neighbours as workers acquired an increased sense of class consciousness. These ties were important in finding a job, sustaining workers before permanent employment and providing for the worker in any downturn or sickness.

Jute textile workers also exhibited a high degree of cooperation. Basu (2004) ascribes this cooperation to 'class consciousness'. Chakrabarty (1989) argues that the mill workers did not develop a modern sense of 'class'. Instead, workers brought their familiar feudal relationships of patronage from the villages to the mills. Habitual patterns of power in the village were thus extended to patterns of power in industry. Just as in cotton textiles, jute workers were recruited by native foremen; in jute these were called *sardars*. The ties between workers and recruiters were an example of these hierarchical relationships. Another example cited by Chakrabarty is that the jute mill workers sought out and then coalesced behind middle-class organizers to formally head their unions. I find Chakrabarty's argument compelling, but I do not think it is inconsistent with cohesive action by the workers. The economic implications of labour force cohesion are very similar whether that cohesion is based on class consciousness as postulated by both Chandavarkar and Basu, semi-feudal habits of collective action as argued by Chakrabarty or formal unions as argued by Gupta. Chakrabarty (1989, p. 116) himself notes that while formal labour unions were very limited in jute textiles, there were several very well-disciplined strikes, and Goswami (1987) claims the jute *sardars* were instrumental in organizing the workers because of the very links Chakrabarty noted. Roy (2008) points out that similar relationships between recruiters and workers were ubiquitous in all Indian industry.

In addition or perhaps complementing these informal labour networks, the formal trade union movement in India greatly expanded across all industries in the 1920s and 1930s. Following the passage of the Indian Trade Disputes Act of 1926, unions registered with the government. In 1927, 29 unions registered. By 1930 there were 119 registered unions, and 562 by 1938. Membership in registered unions rose from 100,619 in 1927 to 399,159 in 1938 (Singh 1965, Appendix A). The data available, however, indicate that the organized strike was a potent tactic. Table 12.5 presents data on strikes in India.[5] Strikes are disaggregated by region and also by industry. The first point to notice is the high percentage of strikes that ended in an outcome indicating a full or partial labour success. This degree of success is consistent both across regions and across industries. The workers in cotton textiles showed a singular ability to strike. Days lost to strikes per worker in cotton and wool textiles according to these data averaged 10.5 per year. Much of the academic discussion on the jute industry suggests the workers were unable to organize effectively. The average days lost to strikes per year per worker in the jute mill industry (3.5) were much lower than in cotton textiles. In coal the average is much lower still (0.17).[6] To put these numbers into perspective, consider similar measures for British industries (Wolcott 2009, p. 471). The average days lost to strikes per worker per year in textiles in the UK between 1921 and 1938 were 1.75. Indian jute workers may have been less strike-prone than Indian cotton workers, but they were not quiescent. Each UK mining and quarrying worker lost approximately 10 days to strikes on average each year, similar to Indian cotton, but much, much more than Indian mining and quarrying workers. Still, UK metal manufacturing workers lost only 0.7 days to strikes per year. Because Indian coal miners were effectively a seasonal labour force, any strikes were a surprise.

The final reason given in the academic literature for low and stagnant labour productivity in colonial India is that Indian labourers were physically incapable of greater productivity. One argument is that low wages caused such poor health and nutrition that greater physical exertion was impossible. The first point, the link

TABLE 12.5 Strikes in India, 1921–1938, by province and by industry

Province	No. of strikes	Men involved	Days lost	Success rate
I. Trade disputes by provinces for the years 1921–1938				
Ajmer-Merwara	4	7,307	433,180	25.0%
Assam	120	62,107	265,161	44.2%
Bengal	1131	2,340,772	30,134,181	32.2%
Bihar & Orissa	96	177,447	5,642,111	44.7%
Bombay	1480	1,990,882	66,581,771	33.2%
Burma	112	123,774	1,535,259	48.2%
Central Provinces	92	135,568	2,732,014	38.0%
Delhi	33	37,523	244,749	30.3%
Madras	323	342,436	5,911,053	52.0%
Punjab	59	34,567	791,742	59.3%
United Provinces	124	234,542	4,842,010	37.9%
II. Classification of disputes by industries for the years 1921–1938				
cotton & woollen	1562	2,152,007	74,761,241	34.2%
jute mills	420	1,495,949	19,552,867	21.9%
engineering	171	153,062	5,311,901	38.0%
railways	113	368,509	9,501,146	28.3%
mines	55	62,918	954,817	38.2%
others	1240	732,728	9,215,523	46.6%

Source: Indian Trade Journal, India (1921–1939).

between nutrition and productivity, and the potential for a 'poverty nutrition trap', is a common theme in development economics today.[7] Wages so low as to restrict productivity advance are unlikely to have been a problem among industrial workers in late-colonial India. Still, working conditions were not good. British labour representatives as well as Indian observers were appalled at the conditions under which Indian labourers worked (Johnston and Sime 1926; Kuczynski 1965). Nonetheless, according to Sivasubramonian's estimates (2000, Table 4.40), the ratio of urban skilled to unskilled wages averaged 2 in the period 1900–1930, and rose to 2.5 in the 1930s. Most industrial workers would be classed as *skilled urban workers.* While these statistics do not reveal whether or not the unskilled workers were caught in a poverty nutrition trap, it is unlikely that workers earning double the wage of the unskilled could have been in a poverty nutrition trap.

A related argument is that harsh Indian work conditions made productivity improvements difficult to achieve. There are two well-known cases where this argument might hold. Chandavarkar (1994) analyses the same Bombay cotton textile rationalization attempts of the 1920s and 1930s that I mentioned earlier. In his judgment, however, workers resisted rationalization not to maintain employment or due to a preference for low effort levels, but rather because management tried to increase labour productivity without making the requisite investments in capital and organizational structures to facilitate productivity advances. Another example is the coal industry. Seth (1941) and Mukhopadhyay (2005) both claim that mine owners contributed to low productivity through the unhealthy conditions at the mines, and also by failure to provide sufficient tubs to miners. The lack of tubs meant that a great deal of time was wasted between cutting the coal and bringing it to the surface. Note that unhealthy conditions are a different problem from wages so low that workers are in a poverty nutrition trap: wages could be high enough to buy sufficient food and yet the environment could still be so unhealthy as to lower productivity.

This discussion has suggested five potential causes of low and stagnant labour productivity in colonial India 1900–1938. One is that low nutrition meant Indian workers were incapable of exerting greater effort. Another is that the dominance of agriculture in the Indian economy and the low level of productivity in agriculture kept wages, and therefore effort levels, low in manufacturing. A third possibility is that there was a culture of low effort levels among individual Indian workers. The fourth possibility is that there was a widespread pattern of incompetence among entrepreneurs in India. The last is that labour was able to collectively resist management's efforts to improve labour productivity.

Examining time series patterns

In this section, I examine patterns in the time series data for the major individual industries 1900–1938. I wish to determine whether these markets were competitive. In competitive labour markets, the wage is determined by workers' opportunity costs and by the hedonic characteristics of the job itself. Assuming job characteristics remain constant or at least are orthogonal to product market conditions, the industry wage will be independent of product market conditions.

I begin with an examination of agricultural wages. Figure 12.1 plots the nominal value of wages for Assam male tea plantation workers and Konkan field labourers 1900–1938. These are the only long series of agricultural wages than I am aware of. Tea was primarily exported, while the agricultural output of the Konkan (food products and cotton) was consumed domestically. Thus it is not surprising that tea garden wages fell during the First World War. But in the first decade of the period as well as the last, the nominal values of these two agricultural wage series from opposite sides of the Indian subcontinent were remarkably similar both in level and trend.

Next, consider industrial wages. Figure 12.2 plots the nominal value of wages for India's large industries: cotton textiles, jute textiles, coal mining and TISCO. Most cover 1900–1938, although the TISCO wage data begin in 1912. There is a great deal of similarity in industrial wages before the First World War. The patterns after the war vary. Bombay cotton wages rose significantly immediately after the war and remained high throughout the period. TISCO wages start much higher than the other industries, but then have similar levels to the Bombay cotton industry until TISCO's wage levels rise even higher in the late 1930s. Jute and Jharia miners' wages never rose very high after the First World War, and began falling almost immediately after the Depression. The jute wage remained above the pre-war level, but Jharia miners' wages fell to about two-thirds of the pre-war level in the 1930s.

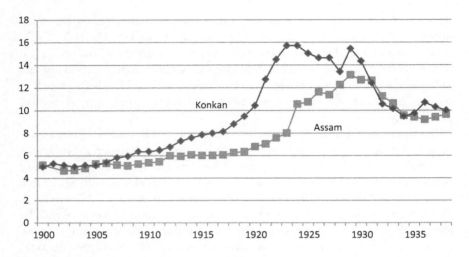

FIGURE 12.1 Male Konkan field labour wages (Rs. per month of 26 days) and male wages in the Assam tea gardens (Rs. per month), 1900–1938.

Sources: Mazumdar (1973) and Government of India, *Indian Trade Journal*, 1912, 1917, 1926, 1943.

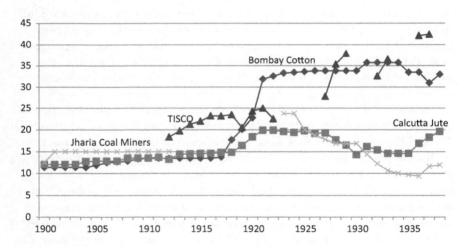

FIGURE 12.2 Monthly male wages (Rs.) of Bombay cotton textiles, jute textiles, and Jharia coal miners, 1900–1938, and TISCO 1912–1938

Sources: Jute – Mukerji (1960); cotton – Mukerji (1959); TISCO – Datta (1986); coal – Datta (1914, vol. 3), and Seth (1941).

These differential patterns are not what would have been expected from competitive labour markets.

Finally, Figure 12.3 plots manufacturing wages relative to agricultural wages. As I have complete series for Bombay cotton and Calcutta jute textiles only, I plot the

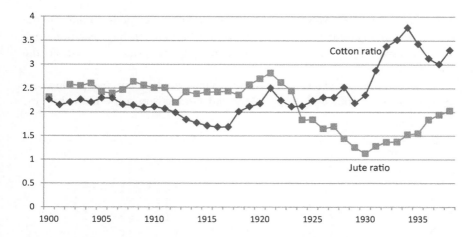

FIGURE 12.3 Jute and cotton mill wages (Rs.) relative to agricultural wages, 1900–1938

Sources: Jute – Mukerji (1960); cotton – Mukerji (1959); TISCO – Datta (1986); coal – Datta (1914, vol. 3), and Seth (1941).

ratio of these industries' wages relative to the appropriate agricultural wages. The cotton series is the ratio of money wages in the City of Bombay cotton textile mills relative to the agricultural money wage in the Konkan, considered the appropriate opportunity wage for Bombay textile labour (Mazumdar 1973). The jute series is the ratio of money wages in jute mills relative to the money wage in tea gardens in Assam. Tea, jute, coal and TISCO all relied on migrant labour from the same relatively small geographic area in Bihar, Orissa and the United Provinces (Das Gupta 1976, pp. 307–308; Seth 1941, p. 32). The groups with the lowest opportunities in their native places migrated to the tea plantations (Das Gupta 1986, p. PE-3; Simmons 1976, p. 472). Thus, the tea plantation wage provides a natural 'opportunity wage' for all other East Indian industries. Both the cotton ratio and the jute ratio are fairly steady before the First World War. In Calcutta the mill wage was about 2.5 times as great as the competing agricultural wage, and in Bombay the ratio was about 2 times the agricultural wage. The Bombay ratio rises slightly in the 1920s relative to its pre-war levels, and then rises significantly in the 1930s. Throughout the 1930s, the ratio suggests Bombay cotton mill wages were 3 times as high as the agricultural wage. In contrast, the Calcutta jute mills ratio falls steadily throughout the 1920s until it almost reaches one, and then gradually rises again. At the end of the period, the ratio is still significantly below its pre-war level. These movements are inconsistent with the hypothesis that the manufacturing wage was determined solely by the agricultural wage.

I next examine patterns of productivity, employment, profit and wage premiums for the four industries. I use the margin between the chief input and final output to proxy profit: the price of cotton cloth vs. raw cotton, gunny bags vs. raw jute, steel vs. iron bars, and coal vs. a market basket of wholesale goods. To measure the wage premium in cotton textiles, I use Konkan field labour as the reservation wage for cotton; and for jute, TISCO and coal, I assume that tea plantation wages are the reservation wage.

The top panels of Figures 12.4 to 12.7 show employment and productivity in each industry. Both coal employment and productivity grow until the First

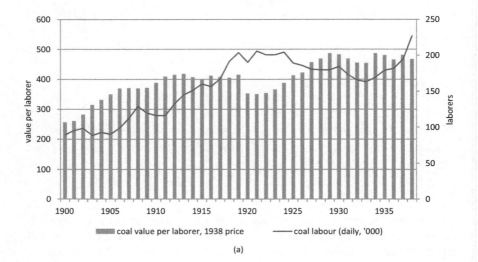

(a)

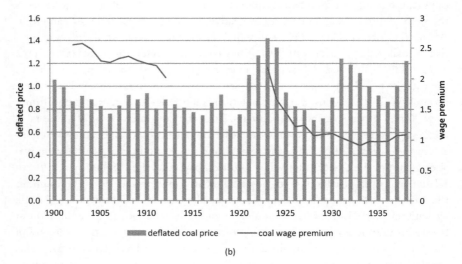

(b)

FIGURE 12.4 Coal mining. Panel A: coal mine employment vs. value of coal per labourer at 1938 prices, 1900–1938. Panel B: coal margin vs. wage premium, 1900–1938

Sources: Sivasubramonian (2000) for production and employment; Figures 12.1 and 12.2 for wages; India, Chief Inspector of the Mines (1908, 1913, 1926) for coal prices; Thingalaya (1969) for Indian price index.

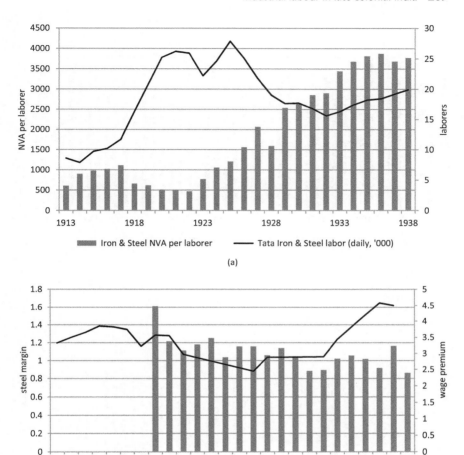

FIGURE 12.5 TISCO. Panel A: TISCO employment vs. net value added per labourer at 1938 prices. Panel B: TISCO margin vs. wage premium, 1920–1938

Sources: Sivasubramonian (2000) for production and employment; Figures 12.1 and 12.2 for wages; Spiegelman (1960) for TISCO steel; Subramanian (1945) for iron bar prices.

World War, then stagnate before falling sharply in the early 1920s. Productivity then resumes an upward trend. Employment falls over most of the post-war period of rising productivity before recovering in the mid-1930s; it ends slightly above its 1920 peak. The relationship between labour productivity and employment at TISCO is similar. Employment peaks in 1925 and then collapses, while productivity advances rapidly until 1932. Employment then resumes an upward trend, though one less steep than that of labour productivity. Average employment at

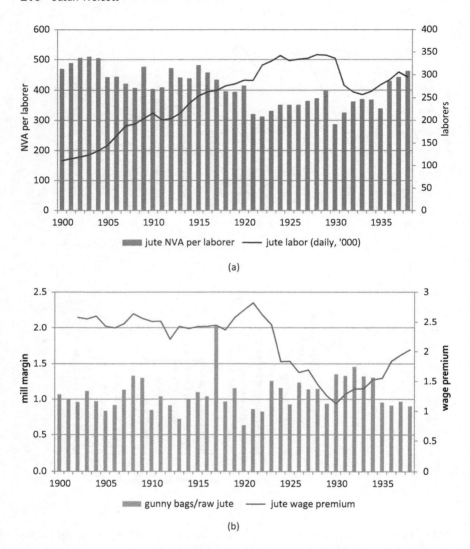

FIGURE 12.6 Jute textiles. Panel A: Jute employment vs. net value added per labourer at 1938 prices, 1900–1938. Panel B: Jute Mill margin vs. wage premium, 1900–1938

Sources: Sivasubramonian (2000) for production and employment; Figures 12.1 and 12.2 for wages; India, Department of Commercial Intelligence and Statistics (1928) for gunny bag price to 1931, then Statistical Abstract for British India; Sivasubramonian (2000, Appendix Table 3d, pp.172–174) for raw jute price.

TISCO 1937–1938 is 18 per cent below the average of 1920–1921. The textile industries are quite different. Before the First World War, productivity has a slight downward trend that accelerates during the war years. In cotton textiles, the fall in productivity in the 1920s is slight, and average labour productivity in the 1930s is

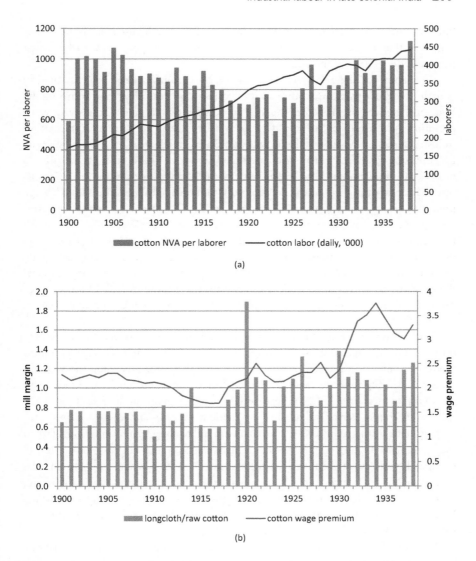

FIGURE 12.7 Cotton textiles. Panel A: Cotton employment vs. net value added per labourer at 1938 prices, 1900–1938. Panel B: cotton mill margin vs. wage premium, 1900–1938

Sources: Sivasubramonian (2000) for production and employment; Figures 12.1 and 12.2 for wages; India, Department of Commercial Intelligence and Statistics (1928) for longcloth price until 1931, then Statistical Abstract for British India; Sivasubramonian (2000, Appendix Table 3d, pp. 172–174) for raw cotton price.

similar to that in the first decade of the twentieth century. In jute mills, however, in the 1920s, fall in labour productivity is more significant. While labour productivity increases in the 1930s as employment drops, it remains below the average level of the first decade of the century. Employment growth 1900–1938 is substantial in both industries. However, in the 1930s, average jute employment is about 14 per cent *lower* than that of the 1920s, while cotton employment *grows* about 14 per cent between the 1920s and the 1930s.

Next consider the relative movement of the manufacturers' product margin and the workers wage premium for the four industries. These series are in the bottom panels of Figures 12.4 to 12.7. In competitive labour markets, the wage premium is unrelated to the profit margin. If labourers can absorb some share of industry rents, the wage premium will be positively related to the profit margin. No industry fits neatly into either predicted scenario. The cotton industry has a positive relationship until the 1930s, but after 1931 the wage premium sustains its upward momentum even though the product margin stabilizes. The TISCO wage premium also goes up in the 1930s while the TISCO product premium remains fairly stable. The coal wage premium collapses after the First World War along with the deflated coal price. The product margin improves in the 1930s, but the wage premium's downward momentum continues. Jute follows an especially odd path: the wage premium falls in the early 1920s along with the product margin, but as the product margin improves, the wage premium continues to fall. The wage premium rises most steeply in the latter part of the 1930s, when the product margin is at its worst.[8]

What is apparent from these graphs when taken together is that the wage premium seems to respond most to changes in employment. The coal wage premium is almost double in the years of rapidly rising employment preceding the war, but then sinks throughout the period of falling employment, and finally picks up again with employment in 1934. The relatively high wage premium at TISCO in 1920 also came after a period of strong employment growth, and then declines with employment through the 1920s. Employment and the wage premium both start to rise again in 1932. Jute employment and the wage premium both rise in the 1930s, though the jute wage premium fell throughout the 1920s when employment was at least steady. For cotton, there is once again the positive relationship between the wage premium and employment. The graphs for cotton are slightly misleading, however. Employment is for India as a whole, while the wage is for Bombay City. Bombay employment did not rise over the 1930s.

The link between employment and wage premiums could indicate labour bargaining power, though it could also indicate labour demand pushing against relatively inelastic labour supply curves in competitive markets. Some degree of bargaining power seems more likely. First, the size of the labour forces in these industries was small relative to the overall labour market. Second, skills were primarily learned on the job. Finally, when employment picks up at the end of the period, the wage premium starts to rise, even though in absolute terms employment was significantly below peak levels for all industries except coal mining. In fact, it is noteworthy that in all four industries, wages and employment rose in the 1930s immediately after production trends turned upward. The expansion caused by the Second World War translated into more employment at higher wages instead of increased productivity.

Conclusion

This chapter reviews the literature and the evidence on the limited growth of labour productivity in the organized industrial sector in colonial India. One potential explanation is that Indian labour was physically incapable of greater effort due to low nutrition. A second is that the dominance of agriculture in the Indian economy caused the manufacturing wage to be determined by the agricultural wage. Management adjusted staffing levels accordingly. A third hypothesis is that labour was unwilling to exert greater effort due to individual preferences. The fourth hypothesis is that management was ineffective in eliciting greater effort. The last hypothesis is that workers collectively resisted increases in productivity that would decrease employment. Given the paucity of detailed wage and production data throughout and the political and economic upheavals of the period from 1920 to Independence, it is probably impossible to definitively isolate the single cause for the lack of productivity improvements in Indian industry outside of TISCO. What this essay has achieved, however, is to bring together a large set of information on labour issues. Also, I believe some hypotheses can be ruled out.

There is no evidence that poor health caused low effort and stagnant productivity in organized industry. In the modern period, research in India shows that better nutrition would lead to more productive workers only for the very lowest paid agricultural workers. In the colonial period, wages were relatively high in the cotton textiles, jute textiles, and iron and steel industries. In cotton textiles in Bombay, even when the wage rose to three times the competing agricultural wage, productivity remained flat. Productivity rose rapidly at TISCO where the average wage was for most years similar to cotton textiles. Thus, nutrition is unlikely to explain the relative pattern of productivity in these two industries. In jute textiles, productivity fell in the 1920s when the nominal wage rose. Thus again, there is limited support for nutrition as a cause of low productivity. Wages were lower in coal mining, and conditions were almost certainly worse. But productivity in the first part of the century (when the underground miner wage was twice the competing tea wage) was not very different than productivity in the 1930s (when the tea wage was approximately the same as the coal wage), and the nominal coal wage had fallen below its pre-war level. Thus, there is limited support for the nutrition argument even in coal mining.

The data presented here indicate that the ratios of industrial wages to agricultural wages moved in response to individual industry demand conditions. The dominance of agriculture in the economy did not preclude independent wage movements in manufacturing. Thus, stagnant agricultural productivity did not automatically imply stagnant manufacturing productivity.

Wages, however, did not move in lockstep with productivity in any of the industries considered. Typically, rising productivity requires greater effort. If individual Indians had a distaste for effort, management would have had to pay workers one-to-one for increasing productivity. Because increased productivity would be completely offset by rising wages, the wage bill would be constant. Thus, management would have had no incentive to increase productivity. But in jute and coal, relative wages fell while productivity was constant. The wage bill must have fallen. In addition, the rising wages at TISCO were more than offset by rising productivity. Thus an underlying distaste for effort cannot alone explain the general stagnation of labour productivity in colonial industry.

The wage premium in individual industries seemed to respond most directly to changes in employment in those industries. The fact that wages responded to market conditions in individual industries is the most interesting and *unexpected* fact presented in this chapter. Organized manufacturing was a small part of the Indian economy. Given that, one would have expected the reservation wage set by agriculture or effort preference to have determined the industrial wage. Why it did not remains unresolved, but it does appear that each industry comprised its own distinct labour market. Given the ease of obtaining the skills needed in each of these industries, it is difficult to understand how that equilibrium could have been maintained. Exploring the labour markets in additional industries is an open and fruitful research question.

Notes

1 For the artisan sector, Sivasubramonian has to rely entirely on wage data to estimate productivity growth as there are no production data available.
2 I have also computed productivity measures for each of these industries separately, but the decomposition is not revealing as all five industries have a pattern similar to the aggregated measure.
3 For an example, see Gilchrist (1924) or Myers (1958, pp. 43–48).
4 Gupta (2011) correctly recognizes that unions were not associated with absolute lower productivity in colonial India.
5 Contemporaries believed that these data represented the most important strikes (Mukhtar 1935, p. 80).
6 To construct these values, employment in cotton was adjusted for the addition of wool, and coal for other mining industries. The adjustments are based on values in the Industrial Census of 1921, the last comprehensive survey.
7 Various scholars have found a relationship between 'weight for height' measures and labour productivity among agricultural workers, including several studies focusing on India; for example, Deolalikar (1988) and Jha, Gaiha and Sharma (2009). Swamy (1997), however, found that even for agricultural workers, wages could be cut and productivity sustained.
8 It is worth noting that India was the monopoly supplier of raw jute, and the world's largest supplier of jute bags. Jute farmers operated in a competitive market, but jute manufacturers had a cartel. Even though it is not clear how effective the cartel was in controlling production, and thus price, interpreting the price movements of gunny bags to raw jute as a measure of market demand for gunny bags is not as straightforward as in the other cases where the prices of both inputs and outputs were clearly determined in competitive world markets (Ahmed 1966; Gupta 2005; Stewart 1998).

References

Ahmed, R. (1966). *The Progress of the Jute Industry and Trade (1855–1966)*, Dacca: Pakistan Central Jute Committee.

Basu, S. (2004). *Does Class Matter? Colonial Capital and Workers' Resistance in Bengal, 1890–1937*, New Delhi: Oxford University Press.

Bloom, N., B. Eifert, A. Mahajan, D. McKenzie, and J. Roberts (2013). 'Does Management Matter? Evidence From India', *The Quarterly Journal of Economics, 128 (1)*, pp. 1–51.

Chakrabarty, D. (1989). *Rethinking Working-Class History. Bengal 1890–1940*, Princeton: Princeton University Press.

Chandavarkar, R. (1994). *The Origins of Industrial Capitalism in India. Business Strategies and the Working Classes in Bombay, 1900–1940*, Cambridge: Cambridge University Press.

———. (1998). *Imperial Power and Popular Politics: Class, Resistance and the State in India, C. 1850–1950*, Cambridge: Cambridge University Press.

Clark, G. (1987). 'Why Isn't the Whole World Developed? Lessons From the Cotton Mills', *Journal of Economic History, 47 (1)*, pp. 141–173.

Das Gupta, R. (1976). 'Factory Labour in Eastern India: Sources of Supply, 1855–1946. Some Preliminary Findings', *Indian Economic and Social History Review, 13 (3)*, pp. 277–329.

———. (1986). 'From Peasants and Tribesmen to Plantation Workers: Colonial Capitalism, Reproduction of Labour Power and Proletarianisation in North East India, 1850s to 1947', *Economic and Political Weekly, 21 (4)*, pp. PE2–PE10.

Datta, K. L. (1914). *Report on the Enquiry into the Rise of Prices in India*, Calcutta: Superintendent Government Printing.

Datta, S. B. (1986). *Capital Accumulation and Workers' Struggle in Indian Industrialisation. The Case of Tata Iron and Steel Company 1910–1970*, Acta Universitatis Stockholmiensis, Stockholm Studies in Economic History 9.

De Haan, A. (1997). 'Unsettled Migrants: Migrant Workers and Industrial Capitalism in Calcutta,' *Modern Asian Studies, 31 (4)*, pp. 919–949.

Deolalikar, A.B. (1988). 'Nutrition and Labour Productivity in Agriculture: Estimates for Rural South India', *Review of Economics and Statistics, 70 (3)*, pp. 406–413.

Gilchrist, R.N. (1924). *The Payment of Wages and Profit Sharing with a chapter on Indian Conditions*, Calcutta: University of Calcutta.

Goswami, O. (1987). 'Multiple Images: Jute Mill Strikes of 1929 and 1937 Seen through Other's Eyes', *Modern Asian Studies, 21 (3)*, pp. 547–583.

Gupta, B. (2005). 'Why Did Collusion Fail? The Indian Jute Industry in the Inter-War Years', *Business History, 47 (4)*, pp. 532–552.

———. (2011). 'Wages, Unions and Labour Productivity: Evidence From Indian Cotton Mills', *The Economic History Review, 64 (S1)*, pp. 76–98.

India, Chief Inspector of the Mines (1908, 1913, 1926). *Annual Reports*.

India, Department of Commercial Intelligence and Statistics (1928). *Index Numbers of Indian prices 1861–1926*, Calcutta: Manager of Publications.

India (1932, 1938, 1943). *Statistical Abstract for British India: Vol. 1920/21 to 1929/30; Vol. 1926/27 to 1935/36; Vol. 1930/31–1939/40*.

Government of India (1912, 1917, 1926, 1943). *Indian Trade Journal*, Calcutta: Department of Commercial Intelligence and Statistics.

Jha, R., R. Gaiha, and A. Sharma (2009). 'Calorie and Micronutrient Deprivation and Poverty Nutrition Traps in Rural India', *World Development, 37 (5)*, pp. 982–991.

Johnston, T., and J.F. Sime (1926). *Exploitation in India*, Dundee: Dundee Jute and Flax Workers Union.

Krishnamurty, J. (1983). 'The Occupational Structure', in D. Kumar and M. Desai, eds., *The Cambridge Economic History of India: Vol. II, c. 1757–1970*, Cambridge: Cambridge University Press, pp. 533–552.

Kuczynski, J. (1965). 'Condition of Workers (1880–1950)', in V.B. Singh, ed., *Economic History of India: 1857–1956*, Bombay: Allied Publishers Private Ltd., pp. 609–637.

Mazumdar, D. (1973). 'Labour Supply in Early Industrialization: The Case of the Bombay Textile Industry', *Economic History Review, 26 (3)*, pp. 477–496.

Morris, M.D. (1965). *The Emergence of an Industrial labour Force in India*, Berkeley and Los Angeles: University of California Press.

———. (1983). 'The Growth of Large-Scale Industry to 1947', in D. Kumar and M. Desai, eds., *The Cambridge Economic History of India: Vol. II, c.1757–1970*, Cambridge: Cambridge University Press, pp. 553–676.

Mukerji, K. (1959). 'Trend in Real Wages in Cotton Textile Mills in Bombay City & Island, From 1900 to 1951', *Artha Vijnana, 1 (1)*, pp. 82–95.

———. (1960). 'Trend in Real Wages in Jute Textile Mills in Bombay City & Island, From 1900 to 1951', *Artha Vijnana, 2 (1)*, pp. 57–69.

Mukhopadhyay, A. (2005). 'Colonial State, Capital, Labour and Industrialisation: Coal Mining and Coal Miners in Colonial India, 1919–39', The *Indian Journal of Labour Economics, 48 (4)*, pp. 1015–1027.

Mukhtar, A. (1935). *Trade Unionism and Labour Disputes in India*, Bombay: Longmans, Green.

Myers, C. (1958). *Labour problems in the Industrialization of India*, Cambridge, MA: Harvard University Press.

Newman, R. (1979). 'Social Factors in the Recruitment of the Bombay Millhands', in K. N. Chaudhuri and C. J. Dewey, eds., *Economy and Society: Essays in Indian Economic and Social History*, Delhi: Oxford University Press.

———. (1981). *Workers and Unions in Bombay, 1918–29: A Study of Organisation in the Cotton Mills*, Canberra: South Asian History Section, Australian National University.

Patel, K.M. (1963). *Rural Labour in Industrial Bombay*, Bombay: Popular Prakashan.

Roy, T. (2005). *Rethinking Economic Change in India. Labour and Livelihood*, New York: Routledge.

———. (2008). 'Sardars, Jobbers, Kanganies: The Labour Contractor and Indian Economic History', *Modern Asian Studies, 42 (5)*, pp. 971–998.

Sen, S. (1999). *Women and Labour in Late Colonial India. The Bengal Jute Industry*, Cambridge: Cambridge University Press.

Seth, B.R. (1941). *Labour in the Indian Coal Industry*, Bombay: D. B. Taraporevala Sons & Co.

Simeon, D. (1993). 'The great TISCO strike and lockout of 1928-Part 1', *Indian Economic and Social History Review, 30 (2)*, pp. 135–161.

Simmons, C.P. (1976). 'Recruiting and Organizing an Industrial Labour Force in Colonial India: The Case of the Coal Mining Industry, c. 1880–1939', *Indian Economic and Social History Review, 13 (4)*, pp. 455–485.

Singh, V.B. (1965). 'Trade Union Movement', in V.B. Singh, ed., *Economic History of India: 1857–1956*, Bombay: Allied Publishers Private Ltd., pp. 563–608.

———, ed. (1965). *Economic History of India: 1857–1956*, Bombay: Allied Publishers Private Ltd.

Sivasubramonian, S. (2000). *The National Income of India in the Twentieth Century*, Oxford: Oxford University Press.

Spiegelman, R.G. (1960). *Protection in India During the Interwar Period with Special Reference to the Steel Industry*, Columbia University, PhD thesis.

Stewart, G.T. (1998). *Jute and Empire: The Calcutta Jute Wallahs and the Culture of Empire*, Manchester: Manchester University Press.

Subramaniam, S. (1945). *Statistical Summary of the Social and Economic Trends in India (In the Period 1918–1939)*, Washington DC: The Govt. of India.

Swamy, A.V. (1997). 'A Simple Test of the Nutrition-based Efficiency Wage Model', *Journal of Development Economics, 53 (1)*, pp. 85–98.

Thingalaya, N.K. (1969). 'A Century of Prices in India', *Economic and Political Weekly, 4 (4)*, pp. 251–256.

Wolcott, S. (1994). 'The Perils of Lifetime Employment: A Comparison of the Indian and Japanese Textile Industries', *Journal of Economic History, 54 (2)*, pp. 307–324.

———. (1997). 'Did Imperial Policies Doom the Indian Textile Industry?' *Research in Economic History, 17*, pp. 135–183.

———. (2009). 'Strikes In Colonial India, 1921–38', *Industrial and Labour Relations Review, 61 (4)*, pp. 460–484.

Wolcott, S., and G. Clark (1999). 'Why Nations Fail: Profits and Managerial Decisions in Indian Cotton Textiles, 1890–38', *Journal of Economic History, 59 (2)*, pp. 397–423.

Yonekura, S. (1994). *The Japanese Iron and Steel Industry, 1850–1990*, New York: St. Martin's Press.

Zeitz, P. (2013). 'Do Local Institutions Affect All Foreign Investors in the Same Way? Evidence from the Interwar Chinese Textile Industry', *The Journal of Economic History, 73 (1)*, pp. 117–983.

13

LAW AND CONTRACT ENFORCEMENT IN COLONIAL INDIA

Anand V. Swamy

Introduction

The "economics of institutions," so influential in the study of economic history and economic development in the last two decades, has given a prominent role to contract enforcement. Economic activity usually requires the combination of inputs (land, labour, credit) that are in the hands of different parties. Occasionally these are one-shot, spot transactions. More typically, two (or more) parties interact over a period of time, and fulfil (or not) their end of the bargain at different times. This leaves room for opportunistic behaviour. If this happens or is expected to happen to a sufficient extent, mutually profitable trades and activities will not occur: cloth may not be woven, peasants may desert their fields, or the wealthy may not lend money. A key question then is: how does a society develop institutions that place limits on opportunism, so that welfare enhancing economic activity can occur (North 1990)? This question is typically not asked in the existing literature on Indian economic history, which tends to focus on distributional issues and exploitative relations between different participants in economic activity.[1] This chapter attempts to partially fill this gap in the literature. In particular, I ask: to what extent was the colonial state able to create a legal and institutional environment that curbed opportunistic behaviour and made economic development possible? I recognize power asymmetries among different participants; indeed I will argue that, in addition to affecting the distribution of income or wealth, they could complicate problems of contract enforcement.

I use a simple framework in my analysis, developed in microeconomic theory. First, each party must be willing to enter the transaction: *participation constraints* must be satisfied. Second, each party must have the motivation and ability to fulfil a reasonable portion of their commitment: *incentive-compatibility constraints* must be satisfied. Failure to satisfy these constraints will result in welfare losses.[2] The legal environment plays an important role in determining whether this happens. In this chapter I discuss transactions between merchant and artisan, lender and borrower, planter and migrant worker.[3]

BOX 13.1 PARTICIPATION AND INCENTIVE-COMPATIBILITY

The design of contracts can be greatly complicated by one party to a transaction having better information than another. This information can pertain to *types* or to *actions*. Suppose, for instance, a lender is approached by a farmer who wants a loan to buy fertilizer. The farmer has no collateral, so repayment depends on the output she will produce. There are "good" (competent) farmers and "bad" (incompetent) farmers. Each farmer knows his or her type, but the lender does not. If defaulting is not very costly, even "bad" borrowers will apply for loans. Not being able to distinguish types, the lender may choose not to advance credit. Alternatively, since defaulting is not costly, the farmer may simply choose to spend the money on (say) a celebration, an action that the lender cannot observe. Because of this concern, the lender may prefer not to provide a loan.

Now suppose a credit bureau is opened. It records repayment information, and borrowers who default will be shunned by lenders in the future. It may no longer be "incentive compatible" for a bad borrower to ask for a loan, or for the farmer to take a loan and fritter away the money. Only "good" borrowers may apply for and receive loans, and use them appropriately. Thus, by creating incentives for borrowers, the credit bureau can facilitate economic activity. But suppose the punishment for defaulting is much harsher: imprisonment. The farmer may worry that if a pest eats the crops, an event over which he or she has no control, the farmer will default and be jailed. The farmer may prefer not to take a loan; his or her "participation constraint" has been violated. Thus, for welfare-enhancing economic activity to occur, the legal and institutional environment should allow both participation constraints and incentive-compatibility constraints to be satisfied.

What does this investigation yield? I find that while the colonial state usually threw its weight behind the stronger party in the transaction (its own agencies, merchants, lenders, planters), its ability to create a contractual environment in which economic surplus could be created was constrained in many ways. First, state capacity was limited. India was the quintessential "non-settler" colony: a small group of British officials was, with the help of many Indian intermediaries, governing a huge population. Company officials had a limited understanding of prevailing institutions and norms. The legal regulations adopted often reflected these administrative shortcomings. Moreover, while Glaeser, Djankov, La Porta, Lopez-de-Silanes, and A. Shleifer (2003) highlight the merits of importation of English legal traditions, they could run afoul of local moral sensibilities (see the "Home production and contract farming" section in this chapter). Second, the Company or the Raj[4] did not simply mirror the short run interests of European capitalists – it could be at loggerheads with them, because of a longer term perspective, and sometimes simply could not control them. Third, the policies of the Company and the Raj were affected by vocal and articulate critics, such as missionaries, and later on Indian nationalists and the press. Fourth, collective resistance by peasants and workers led to concerns about political stability and limited the policies that could be adopted, especially after the "Mutiny." Thus for the Company/Raj, the problem was not just that it reflected the interests of powerful over the weak, the principal over the agent – its capacity to create the appropriate contracting environment was limited. Like many a weak state in a poor country, the problem was not just what it did, but what it could not do.

I tell the story by discussing three sets of transactions: contract farming and home production, lending and borrowing, and migration and retention of plantation workers. In the process I discuss some of the key products of the colonial Indian economy: textiles, indigo, opium, and tea. In each case I clarify the contracting problem, i.e. the conditions that needed to be satisfied for the two parties to engage and produce. I then consider the various factors that facilitated or undermined the satisfaction of participation and incentive-compatibility constraints, including the power asymmetry between the two parties. I find that problems in contract farming and home production were intractable – except in the case of opium, where the huge profits gave the state reason to create an effective system of procurement. The Company and (especially) the Raj struggled with credit market regulation, but its travails were not unique, and they are playing out in various contexts to the present day. With regard to plantation workers, the recruitment methods "worked" in the sense that huge numbers of people did migrate, but workers appear to have been treated very harshly.

To the extent possible, I arrange the examples in chronological order. This is helpful in, for instance, clarifying differences between the administration of the Company and the Raj. In the period of Company rule, especially in the early years, it was still developing its administrative capacity and its eventually famous bureaucracy. After the takeover by the Crown (1858) following the Mutiny, the Raj's political anxieties heavily influenced its choices.

Textiles were the Company's most important exports in the mid-eighteenth century. Next I discuss the contractual problems in the procurement process. I juxtapose a discussion of contract farming where the procurement process was similar, though the products were very different.

Home production and contract farming[5]

The general structure of the contracting problem in this section is as follows: the worker (weaver or peasant) receives an advance and commits to producing goods of a certain quality. The principal in turn commits to a price schedule. The worker can violate the contract by putting the capital to an alternative use, selling the product to another party, adulterating the product, etc. The principal can refuse to honour the price schedule and make arbitrary deductions. I discuss three cases in this section, which cover a range of outcomes, from "success" (opium) to initial success followed by "collapse" (indigo), with textiles being an intermediate outcome.

Textile production in Bengal

By the mid-eighteenth century, cloth was the most important commodity procured and exported by the Company. After it attained political power in Bengal, the expectation was that this trade should grow and become more profitable. Sinha (1965, p. 148) has argued that under Company rule, the buyer (the Company and its intermediaries) gained bargaining power at the expense of the weaver, who had much greater freedom under the Nawab of Bengal. Still, the Company struggled to procure cloth. Why? One part of the story (Gupta 2010) is surely that weavers were reluctant to contract with the Company because its prices were low. But the record reveals that it also struggled to set up the appropriate contractual arrangement.

Textiles were produced at home by weavers scattered over a large area. The Company in its Agency System contracted with the weavers through its agents, the *gumasthas*. The *gumasthas* advanced the capital and collected the output from the weaver. European companies in India had long faced the problem alluded to earlier: a weaver might take an advance, but might then sell the final product to another party. The Company passed regulations to prevent this, giving agents the power to force weavers to work to fulfil their contracts. But this then exposed the weaver to financial exploitation and physical abuse by the *gumastha*, and European Company officials who were in cahoots with him.

The contractual problem was described clearly by Governor Harry Verelst:

> [I]t was thought expedient by the governor and council . . . to make . . . advances to such manufacturers as would otherwise have lain idle. Contracts thus in part executed on one side, afforded a temptation to fraud on the other; and the workman, unless strictly watched, often resold his goods for their full price to a stranger. The gomastahs or agents of the Company were necessarily therefore entrusted with powers which they frequently abused to their own emolument; and an authority given to enforce a just performance of engagements became notwithstanding the vigilance of the higher servants, a source of new oppression.
>
> (Verelst 1772, p. 85)

There were repeated changes in laws, strengthening the powers of the *gumastha* or reining him in (see Mitra 1978, Gupta 2010, Hossain 1988, Sinha 1965, Kranton and Swamy 2008). However, at this early stage the Company simply did not have enough administrative capacity to manage the agents or even its own officials. The records are replete with petitions by weavers complaining of agents – often in collaboration with Company officials – undervaluing cloth, paying in inferior coin, beating them, etc.[6] The Company never quite arrived at a satisfactory set of regulations, and financial pressures meant that the prices offered to the weavers remained low. Weavers remained reluctant to work for the Company (i.e. participation constraints were violated), which struggled to attain procurement targets. Eventually, of course, in the nineteenth century, Bengali cloth ceased to be competitive as cheap manufactured cloth was produced in Europe.

The weakened bargaining strength of the weaver following the transition to colonial rule is also the central element of Parthasarathi's (2001) account of textile production in South India. He also offers some interesting commentary on the roots of weavers' protests. The Company's various coercive interventions, he argues, violated the limits of state power that a "just and moral king in South India" was expected to acknowledge (Parthasarathi 2001, p. 131).

Indigo

Indigo was a major export crop in the first half of the nineteenth century, with Central and Lower Bengal being the major locations. Production was organized by European planters who typically contracted with peasants who were tenants of *zamindars*. The planter advanced capital; the peasant agreed to plant a fixed area and deliver the crop at the end of the season. Planters' complaints are summarized by Roy (2011) as follows:

> They [peasants] could and on some occasions did try to run away with the advance. The contracts did not specify the quantity of crop to be delivered, but the extent of land that could be sown with it. The peasants could sow a smaller area than agreed, under-report the yield or, on the three days when the sowing had to be completed, make themselves scarce.
>
> (p. 64)[7]

The peasants in turn complained of abuse by planters and their agents: they were coerced into sowing indigo; the planter did not pay the contracted price; he imprisoned and beat them. A Faridpur magistrate commented that from its inception the system of indigo production was a "system of bloodshed;" "Not a chest of indigo reached England without being stained with human blood" (Kolsky 2010, p. 58). Eventually in 1860, peasants refused to sow indigo and attacked European managers and factories, events that came to be known as the Blue Mutiny (Kling 1966; Das 1992, p. 2).

There were two administrative responses: for a period of six months, non-fulfilment of contract by peasants was made a criminal offence for which they could be imprisoned, and a Commission was appointed to investigate the indigo industry and recommend a policy. The Commission produced a report (with some internal dissent) that was sympathetic to the peasants and complained of the low remuneration they received. This intervention was largely ineffectual; problems were not resolved, and in the 1860s, the indigo industry in Bengal was "practically destroyed" (Roy 2011, p. 72), with planters and agency houses closing shop or moving elsewhere.

The example of indigo, like that of tea, which I discuss later, is useful because it illustrates the range of factors that affected contracting and dispute resolution. There is of course the fundamental problem of the inability of the legal system to enforce contracts. For the planters, the civil courts were largely useless for ensuring performance by the peasant (Roy 2011). It is even less likely that a peasant could take a better connected and sophisticated European planter to court. There is nothing surprising about this: the tardiness and corruptibility of the legal system is a feature of developing economies even today. However, the colonial context introduced a special element that perhaps is not so common in present-day developing economies: the impunity of the planter. Kolsky (2010) argues that "White Violence" by the non-official European, which was difficult to control, was a fundamental problem for the colonial state. The literature on indigo is replete with graphic descriptions of stocks, whips, and other instruments for torture and imprisonment, and accounts of abuse of various kinds, including sexual. It is not easy to quantify the frequency of these occurrences, and there are examples of progressive planters who treated their workers well, building hospitals and schools (Kling 1966, p. 59). Still, the central conclusion of much of the literature – that unchecked planter violence played a role in undermining the indigo industry – is plausible.[8]

The controversy over indigo also brought to prominence pressure groups that would henceforth play an important role: the urban Indian middle class, the Indian press, and the missionaries. Racial relations had been soured by the 1850s in part by controversies over "Black Acts" (which put Europeans under the jurisdiction of Indian judges). British commercial interests had always been well represented, but the Indigo Planters' Association, with influence in India and in London (including lobbyists), was formed in 1851. The Indigo Planters' Association supported two journals, the *Englishman* and the *Bengal Hurkuru*. *Zamindars* and Bengali urban middle classes formed the British Indian Association, which supported the *Hindoo Patriot*, and the *Indian Field*. These English-language newspapers and the Bengali-language *Som Prakash* (Kling 1966, pp. 118–119) campaigned against the indigo planters. Missionaries, who were critical of the planters, were also highly visible in public discussion. They were well connected with various parties: they worked with the peasants in remote locations, engaged with English-speaking Indian urban middle classes, and had access to the administration in India as well as the public sphere in London. We will encounter missionaries again in our discussion of tea plantations later.

Opium

In contrast with the two cases mentioned earlier, especially indigo, the opium enterprise must be considered a resounding success, at least in the sense of being a productive and hugely profitable enterprise for over a century.[9] The Opium Monopoly was the biggest revenue earner for the state, aside from land taxes, providing as much as 17 per cent of the revenues of the Government of India in 1861 (D. Kumar 1983, p. 916).[10] Opium was also grown via a contract farming arrangement of the type described earlier, with two major differences: it was run by the government, and it was a monopoly. The government was the only legal buyer. At the centre of the procurement system were two "Agencies" centred in Patna and Banaras.

In the early nineteenth century there were complaints about low prices, coercion by government employees, and forced cultivation along the lines we have seen earlier. There were also the usual complaints about peasants not growing the agreed amounts, adulterating the produce, etc. But eventually the Opium Monopoly worked relatively smoothly. Like a textbook monopolist, the Company was able to increase or decrease its output, depending on the market price (Kranton and Swamy 2008, p. 982). The Indigo Commission also commented favourably on the freedom of the opium cultivators, as compared to indigo. In 1850, when the price of competing crops increased, *raiyats* growing poppy were allowed to switch to other crops; then, to lure them back, the price of poppy was increased. In contrast, regarding indigo the Commission writes:

> No one pretends the same rise of prices [of competing crops] has not been felt throughout Lower Bengal, during the same period, and probably owing to the same causes; nor does anyone tell us, in all Bengal, whether any number of ryots, or if any, were allowed to abandon the production of indigo. The inference is plain: while the asamis [peasants] of Behar and Benaros [sic] have been free agents in their choice, the ryots of Bengal, from the causes already enumerated, have, practically, had no choice at all.
>
> (Das 1992, p. 60)

This claim is likely too broad; as Roy (2011) points out, it is not likely that the entire indigo industry, over a long period, was run primarily via forced cultivation. Still, it does appear that the opium enterprise was better managed, and more successful at procurement.[11] Why?

In principle, price could have paid a role: the margin in opium was large and hence there was more surplus to share, and room to raise the price to increase production.[12] This cannot be an adequate explanation in itself because indigo was profitable too. Roy (2011, p. 63) documents that planters received Rs.7.4 per *bigha* (1 *bigha* = 0.49 acres) planted with indigo, of which the peasant received Rs.2. There was an adequate margin here, even after allowing for rent, transportation, and processing.

Perhaps more significantly, in the case of opium, the government – taking a long-term perspective – had invested in an elaborate system of supervision. This ranged from the Agency headed by an Indian Civil Service officer to the sub-agency managed by the Sub-Deputy Opium Agent, to the sub-divisional office managed by the *gumastha* with a staff of roughly twenty-five, which dealt directly with the peasant or the village headman (Richards 1981, p. 70). Procedures for evaluating quality were systematized: by the 1860s, chemical tests were being performed for adulteration. It is likely that, as a result of these measures, poppy growing peasants were more confident that their contracts would be honoured.

However, to understand the indigo-opium contrast, we also cannot rule out the factor alluded to earlier: the government's failure to regulate the behaviour of the indigo planters. No doubt the employees of the Opium Agency also could be corrupt or violent, but probably not on the scale or with the sense of impunity the planters possessed, given their racial arrogance and relationship with the powers-that-be. It appears that in the case of indigo, this specific feature of the colonial setting aggravated a common contracting problem.

Some of the most important legal changes in the colonial period concerned the enforcement of credit contracts, which is the subject of the next section.

Lenders and debtors

The contracting issues between lender and debtor have already been discussed in Box 13.1. A lender usually wants to have recourse to collateral or other devices that protect him or her from default. However, as recent events have amply demonstrated, lenders can be opportunistic as well, and engage in predatory behaviour. The right regulatory mix between protection for lenders and protection for borrowers is still being debated.

Colonial era innovations initially moved decisively in the direction of favouring the lender. First, because titles to land were defined more clearly (see Chapter 7, in this volume, on agriculture), it became easier to use land as collateral, or to seize it in lieu of debt repayment. Second, enforcement of credit contracts – which had often relied on community institutions like the *Panchayat* or village council – now moved into formal courts. Consider, for instance, a Gujarati or Marwari moneylender operating in a rural area in the Bombay Deccan. In pre-colonial India, two factors would have limited this lending: first, while land transfers did occur (Guha 1985), there was not much history of seizure for debt; second, in any dispute with a peasant, the moneylender would have to go to the village *Panchayat* for adjudication. The *Panchayat's* sympathies would more likely be with the peasant than with an immigrant lender (R. Kumar 1965, 1968). Even if the *Panchayat* ruled in his favour, it would not necessarily enforce its decision, and the lender might have to use his private coercive capacity. Now, under colonial rule, if he could take the written contract ("bond") to the district court, he might well get a quick decision, even in the absence of the defendant (*ex-parte*), and be able to acquire his debtor's land and other assets.[13] The wealthier and more educated lender could also negotiate the courts better than his poor and likely illiterate client.

These changes encouraged lending and facilitated the expansion of commercial agriculture. However, as recent events around the world have demonstrated, the availability of new financial instruments can have unexpected outcomes. Indeed, from the mid-nineteenth century we see descriptions (some no doubt overdrawn) of gullible borrowers incapable of handling the resources now at their disposal, and predatory lenders eager to lend to their unsophisticated clients.[14]

In the Bombay Deccan as well as other regions (e.g. Punjab or tribal regions like the Santal Parganas) lenders might be "other" than the peasants: immigrants (Bombay Deccan) or from a different religion (Punjab) or both (Santal Parganas). Prominent officials in all these regions argued that peasants were being dispossessed at an alarming rate. These concerns were particularly salient after 1857 because the "Mutiny" was viewed as a consequence of disruptions of traditional Indian society by British rule. As we will see in the remainder of this section, henceforth, the Raj would take a cautious approach.

Concerns about deteriorating moneylender-peasant relations were borne out when in 1875, peasants in two districts in the Deccan, Poona and Ahmednagar, attacked moneylenders and tore up the bonds, occasionally inflicting injury. British officialdom viewed this as evidence that the legal innovations introduced during colonial rule were inappropriate for the Indian setting. Evidence in support of this perspective was marshalled and consolidated in the famous Report of the Deccan Riots Commission of 1876. The resulting policy change, the Deccan Agriculturist's Relief Act (DARA), was enacted a few years later, in 1879.

DARA had many provisions involving registration of bonds, ceilings on interest accumulation,[15] and court procedure, but the key provisions gave the judge discretion to go "behind the bond." Because the borrower was viewed as gullible and the lender as predatory, the judge would not be bound by the written terms of the contract and could use his own judgment in awarding repayment. This represented a significant weakening of the lender's power to recover loans, at least in the legal system. One might expect that this would lead to a drying up of credit. Ongoing research (Chaudhary and Swamy 2014) suggests that DARA did initially lead to some reduction in credit availability, but that lenders learned to sidestep it by, for instance, disguising loans with land as collateral as land sales. There is also anecdotal evidence suggesting that lenders investigated borrowers more carefully, and were less willing to lend for "unproductive" purposes like weddings and funerals. There is no evidence of any adverse impact of DARA on "real outcomes," in particular, cropped area, ownership of bullocks, or yields. It appears that in DARA, the Raj got the power balance between lender and debtor approximately right, creating a reasonable structure of incentives for both parties, and satisfying participation constraints.

Punjab witnessed a sequence of events similar to the Deccan. After extensive discussion, the Punjab Land Alienation Act was passed in 1900, which prohibited land transfer from "agricultural tribes" to "non-agricultural tribes." The argument in Box 13.1 suggests that the loss of land as potential collateral would create a perverse incentive for borrowers and weaken the position of the non-agriculturist lender. Consistent with this intuition, according to Bhattacharya (1985), the Punjab Land Alienation Act reduced the presence of the professional non-agriculturist moneylender and strengthened the hand of the richer peasants (belonging to agricultural tribes) who also loaned money. Thus, in this instance, the colonial state's intervention was likely too heavy-handed.

It is difficult to arrive at an overall assessment of the colonial state's performance in the sphere of credit market regulation because so many of the problems it struggled to address – predatory lenders, excessive borrowing, foreclosures, threats to indigenous communities – persist in India and elsewhere. For instance, the state of Uttarakhand recently passed restrictions on non-residents owning land, which have been debated as well as legally challenged. Special rules to protect tribals from land transfer were written into the Indian constitution, and are the subject of ongoing controversy.[16] Indeed, in the wake of the global financial crisis, the debate on how to regulate financial markets is ongoing around the world. The Raj's struggles in this dimension do not seem exceptional.

Plantations and indentured labour

Our final example pertains to an organizational form I have not yet discussed: the plantation, and a different category of workers, the migrant. The product in question is tea, a major export crop from the late nineteenth century. Tea plantations in Assam acquired a special notoriety for the restrictions placed on plantation workers as well as the violence and poor working conditions to which they were subject. This example is especially useful for this chapter because it features a huge power asymmetry between principal and agent as well as an intrinsically difficult contractual problem.

After tea was "discovered" in Assam in the 1830s, the first enterprise (Assam Company) was formed. Planters (European) received land leases at concessional rates. It was difficult for them to find workers: the local population was sparse, and planters considered local workers unproductive. Therefore, workers had to be hired from more densely populated regions.

The contractual problem was as follows. Assam, especially upper Assam,[17] was very far away from key recruitment regions (Chota Nagpur and Santal Parganas). Workers were too poor to pay the substantial travel costs, so employers bore this expense. Also, it could take a worker up to a year to become proficient on the job. An employer faced the risk that the worker in whose travel he had invested could be "enticed" away by another planter before he had recouped his upfront cost. There are, in theory, several potential solutions to this problem: employers could offer bonuses (such as small plots of land) to workers who stayed on, they could form associations and agree not to "entice" workers, or legislation could be passed to fine an employer who enticed a worker under contract with another planter. All these methods were tried in Assam at various times, but were not sufficient for reasons that are not entirely clear.[18] The method chosen to protect the planter was a particularly harsh form of indenture that permitted *private arrest* by the employer. This form of protection to the planter of course made the worker vulnerable to abuse by his/her employer, who might virtually imprison him/her in a remote region of Assam, from which there was little chance to return. This problem was exacerbated by the fact that workers often did not know their rights, and employers used the coercive provisions of the Special Act (which permitted private arrest) even on workers who were not under its purview (Mohapatra 2004, p. 266). Given this, historians have argued that workers were often reluctant to migrate to Assam (their participation constraints had been violated).[19]

How well did the Raj address the concerns of planter and worker? It faced a now-familiar set of figures in passing legislation. On the one hand, the planters' associations in India and in London constituted a powerful and effective lobby in favour of Assam's Special Acts, which permitted private arrest of workers by planters. But conditions in Assam plantations also attracted criticism from idealistic officials and humanitarians, missionaries, nationalist critics, and the Indian press. Reverend Dowding, a long-time critic of the tea industry, wrote to the Secretary of State in 1896 that a "coolie is not to be classified with livestock" (Kolsky 2010, p. 165). Bengali publications like *Bengalee* and *Sanjibani* produced scathing accounts of conditions on the plantations (Kolsky 2010, pp. 165, 181). Kolsky also argues that, because the planters were European, the nationalist movement was able to support tea workers without generating class antagonisms among Indians.

For all the protests, changes in the contracts actually used as well as legislative changes seem to have been driven primarily by declining travel costs, consistent with a view of indenture as a response to the planter's need to recover his initial expense. This is evident from comparisons both across and within regions. The same European firms that operated in Assam, relying on the same managing agencies, did *not* use any type of indenture in the Dooars, an important tea growing region in Bengal, because the Dooars were closer to the recruiting regions and connected early by rail. Within Assam, the Surma Valley (which was closer to the recruiting regions) abandoned the use of Assam's Special Acts as transportation improved. By 1900, the Surma Valley relied almost exclusively on a weaker form of indenture, which did not permit private arrest.[20] Eventually, starting in 1908, various aspects of penal legislation in Assam were chipped away, and penal contracting ended altogether in 1926.

Judged by the extent of migration, Assam's penal legislation may be considered a success. In 1883 close to 14,000 workers migrated to the remote Brahmaputra Valley alone, with contracts written under the notorious Special Act. In 1900, more than 28,000 workers migrated under similar terms.[21] We do not know the counterfactual; maybe even more would have migrated absent the Special Acts. Still, the sheer volume of migration, from some of the poorest regions in India, is impressive. However, the record of penal legislation with respect to the treatment of workers once at the plantation was dismal. The abuse of workers and the planters' sense of impunity persisted. The Royal Commission on Labour in India (1931) received complaints along these lines even after all penal legislation was abolished.[22]

Conclusion

The introduction to this chapter argued that the literature to date has typically (and appropriately) emphasized power asymmetries between "principal" and "agent" but that intrinsic contractual problems common to developing economies deserve more consideration. The creation of economic surplus, I argued, requires that both parties to the contract honour it to some minimal extent, and ensuring this can be difficult in a variety of power configurations.

What has this approach yielded? Overall, my conclusion is that both Company and Raj struggled to create a legal and regulatory environment that would promote economic welfare. There were some spectacular failures, like indigo. There were some successes, like opium, where – at least at the Indian end – both the state and the peasant likely gained from a huge export trade (Richards 1981, 2002). In the case of tea, economic surplus was surely created, but how much of it accrued to the worker is open to question. However, in the aggregate, the colonial state's performance cannot be viewed favourably. In its early (Company) phase, its administrative capacity was limited: it overly empowered intermediaries (e.g. in textiles), whose behaviour it could not control. The later Raj was more capable, but much more cautious, enacting laws it viewed as politically beneficial (especially the Punjab Land Alienation Act) but whose economic advantages were questionable. And throughout the colonial period, from indigo to tea, it struggled to restrain European principals.

Still, a cautionary note about benchmarks is warranted: while many regulations and contract enforcement methods allowed or used by the Company/Raj would strike the contemporary observer as cruel, or ineffective, they fare better in a comparative perspective. For instance, "putting-out" systems (home production with an advance) and contract farming have been difficult to sustain the world over. Debtors, especially if they were poor, could be treated harshly even in nineteenth-century England – and migrant workers are misled or underpaid even in the present day. There is no doubt the Company/Raj struggled to create the appropriate legal and regulatory environment in part because this was a *colonial* regime favouring narrow interests, but the contractual issues that it grappled with plague many economies, colonial or not. This short chapter has provided a few examples of this, but there are many other areas in which incentive issues are central, from corporate law to patents and trademarks, to rights over water and forests. These remain promising areas for future research on colonial India.

Notes

I thank – but do not implicate – Latika Chaudhary, Bishnupriya Gupta, Tirthankar Roy, Arafaat Valiani, and seminar participants at Columbia University and the University of Warwick for comments on an earlier version of this chapter.

1 Some exceptions are Hejeebu (2005), Gupta (2010), Kranton and Swamy (2008), and Roy (2011).

2 This chapter focuses exclusively on relations between relatively powerful parties ("principals") and weaker ones ("agents"). See Roy (2010) for a discussion of relationships among groups of artisans, workers, etc., which were often adjudicated within communities, outside the formal legal system.

3 Of course, the contractual issues I discuss emerge in a range of other settings as well, including industry and landlord-tenant relations.

4 The East India Company's administration was replaced by direct administration by the Crown (British Raj) in 1858.

5 The discussion of textiles and opium in this section draws on Kranton and Swamy (2008).

6 See, for instance, Mitra (1978, pp. 234–235).

7 It is worth noting that the enforcement problems associated with contract farming are not specific to colonial Bengal, or to India. Jaffee (1994) reports on the breakdown of operations of Kenya Horticultural Exports (KHE) because a drought increased the price, and farmers who had contracted with KHE chose to sell elsewhere. Hightower (1975, p. 17) describes opportunism on the part of buyers of asparagus in the United States, who paid growers arbitrarily low prices.

8 It is also conceivable that, as in the case of South Indian weavers discussed earlier, while certain forms of coercion (e.g. by *zamindars*) were tolerated, the violence of planters had no moral sanction and was hence resisted to a greater extent. I thank Tirthankar Roy for this observation.

9 The Patna Agency was opened in 1797 and closed in 1910.

10 This 17% includes taxes on opium exports from the Princely States.

11 John Rivett-Carnac, who managed the Benares Agency from 1874–1894, wrote in his memoir that the job was not very challenging and that it offered a "quiet haven" (Rivett-Carnac 1910/2005, p. 304). It is hard to imagine anyone associated with the indigo industry using similar language.

12 In the second half of the 1850s, faced with the decline in production mentioned earlier, the price paid to the peasant had been increased by 42% (Chaudhuri 1983, p. 314).

13 In a famous paper titled "From Indian Status to British Contract," Cohn (1961) identified a broad pattern of formalization of economic relationships during colonial rule.

14 See, for instance, Deccan Riots Commission (1876, p. 31).

15 DARA reinstituted *Damdupat*, a traditional Hindu rule that limits interest accumulation to the amount of the principal. Interestingly, this is also a feature of recent legislation on micro finance in Andhra Pradesh.

16 See the famous Samatha judgment of the Supreme Court in 1997 regarding restrictions on the government's right to lease land in "Scheduled Areas" to private parties: http://cseindia.org/mining/pdf/samata_vs_AP.pdf.

17 The two main tea growing regions in Assam were the Brahmaputra Valley (Upper Assam) and the Surma Valley.

18 These are the subject of ongoing research by the author and Bishnupriya Gupta (Gupta and Swamy 2014). This section of the chapter draws on our ongoing work.

19 The Assam Labour Enquiry of 1906 reported that of thirty-one witnesses interviewed in the recruiting areas, twenty-eight were reluctant to go to Assam because of the penal contract and its consequences (Behal 2006, p. 144). This raised recruitment costs, leading, as Behal and Mohapatra (1992) put it, to "*high cost of cheap labour*" (p. 170, their italics).

20 The Workman's Breach of Contract Act of 1859, originally devised for the Presidency towns of Bombay, Madras, and Calcutta, allowed imprisonment of a worker who had taken an advance and "absconded," but did not permit private arrest by the employer.

21 These are the author's calculations from the *Annual report of labour immigration into Assam* for 1883 and 1900.

22 For instance, a woman worker, Mt. Miriam Musalmani, testified that both she and her son (a child) had been beaten. The Commission's doctor did not think her wounds were

caused by a cane, but confirmed that her son's injuries were (Royal Commission 1931, vol. 6, part 1, p. 117). Also see the interview with worker Khudiran (Royal Commission 1931, vol. 6, part 2, p. 99).

References

Assam (India) (1883/1900). *Annual report of Labour Immigration into Assam*. Shillong: General Department, Government Central Press.

Behal, R.P. (2006). 'Power Structure, Discipline, and Labour in Assam Tea Plantations Under Colonial Rule', *International Review of Social History 51, Supplement*, pp. 143–172.

Behal, R. P., and P. Mohapatra (1992). 'Tea and Money versus Human Life: The Rise and Fall of the Indenture System in the Assam Tea Plantations 1840–1908', in E.V. Daniel, H. Bernstein, and T. Brass, eds., *Plantation, Peasants and Proletarians in Colonial Asia*, London: Frank Cass.

Bhattacharya, N. (1985). 'Lenders and Debtors in the Punjab Countryside, 1880–1940', *Studies in History, 1 (2)*, pp. 305–342.

Chaudhary, L., and A.V. Swamy (2014). 'Protecting the Borrower: An Experiment in Colonial India'. Retrieved from the Social Science Research Network (SSRN): http://ssrn.com/abstract=2439833 or http://dx.doi.org/10.2139/ssrn.2439833

Chaudhuri, B. (1983). 'Eastern India II', in D. Kumar and M. Desai, eds., *The Cambridge Economic History of India: Vol. II, c.1757–1970*, Cambridge: Cambridge University Press, pp. 270–331.

Cohn, B. (1961). 'From Indian Status to British Contract', *Journal of Economic History, 21 (4)*, pp. 613–628.

Das, P., ed. (1992). *Report of the Indigo Commission 1860*, Calcutta: Publication Bureau, North Bengal University.

Deccan Riots Commission (1876). *Report of the Committee on the Riots in Poona and Ahmednagar 1875*, Bombay: Government Central Press.

Glaeser, E., S. Djankov, R. La Porta, F. Lopez-de-Silanes, and A. Shleifer (2003). 'Courts: The Lex Mundi Project', *Quarterly Journal of Economics, May, 118 (2)*, pp. 453–512.

Guha, S. (1985). *The Agrarian Economy of the Bombay Deccan 1818–1941*, Delhi: Oxford University Press.

Gupta, B. (2010). 'Competition and Control in the Market for Textiles: The Indian Weavers and the East India Company', in G. Riello and T. Roy, eds., *How India Clothed the World: The World of South Asian Textiles, 1500–1850*, Leiden: Brill.

Gupta, B., and A.V. Swamy (2014). 'Unfree Labour: Did Indenture Reduce Labour Supply to Tea Plantations in Assam?' CAGE Working Paper, University of Warwick. Retrieved from http://econpapers.repec.org/paper/cgewacage/177.htm.

Hejeebu, S. (2005). 'Contract Enforcement in the English East India Company', *Journal of Economic History, 65 (2)*, pp. 496–523.

Hightower, J. (1975). *Eat Your Heart Out: Food Profiteering in America*, New York: Crown Publishers.

Hossain, H. (1988). *The Company Weavers of Bengal*, Delhi: Oxford University Press.

Jaffee, S. M. (1994). 'Contract Farming in the Shadow of Competitive Markets: The Experience of Kenyan Horticulture', in P.D. Little and M.J. Watts, eds., *Living Under Contract: Contract Farming and Agrarian Transformation in Sub-Saharan Africa*, Madison, WI: University of Wisconsin Press.

Kling, B. (1966). *The Blue Mutiny: The Indigo Disturbances in Bengal 1859–62*, Philadelphia: University of Pennsylvania Press.

Kolsky, E. (2010). *Colonial Justice in British India: White Violence and the Rule of Law*, Cambridge: Cambridge University Press.

Kranton, R., and A.V. Swamy (2008). 'Contracts, Hold-Up and Exports: Textiles and Opium in Colonial India', *American Economic Review, 98 (3)*, pp. 967–989.

Kumar, D. (1983). 'The Fiscal System', in D. Kumar and M. Desai, eds., *The Cambridge Economic History of India, Vol. II, c.1757–c.1970*, Cambridge: Cambridge University Press, pp. 905–946.

Kumar, R. (1965). 'The Deccan Riots of 1875', *Journal of Asian Studies, 24 (4)*, pp. 613–635.

———. (1968). *Western India in the Nineteenth Century*, London: Routledge and Kegan Paul.

Mitra, D. B. (1978). *The Cotton Weavers of Bengal, 1757–1833*, Calcutta: Firma Mukhopadyay.

Mohapatra, P. (2004). 'Assam and the West Indies, 1860–1920: Immobilizing Plantation Labor', in D. Hay and P. Craven, eds., *Masters, Servants, and Magistrates in Britain and the Empire, 1562–1955*, pp. 455–480.

North, D. C. (1990). *Institutions, Institutional Change and Economic Performance*, New York: Cambridge University Press.

Parthasarathi, P. (2001). *The Transition to a Colonial Economy: Weavers, Merchants, and Kings in South India, 1720–1800*, Cambridge: Cambridge University Press.

Richards, J. F. (1981). 'The Indian Empire and the Peasant Production of Opium in the Nineteenth Century', *Modern Asian Studies, 15 (1)*, pp. 59–82.

———. (2002). 'The Opium Industry in British India', *Indian Economic and Social History Review, 39 (2–3)*, pp. 149–180.

Rivett-Carnac, J.H. (1910/2005). *Many Memories of Life in India, at Home and Abroad*, Elibron Classics.

Roy, T. (2010). *Company of Kinsmen: Enterprise and Community in South Asian History, 1700–1940*, New York: Oxford University Press.

———. (2011). 'Indigo and Law in Colonial India,' *Economic History Review, 64 (S1)*, pp. 60–75.

Royal Commission on Labour in India (1931). *Report of the Royal Commission on Labour in India*. London: His Majesty's Stationery Office.

Sinha, N.K. (1965). *The Economic History of Bengal: from Plassey to the Permanent Settlement: Vol. I*, Calcutta: Firma Mukhopadhyay.

Verelst, H. (1772). *A View of the Rise, Progress, and Present State of the English Government in Bengal*, London: J. Nourse, Brotherton and Sewell, G. Robinson, and T. Evans.

14

THE PARTITION AND ITS AFTERMATH

Empirical investigations

Prashant Bharadwaj and Kevin Quirolo

Introduction

When Britain relinquished control of its Indian Colony in 1947, it divided the territory into three regions separated by international borders, resulting in one of the largest and most rapid migrations in human history. Over 17 million people were pushed across the new boundaries. The study of the Partition of India is of central importance not only to Indian, Pakistani, and Bangladeshi history,[1] but also to understanding involuntary migration in the twenty-first century. For example, increasingly worse floods have recently imposed migration on some in Bangladesh, and descriptions of refugee struggles have emerged in the popular press, along with speculation that some 30 million Bangladeshis could be displaced by climate change (Harrabin 2006; Kakissis 2010). Mass movement followed the 1983 civil war in Sudan and the continuing conflict in Iraq, the latter resulting in Jordan and Syria having the highest concentrations of refugees per capita in the world (Frelick 2007). What are the demographic and economic implications of such mass migrations? We use the partition of British India into India, Pakistan, and Bangladesh as a case study for understanding the characteristics, dynamics, and economic consequences of involuntary migrations.

While the trauma and politics of partition is well recorded in various forms of popular media and literature,[2] there is surprisingly little detailed empirical work examining the consequences of such an enormous and rapid migration. Other large-scale migrations (such as the migration from Europe to the New World starting in the 1850s) have been well studied by economic historians, yet the population exchange after partition appears relatively understudied. Even basic questions of who, where, and how many moved appear not to have been studied at a disaggregated level with available data. As a result, the more important questions of whether sending and receiving communities experienced demographic or economic changes remain largely unanswered. Yet such answers are vital to explain the subsequent growth of the newly formed countries. For example, our empirical analysis corroborates anecdotal evidence that migration created a new class of educated and skilled migrants in urban areas of Pakistan, which likely helped shape the latter's economic and political future.

This chapter covers three aspects of the flow of migration: first, we examine the basics of who moved, where, and how many. Our study shows a high degree of variation in the amount of migration across geographical areas at country, state, and district levels. Moreover, levels of in- and out-migration in a district were influenced by that district's distance to the partition border. A key contribution of our study is the examination of outflows (people leaving a certain area). Since this variable was not collected in surveys or censuses, we develop a simple yet effective methodology to examine characteristics of people who left affected areas.

Second, we examine the impacts of migration on literacy and occupation rates at the district level. Since religion was the deciding factor in population exchange, it is likely that literacy and occupation rates of migrants differed from those of non-migrants. For instance, our analysis suggests that the partition resulted in greater concentration of literate migrants in urban areas of Pakistan. Since the level of migration was unmatched by availability of arable land, agricultural professions declined in areas affected by migration.

Third, we study the specific case of jute cultivation in Bengal and Bangladesh to assess whether economies incorporate and benefit from migrants. The ability of the receiving economy to assimilate migrants is related in turn to three broader questions: 1) What economic impact did the partition have on India? 2) To what extent are migrants and refugees "good" or "bad" for the receiving economy? 3) Can migration act as a substitute for trade?

Jute is significant because pre-partition Bengal was one of the largest centres in the world for jute manufacturing. However, what became Bangladesh contained all the jute farms and what became Indian Bengal housed all jute-processing mills. Partition therefore created an artificial shortage of raw jute in West Bengal. We examine whether partition-related migratory flows determined which areas produced jute in response to this sudden supply shock.

Partition lends itself well to empirical study, with reliable data sources before and after the resulting migration. Extensive, district-level data allow us to quantify some aspects of the migratory movement and examine its demographic and economic consequences. However, this is not to say that our studies are without limitations. While we do our best to account for factors other than migration that might affect observed demographic and economic changes, the partition coincided with massive unaccounted social changes like the 1943 Bengal famine and governmental programs specifically responding to migration. Therefore, while we relate the demographic and economic changes examined in this chapter to the influx of new migrants, we are neither able to examine the mechanisms of these relationships nor to claim "causal" relationships in the strict sense of the word. Fleshing out mechanisms that link the migratory flows to the observed impacts is a fruitful course for future research in this area.

The rest of this chapter is organized as follows: The next section provides a brief history of the political events surrounding partition. The sections following discuss (in this order) other empirical works on the partition, the characteristics of the migratory flows, the impacts that these flows had on literacy, occupation, and gender ratios, and the link between partition-related migration and the jute industry in West Bengal. The last section concludes.

Background on the partition

As the talk for independence gathered steam in the 1930s, the Muslim League, led by Muhammad Ali Jinnah, was concerned about a Hindu-dominated independent India. In 1940, the League called for the creation of a separate Muslim state. England's partition plan of 3 June 1947 laid the foundations for this separation, placing Sir Cyril Radcliffe in charge of both the Bengal and Punjab Boundary Commissions. In a speedy two months, undivided India was carved into the independent states of India and Pakistan (what became Bangladesh was called *East Pakistan*). The *Radcliffe Award*, as the Boundary Commissions' reports were called, was aimed at calming religious tensions but instead caused controversy. In some ways, "no man-made boundary has caused so many troubles and effectively impeded the advent of peace in South Asia as has the Punjab boundary resulting from the Commission's verdict" (Cheema 2000, p. 1). Radcliffe, a lawyer by profession, was unfamiliar with boundary making and his selection as chairman of the Boundary Commissions was ostensibly based on his "impartial" relations with India. Along with this impartiality, however, came a lack of knowledge of the people and land that he was assigned to divide (Tan and Kudaisya 2000, p. 84). Moreover, at his first meeting with the then-Viceroy, Lord Mountbatten, on 8 June, Radcliffe was evidently shocked to hear he had only five weeks to draw the lines. In his opinion it would take "the most careful of arbitrators years to decide on a boundary that would certainly cut across homes and populations" (Tan and Kudaisya 2000, p. 81).

The ambiguity in the terms of boundary making further complicated Radcliffe's task. The political parties had only agreed that boundaries would be set by "ascertaining the contiguous majority areas of Muslims and Non-Muslims" and considering "other factors." Furthermore, the boundary decisions were kept secret until the last minute before they were released, heightening the speculation regarding Radcliffe's methods of deciding where the borders should fall. It was alleged that Radcliffe calculated some districts' religious majorities using the 1941 Census, which many feared was rigged to under-report certain religious populations.

Upon the insistence of Jawaharlal Nehru, Radcliffe was asked to release the boundary award by 15 August 1947, the day of Indian Independence. However, the Commission's report was not made public until 17 August – and upon its release, the report was received with considerable criticism. Radcliffe, well aware of the dissent he might have caused, wrote:

The many factors that bore upon each problem were not ponderable in their effect upon each other. . . . each decision at each point was debatable and formed of necessity under great pressure of time, conditions, and with knowledge that, in any ideal sense, was deficient.

(Tan and Kudaisya 2000, p. 93)

The multiple factors that Radcliffe had to consider in a short period of time made the boundary decision process rather murky and haphazard. He later lamented, "Nobody in India will love me for the award about the Punjab and Bengal and there will be roughly 80 million people with a grievance who will begin looking for me" (Khilnani 1997, p. 201).

Though the boundary decisions were bound to cause problems, the governments on either side and the departing British had made very little preparations for the affected populations to be evacuated until it was too late (Tan and Kudaisya 2000, p. 98). When the Award was made public, hundreds of thousands found themselves on the wrong side of the border in Punjab, resulting in tremendous violence and forced migration. Even before the declaration of independence, the violence in Punjab had started to take its toll. In March 1947 the scale of rioting was such that several thousand villagers in the Lahore and Rawalpindi districts were forced to leave their villages.

Other empirical works on partition

One of the first and most comprehensive empirical studies of partition was *Economic Consequences of Divided India*, by C.N. Vakil, published in 1950. The book includes ten extensive studies of different sectors of the economy, including jute, which underline the challenges created by partition. Vakil estimates that over 17 million people were displaced due to partition: 6 million from West Pakistan to India, 6.5 million from the East Punjab area to Pakistan, 4 million from East Bengal to India, and 1 million moving from West Bengal to East Bengal (Vakil 1950, p. 25). Unfortunately, this study used data from the 1947–1948 Annual Report of the Ministry of Relief and Rehabilitation, whose procedural details are unknown (Vakil 1950, p. 76; Visaria 1969). While the book's scope is ambitious, a review conceded that it is "more documentary than analytical" (Basch 1952).

An even earlier study published in 1949 corroborates the economic disintegration from partition. Furthermore, this early investigation found that migration increased Indian literacy and resulted in drastic religious homogenization. This study estimated similar migration numbers for Punjab, and approximately 1 million deaths due to partition (Davis 1949). Other sources have pegged migration from 12 million to 17 million, and mortality from 200,000 to 1 million, although sources and methodology are not forthcoming (see sources cited in Hill et al. 2008).

More recent empirical studies of India and Pakistan focus on post-partition demographic changes (Visaria 1969; Retherford and Mirza 1982; Preston and Bhat 1984; Bhat 1998; Srivastava and Sasikumar 2003). These studies often note the difficulty of analyzing partition period data. Indeed, boundary relocation and data quality have been major obstacles since before the partition (Yeatts 1942; Davis 1949; Visaria 1969). This chapter builds on recent work done by Hill, Seltzer, Leaning, Malik, and Russell (2005) on the demographic impact of partition. Their two studies on Punjab and Bengal use data from the 1931, 1941, 1951, and 1961 Censuses. In Punjab they found that partition resulted in a high degree of religious homogenization. They report that Indian Punjab lost 1.4 million Pakistan bound out-migrants, Pakistani Punjab gained 1.5 million Indian in-migrants, and in all of Punjab an estimated 2.3–3.2 million people were "missing" (assumed to be deaths or unrecorded migrations). In Bengal they found a lesser degree of religious homogenization. While Bangladesh experienced 1.4 million out-migrants, West Bengal gained a similar number, and an estimated 9 million people were "missing." However, this last estimation was unable to distinguish between deaths due to the Bengal Famine, deaths due to partition related violence, and migration out of the area of undivided Bengal.

Characteristics of the migratory flows

Data and methodology

Our primary sources of data are the 1931 Census of British India and the 1951 Censuses of India and Pakistan. The 1941 Census is avoided since there is some controversy over its reliability.[3] The district is the smallest administrative unit for which consistent data is available, making it indispensable for conducting a detailed analysis.[4] Hence, we undertook the construction of comparable district-level mappings for the two censuses,[5] testing visual matches with acreage calculation. This process resulted in 287 comparable "districts" between the two censuses. Mapping is explained in detail in Bharadwaj, Khwaja, and Mian (2008; 2009).

The post-partition 1951 Census contains a question that specifically asks whether people moved due to the partition, allowing a direct count of "inflows" to that district. However, outflows (how many people left a given district) are estimated assuming 1) only religious minorities are migrants out of each country, and 2) our estimated minority growth rate is accurate.

The magnitude of migration

We find significant variation in the amount of migration between countries, states, and districts for both inflows and outflows. Migration in either direction was more likely closer to the border. Migrants tended to leave districts that initially had many minorities[6] and settle in districts across the border vacated by migrants travelling in the opposite direction.

Inflows

Migration into countries is calculated from the 1951 Censuses using tallies of *displaced persons* in India and *muhajir* in Pakistan, which refer specifically to people displaced across national borders due to partition and do not reflect the effects of domestic migration.[7] Thus, total inflows for all three countries combined is measured at 14.49 million or 3.3 per cent of the total population.

However, there was substantial variation between countries, states, and even districts. India received 7.3 million migrants (2.04 per cent of its population),[8] Pakistan 6.5 million (20.9 per cent), and Bangladesh 0.7 million (1.66 per cent). Thus, in Pakistan, in-migrants formed a substantially larger portion of the population. At the state and district level, inflows are concentrated at the borders, with three times more on the western border than the eastern. Figure 14.1 and some of the subsequent figures are to be interpreted as moving from Pakistan to Bangladesh from left

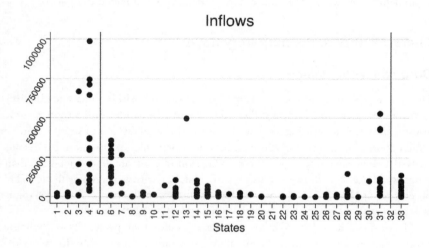

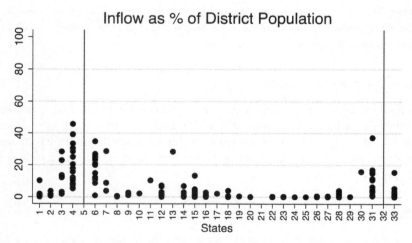

FIGURE 14.1 Inflows of population into India, Pakistan, and Bangladesh

to right with the vertical lines representing the two borders. Each number on the x-axis represents a state in the country arranged by distance to the closest border. For example, State 6 is Punjab in India since it was closest to the western border, while State 31 is West Bengal since it was closest to the eastern border.

Measuring each district's inflow as a percentage of the country's total inflow, the regression analysis shows 1) a "distance effect," 2) an "urbanization effect," and 3) a "replacement effect." That is, migrants tended to settle 1) closer to the border, 2) in big cities, and 3) in areas with large out-migration, respectively. Only in India was the distance effect a statistically significant factor, although the magnitude is quite small. Inflows to India decrease by 0.23 per cent 100 miles from the border. When we analyze distances within states, rather than within a country by using state fixed effects (see Box 14.1), the distance effect becomes statistically insignificant (perhaps because migrants remained within linguistically homogenous areas[9] or because state geography closely aligns with distance to the border). The replacement effect is strong and statistically significant in all three countries, even controlling for district size and differences between states. In Pakistan migrants replaced one another almost one-to-one. Finally, having a big city (defined as one of the twenty-four largest cities in 1931) made Indian districts statistically significantly more likely to receive migrants. The small number of "big cities" in Pakistan and Bangladesh impeded reliable statistical analysis. Tables and more detailed analysis for both this and the following section can be found in Bharadwaj, Khwaja, and Mian (2009).

BOX 14.1   WHAT ARE FIXED EFFECTS?

Most of the analysis in this chapter includes a *state fixed effect*. In this case, a state fixed effect is used to control for time invariant characteristics of a given state. For example, if the state of Bihar receives fewer migrants and has low jute yields compared to other states due to its lack (or abundance) of rivers, we ought to control for this lack (or abundance) of rivers to obtain estimates that more closely link migratory flows and yields. However, rivers might not be the only such attribute of the state of Bihar that affects our outcome (yield) and independent variable (migratory flows) of interest. A fixed effect at the state level captures all such *time invariant* characteristics by including a dummy variable for that state. It should be noted that time varying characteristics, such as state level growth in output, are *not* captured by fixed effects.

Outflows

Since there is no *direct* measure of out-migration, and because out-migrants were predominantly religious minorities, outflows are estimated as the difference between the observed and expected 1951 minority population.[10] Computing the expected minority population in 1951 rests on two assumptions: 1) out-migrants are strictly minorities, and 2) the growth rate in the minority population is computed accurately. The first is generally supported by anecdotal and statistical evidence.[11] The second requires special consideration.

Since we assume the majority population is unchanged by partition, we estimate the minority growth rate by scaling the majority growth rate between 1931 and 1951. Importantly, the majority growth rate for this period incorporates the population losses due to the Bengal Famine.[12] However, we must scale this rate because the Muslim growth rate tended to be higher pre-partition.

Our method calculates total outflows from all three countries as 17.9 million,[13] though given the necessary assumptions, this is a rather rough estimate. Our outflow measure followed roughly the same pattern of spatial variation as inflows. Outflows for India were 9.6 million (2.68 per cent of total population); for Pakistan 5.4 million (18.01 per cent); and for Bangladesh 2.9 million (6.51 per cent). Note that outflows were similar to inflows in terms of percentages, except in Bangladesh where outflows exceeded inflows as a percentage as well as in absolute number. This is verified by the rather one-sided nature of the migration along the eastern border (i.e. more migrants left East Pakistan/Bangladesh to enter West Bengal). Figure 14.2 shows that outflows had a largely similar pattern to inflows.

Regression analysis of outflows[14] suggests that they too were subject to a "distance effect" as well as an "unwelcome effect," i.e. minorities were more likely to leave districts with large minority populations pre-partition. The effect of distance to the border is negative and statistically significant for India: districts on the border had 0.36 per cent higher outflows than those 100 miles away. The size of the minority population had significant influence for both India and Pakistan. A district with a 1 per cent higher 1931 minority population ratio could expect 0.78 per cent higher outflows in India and 0.67 per cent in Pakistan. The irrelevance of distance and minority population in the Bengal area is consistent with suggestions that migration decisions included other considerations (Tan and Kudaisya 2000, pp. 144–161). More detailed analysis can be found in Bharadwaj, Khwaja, and Mian (2008).

Total population and missing persons

The mutual exchange of populations attenuated the net effects of migration. There were net outflows from India and Bangladesh of 2.3 million and 2.1 million, respectively, and a net inflow into Pakistan of 1.1 million. Subtracting total inflows from total outflows gives us an estimate of the number of "missing" people due to partition (either from mortality or migration out of these countries all together), totalling 3.4 million. Although precise numbers are unavailable for migration out of all three countries collectively, it is unlikely to be significant and most of those "missing" should be attributed to mortality.

This is a large number, but it is consistent with accounts in the literature. The 1.3 million Muslim deaths in Punjab and Karachi estimated by British leaders (James 1998, p. 636) match our estimate of 1.26 million Muslims who left western

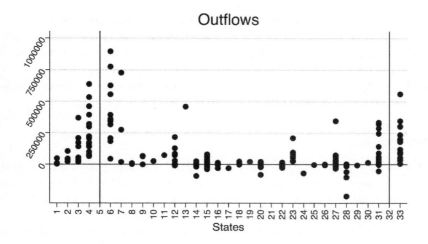

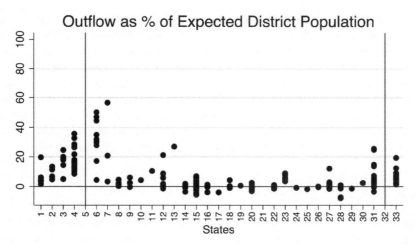

FIGURE 14.2 Outflow of population from India, Pakistan, and Bangladesh

India[15] but did not arrive in Pakistan. The number of missing non-Muslims in the same area is 0.84 million, making a total of 2.1 million missing people along the western border. This total is comparable with the 2.2–2.9 million estimate of Hill et al. (2008). On the eastern border we estimate the total missing to be 1.34 million, which is far smaller than the 9 million estimated by Hill et al. (2005), but they attribute the size of their number to the Bengal Famine. However, for this region, our estimate likely reflects internal migration to Assam, since anecdotal accounts report a lower level of partition-related violence on the eastern border than the western.

Demographic impact of the population exchange

The simple tally of bodies as in the previous section misses the fundamental changes in population composition along three important outcome variables: literacy, gender, and occupation. Arriving migrants tended to raise literacy, lower the ratio of men to women, and lower the portion of workers in agriculture. However, results for Bangladesh were mostly insignificant, likely due to the small sample size. In this section, we examine changes in literacy and occupation.

Methodology

One of the main challenges of analyzing the impact of migration due to partition is distinguishing such impact from changes that would have occurred anyway. One potential solution is to find relevant control districts, i.e. districts that are similar along various dimensions but are relatively unaffected by partition-related migration. Thus, our strategy is to compare neighbouring districts *within* a state that received different numbers of migrants.

In the preceding section, we established that while partition had large migratory flows, movements in either direction tended to balance out, thus making the net population impact much smaller. Therefore, any demographic changes due to partition must mainly arise as a result of compositional differences between movers (inflows and outflows) and non-migrants. With this in mind, we constructed a regression equation to measure the effect of inflows and outflows on the change in a given outcome variable (such as literacy) while controlling for changes in the outcome for non-migrants, and unobserved time invariant state characteristics (state fixed effects). Further discussion of our methodology is available in Bharadwaj, Khwaja, and Mian (2009).

Literacy

Anecdotal evidence from Pakistan, especially accounts from Karachi, suggests that migrants were more educated. Figure 14.3 illustrates this for each district using a "linear" map of British India as in the preceding section. Since data on migrant literacy for India was not tabulated in the 1951 Census, we can only provide results for Pakistan and Bangladesh. The y-axis is the difference in 1951 literacy rates (in per cent) between the migrants into a district and non-migrant residents. Districts with larger overall inflows have larger circles on the graph, which is important because some areas received few, but highly literate, migrants.[16] In order to get a sense of the overall impact of inflows on literacy rates, one should focus more on the larger circles.

The figure shows that, for the most part, migrants into Pakistani and Bangladeshi districts were significantly more literate than the resident population. In some cases, the differences were quite large: an example is Larkana district, which received more than 600,000 migrants and had a difference of 21 per cent in the literacy rates between migrants and residents. Tests reveal that these differences are statistically significant and relatively large: for Pakistani districts, the migrant literacy rate was

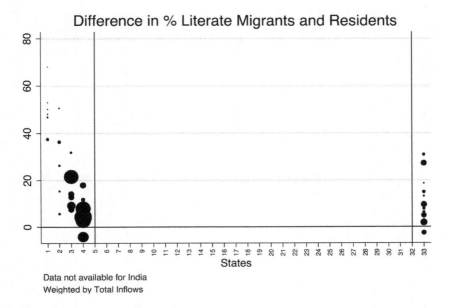

FIGURE 14.3 Difference in literacy between migrants and residents

7.1 percentage points higher than the resident literacy rate. The corresponding difference for Bangladesh was 8.1 percentage points. This suggests that the coefficient on inflows should be positive for Pakistan and Bangladesh.

Table 14.1 presents results with literacy as the outcome variable of interest. The effects for western India reveal that for a 10 per cent increase in inflows, literacy increases by around 2.8 percentage points (Column 3 of the first panel of Table 14.1), an increase of 36 per cent over the 1931–1951 average change in literacy. Hence, incoming migrants have a large positive effect on the overall literacy rates in Indian districts. In Pakistan, outflows decreased literacy rates, while inflows increased literacy rates. However, as we can tell from the coefficients in Column 6, outflows decreased literacy by more than the gains in literacy due to the inflows. A 10 per cent increase in outflows tended to decrease literacy rates by 13.1 per cent, while a similar increase in inflows increased literacy rates by 6.5 per cent. Hence, in places with large inflows and outflows, the overall effect could be muted, but in places with more one-sided movements, these effects could be quite large. A striking example is the case of Karachi, one of the largest cities in Pakistan. Nearly 20 per cent of all literate migrants into Pakistan settled in this city. While in 1931, Karachi contributed around 9 per cent of all literates in Pakistan, by 1951, it contributed nearly 20 per cent, with most of this increase coming from the influx of educated migrants. In Bangladesh and eastern Indian states, the effect of migration on literacy is small and statistically insignificant.

TABLE 14.1 Impact of migration on literacy at district level

Dependent Variable: Difference in % Literate (in District Population) – 1951 minus 1931

	(1)	(2)	(3)	(4)	(5)	(6)
	Western India			Pakistan		
Inflow as % of district population	0.185		0.281	0.041		0.063
	[0.068]***		[0.128]**	[0.021]*		[0.017]***
Outflow as % of district population		0.051	−0.047		−0.089	−0.122
		[0.028]*	[0.053]		[0.033]**	[0.029]***
Constant	2.886	4.143	2.411	0.405	1.085	0.378
	[2.949]	[2.931]	[3.000]	[0.753]	[0.672]	[0.586]
Controls used	Basic + A			Basic + B		
Observations	174	174	174	35	35	35
R−squared	0.63	0.62	0.63	0.97	0.97	0.98

Dependent Variable: Difference in % Literate (in District Population) – 1951 minus 1931

	(1)	(2)	(3)	(4)	(5)	(6)
	Eastern India			Bangladesh		
Inflow as % of district population	0.054		0.126	−0.308		−0.093
	[0.114]		[0.126]	[0.253]		[0.385]

Outflow as % of district population		-0.08	-0.12		-0.245	-0.198
		[0.083]	[0.092]		[0.168]	[0.263]
Constant	6.441	7.291	6.81	6.173	5.944	6.274
	[1.596]***	[1.534]***	[1.608]***	[3.568]	[3.231]*	[3.643]
Controls used	Basic + A			Basic + A		
Observations	50	50	50	17	17	17
R–squared	0.3	0.31	0.33	0.65	0.67	0.67

Std Errors in brackets. * significant at 10%, ** significant at 5%, ***significant at 1%

This table examines the impact of inflows and outflows in a district on that district's percentage literate in 1951. Per cent literate is defined in terms of the population. Inflows are people moving into a given district due to partition; outflows are those moving out. The observations for India are fewer than the usual 234 because we do not have 1921 information for seven districts. We lose an additional three districts to outliers: Bombay (city), Cochin, and Muzaffarnagar. "Residents" in 1951 are just the people who did not move due to Partition. "Majority" is defined as Muslims in Pakistan/Bangladesh and Non-Muslims in India. Resident literacy (1951) cannot be computed for India as data on literacy of migrants was not collected.

Basic controls: State fixed effects, per cent Majority and Minority literacy in 1931, dummy for whether the district had a big city (defined as one of the twenty-four largest cities in 1931).

A: difference in Majority literacy (1931–1921)

B: difference in Resident literacy (1951–1931)

Occupation

Did migrants differ in the occupations they took up after migrating? Were these occupational differences large enough to affect the overall distribution of occupation in a district? Our results show that migrants were more likely to enter non-agricultural professions.

Figure 14.4 illustrates this result by plotting the percentage of migrants in agricultural professions minus the percentage of residents in agriculture in districts in 1951. Each dot indicates whether arriving migrants were more (positive values) or less (negative values) likely to work in agriculture relative to non-migrant residents. Districts with larger overall inflows are displayed as larger dots.

The figure shows migrants in all three countries were significantly less likely to be in agricultural professions, although this difference is largest for districts in India and Bangladesh. This is not surprising given accounts that the level of migration sometimes outstripped the availability of farm land vacated (Tan and Kudaisya 2000, p. 127). Moreover, while the Indian Government in the Punjab engaged in a massive land redistribution project, no serious effort was made in Bengal (Chatterji 2007). Indeed, the land redistribution by the government in Indian Punjab was crucial to the region's future success in agriculture (Sims 1988). Despite these efforts, in general, a land to land transfer of occupation was difficult due to the complexities of land tenure, its legal regulations, and the political influence of landowners

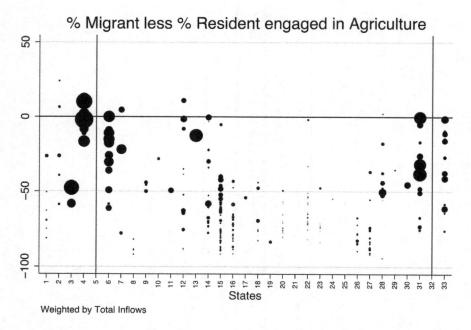

FIGURE 14.4 Share of migrants minus share of residents engaged in agriculture

themselves. Thus, the complex political and legal issues surrounding land are likely responsible for the drop in agricultural professions among refugees who moved.

Table 14.2 examines agricultural professions as the outcome of interest in a similar set-up to that of Table 14.1.[17] The results show that migration substantially restructured agricultural occupation in India. In western India, a 10 per cent increase in inflows was associated with an almost 14 percentage point drop in the population engaged in agriculture and a 10 per cent increase in outflows was associated with only around a six point increase. These are large changes considering that the percentage engaged in agriculture was relatively constant between 1931 and 1951. The opposing influences of inflows and outflows suggest that both those who left India and those who entered it were less likely to be agriculturists or to choose agricultural professions. Anecdotal evidence suggests that in addition to land scarcity, those leaving Pakistan may have also been more likely to have non-agricultural vocations, leaving many white collar positions empty (Tan and Kudaisya 2000, p. 179).

In eastern India, we find that for a 10 per cent increase in inflows, the percentage of the population engaged in agriculture dropped by 9 percentage points. This finding is supported in Joya Chatterji's work focusing on the eastern border of partition. While she notes that the educated and non-agriculturalist migrants moved to cities like Calcutta in hopes of better job prospects, peasant migrants tended to settle in tracts of land between the two Bengals. However, the quality of land in these tracts tended to be poor, and as a result, many migrants gave up agriculture altogether to move to more urban areas (Chatterji 2007, p. 126). Even the Census of 1951 noted the "sizeable proportion" of refugee agriculturists "living, strangely enough, in towns" (Chatterji 2007, p. 126). Hence, at least in India, it appears that the overall impact of partition-related migration seems to have been a decrease in entry into agricultural occupations.

Partition and the jute industry

Although migrants were unlikely to pursue agriculture, those that did so in Indian Bengal fulfilled a special need. Of the many industries subject to economic disintegration noted by Vakil (1950), jute production in Bengal may have been the worst hit and most crucial.

In 1921 jute (a labour-intensive herbaceous crop used to make textiles) was India's largest export and the state of Bengal held a near world monopoly in its production (Sen 1999, p. 13; Stewart 1998, p. 12). However, partition severed factors of production: 81 per cent of existing jute cultivation went to Bangladesh, all of the mills went to India, and trade restrictions obstructed their coordination (T. Ghosh 1999, p. 63). In India, shortages in the supply of raw jute pushed up prices.

In this context, we find that the inflow of migrants from Bangladesh increased jute acreage and yields in India, with no evidence of such flows lowering jute prices or agricultural wages, or increasing acreage of other crops. This is suggestive evidence that migrants from Bangladesh may have aided jute cultivation with special skills, rather than a simple increase in labour supply.

TABLE 14.2 Impact on agricultural occupation at district level

Dependent variable: Difference in % engaged in agriculture (in district population) — 1951 minus 1931

	(1)	(2)	(3)	(4)	(5)	(6)
	Western India			Pakistan		
Inflow as % of district population	0.045		−1.415	0.035		0.031
	[0.286]		[0.508]***	[0.135]		[0.148]
Outflow as % of district population		0.213	0.68		0.042	0.023
		[0.111]*	[0.199]***		[0.262]	[0.287]
Constant	−20.826	−21.646	−15.878	6.487	6.773	2.545
	[11.472]*	[11.193]*	[11.078]	[6.704]	[7.964]	[10.820]
Controls used	Basic + A			Basic + A		
Observations	136	136	136	21	21	21
R−squared	0.48	0.49	0.52	0.87	0.87	0.87

	(1)	(2)	(3)	(4)	(5)	(6)
	Eastern India			Bangladesh		
Inflow as % of district population	−1.011		−0.976	0.758		0.934
	[0.457]**		[0.518]*	[1.060]		[1.085]
Outflow as % of district population		−0.383	−0.058		−0.222	−0.265
		[0.359]	[0.387]		[0.276]	[0.284]
Constant	12.946	10.276	12.963	5.315	8.939	5.787
	[7.433]*	[7.669]	[7.540]*	[5.415]	[4.016]*	[5.478]
Controls used	Basic + A			Basic + A		
Observations	44	44	44	15	15	15
R−squared	0.32	0.25	0.32	0.18	0.19	0.26

Std Errors in brackets. * significant at 10%, ** significant at 5%, *** significant at 1%

This table examines the impact of inflows and outflows in a district on the % engaged in agriculture in that district in 1951. Computation of outflow is discussed in the online Appendix. Inflows are people moving into a given district due to partition, outflows are those moving out. Per cent agriculture in India in 1951 includes dependents of the workers, while for Pakistan *and* Bangladesh, they are excluded. It is not possible to separate out dependents in the Indian figure, or include dependents in the Pakistani figure. In 1931 the per cent agriculture figure includes dependents for India, but not for Pakistan and Bangladesh. Observations are fewer in these regressions as occupation data was collected only for some states in 1931. States included are Ajmer, Assam, Baluchistan, Bihar and Orissa, Bengal, Gwalior, Central India Agency, Hyderabad, Madhya Bharat, Madras, Mysore, NWFP, Punjab, Rajputana, Uttar Pradesh, and Western Agencies. State fixed effects used in all regressions. "Residents" in 1951 are just the people who did not move due to Partition. "Majority" is defined as Muslims in Pakistan/Bangladesh and Non-Muslims in India.

Basic controls: State fixed effects, per cent Majority and Minority literacy in 1931, dummy for whether the district had a big city (defined as one of the twenty-four largest cities in 1931)

A: difference in Majority literacy (1931–1921)

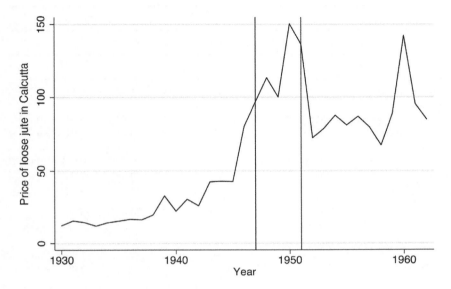

FIGURE 14.5 The price of raw jute in Calcutta

Note: The price is in Rupees per 100 Kg. Data are taken from IJMA (1963). Vertical lines denote 1947 and 1951.

Data and methodology

For agricultural information on jute and other crop acreage and yield, we use the 1931 Agricultural Census and the World Bank Agricultural and Climate dataset. The former provides pre-partition, district-level data on acreage and yields of various crops, which we match with the districts in the Census data. From the latter dataset, we use the 1956 data on yields and acreage because they are the earliest post-partition information at the district level. Jute output is imputed as the product of acreage and estimated yield.

Our main worry here is unobserved selection; that is to say, migrants likely chose districts that promised superior jute cultivation for reasons that we do not observe in the data. In that case, standard regression analysis (OLS) would falsely attribute a district's higher output from suitability for cultivation to the higher numbers of migrants in those districts. Accordingly, we use an instrumental variable (IV) approach using log distance from the border to predict the square root of migrants,[18] with the idea that distance incurs travel costs unrelated to suitability for jute cultivation. We include a number of controls for district suitability, human capital, and time invariant state characteristics (state fixed effects).

Migrant effect on acreage

Table 14.3 reports OLS and IV estimates for districts in the eastern Indian states, which received the most migrants and cultivated the most jute.[19]

TABLE 14.3 The impact of migrants on jute acreage

	(1)	(2)	(3)	(4)	(5)	(6)	(7)	(8)
	Dependent variable: Jute acres per capita × 100, 1956							
	OLS				IV			
Sqrt. of migrant share	1.61[1]	1.16[2]	1.33	1.48	2.26[1]	1.30[1]	2.11[1]	2.20[1]
	(0.43)	(0.58)	(0.87)	(0.95)	(0.58)	(0.41)	(0.66)	(0.78)
Jute acres/100, 1931		0.01[1]	0.01[1]	−0.01		0.01[1]	0.01[1]	−0.01
		(0.00)	(0.00)	(0.01)		(0.00)	(0.00)	(0.01)
Pop. density/100, 1956		−0.10[2]	−0.06	0.26		−0.09[3]	−0.02	0.35[2]
		(0.05)	(0.05)	(0.17)		(0.05)	(0.05)	(0.18)
Big city dummy		1.07	0.52	−8.03[1]*		1.06	−0.00	−9.33[1]
		(1.33)	(1.73)	(3.04)		(1.33)	(1.51)	(3.05)
Male literacy, 1956		−0.08	−0.07	0.01		−0.09	−0.08	−0.00
		(0.06)	(0.07)	(0.05)		(0.07)	(0.08)	(0.05)
Minority share, 1931		0.10[1]	0.11[1]	0.13[1]		0.09[1]	0.09[1]	0.10[2]
		(0.02)	(0.02)	(0.04)		(0.02)	(0.03)	(0.05)
Nadia dummy		−7.17[2]	−7.90[2]	−6.10[3]		−7.63[1]	−10.42[1]	−8.32[1]
		(2.81)	(3.72)	(3.35)		(2.05)	(2.68)	(2.66)
Observations	35	35	35	35	35	35	35	35
Other 1931 acreages	No	No	No	Yes	No	No	No	Yes
State FE	No	No	Yes	Yes	No	No	Yes	Yes
KPF Statistic					47.21	17.78	7.869	5.480

Notes: [1]Significant at 1%, [2]Significant at 5%, [3]Significant at 10%. Robust z statistics in parentheses. All regressions include a constant.

Sources: Data are taken from the 1931 and 1951 Censuses of India, the 1931 Agricultural Census, and the World Bank Agricultural and Climate dataset.

The positive and statistically significant effect of migration in our OLS regression in Column 1 (Table 14.3) is robust to the inclusion of controls[20] in Column 2. Column 3 adds state fixed effects,[21] and Column 4 adds acreage of all other crops in the data.[22] Given the average increase of 1.19 in our measure of arriving migration, these OLS estimates suggest between a 1.38 and 1.92 unit increase in our measure of jute acreage per capita, explaining 63 per cent to 87 per cent of the average increase (2.20 units).

Columns 5–8 replicate Columns 1–4 using our instrumental variables approach. The KP F-Statistic suggests that our instrument (log distance to border) does well in terms of predicting the square root of migrant share in Column 4. In all four columns, the impact of migrants on jute production is statistically significant despite controlling for location selection. Using the same process as earlier, our IV results suggest that on average, migrants, explain between 70 per cent and 122 per cent of average jute acreage per capita. Results for jute output had similar results. Furthermore, these effects were not seen in other crops.

Migrant effect on yields

Migrants increased yields, controlling for population density, ruling out increased labour supply or expansion of farming as alternative explanations. Therefore, we argue that the increase in output was likely due to skills specific to jute that migrants brought over. However, our data cannot directly demonstrate any particular mechanism, so we cannot rule out the possibility that migrant populous districts received more government services or agricultural technologies specifically related to jute.

Table 14.4 reports an analysis of jute yields parallel to that of jute acreage (Table 14.3), although economic significance is less precisely estimated. Across OLS columns, a standard deviation increase of 1 in our migration measure predicts an increase in yields from 0.22 to 0.50 standard deviations; for IV, the comparable range is 0.33 to 0.94. An increase in acreage, output, and yield of jute does not necessarily mean that the resident population benefited from such an expansion. In fact, these effects could lower prices and wages, seriously harming residents; however, this is not what we see in the post-partition data (Bharadwaj and Fenske 2011).

Robustness checks

Several falsification tests support our jute-specific skills story. If similar effects are found for other crops, then it may be argued that the migrants' effect on jute is only a statistical artefact or simply not due to special skills. However, we find that this is not the case. For a variety of crops examined, we find little positive correlation between migratory flows and cultivation. The effect of migrants is largely either negative or insignificant (even for rice, a particularly labour-intensive crop).

It could also be the case that migrants selected districts with good jute markets, and that this is correlated with distance to the border. However, our results are robust to the inclusion of controls for market quality. We account for this by controlling for the price of raw jute and the normalized distance from Calcutta, the principal market for jute. These measures of market quality both have a positive impact on jute acreage, as may be expected. However, our migration measure remains robust and in many cases, the coefficient is largely unaffected. More detailed accounts of these and two other procedures are included in Bharadwaj and Fenske (2011).

Conclusion

Partition had wide-ranging effects on the location, composition, and occupation of the underlying population. The construction of accurate, district-level data allows us to dissect the various, simultaneous, and countervailing effects bringing

TABLE 14.4 The impact of migrants on jute yields

	(1)	(2)	(3)	(4)	(5)	(6)	(7)	(8)
	Dependent variable: Jute yield × 100, 1956							
	OLS				IV			
Sqrt. of Migrant Share	9.83***	22.29***	11.31	16.04*	14.97***	34.86***	42.26**	42.10***
	(3.10)	(6.98)	(7.94)	(8.29)	(5.31)	(11.74)	(20.79)	(15.89)
Jute acres/100, 1931		0.06***	0.07***	0.10*		0.07***	0.07***	0.06
		(0.02)	(0.01)	(0.05)		(0.02)	(0.02)	(0.07)
Pop. Density/100, 1956		5.51***	6.06***	10.47***		6.25***	7.81***	13.68***
		(1.22)	(1.57)	(3.44)		(1.50)	(1.87)	(3.54)
Big City Dummy		−89.87***	−83.63***	−219.57***		−90.08***	−104.17***	−267.01***
		(21.09)	(30.80)	(68.88)		(25.50)	(38.72)	(76.22)
Male Literacy, 1956		−0.91	−1.35	−1.20		−1.59	−1.68*	−1.51
		(0.95)	(0.85)	(1.28)		(1.04)	(0.96)	(1.20)
Minority Share, 1931		−1.49**	−1.17*	−1.91***		−2.22**	−2.06*	−2.79***
		(0.72)	(0.62)	(0.54)		(0.94)	(1.07)	(0.80)
Nadia Dummy		−55.98***	−30.90	−27.57		−97.08**	−129.75*	−107.82**
		(19.79)	(20.40)	(26.56)		(40.20)	(68.24)	(49.48)
Observations	35	35	35	35	35	35	35	35
Other 1931 acreages	No	No	No	Yes	No	No	No	Yes
State F.E.	No	No	Yes	Yes	No	No	Yes	Yes
KP F Statistic					47.21	17.78	7.869	5.480

Notes: ***Significant at 1%, **Significant at 5%, *Significant at 10%. Robust z statistics in parentheses. All regressions include a constant.

Sources: Data are taken from the 1931 and 1951 Censuses of India, the 1931 Agricultural Census, and the World Bank Agricultural and Climate dataset.

about these effects. Over 17 million people were forced from their native countries, 3.7 million of whom likely died. Migrants brought higher literacy rates across the border with them and were less likely to enter into agricultural work. When migrants did engage in agriculture in Indian Bengal, they appear to have improved jute cultivation without harming the resident economy. Understanding complicated human movements with this level of detail and better methods will be crucial for policy and scholarship for Indian economic history. Future work can elaborate on long-term consequences of these migratory flows. One exciting avenue for new research could be linking partition related flows to subsequent ethnic violence as in some of the recent work by Jha and Wilkinson (2012).

Notes

This chapter is largely based on and heavily borrows from three papers: Bharadwaj, Khwaja, and Mian (2008); Bharadwaj, Khwaja, and Mian (2009); and Bharadwaj and Fenske (2011). Bharadwaj is indebted to his co-authors, Asim Khwaja, Atif Mian, and James Fenske, for their support with the papers that are summarized in his chapter. We thank the editors for helpful comments. Any errors are our own.

 1 While partition technically resulted in the formation of East Pakistan, which later became Bangladesh, we use the term *Bangladesh* throughout this chapter.
 2 General texts (Bose and Jalal 1998; Brass 1990; Sarkar 1993; Tan and Kudaisya 2000), anecdotal accounts (Butalia 2000; Shahid Hamid 1993), urban sociological work (Bopegamage 1957; Qadeer 1983), and fiction (A. Ghosh 1988; Manto 1997) are representative of the large body of important qualitative work.
 3 In the 1941 Census's own introduction, the Census commissioner notes that "the great population regions of the Indus and Ganges systems in which nearly half the total population of India lies have only a limited representation in the Census figures" (Yeatts 1942, p. 11).
 4 For more on the British spatial system, see Kant (1988).
 5 The studies by Hill et al. (2005) address the problem of boundary changes i) by focusing on demographics of the whole area of undivided Punjab and undivided Bengal; and ii) by using the 1951 Census's re-tabulation of 1931 and 1941 total population using post-partition districts.
 6 The term *minority* refers to the religious minority in a given country. In India minorities are Muslims, and in Pakistan and Bangladesh, minorities are Hindus and Sikhs.
 7 This variable would be inaccurate if individuals misreported migrant status, but there is little reason to suspect there were significant incentives to do so.
 8 To put the number for India in perspective, we calculate from Srivastava and Sasikumar (2003) that internal migration rate in India was around 11 per cent in 1992. Hence, an impact of 2 per cent in migration in 1951 is potentially a large effect.
 9 Thanks to Bishnupriya Gupta for this observation.
10 Expected 1951 minority population = 1931 minority population × minority growth rate.
11 This does not hold for some districts, particularly in Bengal. However, the Census does not record the religion of migrants so it is difficult to directly test this.
12 However, in our method, we assume that Muslims and non-Muslims were equally likely to die from the Bengal Famine.
13 In terms of 1951 population levels, which includes infants born post-partition to out-migrants. This is done to remain consistent with inflow methodology and because migration did continue after 1947.

14 Measured by district outflows as a per cent of total outflows.
15 *Western India* is defined by districts whose closest border is the Punjab border. This calculation also assumes that outflows from these districts moved toward Pakistan, and not Bangladesh.
16 For example, Baluchistan in Pakistan had an average migrant literacy of around 63 per cent, but less than 28,000 in-migrants – a relatively small number given the large inflows in other states.
17 Due to non-availability of data as well as some reshaping problems, the data for 1931 occupation is incomplete for parts of India and Pakistan.
18 We use the square root of the migrant share of the population because visual inspection of the data suggests that the relationship is concave. Since some districts received either few migrants or none at all, the square root is a more appropriate transformation than the natural log.
19 These states are Bihar, West Bengal, and Orissa.
20 For more detail on controls, please see Bharadwaj and Fenske (2011).
21 The insignificance of migration in Column 3 is likely due to multi-collinearity since the coefficient has increased but the *t*-statistic is still 1.53.
22 Unfortunately, there are few degrees of freedom in this regression so the results ought to be viewed with caution.

References

Basch, A. (1952). 'Review: Economic Consequences of Divided India by CN Vakil', *American Economic Review, 42 (4)*, pp. 632–633.

Bharadwaj, P., and J. Fenske (2011). 'Partition, Migration, and Jute Cultivation in India', *Journal of Development Studies, 48 (8)*, pp. 1084–1107.

Bharadwaj, P., A. Khwaja, and A. Mian (2008). 'The Big March: Migratory Flows after Partition of British India', *Economic and Political Weekly. 43 (35)*, pp. 39–49.

———. (2009). 'The Partition of India: Demographic Consequences', UC San Diego Working Paper.

Bhat, P.N.M. (1998). 'Demographic estimates for post- independence India: A new integration', *Demography India, 27 (1)*, pp. 23–57.

Bopegamage, A. (1957). *Delhi: A Study in Urban Sociology, Sociology Series No. 7*, Bombay: University of Bombay Publications.

Bose, S., and A. Jalal (1998). *Modern South Asia: History, Culture, Political Economy*, New York: Routledge.

Brass, P. (1990). *The Politics of India since Independence*, London: Cambridge University Press.

Butalia, U. (2000). *The Other Side of Silence: Voices from the Partition of India*, Durham, NC: Duke University Press.

Chatterji, J. (2007). '"Dispersal" and the failure of rehabilitation. Refugee camp-dwellers and squatters in West Bengal', *Modern Asian Studies, 41 (5)*, pp. 995–1032.

Cheema, P. I. (2000). 'The Politics of the Punjab Boundary Award', Heidelberg Papers in South Asian and Comparative Politics, Working Paper No.1.

Davis, K. (1949). 'India and Pakistan: The demography of Partition', *Pacific Affairs, 22 (3)*, pp. 254–264.

Frelick, B. (2007). 'Iraqis denied right to asylum', *Forced Migration Review, Special issue: Iraq's displacement crisis: the search for solutions, June*, pp. 24–26.

Ghosh, A. (1988). *The Shadow Lines*, Delhi: Ravi Dayal Publishers.

Ghosh, T. (1999). 'Income and productivity in the Jute industry across the 1947 divide', in A. de Haan and S. Sen, eds., *Case for Labour History: The Jute Industry in Eastern India*, Calcutta: K. P. Bagchi and Co., pp. 54–81.

Harrabin, R. (2006). *Climate fears for Bangladesh's future*, BBC News, 14 September. Retrieved from http://news.bbc.co.uk/1/hi/5344002.stm.

Hill, K., W. Seltzer, J. Leaning, S.J. Malik, and S.S. Russell (2005). 'The demographic impact of partition: Bengal in 1947', Working Paper. Retrieved from http://iussp2005.princeton.edu/papers/52236.

———. (2008). 'The Demographic Impact of Partition: The Punjab in 1947', *Population Studies Cambridge, 62 (2)*, pp. 155–170.

James, L. R. (1998). *The Making and Unmaking of British India*, New York: St. Martin's Press.

Jha, S., and S. Wilkinson (2012). 'Does Combat Experience Foster Organizational Skill? Evidence from Ethnic Cleansing during the Partition of South Asia', *American Political Science Review, 106 (4)*, pp. 883–907.

Kakissis, J. (2010). 'Environmental Refugees Unable to Return Home', *New York Times*, 3 January.

Kant, S. (1988). *Administrative Geography of India*, Jaipur: Rawat Publications.

Khilnani, S. (1997). *The Idea of India*, United Kingdom: Hamish Hamilton Ltd.

Manto, S.H. (1997). *Mottled Dawn; Fifty Sketches and Stories of Partition*, Delhi: Penguin Books.

Preston, S.H., and P.N.M. Bhat (1984). 'New Evidence on Fertility and Mortality Trends in India', *Population and Development Review, 10 (3)*, pp. 481–503.

Qadeer, M. A. (1983). *Lahore: Urban Development in the Third World*, Lahore: Vanguard Books Limited.

Retherford, R.D., and G.M. Mirza (1982). 'Evidence of Age Exaggeration in Demographic Estimates for Pakistan', *Population Studies, 36 (2)*, pp. 257–270.

Sarkar, S. (1993). *Modern India 1885–1947*, Basingstoke: Macmillan.

Sen, S. (1999). *Women and Labour in Late Colonial India: The Bengal Jute Industry*, Cambridge: Cambridge University Press.

Shahid Hamid, S. (1993). *Disastrous Twilight: A Personal Record of the Partition of India*, London: Leo Cooper.

Sims, H. (1988). *Political Regimes, Public Policy and Economic Development: Agricultural Performance and Rural Change in the Two Punjabs*, Delhi: Sage Publications.

Srivastava, R., and S.K. Sasikumar (2003). 'An Overview of Migration in India, Its Impacts and Key Issues', Paper presented at the Regional Conference on Migration, Development and Pro-Poor Policy Choices in Asia, 22–24 June, in Dhaka, Bangladesh. Retrieved from http://www.eldis.org/go/topics&id=17521&type=Document#.U9VXkeNdVNt.

Stewart, G.T. (1998). *Jute and Empire: The Calcutta Jute Wallahs and the Landscapes of Empire*, Manchester: Manchester University Press.

Tan, T.Y., and G. Kudaisya (2000). *The Aftermath of Partition in South Asia*, London: Routledge.

Vakil, C.N. (1950). *Economic Consequences of Divided India*, Bombay: Vora & Co.

Visaria, P.M. (1969). 'Migration between India and Pakistan, 1951–61', *Demography, 6 (3)*, pp. 323–334.

Yeatts, M.W.M. (1942). *Census of India, 1941: Vol. 1, India. Part II, Administration Report*, Simla: Government of India Press.

INDEX

Page number for boxes, figures, tables and boxes are shown in *italic* type.